TRANSFORMATECH INSTITUTE

Creating Production-Ready LLMs

A Comprehensive Guide to Building, Optimizing, and Deploying Large Language Models for Production Use

First edition

This book was professionally typeset on Reedsy.
Find out more at reedsy.com

Contents

III Part III: Advanced Techniques and Concepts

Introduction to Large Language Models (LLMs) and Their Impact on AI.

Large Language Models, or LLMs, have become a central focus in the field of artificial intelligence, especially over the past few years. These models have made it possible to generate human-like text, understand and respond to complex queries, and even perform tasks that require a degree of creativity and reasoning that was previously thought to be the exclusive domain of humans.

LLMs are essentially deep learning models that have been trained on vast amounts of text data. They learn to predict the next word in a sentence, understand context, and generate coherent and contextually relevant text based on the input they receive. The most well-known examples of LLMs include models like GPT-3, BERT, and T5, all of which have demonstrated remarkable abilities in natural language processing (NLP) tasks.

The Impact of LLMs on AI and Beyond

The introduction and development of LLMs have significantly impacted not only the field of AI but also many other areas, including business, healthcare, education, and entertainment. Here's how LLMs are shaping these fields:

1) Enhancing Natural Language Understanding:

- LLMs have vastly improved machines' ability to understand and generate human language. This has led to more accurate and context-aware chatbots, virtual assistants, and other AI-driven communication tools.

2) Revolutionizing Content Creation:

- With the ability to generate text that is often indistinguishable from that written by humans, LLMs are being used to create content ranging from news articles to marketing copy. This has opened new possibilities for content creation but also raised questions about authenticity and the future of creative work.

3) Advancing Research and Development:

- Researchers use LLMs to sift through vast amounts of academic papers, extract relevant information, and even suggest new hypotheses. This has accelerated the pace of discovery in fields like medicine, where LLMs help in literature reviews and drug discovery.

4) Improving Accessibility:

- LLMs play a crucial role in creating more accessible technology. For instance, they power translation tools that break down language barriers and assistive technologies that help people with disabilities interact with digital content more easily.

5) Transforming Business Operations:

- Businesses are leveraging LLMs to automate customer service, streamline operations, and gain insights from large datasets. The ability to analyze and generate human language at scale has enabled companies to better understand customer needs, optimize marketing strategies, and make data-driven decisions more effectively.

Why LLMs Matter

The significance of LLMs extends beyond their technical capabilities. They represent a shift in how we interact with technology, bringing us closer to machines that can understand and respond to us in ways that feel natural and intuitive. This has profound implications for everything from personal computing to global industries.

However, with great power comes great responsibility. The deployment of LLMs in real-world applications must be done thoughtfully, considering ethical concerns, potential biases, and the societal impacts of these technologies. This book aims to equip you with the knowledge and tools needed to build, optimize, and deploy LLMs responsibly and effectively in production environments.

By the end of this book, you'll not only understand the mechanics of LLMs but also their broader implications and how to harness their potential while mitigating their risks. Whether you're a data scientist, an AI engineer, a researcher, or a professional looking to integrate LLMs into your work, this book will guide you through every step of the process.

Purpose of the Book

The goal of this book is straightforward: to equip you with the knowledge and practical skills needed to successfully deploy Large Language Models (LLMs) in production environments. While LLMs are powerful tools with the potential to revolutionize various industries, getting them from a research or development phase into a stable, efficient, and scalable production environment comes with its own set of challenges. This book is designed to help you overcome those challenges.

Why This Book is Important

Deploying LLMs in production isn't just about knowing how to code or understanding the underlying algorithms. It requires a comprehensive approach that includes everything from model optimization and fine-tuning to ensuring that your deployment is ethical, secure, and capable of scaling as needed. This book is intended to serve as a complete guide, covering all aspects of this process.

Here's what you can expect:

1) Thorough Coverage of Core Concepts:

- Before diving into the practical aspects, the book will first ensure you have a solid understanding of the fundamentals of LLMs. We'll discuss the architecture, the theory behind these models, and why they perform as they do. This foundation is crucial for making informed decisions throughout the deployment process.

2) Step-by-Step Guidance on Practical Implementation:

- We'll walk you through the entire process of deploying LLMs, from setting up your development environment to fine-tuning your model for specific tasks. Whether you're working with a pre-trained model or training one from scratch, you'll find practical advice and examples that can be directly applied to your projects.

4) Addressing Common Pitfalls:

- Many who attempt to deploy LLMs in production encounter similar challenges—whether it's dealing with model scalability, optimizing performance, or ensuring data privacy. This book doesn't just point out these potential pitfalls; it offers clear strategies to avoid or mitigate them.

5) Advanced Techniques for Enhanced Performance:

- For those looking to go beyond the basics, this book includes advanced techniques to help you optimize your models for production. Topics like prompt engineering, retrieval-augmented generation, and model compression are covered in depth, providing you with the tools to make your deployments more efficient and effective.

6) Ethical and Responsible Deployment:

- With great power comes the responsibility to deploy these models ethically. Throughout the book, we'll discuss best practices for ensuring your deployments are not only effective but also responsible. This includes addressing potential biases in your models and ensuring they comply with legal and regulatory standards.

Who Will Benefit from This Book

This book is tailored for a wide range of professionals, from data scientists and AI engineers to researchers and tech leads. Whether you're someone who is just beginning to work with LLMs or a seasoned professional looking to refine your skills and approach, you'll find valuable insights and actionable advice throughout these pages.

The purpose of this book is not just to provide information, but to empower you to apply what you've learned in real-world scenarios. By the time you reach the final chapter, you should feel confident in your ability to bring LLMs into production, optimize them for your specific needs, and do so in a way that is both efficient and ethically sound.

Who Should Read This Book?

This book is designed for anyone who wants to understand Large Language Models (LLMs) on a deeper level and apply that understanding in a practical, real-world setting. Whether you're a data scientist, an AI engineer, a researcher, or a professional working with technology, you'll find the insights and guidance here valuable.

Data Scientists

If you're a data scientist, you likely already have experience with machine learning models, data preprocessing, and analytics. This book will build on that foundation, helping you understand how LLMs work and how to integrate them into your workflows. We'll cover everything from fine-tuning pre-trained models to optimizing their performance for specific tasks. By the end, you'll be equipped to not only use LLMs but also to tailor them to meet the unique challenges of your projects.

AI Engineers

As an AI engineer, you're at the forefront of bringing AI models from concept to production. This book is geared toward providing you with the practical tools and techniques needed to deploy LLMs effectively. We'll address common challenges such as scalability, latency, and integration into existing systems. You'll also learn advanced techniques to optimize and maintain LLMs in a production environment, ensuring they perform reliably and efficiently.

Researchers

For researchers, especially those focused on natural language processing

(NLP) and AI, this book offers a comprehensive look at both the theoretical underpinnings and practical applications of LLMs. You'll gain insights into the latest developments in LLM architecture, as well as learn how to conduct experiments and push the boundaries of what these models can do. The book is also a valuable resource for understanding the broader implications of LLMs, including ethical considerations and potential societal impacts.

Professionals

If you're a professional working in a field where AI and machine learning are becoming increasingly important, this book will help you stay ahead of the curve. Whether you're in business, healthcare, finance, or any other industry, understanding LLMs will be crucial as these models continue to shape the future of technology. You don't need to be a machine learning expert to benefit from this book—each concept is explained clearly, with practical examples that you can apply directly to your work.

In short, this book is for anyone who wants to gain a deeper understanding of LLMs and how to apply them effectively in a production environment. Whether you're looking to build your first LLM-based application or optimize an existing system, the information here is designed to be both accessible and actionable, helping you achieve your goals with confidence.

How to Use This Book

This book is organized to guide you through the entire process of working with Large Language Models (LLMs), from the fundamental concepts to the advanced techniques required for deploying them in production. The content is structured to be both comprehensive and practical, ensuring you can easily apply what you learn to your own projects.

Understanding the Book's Structure

The book is divided into several parts, each focusing on a different aspect of LLMs.

Here's how it's laid out:

1) Foundations of Large Language Models:

- This section covers the basics you need to understand before diving into more complex topics. We'll discuss the architecture of LLMs, the theory behind their operation, and the mathematical concepts that underpin them. Even if you're familiar with some of these ideas, this section will ensure you have a solid foundation to build on.

2) Practical Implementation of LLMs:

- Here, we move from theory to practice. You'll learn how to collect and preprocess data, train LLMs from scratch, and fine-tune pre-trained models for specific tasks. This section is full of step-by-step instructions and code examples, making it easy to follow along and apply the concepts to your own work.

3) Advanced Techniques and Concepts:

- Once you've mastered the basics, this section introduces more advanced topics such as prompt engineering, retrieval-augmented generation, and model optimization. These techniques will help you push the performance of your models even further, making them more efficient and effective in a production environment.

4) Deployment and Scaling:

- This part of the book is dedicated to getting your LLMs ready for production. We'll cover the best practices for deployment, including how to ensure your models are robust, scalable, and secure. We'll also discuss common challenges in production environments and how to overcome them.

5) Case Studies and Real-World Applications:

- To help you see how these concepts are applied in real life, this section includes case studies from various industries. You'll learn how LLMs are being used in healthcare, finance, education, and more, giving you insights into the practical applications of these models.

6) Future of Large Language Models:

- Finally, we'll look at the emerging trends in LLMs and what the future might hold. This section will help you stay ahead of the curve and prepare for the next advancements in the field.

Practical Projects

Throughout the book, you'll find practical projects that you can work on to reinforce your understanding of the material. These projects are designed to be hands-on and directly applicable to real-world scenarios. By the time you finish the book, you should have a portfolio of projects that demonstrate your ability to work with LLMs in a production setting.

Theoretical Insights

While this book is very much focused on practical application, we don't ignore the theory. Understanding why and how LLMs work is crucial to making the right decisions when building and deploying them. Each section includes discussions of the theoretical concepts that underpin the techniques you'll be using, giving you a deeper understanding of the models and how to optimize them.

Deployment Strategies

Deploying LLMs in production is a complex task that involves more than just coding. This book will guide you through the entire deployment process, from setting up your environment to monitoring your models once they're live. We'll also cover the ethical and legal considerations that come with deploying AI models, ensuring that you're not only effective but also responsible in your approach.

By following the structure of this book, you'll be able to build a strong foundation in LLMs, apply advanced techniques to optimize your models, and confidently deploy them in production environments. Whether you're working on a small project or looking to scale up to enterprise-level applications, the guidance provided here will help you succeed.

I

Part I: Foundations of Large Language Models

Chapter 1: Understanding Language Models

1.1 Definition and History of Language Models

Language models are at the heart of many modern natural language processing (NLP) applications, but the concept itself has been around for quite some time. In simple terms, a language model is a statistical or machine learning model that can predict the next word in a sequence, given the words that precede it. This ability to understand and generate human language has made language models a fundamental tool in AI, powering everything from search engines to voice assistants.

What Exactly is a Language Model?

At its core, a language model is designed to capture the patterns and structures in text. By analyzing large amounts of text data, it learns the probability of a word or sequence of words occurring in a particular context. For example, in the sentence "The cat is on the," a well-trained language model would predict that the next word is likely "mat" because it has seen this phrase frequently in its training data.

Language models come in various forms, from simple statistical models that look at word frequencies to complex neural networks that understand deep contextual relationships between words. Regardless of the type, the goal remains the same: to generate or understand human language in a way that is both meaningful and coherent.

A Brief History of Language Models

The development of language models can be traced back to the early days of computational linguistics, long before the advent of neural networks. Here's a brief overview of how language models have evolved over the years:

1) N-gram Models: The Beginning

- One of the earliest types of language models was the n-gram model, which dates back to the mid-20th century. N-gram models are simple statistical models that predict the next word in a sequence based on the previous *n* words. For example, a bigram model (n=2) would predict the next word based on the previous one word, while a trigram model (n=3) would consider the previous two words.
- These models are relatively easy to build and interpret, but they have limitations. Because they rely on fixed-length word sequences, n-gram models often struggle with long-range dependencies—when the meaning of a word depends on something that occurred much earlier in the text.

2) Hidden Markov Models (HMMs): A Step Forward

- In the 1970s and 1980s, Hidden Markov Models (HMMs) became popular in the field of speech recognition and NLP. HMMs are probabilistic models that use hidden states to represent the underlying structure of sequences, making them more powerful than simple n-grams.
- HMMs allowed for more sophisticated language models that could capture some of the context and structure of language, but they still had limitations, particularly in handling complex, nuanced language

patterns.

3) The Rise of Neural Networks: A Paradigm Shift

- The late 1990s and early 2000s saw the introduction of neural networks into language modeling. Recurrent Neural Networks (RNNs), in particular, were a game-changer because they could process sequences of variable length and maintain a "memory" of previous inputs. This made RNNs much better at capturing long-range dependencies in text.
- However, RNNs also had their shortcomings, particularly in dealing with very long sequences, which led to the development of Long Short-Term Memory (LSTM) networks and Gated Recurrent Units (GRUs). These models improved the ability to handle long-term dependencies by mitigating the vanishing gradient problem that plagued earlier RNNs.

4) Transformers: The Modern Era of Language Models

- The most significant leap in language modeling came with the introduction of the Transformer architecture in 2017, which formed the basis of many modern LLMs like BERT, GPT, and T5. Unlike RNNs, Transformers don't process data sequentially. Instead, they use a mechanism called "attention" to weigh the importance of different words in a sentence, regardless of their position. This allows Transformers to understand context more effectively and capture complex relationships in text.
- Transformers have revolutionized NLP, enabling the development of LLMs that can generate coherent text, translate languages, summarize documents, and much more, with a level of fluency and accuracy that was previously unattainable.

The Importance of Understanding Language Models

Understanding the history and evolution of language models is crucial because it helps us appreciate the advances that have led to the powerful models we have today. Each stage of development—from n-grams to Transformers—has contributed to our current ability to create models that can process, understand, and generate human language with remarkable accuracy.

In this book, we'll dive deeper into these concepts, building on this historical context to show you how to apply modern LLMs effectively. Whether you're new to the field or looking to refine your skills, this foundational knowledge will be essential as you work through the more advanced topics in the chapters to come.

1.2 Evolution from Statistical to Neural Language Models

The evolution of language models from simple statistical methods to advanced neural networks marks one of the most significant shifts in the field of natural language processing (NLP). This progression not only enhanced our ability to understand and generate human language but also opened up new possibilities for applications that were previously unimaginable. In this section, we'll walk through this evolution, highlighting key milestones and explaining why each step was important.

Statistical Language Models: The Early Days

Before the rise of neural networks, language models were primarily based on statistical methods. These models relied on probabilities and statistics to predict the likelihood of a word or sequence of words in a given context.

1) N-gram Models:

- **How They Work:** N-gram models are the simplest form of statistical language models. They predict the next word in a sequence based on the previous *n* words. For example, a trigram model (where $n = 3$) predicts the next word using the previous two words. If your sentence is "The cat is on the," the trigram model might predict "mat" as the next word because "on the mat" is a common phrase.
- **Limitations:** While n-gram models are straightforward and easy to implement, they have notable limitations. They struggle with long-range dependencies because they only consider a fixed number of preceding words. This makes them less effective at capturing the broader context of a sentence or document. Additionally, n-gram models require large amounts of data to produce accurate predictions, as they need to observe every possible word sequence during training.

2) Hidden Markov Models (HMMs):

- **How They Work:** HMMs represent a more sophisticated approach, using hidden states to model sequences. In the context of language, these hidden states can represent various linguistic structures, such as parts of speech. HMMs calculate the probability of a sequence by considering both the observed words and the underlying hidden states that generate them.
- **Limitations:** Although HMMs provided a significant improvement over n-gram models by capturing more structure in language, they still had their downsides. They often struggled with ambiguity and could not easily capture the complex dependencies found in natural language. As a result, HMMs were eventually surpassed by more powerful methods.

The Shift to Neural Language Models

The limitations of statistical models, particularly their inability to handle complex and long-range dependencies, led to the development of neural language models. These models leverage the power of neural networks to process and generate language in a way that more closely resembles human cognition.

1) Recurrent Neural Networks (RNNs):

- **How They Work:** RNNs introduced a major breakthrough by allowing models to process sequences of variable length and maintain a form of "memory" through their hidden states. Unlike n-grams, which only look at a fixed number of words, RNNs can theoretically consider all previous words in a sentence when predicting the next word. This is achieved through a feedback loop that passes information from one step of the sequence to the next.
- **Limitations:** Despite their advantages, RNNs have a significant drawback known as the vanishing gradient problem. This issue arises during training when the gradients that update the network's weights become too small, effectively preventing the model from learning long-range dependencies. As a result, RNNs often struggle with very long sequences.

2) Long Short-Term Memory Networks (LSTMs) and Gated Recurrent Units (GRUs):

- **How They Work:** LSTMs and GRUs were developed to address the vanishing gradient problem in RNNs. These models introduce gating mechanisms that control the flow of information, allowing them to "remember" important details over longer periods and "forget" irrelevant information. This makes LSTMs and GRUs more effective at handling long-range dependencies, such as those found in lengthy sentences or paragraphs.

- **Limitations:** While LSTMs and GRUs significantly improved the performance of neural language models, they still had limitations. Training these models can be computationally expensive, and they often require extensive fine-tuning to achieve optimal performance. Additionally, even with gating mechanisms, these models can still struggle with extremely long sequences or complex hierarchical structures.

The Transformer Revolution

The introduction of the Transformer architecture in 2017 marked a turning point in the evolution of language models. Transformers eliminated many of the challenges faced by RNNs and their variants, leading to the development of today's Large Language Models (LLMs).

1) How Transformers Work:

- Transformers use a mechanism called "self-attention" to weigh the importance of each word in a sequence relative to all other words, regardless of their position. This allows the model to capture long-range dependencies and complex relationships between words more effectively than previous models. Transformers also process entire sequences in parallel, rather than sequentially, which significantly speeds up training and inference.

2) The Impact of Transformers:

- Transformers have become the foundation of many state-of-the-art LLMs, including BERT, GPT, and T5. These models have achieved unprecedented levels of performance on a wide range of NLP tasks, from translation and summarization to question answering and text generation. The scalability and flexibility of Transformers have made them the go-to architecture for modern language models, enabling the creation of models with billions of parameters that can handle a vast array of tasks.

Why This Evolution Matters

Understanding the evolution from statistical to neural language models helps highlight the strengths and limitations of different approaches. It also provides insight into why modern LLMs are so powerful and why they represent a significant advancement in NLP. As you work with these models, recognizing the history and development of the underlying technologies will enable you to make better decisions about how to implement and optimize them in your own projects.

In the next section, we'll dive deeper into what makes Large Language Models special and how they've become the cornerstone of modern AI applications.

1.3 Overview of Large Language Models (LLMs)

Large Language Models (LLMs) have become one of the most talked-about advancements in artificial intelligence, particularly in natural language processing (NLP). But what exactly are LLMs, and why are they so important? In this section, we'll break down what makes these models unique, how they work, and why they've gained such prominence in the world of AI.

What Are Large Language Models?

At their core, Large Language Models are deep learning models that have been trained on vast amounts of text data. They are designed to understand and generate human language in a way that is contextually relevant and coherent. LLMs achieve this by learning the statistical patterns and relationships between words, phrases, and even entire sentences in the data they are trained on.

What sets LLMs apart from earlier models is their size—both in terms of the number of parameters (the weights and biases that the model learns during training) and the amount of data they are trained on. Modern LLMs like GPT-3, for example, have billions of parameters, allowing them to capture a much richer understanding of language than smaller models.

Key Features of LLMs

1) Scale and Size:

- LLMs are characterized by their sheer size. Models like GPT-3, which has 175 billion parameters, represent a massive leap in scale compared to previous generations of language models. This size enables LLMs to store and process a vast amount of information, which allows them to generate text that is remarkably coherent and contextually appropriate.

2) Pre-training and Fine-tuning:

- LLMs typically go through two main phases: pre-training and fine-tuning. During pre-training, the model is exposed to a large corpus of text data, where it learns to predict the next word in a sentence based on the context provided by the preceding words. This phase is usually unsupervised, meaning the model learns from raw text without labeled data.
- Fine-tuning comes next, where the model is adjusted on a smaller, task-specific dataset. This process helps tailor the LLM to perform specific tasks like answering questions, translating languages, or summarizing text. Fine-tuning is often supervised, with the model

learning from labeled examples that guide it toward the desired output.

3) Transfer Learning:

- One of the most powerful aspects of LLMs is their ability to transfer knowledge from one task to another. Because they are pre-trained on diverse text data, LLMs can be fine-tuned for specific tasks with relatively little additional data. This makes them incredibly versatile and capable of performing well on a wide range of NLP tasks with minimal additional training.

4) Contextual Understanding:

- LLMs excel at understanding the context in which words and phrases are used. This is largely thanks to the attention mechanisms in Transformer architectures, which allow the model to focus on relevant parts of the input text while generating or processing language. As a result, LLMs can produce text that is not only grammatically correct but also contextually meaningful.

5) Generative Capabilities:

- Beyond understanding language, LLMs are also capable of generating text. This means they can write essays, generate dialogue, create summaries, and even produce poetry—all based on the input they receive. The generative abilities of LLMs have led to the development of a wide range of applications, from chatbots to content creation tools.

Why LLMs Are Important

The rise of LLMs has had a profound impact on the field of AI and beyond. Here's why they matter:

1) Versatility:

- LLMs are incredibly versatile, able to perform a wide range of tasks without needing to be trained from scratch for each one. This versatility makes them valuable in various industries, from customer service to healthcare, where they can be applied to different problems with minimal modification.

2) Accessibility:

- As LLMs have become more widespread, they've also become more accessible. Frameworks like Hugging Face's Transformers library allow developers to easily integrate powerful LLMs into their applications, making advanced NLP capabilities available to a broader audience.

3) Innovation:

- The capabilities of LLMs are driving innovation across numerous fields. From automating routine tasks to assisting with creative processes, LLMs are being used in ways that are transforming how we interact with technology. They are not just tools for processing language; they are becoming partners in problem-solving and content creation.

4) Ethical and Societal Implications:

- The widespread use of LLMs also brings with it important ethical and societal considerations. As these models become more integrated into our daily lives, questions about bias, misinformation, and the potential misuse of AI-generated content have come to the forefront. Understanding these implications is crucial for anyone working with LLMs, and this book will address these challenges in depth.

A Glimpse into the Applications of LLMs

LLMs are already being used in a variety of applications, from virtual assistants like Google Assistant and Amazon Alexa to tools that help automate writing, such as OpenAI's GPT-3-powered applications. In healthcare, LLMs assist in summarizing patient notes, while in finance, they help analyze and interpret vast amounts of textual data.

The ability of LLMs to understand and generate language makes them a key technology in the ongoing development of AI. Whether you're looking to build chatbots, automate content creation, or develop new AI applications, LLMs offer a powerful toolset that can be adapted to a wide range of tasks.

In the next section, we'll dive into the key concepts that underpin LLMs, such as tokens, embeddings, and the Transformer architecture, which are essential for understanding how these models function and how to work with them effectively.

1.4 Key Concepts in NLP (Tokens, Embeddings, Transformers)

To work effectively with Large Language Models (LLMs), it's essential to understand the key concepts that form the foundation of how these models operate. In this section, we'll break down three critical concepts in natural language processing (NLP): tokens, embeddings, and the Transformer architecture. These elements are the building blocks that enable LLMs to understand, process, and generate human language.

Tokens: The Building Blocks of Language Models

Before a language model can process text, the text needs to be broken down into smaller, manageable pieces called tokens. Tokens can be words, subwords, characters, or even larger units like phrases, depending on the tokenization strategy used. Tokenization is the first step in preparing text data for a language model.

1) What Are Tokens?

- **Words as Tokens:** In the simplest case, each word in a sentence is treated as a token. For example, the sentence "The cat sat on the mat" would be split into six tokens: "The," "cat," "sat," "on," "the," and "mat."
- **Subword Tokens:** In many modern language models, particularly those dealing with large vocabularies or multiple languages, words are often broken down into subword tokens. This approach helps the model handle rare or unseen words by breaking them into smaller, more common parts. For example, the word "unhappiness" might be tokenized into "un," "happi," and "ness."
- **Character Tokens:** Some models, particularly those dealing with very diverse or complex languages, use individual characters as tokens. This allows for maximum flexibility but can result in much longer sequences.

2) Why Tokens Matter:

- Tokenization is crucial because it directly impacts how the model processes and understands text. The choice of tokenization strategy can affect the model's performance, especially in handling out-of-vocabulary words or dealing with different languages. Tokens are the interface between raw text and the model's internal workings, making them a fundamental concept in NLP.

Embeddings: Transforming Text into Vectors

Once text is tokenized, each token needs to be converted into a numerical format that the model can process. This is where embeddings come in. Embeddings are dense vector representations of tokens, where each token is represented as a point in a high-dimensional space.

1) What Are Embeddings?

- **Vectors in High-Dimensional Space:** An embedding is essentially a vector—a list of numbers—that represents a token. The idea is to map tokens that have similar meanings to vectors that are close to each other in this high-dimensional space. For example, the words "king" and "queen" might have embeddings that are similar to each other, reflecting their related meanings.
- **Learning Embeddings:** Embeddings are typically learned during the training of the language model. The model adjusts the embeddings to capture semantic relationships between words based on the context in which they appear in the training data.

2) Why Embeddings Matter:

- Embeddings are powerful because they allow the model to capture complex relationships between words. Unlike simple one-hot encoding, where each word is represented by a unique binary vector, embeddings enable the model to understand that words can have similar meanings, even if they're not identical. This capability is critical for tasks like word similarity, analogy reasoning, and more.

3) Popular Embedding Techniques:

- **Word2Vec:** One of the earliest and most well-known embedding techniques, Word2Vec, uses shallow neural networks to learn word embeddings based on the context in which words appear.

- **GloVe:** GloVe (Global Vectors for Word Representation) is another popular embedding technique that focuses on aggregating global word-word co-occurrence statistics from a corpus.
- **Transformer-Based Embeddings:** Modern LLMs often generate embeddings dynamically based on the context in which a word appears, thanks to the Transformer architecture.

Transformers: The Architecture Behind LLMs

The Transformer architecture is the backbone of most modern LLMs. Introduced in a 2017 paper by Vaswani et al., Transformers revolutionized NLP by addressing the limitations of earlier models like Recurrent Neural Networks (RNNs) and Long Short-Term Memory (LSTM) networks.

1) How Transformers Work:

- **Self-Attention Mechanism:** The key innovation of Transformers is the self-attention mechanism, which allows the model to weigh the importance of different words in a sequence relative to each other, regardless of their position. This means the model can focus on the most relevant parts of the input text when generating predictions, leading to better understanding and generation of language.
- **Parallel Processing:** Unlike RNNs, which process input sequentially, Transformers can process entire sequences of tokens in parallel. This dramatically speeds up training and inference, making Transformers much more efficient for large-scale models.
- **Layers and Heads:** Transformers consist of multiple layers, each containing multiple attention heads. Each head in a layer processes the input data differently, capturing different aspects of the text. The outputs from these heads are then combined and passed on to the next layer, allowing the model to build increasingly complex representations of the input text.

2) Why Transformers Matter:

- **State-of-the-Art Performance:** Transformers have set new benchmarks in a wide range of NLP tasks, from translation and summarization to question answering and text generation. Their ability to handle long-range dependencies and process data efficiently has made them the architecture of choice for LLMs.
- **Scalability:** Transformers scale remarkably well with data and computational resources. This scalability is why they are used in models with billions of parameters, enabling the creation of powerful LLMs that can perform complex tasks with high accuracy.

Putting It All Together

Tokens, embeddings, and the Transformer architecture are the key concepts that make LLMs work. Tokens are the basic units of text that the model processes, embeddings are the numerical representations that capture the meaning of these tokens, and Transformers are the architecture that brings it all together, allowing the model to understand and generate human language in sophisticated ways.

Understanding these concepts is crucial for anyone working with LLMs. As you progress through this book, you'll see how these elements are applied in practice, helping you to build, optimize, and deploy LLMs in real-world scenarios. In the next section, we'll dive deeper into the theoretical underpinnings that explain why LLMs are so effective at what they do.

1.5 Why LLMs Work: The Theoretical Underpinnings

Large Language Models (LLMs) might seem almost magical in their ability to understand and generate human language, but their effectiveness is grounded in solid theoretical principles. Understanding these principles can give you deeper insights into why LLMs are so powerful and how they can be applied effectively in various tasks. In this section, we'll break down the key theoretical underpinnings that make LLMs work so well.

The Principle of Language Modeling: Predicting the Next Word

At the core of LLMs is a fundamental concept: predicting the next word in a sequence based on the context provided by the previous words. This process is known as language modeling, and it's what enables LLMs to generate coherent and contextually appropriate text.

1. **Conditional Probability:**
   - Language modeling involves calculating the conditional probability of a word given the preceding words in a sentence. For example, if you have the sequence "The cat sat on the," the model might predict "mat" as the next word because it's a common phrase.
   - Formally, this is expressed as $P(w_n|w_1, w_2, \ldots, w_{n-1})$, where $P(w_n)$ is the probability of the next word w_n given the previous words $w_1, w_2, \ldots, w_{n-1}$. The model is trained to maximize this probability across a large dataset, learning patterns and relationships in the process.
2. **Chain Rule of Probability:**
   - The chain rule of probability is used to break down the probability of a sequence of words into the product of conditional probabilities. For a sequence of words $w_1, w_2, \ldots, w_n$, the probability of the entire sequence is:

     $$P(w_1, w_2, \ldots, w_n) = P(w_1) \times P(w_2|w_1) \times P(w_3|w_1, w_2) \times \cdots \times P(w_n|w_1, w_2, .$$
   - This decomposition allows the model to learn the structure of language by focusing on one word at a time, in the context of its preceding words.

Attention Mechanism: Focusing on What's Important

A key innovation that made LLMs particularly powerful is the attention mechanism, introduced with the Transformer architecture. The attention mechanism allows the model to weigh the importance of different words in a sentence when making predictions.

1) Self-Attention:

- In self-attention, every word in a sentence is compared to every other word to determine how much attention should be paid to each one. This means that when the model is processing a word, it can "attend" to other relevant words in the sentence, regardless of their position. This is particularly important for capturing long-range dependencies in text, where the meaning of a word might depend on something that appeared much earlier in the sentence.
- For example, in the sentence "The cat, which was sitting on the mat, looked content," the model needs to recognize that "cat" and "looked" are related, even though they are separated by several words.

2) Scaled Dot-Product Attention:

- The attention mechanism in Transformers is typically implemented as scaled dot-product attention, where the relevance of one word to another is calculated as the dot product of their respective vectors, scaled by the square root of the dimension of the vectors. This approach allows the model to efficiently compute the attention scores that determine how much focus to give to each word.

3) Multi-Head Attention:

- Transformers use multi-head attention, where multiple attention mechanisms (or heads) operate in parallel. Each head captures different aspects of the relationships between words, allowing the model to consider various perspectives when processing a sentence. The outputs from all heads are then combined, providing a richer representation of the input text.

Transformers: Parallel Processing and Scalability

The Transformer architecture, which underpins most modern LLMs, brought a significant leap in performance by allowing models to process data in parallel, rather than sequentially, as with earlier architectures like RNNs.

1) Parallelism:

- Transformers process entire sequences of text simultaneously, rather than one word at a time. This parallelism makes training much faster and allows for scaling up to handle large datasets and complex models with billions of parameters.
- Parallel processing also helps the model handle long sequences more effectively, as it can consider the entire context at once rather than relying on a step-by-step approach.

2) Positional Encoding:

- Because Transformers process all words in a sequence simultaneously, they need a way to understand the order of words. This is where positional encoding comes in. Positional encodings are added to the word embeddings to give the model information about the position of each word in the sequence. These encodings help the model distinguish between different word orders, which is crucial for understanding meaning.

Deep Learning and Backpropagation: Learning from Data

At the heart of training LLMs is deep learning, a subfield of machine learning that involves training neural networks with many layers to learn from data.

1) Neural Networks:

- LLMs are built on deep neural networks, which consist of multiple layers of interconnected nodes (or neurons). Each layer transforms the input data into a more abstract representation, allowing the model to capture increasingly complex patterns.
- In the context of LLMs, these layers help the model understand not just the immediate context of a word but also its broader meaning in relation to the entire sentence or document.

2) Backpropagation and Gradient Descent:

- During training, the model makes predictions and compares them to the actual data to calculate errors. Backpropagation is the process of sending these errors backward through the network to update the weights of the connections between nodes.
- Gradient descent is the optimization algorithm that adjusts the weights to minimize the error. Over many iterations, this process fine-tunes the model's parameters, enabling it to make increasingly accurate predictions.

Language as a Distribution: Modeling the Probabilities

One of the key reasons LLMs are effective is their ability to model language as a probability distribution. By understanding language in terms of probabilities, LLMs can generate text that is both coherent and contextually appropriate.

1) Softmax Function:

- At the final layer of the model, the softmax function is used to convert the model's outputs into a probability distribution over the vocabulary. This distribution tells us the likelihood of each word being the next word in the sequence. The model then chooses the word with the highest probability or samples from the distribution, depending on the application.

2) Learning the Distribution:

- The model learns the distribution of language by being exposed to vast amounts of text during training. As it encounters more data, it refines its understanding of how words are typically used, which improves its ability to generate or predict text in new contexts.

Putting It All Together: The Power of LLMs

The effectiveness of LLMs comes from the combination of these theoretical principles. By predicting the next word based on context, focusing on the most relevant parts of the input through attention, and leveraging deep learning to fine-tune these predictions, LLMs can produce text that is both meaningful and contextually appropriate.

Understanding these theoretical underpinnings helps to demystify how LLMs work and provides a foundation for using these models effectively. Whether you're training your own LLM, fine-tuning a pre-trained model, or deploying one in production, grasping these concepts will enable you to make informed decisions and optimize the performance of your models.

In the next section, we'll discuss the limitations and challenges of LLMs, providing a balanced view of what these models can and cannot do, and how to address some of the common issues that arise when working with them.

1.6 Limitations and Challenges of LLMs

Large Language Models (LLMs) have revolutionized the field of natural language processing (NLP) and have opened up new possibilities in AI. However, like any technology, LLMs come with their own set of limitations and challenges. Understanding these constraints is crucial for anyone looking to use or develop LLMs effectively. In this section, we'll discuss some of the key limitations and challenges associated with LLMs.

1. Scale and Resource Intensity

One of the most significant challenges with LLMs is their sheer size and the computational resources required to train and deploy them.

1) Training Costs:

- Training LLMs involves enormous computational resources. For example, training a model like GPT-3 requires powerful GPUs or TPUs running for extended periods, often leading to high energy consumption and significant costs. This resource intensity makes it difficult for smaller organizations or independent researchers to train large models from scratch.

2) Deployment Challenges:

- Even after training, deploying LLMs in production can be challenging. These models require substantial memory and processing power to run efficiently, which can lead to increased costs for cloud infrastructure or specialized hardware. Moreover, latency can become an issue, particularly for real-time applications where quick responses are essential.

3) Environmental Impact:

- The environmental impact of training large models is also a growing concern. The energy required to train LLMs contributes to carbon emissions, raising ethical questions about the sustainability of this technology. As the field advances, finding ways to reduce the carbon footprint of LLMs will be an important area of focus.

2. Interpretability and Transparency

LLMs are often described as "black boxes," meaning that while they can produce highly accurate results, understanding how they arrive at those results is not always straightforward.

1) Lack of Transparency:

- The complexity of LLMs makes it difficult to interpret their decision-making processes. For instance, while a model might generate a coherent response, the reasons behind why it chose specific words or phrases over others are not always clear. This lack of transparency can be a significant drawback in applications where understanding the rationale behind decisions is critical, such as in healthcare or legal contexts.

2) Challenges in Debugging:

- Debugging LLMs can be challenging due to their size and complexity. When an LLM produces an incorrect or biased output, it's not always easy to pinpoint the cause. This can make it difficult to improve the model or to ensure that it behaves as expected in all scenarios.

3. Bias and Fairness

Bias in LLMs is one of the most pressing issues facing the AI community today. Because LLMs learn from large datasets that often contain biases, they can inadvertently perpetuate or even amplify those biases.

1) Source of Bias:

- LLMs are trained on vast amounts of text from the internet, which includes biased language, stereotypes, and potentially harmful content. If these biases are not addressed, the models can generate outputs that reflect and reinforce those biases, leading to unfair or discriminatory outcomes.

2) Impact on Decision-Making:

- In applications like hiring, lending, or law enforcement, biased outputs from LLMs can have serious consequences. For example, if an LLM is used to screen job applicants, it might favor certain demographics over others based on biased training data. Addressing bias in LLMs is crucial to ensure that these models are fair and ethical.

3) Mitigation Strategies:

- Researchers are actively working on strategies to mitigate bias in LLMs, such as fine-tuning models on curated datasets, using fairness constraints during training, or applying post-processing techniques to adjust biased outputs. However, completely eliminating bias remains a challenging task.

4. Generalization and Context Understanding

While LLMs are remarkably good at generating text that appears human-like, they can struggle with certain types of generalization and understanding complex contexts.

1) Surface-Level Understanding:

- LLMs are excellent at capturing patterns in text but may lack a deep understanding of the underlying concepts. They can produce coherent sentences that make sense on the surface but fail when more in-depth reasoning or domain-specific knowledge is required. For example, an LLM might generate a convincing but factually incorrect explanation for a scientific phenomenon.

2) Struggles with Novel Contexts:

- When faced with contexts that differ significantly from the training data, LLMs can struggle to generalize appropriately. This can lead to outputs that are nonsensical or irrelevant in novel situations. Ensuring that LLMs can adapt to new contexts without retraining is an ongoing challenge.

5. Ethical and Societal Implications

As LLMs become more integrated into society, they raise a host of ethical and societal questions that need to be carefully considered.

1) Misinformation and Manipulation:

- LLMs can be used to generate highly convincing fake news, deepfakes, or other forms of misinformation. The ease with which these models can produce misleading content poses significant risks, especially in the context of social media and online communication.

2) Privacy Concerns:

- LLMs trained on large datasets might inadvertently memorize sensitive information, which can then be reproduced in generated text. This raises concerns about data privacy, particularly when models are trained on personal or proprietary data.

3) Autonomy and Control:

- As LLMs become more capable, there is a growing debate about the level of autonomy these models should have. Questions about human oversight, accountability, and control are central to the responsible deployment of LLMs in various applications.

6. Continuous Learning and Adaptation

Another limitation of current LLMs is their difficulty in learning continuously from new data without forgetting what they've previously learned.

1) Catastrophic Forgetting:

- When an LLM is fine-tuned on a new dataset, it can suffer from catastrophic forgetting, where it loses information learned during its initial training. This makes it challenging to keep models up to date with the latest information without retraining from scratch.

2) Adaptation to New Knowledge:

- LLMs typically require significant retraining to incorporate new knowledge. Unlike humans, who can learn incrementally and adapt to new information quickly, LLMs need large amounts of data and compute resources to update their knowledge, which limits their flexibility in dynamic environments.

Addressing the Challenges

While these limitations are significant, they are not insurmountable. Researchers and practitioners are actively working on solutions to improve the transparency, fairness, efficiency, and adaptability of LLMs. By understanding these challenges, you'll be better equipped to work with LLMs effectively and responsibly.

As we move forward in this book, we'll delve into practical strategies for addressing some of these challenges and optimizing LLMs for real-world applications. By being aware of the limitations, you can make more informed decisions about how to deploy and refine these powerful tools.

Chapter 2: Architectures and Frameworks

2.1 The Transformer Architecture: In-Depth Explanation

The Transformer architecture is the backbone of most modern Large Language Models (LLMs), and understanding how it works is key to grasping why these models are so powerful. Introduced in 2017 by Vaswani et al., the Transformer brought a fundamental shift in how we approach natural language processing (NLP), making it possible to train models that are both more efficient and more capable than their predecessors.

What Makes the Transformer Different?

Before the Transformer, Recurrent Neural Networks (RNNs) and their variants, like Long Short-Term Memory (LSTM) networks, were the go-to architectures for sequence-based tasks. However, these models processed input sequentially, word by word, which made them slow and prone to issues like vanishing gradients. The Transformer, in contrast, processes entire sequences in parallel, which not only speeds up training but also allows it to capture long-range dependencies more effectively.

The Self-Attention Mechanism

At the heart of the Transformer is the self-attention mechanism. This is what allows the model to weigh the importance of different words in a sequence relative to each other, regardless of their position. Here's how it works:

1) Attention Scores:

- For each word in the input sequence, the Transformer calculates a set of attention scores. These scores determine how much attention the model should pay to each word in the sequence when processing a particular word. The attention scores are based on the dot product of the word's query vector with the key vectors of all other words in the sequence.

2) Queries, Keys, and Values:

- In the Transformer, each word in the sequence is transformed into three vectors: a query, a key, and a value. The query and key vectors are used to calculate the attention scores, while the value vectors are combined according to these scores to produce the final output. This process allows the model to focus on the most relevant parts of the sequence when making predictions.

3) Scaled Dot-Product Attention:

- The raw attention scores are scaled by the square root of the dimensionality of the key vectors. This scaling prevents the dot products from becoming too large when the dimensionality is high, which could otherwise cause the softmax function to produce very small gradients, making the model harder to train.

4) Softmax Function:

- The scaled attention scores are passed through a softmax function to convert them into probabilities. These probabilities indicate the importance of each word in the sequence, allowing the model to focus on the most relevant words while processing the input.

Multi-Head Attention

One of the key innovations of the Transformer is its use of multi-head attention. Instead of having just one set of attention scores, the model calculates several different sets, or "heads," in parallel. Each head looks at the sequence from a different perspective, allowing the model to capture a variety of relationships between words.

1) Why Multi-Head Attention Matters:

- Multi-head attention enables the model to focus on different aspects of the input simultaneously. For example, one head might focus on the syntactic structure of a sentence, while another head focuses on semantic meaning. By combining these different perspectives, the model can build a richer, more nuanced understanding of the text.

2) Combining the Heads:

- After processing the input through multiple attention heads, the outputs are concatenated and passed through a final linear layer. This allows the model to integrate the different perspectives from each head into a single representation that captures both the local and global context of the input.

Positional Encoding: Handling the Sequence Order

Because the Transformer processes all words in a sequence in parallel, it needs a way to keep track of the order of the words. This is where positional encoding comes in.

1) What Is Positional Encoding?

- Positional encoding adds information about the position of each word in the sequence to its corresponding word embedding. This is typically done by adding sine and cosine functions of different frequencies to the embeddings. These functions are designed so that each position in the sequence has a unique encoding, allowing the model to distinguish between different word orders.

2) Why It's Important:

- Without positional encoding, the Transformer would treat the sequence as a "bag of words," ignoring the order in which words appear. This would be problematic for tasks like translation, where word order is crucial to meaning. Positional encoding ensures that the model can take the sequence order into account when processing text.

The Transformer's Layer Structure

The Transformer is made up of multiple layers, each consisting of two main components: the multi-head attention mechanism and a feed-forward neural network.

1) Multi-Head Attention Layer:

- As described earlier, this layer allows the model to focus on different parts of the input sequence simultaneously. Each attention head processes the input independently, and their outputs are combined to form the final output of the layer.

2) Feed-Forward Neural Network:

- After the multi-head attention layer, the output is passed through a feed-forward neural network. This network consists of two linear layers with a ReLU activation function in between. The feed-forward network processes each position in the sequence independently, applying the same transformation to all positions.

3) Layer Normalization and Residual Connections:

- To stabilize training, each layer in the Transformer includes layer normalization and residual connections. Layer normalization helps to normalize the input to each layer, improving training efficiency. Residual connections add the original input to the output of the layer, which helps to prevent the gradient from vanishing during backpropagation, making the model easier to train.

Encoder-Decoder Structure

The original Transformer architecture is designed as an encoder-decoder model, which is particularly useful for tasks like translation. However, many LLMs use just the encoder (e.g., BERT) or the decoder (e.g., GPT) portions of the Transformer.

1) Encoder:

- The encoder processes the input sequence and generates a set of representations that capture the meaning of the input. Each layer of the encoder builds on the previous one, gradually refining these representations.

2) Decoder:

- The decoder generates the output sequence, using the representations produced by the encoder. It also includes a mechanism to attend to the encoder's output, ensuring that the generated sequence is consistent with the input. In models like GPT, the decoder is used on its own to generate text based on a given prompt.

Why the Transformer Architecture Matters

The Transformer architecture's ability to process sequences in parallel, capture long-range dependencies, and handle large datasets efficiently is what makes it the foundation of modern LLMs. Its flexibility allows it to be adapted to a wide range of tasks, from translation and summarization to question answering and text generation.

Understanding the details of how the Transformer works is crucial for anyone looking to work with LLMs. Whether you're building your own model, fine-tuning a pre-trained one, or simply trying to optimize performance, a solid grasp of the Transformer architecture will give you the tools you need to succeed.

In the next section, we'll explore the different variants of the Transformer architecture, such as BERT, GPT, and T5, and discuss how these models have been adapted to tackle specific NLP tasks.

2.2 Variants of Transformers: BERT, GPT, T5, etc.

The Transformer architecture has become the foundation for a wide range of powerful models in natural language processing (NLP). While the basic principles of the Transformer remain the same, different models have been developed to address specific tasks and challenges within NLP. In this section, we'll look at some of the most important Transformer variants—BERT, GPT, T5, and others—and understand what makes each of them unique.

BERT (Bidirectional Encoder Representations from Transformers)

BERT is one of the most influential Transformer-based models and represents a significant shift in how we approach NLP tasks. Introduced by Google in 2018, BERT is designed to understand the context of words in a sentence by looking at both the words that come before and after a given word—hence the term "bidirectional."

1) Bidirectional Training:

- Traditional models like GPT process text in one direction—either from left to right or right to left. BERT, however, processes text in both directions simultaneously. This means BERT can capture more context and understand words in relation to the entire sentence, not just the preceding words.

2) Masked Language Modeling:

- BERT is pre-trained using a technique called Masked Language Modeling (MLM). During training, random words in a sentence are "masked" or hidden, and the model is tasked with predicting these masked words based on the surrounding context. This approach forces BERT to learn a deep understanding of language structure and context.

3) Next Sentence Prediction:

- Another aspect of BERT's pre-training involves predicting whether a given sentence logically follows another sentence. This helps BERT understand relationships between sentences, making it particularly effective for tasks like question answering and natural language inference.

4) Applications of BERT:

- BERT has been fine-tuned for a wide range of tasks, including sentiment analysis, named entity recognition, and more. Its ability to understand context deeply makes it highly effective for tasks where nuanced understanding of language is crucial.

GPT (Generative Pre-trained Transformer)

GPT, developed by OpenAI, is another landmark model in the Transformer family. Unlike BERT, which focuses on understanding text, GPT is designed to generate text. This makes it particularly useful for tasks like text completion, content creation, and conversational agents.

1) Autoregressive Language Modeling:

- GPT uses an autoregressive approach, meaning it generates text one word at a time, using the previous words to predict the next one. This sequential generation allows GPT to produce coherent and contextually appropriate text.

2) Unidirectional Context:

- Unlike BERT, which is bidirectional, GPT processes text in one direction—typically left to right. This makes GPT particularly good at generating long-form content where maintaining a coherent narrative over many words or sentences is important.

3) Transfer Learning with GPT:

- Like BERT, GPT is pre-trained on large amounts of text data and can be fine-tuned for specific tasks. However, because GPT is a generative model, it excels at tasks that require text generation, such as writing essays, generating code, or even creating poetry.

4) GPT-2 and GPT-3:

- Subsequent versions of GPT, such as GPT-2 and GPT-3, have significantly increased the model's size and capabilities. GPT-3, with 175 billion parameters, is one of the largest language models ever created and can perform a wide range of tasks with minimal fine-tuning, simply by providing it with the right prompt.

T5 (Text-To-Text Transfer Transformer)

T5, developed by Google, takes a different approach by framing all NLP tasks as a text-to-text problem. Whether it's translation, summarization, or classification, T5 converts the input into text and expects the output to be text as well.

1) Unified Framework:

- T5's text-to-text framework allows it to be applied to a wide range of tasks without needing to change the model architecture. This simplifies the process of fine-tuning the model for different tasks since the same basic approach is used for everything.

2) Pre-training with Span Corruption:

- During pre-training, T5 uses a technique called span corruption. This involves randomly selecting spans of text (rather than individual words) to mask and then training the model to predict the missing spans based on the surrounding context. This helps T5 learn to generate coherent text over longer sequences.

3) Versatility:

- T5's versatility makes it a strong choice for many NLP applications. It's particularly effective for tasks that involve transforming one type of text into another, such as translation, summarization, and even question answering.

Other Notable Transformer Variants

In addition to BERT, GPT, and T5, several other Transformer variants have been developed to tackle specific challenges in NLP:

1) RoBERTa (Robustly Optimized BERT Pretraining Approach):

- RoBERTa is a variant of BERT that modifies the pre-training process by removing the Next Sentence Prediction task and using larger batch sizes and more training data. These changes result in improved performance across a range of tasks.

2) ALBERT (A Lite BERT):

- ALBERT is designed to be a lighter, more efficient version of BERT. It reduces the size of the model by sharing parameters across layers and using factorized embeddings, making it faster and less resource-intensive while maintaining strong performance.

3) DistilBERT:

- DistilBERT is a smaller, faster version of BERT that is designed to run efficiently on less powerful hardware. It's created using a technique called knowledge distillation, where a smaller model is trained to replicate the behavior of a larger model, resulting in a model that is 60% faster and half the size of BERT, with 97% of its performance.

4) XLNet:

- XLNet combines ideas from BERT and autoregressive models like GPT. It uses a permutation-based training approach to capture bidirectional context without relying on masking. This allows it to model dependencies between all positions in a sequence more effectively.

Choosing the Right Transformer Variant

When working with Transformers, it's important to choose the right variant for your specific task. BERT is often the go-to model for understanding text, while GPT excels at text generation. T5's versatility makes it a strong contender for tasks that involve transforming text, and lighter models like ALBERT and DistilBERT are ideal when computational resources are limited.

Each of these models builds on the Transformer architecture in different ways, optimizing it for particular use cases. Understanding the strengths and weaknesses of each variant can help you make informed decisions about which model to use for your project.

In the next section, we'll compare these LLM architectures in more detail, examining their performance, resource requirements, and suitability for various tasks. This will help you better understand the trade-offs involved in choosing one model over another.

2.3 Comparison of LLM Architectures

With so many Transformer-based models available, choosing the right one for your specific task can be challenging. Each model, whether it's BERT, GPT, T5, or others, has its strengths and trade-offs. In this section, we'll compare these Large Language Model (LLM) architectures across several key dimensions: training objectives, directional context, scalability, and suitability for different NLP tasks. Understanding these differences will help you select the best model for your needs.

1. Training Objectives

One of the primary ways LLMs differ is in their training objectives, which shape how they learn to process and generate language.

BERT (Bidirectional Encoding):

- BERT is trained using a combination of Masked Language Modeling (MLM) and Next Sentence Prediction (NSP). In MLM, BERT randomly masks words in a sentence and then tries to predict them, forcing the model to understand the context surrounding each word. NSP further helps BERT understand the relationships between sentences, making it well-suited for tasks like question answering and sentence classification.

GPT (Autoregressive Generation):

- GPT models are trained using an autoregressive objective, which means they generate text by predicting the next word in a sequence based on the preceding words. This makes GPT particularly effective for text generation tasks, such as story writing or dialogue generation, where maintaining coherence over long sequences is important.

T5 (Text-to-Text Framework):

- T5 adopts a unified text-to-text framework, where all tasks are framed as converting one type of text into another. Whether it's translation, summarization, or classification, the input is treated as text, and the output is also text. T5's training objective is based on span corruption, where spans of text are masked, and the model is trained to predict the missing spans.

2. Directional Context

The directionality of a model—whether it processes text unidirectionally or bidirectionally—affects how it understands and generates language.

BERT (Bidirectional):

- BERT processes text bidirectionally, meaning it considers both the left and right context when predicting masked words. This allows BERT to develop a deeper understanding of context, making it particularly effective for tasks where understanding the meaning of a word in relation to the entire sentence is important.

GPT (Unidirectional):

- GPT processes text unidirectionally, typically from left to right. This makes GPT better suited for tasks that require generating text sequentially, such as language modeling and creative writing, where the model builds up context as it generates each word.

T5 (Bidirectional for Encoding, Autoregressive for Decoding):

- T5 uses a bidirectional approach during the encoding phase to understand the context fully, but it switches to an autoregressive approach during decoding for text generation. This hybrid approach allows T5 to excel at both understanding and generating text, making it versatile across a range of tasks.

3. Scalability and Resource Requirements

The size of an LLM, in terms of the number of parameters, directly impacts its performance, training time, and resource requirements.

BERT:

- BERT comes in several sizes, from BERT-Base with 110 million parameters to BERT-Large with 340 million parameters. While BERT-Large offers better performance, it also requires more computational resources and longer training times.

GPT:

- GPT models have progressively scaled up, with GPT-3 being the largest with 175 billion parameters. While this makes GPT-3 incredibly powerful, it also means that training and deploying such a model require significant computational resources, making it accessible primarily to organizations with extensive resources.

T5:

- T5 also comes in various sizes, from T5-Small (60 million parameters) to T5-XXL (11 billion parameters). The smaller versions of T5 are more accessible for tasks requiring less computational power, while the larger versions provide state-of-the-art performance at the cost of increased resource demands.

4. Suitability for Different NLP Tasks

Different LLMs are optimized for different types of NLP tasks. Here's how they compare:

BERT:

- **Best For:** Understanding tasks such as sentiment analysis, named entity recognition, and question answering. BERT's bidirectional context makes it especially strong for tasks where the relationship between words and their context matters.
- **Not Ideal For:** Text generation tasks, where a unidirectional model like GPT might perform better.

GPT:

- **Best For:** Text generation tasks like content creation, storytelling, and conversational AI. GPT's autoregressive nature allows it to generate coherent and contextually appropriate text over long sequences.
- **Not Ideal For:** Tasks requiring a deep understanding of context within a sentence, such as certain types of comprehension tasks.

T5:

- **Best For:** A wide range of tasks including translation, summarization, and text classification, thanks to its unified text-to-text approach. T5's flexibility makes it a good choice for projects where multiple NLP tasks need to be handled by the same model.
- **Not Ideal For:** Tasks where extreme efficiency or minimal resource use is critical, especially when using larger versions of T5.

5. Flexibility and Adaptability

Flexibility refers to how easily an LLM can be adapted to different tasks through fine-tuning or modification.

BERT:

- BERT's structure makes it highly adaptable for fine-tuning on various NLP tasks. It has become a standard model for many NLP benchmarks due to its versatility and strong performance across different tasks.

GPT:

- GPT is also highly adaptable, especially for tasks requiring text generation. It can be fine-tuned for specific applications, but its unidirectional nature makes it less flexible for tasks that require understanding context from both directions.

T5:

- T5's text-to-text framework provides a high degree of flexibility, allowing it to be applied to virtually any NLP task that can be framed as text-to-text. This makes T5 particularly useful in scenarios where you need a single model to perform a variety of tasks.

Summary of Key Differences

- **BERT** excels in understanding tasks due to its bidirectional context and is well-suited for fine-tuning on a range of NLP applications.
- **GPT** shines in text generation with its autoregressive approach, making it ideal for creative tasks and conversational AI.
- **T5** offers a versatile, unified approach to NLP tasks, providing a balance between understanding and generating text across a wide

range of applications.

When choosing between these models, consider the specific requirements of your task, the computational resources available, and the desired outcome. Understanding the strengths and limitations of each architecture will enable you to select the most appropriate model for your needs.

In the next section, we'll explore the frameworks available for building and deploying these LLMs, such as TensorFlow, PyTorch, and Hugging Face Transformers, which provide the tools you need to implement and customize these models effectively.

2.4 Frameworks for Building LLMs: TensorFlow, PyTorch, Hugging Face Transformers

Building and deploying Large Language Models (LLMs) requires robust and flexible frameworks that can handle the complexities of training, fine-tuning, and serving these models. Three of the most popular frameworks in the AI community today are TensorFlow, PyTorch, and Hugging Face Transformers. Each of these frameworks offers unique features and tools that cater to different needs and preferences. In this section, we'll explore what each framework offers and how they can be used effectively in building LLMs.

TensorFlow

TensorFlow, developed by Google, is one of the most widely used deep learning frameworks. It's known for its flexibility, scalability, and strong support for production deployment, making it a popular choice for both research and industry.

1) Key Features:

- **Ecosystem:** TensorFlow has a rich ecosystem of tools and libraries, including TensorBoard for visualization, TensorFlow Lite for mobile and embedded devices, and TensorFlow Serving for deploying models in production environments. This makes it an all-in-one solution for developing, training, and deploying LLMs.
- **Keras Integration:** TensorFlow's integration with Keras, a high-level API, makes it easier to build and experiment with neural networks. Keras provides a user-friendly interface for quickly prototyping models, which is especially useful when working with complex architectures like Transformers.
- **TF Hub and Model Garden:** TensorFlow Hub is a repository of pre-trained models that can be easily integrated into your projects. The Model Garden contains state-of-the-art models, including LLMs, that you can fine-tune or use out of the box.

2) Advantages:

- **Scalability:** TensorFlow is designed to scale from individual experiments on a single GPU to distributed training across multiple GPUs and TPUs. This makes it suitable for large-scale LLM projects where you need to process vast amounts of data.
- **Production-Ready:** TensorFlow's strong focus on production deployment means that it provides tools to efficiently move models from research to production. TensorFlow Serving, in particular, is widely used to deploy LLMs in real-world applications, offering high-performance inference at scale.

3) Considerations:

- **Learning Curve:** TensorFlow's flexibility comes with a steeper learning curve, especially for beginners. While Keras simplifies some aspects, mastering TensorFlow's full capabilities requires a good understanding of its computational graph and other advanced features.

PyTorch

PyTorch, developed by Facebook's AI Research lab, has quickly become a favorite among researchers and practitioners due to its ease of use, dynamic computation graph, and strong community support. It's particularly popular in academic research but is also increasingly being used in production environments.

1) Key Features:

- **Dynamic Computation Graph:** PyTorch uses a dynamic computation graph, meaning that the graph is built on-the-fly as operations are executed. This makes debugging and model experimentation more intuitive compared to static graph frameworks like TensorFlow.
- **Native Python Integration:** PyTorch integrates seamlessly with Python, making it feel more natural for Python developers. This integration simplifies the process of writing custom layers, loss functions, and other components.
- **TorchServe:** For production deployment, PyTorch offers TorchServe, an easy-to-use tool for serving PyTorch models at scale. TorchServe provides features like multi-model serving, model versioning, and metrics, making it easier to deploy and manage LLMs.

2) Advantages:

- **User-Friendly:** PyTorch's straightforward API and dynamic graph make it easier to learn and use, especially for those new to deep learning. This has led to its rapid adoption in the research community, where quick prototyping is often necessary.
- **Strong Community and Ecosystem:** PyTorch has a vibrant community that contributes to its continuous development. The framework also has a growing ecosystem of tools, including PyTorch Lightning for organizing code, and Hugging Face Transformers, which is built on

top of PyTorch.

3) Considerations:

- **Production Deployment:** While PyTorch has made strides in production readiness with TorchServe and other tools, TensorFlow is still often considered more mature for large-scale deployment in enterprise environments. However, PyTorch's rapid development is closing this gap.

Hugging Face Transformers

Hugging Face Transformers is a specialized library that provides implementations of state-of-the-art LLMs like BERT, GPT, T5, and others. It's built on top of PyTorch and TensorFlow, making it incredibly versatile and accessible.

1) Key Features:

- **Pre-trained Models:** Hugging Face Transformers offers a wide range of pre-trained models that can be easily fine-tuned or used as-is. This includes models for tasks like text classification, question answering, and text generation.
- **Tokenizer and Pipeline APIs:** The library provides powerful tokenizer utilities that handle text preprocessing, as well as pipeline APIs that simplify the process of setting up end-to-end NLP workflows. This makes it easier to integrate LLMs into your projects without needing to dive into the complexities of model training.
- **Model Hub:** Hugging Face Model Hub is an open repository where researchers and developers can share their trained models. This allows you to leverage models trained by others or contribute your own, fostering collaboration within the AI community.

2) Advantages:

- **Ease of Use:** Hugging Face Transformers is designed to be user-friendly, with well-documented code and examples. Whether you're a beginner or an experienced developer, you can quickly get started with LLMs using the tools provided by Hugging Face.
- **Flexibility:** The library supports both PyTorch and TensorFlow, allowing you to choose the backend that best suits your needs. It also integrates easily with other libraries and tools, making it a versatile addition to any NLP project.

3) Considerations:

- **Specialized Use:** While Hugging Face Transformers is incredibly powerful for NLP tasks, it's more specialized compared to general-purpose frameworks like TensorFlow and PyTorch. If you're working on projects outside of NLP, you might need to rely on other tools or frameworks.

Choosing the Right Framework

The choice between TensorFlow, PyTorch, and Hugging Face Transformers depends on your specific needs, experience level, and the nature of your project:

- **TensorFlow** is ideal if you need a robust, production-ready framework that scales well across large projects and offers a comprehensive ecosystem of tools.
- **PyTorch** is a great choice for research and development, particularly if you value ease of use, dynamic graph execution, and seamless Python integration.
- **Hugging Face Transformers** is perfect if your work focuses on NLP and you want access to state-of-the-art LLMs with minimal setup and

configuration.

Each of these frameworks has its strengths, and the best choice will depend on the specific requirements of your project. By understanding what each framework offers, you can select the one that aligns best with your goals and workflow.

In the next section, we'll discuss scalability considerations in LLM architectures, exploring how these frameworks handle the challenges of training and deploying large models at scale.

2.5 Scalability Considerations in LLM Architectures

Scaling Large Language Models (LLMs) is a critical aspect of their development and deployment, particularly as the demand for more powerful and efficient models continues to grow. The ability to scale effectively impacts not only the performance of these models but also the feasibility of deploying them in real-world applications. In this section, we'll discuss the key scalability considerations in LLM architectures, focusing on data parallelism, model parallelism, hardware requirements, and the challenges of maintaining performance as models grow in size.

1. Data Parallelism

Data parallelism is one of the most common strategies used to scale the training of LLMs. It involves splitting the training data across multiple processors or machines so that each one processes a different subset of the data simultaneously.

1) How It Works:

- In data parallelism, a copy of the model is replicated across multiple

GPUs or TPUs, and each copy processes a different mini-batch of data. After each forward and backward pass, the gradients computed by each copy are averaged and used to update the model parameters, ensuring that all copies remain synchronized.

2) Advantages:

- **Efficiency:** Data parallelism can significantly speed up training by utilizing multiple processors to handle large datasets simultaneously. This approach is particularly effective when the model itself can fit into the memory of a single GPU or TPU.
- **Simplicity:** Implementing data parallelism is relatively straightforward, especially with frameworks like TensorFlow and PyTorch that provide built-in support for distributed training.

3) Considerations:

- **Communication Overhead:** As the number of GPUs or TPUs increases, the time required to communicate and synchronize gradients across devices can become a bottleneck. Efficient communication strategies, such as reducing the precision of gradients (e.g., using float16 instead of float32), can help mitigate this issue.

2. Model Parallelism

Model parallelism is another approach to scaling LLMs, particularly when the model is too large to fit into the memory of a single GPU or TPU. In this case, the model itself is split across multiple devices.

1) How It Works:

- In model parallelism, different layers or parts of the model are placed on different devices. During the forward pass, data is passed through the layers sequentially across devices. For example, the first few layers might be on one GPU, the middle layers on another, and the final layers on a third.

2) Advantages:

- **Handling Large Models:** Model parallelism allows you to train models that exceed the memory capacity of a single GPU or TPU. This is essential for very large LLMs like GPT-3, which have billions of parameters.

3) Considerations:

- **Complexity:** Implementing model parallelism is more complex than data parallelism. It requires careful partitioning of the model and efficient management of data transfers between devices to minimize latency.
- **Load Balancing:** Ensuring that all devices are utilized effectively can be challenging. If one part of the model is significantly more computationally intensive than others, it can lead to imbalances and reduced efficiency.

3. Pipeline Parallelism

Pipeline parallelism is a hybrid approach that combines elements of both data and model parallelism. It involves partitioning the model into stages and then feeding different mini-batches of data through these stages in a staggered manner.

1) How It Works:

- The model is divided into several stages, with each stage running on a different GPU or TPU. As soon as the first stage finishes processing one mini-batch, it starts processing the next one while the second stage processes the output of the first mini-batch. This creates a pipeline of data flowing through the model.

2) Advantages:

- **Improved Resource Utilization:** By overlapping the execution of different stages, pipeline parallelism can reduce idle time for each device, leading to better utilization of resources.
- **Scalability:** This approach can scale effectively with the number of devices, making it suitable for very large models that require both data and model parallelism.

3) Considerations:

- **Latency:** Pipeline parallelism introduces some latency due to the staggered execution, which can affect training speed. However, this is often outweighed by the overall efficiency gains.
- **Complexity:** Like model parallelism, pipeline parallelism is complex to implement and requires careful management of data flow between stages.

4. Hardware Requirements

The scalability of LLMs is also heavily dependent on the underlying hardware. As models grow in size, the demand for computational power, memory, and bandwidth increases, making the choice of hardware critical.

1) GPUs vs. TPUs:

- **GPUs (Graphics Processing Units):** GPUs are widely used for training LLMs due to their high parallel processing capabilities. NVIDIA GPUs, in particular, are commonly used in both research and production environments, with libraries like CUDA and cuDNN providing the necessary tools for deep learning.

- **TPUs (Tensor Processing Units):** Developed by Google, TPUs are specialized hardware designed specifically for machine learning tasks. They offer high performance and efficiency, particularly for training large models at scale. TPUs are often used in cloud environments where scalability and speed are critical.

2) Memory Considerations:

- As LLMs grow in size, the memory requirements for storing model parameters and intermediate computations also increase. High-end GPUs and TPUs with large amounts of VRAM (Video RAM) are essential for training and deploying large models. Techniques like mixed precision training, where some calculations are done in lower precision (e.g., float16), can help reduce memory usage without significantly impacting performance.

3) Distributed Training Infrastructure:

- Scaling LLMs often requires distributed training across multiple GPUs or TPUs. This involves setting up clusters of machines, each equipped with multiple GPUs or TPUs, and managing the distribution of data and model parameters across these machines. Cloud platforms like Google Cloud, AWS, and Azure offer tools and services that simplify the deployment of distributed training environments.

5. Maintaining Performance at Scale

As LLMs scale up, maintaining performance becomes increasingly challenging. Larger models tend to require more data, more computation, and more careful tuning to achieve optimal results.

1) Hyperparameter Tuning:

- Hyperparameter tuning is critical when scaling LLMs. Parameters like learning rate, batch size, and the number of layers need to be carefully adjusted to ensure that the model trains efficiently and converges to a good solution. Automated hyperparameter tuning tools, such as Google's Vizier or Ray Tune, can help manage this process at scale.

2) Gradient Accumulation:

- Gradient accumulation is a technique used to simulate larger batch sizes without requiring more memory. Gradients are accumulated over several mini-batches before performing a weight update. This allows for more stable training and can be particularly useful when working with large models on limited hardware.

3) Checkpointing and Fault Tolerance:

- Training large LLMs can take days or even weeks, making fault tolerance essential. Checkpointing involves periodically saving the model's state so that training can resume from the last checkpoint in case of a failure. This is crucial for avoiding the loss of progress during long training runs.

4) Optimizing Communication:

- Efficient communication between devices is essential for maintaining performance in distributed training. Techniques like gradient compression, where gradients are compressed before being sent across devices, and using high-bandwidth interconnects like NVIDIA's NVLink can help reduce communication overhead.

6. Energy Efficiency and Environmental Impact

As LLMs scale up, their energy consumption becomes a significant concern, both in terms of cost and environmental impact.

1) Energy-Efficient Hardware:

- Using energy-efficient hardware, such as TPUs or GPUs with better power efficiency, can help reduce the overall energy consumption of training and deploying LLMs. Additionally, optimizing the use of cloud resources to run models during off-peak hours can also lead to energy savings.

2) Sustainable AI Practices:

- Researchers and practitioners are increasingly focusing on sustainable AI practices, such as using pre-trained models and fine-tuning them rather than training large models from scratch. This not only reduces energy consumption but also speeds up the development process.

3) Carbon Footprint Reduction:

- Some organizations are exploring ways to offset the carbon footprint of training large models, such as investing in renewable energy or participating in carbon offset programs. As the AI community becomes more aware of the environmental impact of large-scale models, these practices are likely to become more common.

Scaling LLMs involves a careful balance of data and model parallelism, appropriate hardware selection, and techniques to maintain performance as models grow in size. Understanding these scalability considerations is crucial for successfully developing and deploying LLMs, particularly as the demand for larger and more powerful models continues to rise.

In the next section, we'll look at future trends in LLM architectures, exploring how the field is evolving and what innovations are on the horizon to address the challenges of scaling and deploying these models.

2.6 Future Trends in LLM Architectures

The field of Large Language Models (LLMs) is evolving rapidly, with new architectures, techniques, and applications emerging regularly. As the demand for more powerful, efficient, and versatile models grows, researchers and developers are pushing the boundaries of what LLMs can achieve. In this section, we'll look at some of the key trends shaping the future of LLM architectures and how these developments might impact the landscape of natural language processing (NLP).

1. Smaller, More Efficient Models

While large models like GPT-3 have demonstrated impressive capabilities, their size and resource requirements make them difficult to deploy and scale. As a result, there is a growing focus on developing smaller, more efficient models that can deliver similar performance with fewer resources.

1) Model Compression Techniques:

- Techniques such as pruning, quantization, and knowledge distillation are becoming increasingly important. These methods reduce the size of LLMs by removing redundant parameters, lowering the precision of computations, or training smaller models to mimic the behavior of larger ones. These techniques not only reduce the computational footprint but also make it easier to deploy models on edge devices and in low-resource environments.

2) Sparse Models:

- Sparse models, which selectively activate only a portion of their neurons or parameters for each input, are gaining attention as a way to maintain model performance while reducing computational demands. Approaches like Mixture of Experts (MoE) allow different parts of the model to specialize in handling different types of inputs, leading to more efficient use of resources.

3) Adaptive Computation:

- Adaptive computation techniques enable models to dynamically adjust their complexity based on the difficulty of the input. For example, a model might use fewer layers or parameters when processing simpler inputs and more for complex ones. This approach helps balance performance and efficiency, particularly in real-time applications.

2. Multimodal Models

The future of LLMs isn't limited to text alone. There is a growing interest in developing multimodal models that can process and generate content across multiple modalities, such as text, images, and audio.

1) Vision-Language Models:

- Models like OpenAI's CLIP and DALL-E have shown that combining text and visual data can lead to powerful new capabilities. These models can generate images from textual descriptions or understand images in the context of related text. As research in this area progresses, we can expect to see more models that integrate language with other modalities, opening up new possibilities for applications in areas like content creation, virtual reality, and human-computer interaction.

2) Audio and Speech Integration:

- Integrating audio and speech processing with LLMs is another emerging trend. By combining speech recognition, natural language understanding, and text-to-speech generation, multimodal models could enhance voice assistants, improve accessibility tools, and enable more natural interactions between humans and machines.

3) Unified Multimodal Frameworks:

- Researchers are also working on unified frameworks that can handle multiple modalities within a single architecture. These frameworks aim to create models that can seamlessly switch between or combine different types of inputs and outputs, making them more versatile and capable of handling complex tasks that require an understanding of diverse data types.

3. Continuous Learning and Adaptation

One of the limitations of current LLMs is their static nature: once trained, they are not easily updated with new information without retraining. Future LLM architectures are likely to incorporate continuous learning capabilities, allowing models to adapt to new data and evolving contexts more effectively.

1) Lifelong Learning:

- Lifelong learning refers to the ability of a model to continuously learn from new data without forgetting previously acquired knowledge. This is crucial for applications where the information changes frequently, such as news summarization or financial analysis. Techniques like elastic weight consolidation and memory-augmented networks are being explored to enable this capability.

2) Few-Shot and Zero-Shot Learning:

- Few-shot and zero-shot learning enable models to perform new tasks with little to no additional training data. These capabilities are particularly useful in scenarios where labeled data is scarce or where the model needs to generalize to unseen tasks. Future architectures may further enhance these abilities, making LLMs even more versatile and applicable to a broader range of problems.

3) Real-Time Adaptation:

- Real-time adaptation involves adjusting the model's behavior based on immediate feedback from users or the environment. This could lead to more interactive and responsive applications, such as adaptive chatbots that learn user preferences over time or recommendation systems that update in real-time based on user interactions.

4. Ethics and Explainability

As LLMs become more integrated into critical applications, the need for ethical AI and explainability will continue to grow. Future architectures will likely include features that address these concerns more directly.

1) Bias Mitigation:

- There is ongoing research into methods for detecting and mitigating bias in LLMs. This includes developing fairer training practices, using balanced datasets, and applying post-processing techniques to reduce biased outputs. As ethical considerations become more central to AI development, future models will likely incorporate these practices from the ground up.

2) Explainable AI (XAI):

- Explainability is crucial for understanding how LLMs make decisions, particularly in high-stakes applications like healthcare or legal systems. Future LLM architectures may include built-in mechanisms for generating explanations for their outputs, helping users and developers understand the reasoning behind a model's decisions.

3) Regulatory Compliance:

- As governments and organizations introduce regulations around AI usage, future LLMs will need to be designed with compliance in mind. This includes ensuring data privacy, meeting transparency requirements, and providing mechanisms for auditing and accountability.

5. Decentralized and Federated Learning

The traditional approach to training LLMs involves centralizing large datasets in one location, which can raise privacy concerns and logistical challenges. Decentralized and federated learning are emerging as alternatives that address these issues by allowing models to be trained across multiple locations while keeping data local.

1) Federated Learning:

- In federated learning, the model is trained across multiple decentralized devices or servers, each with its local data. The model updates are aggregated centrally, but the data never leaves the local devices. This approach enhances privacy and reduces the need for massive centralized datasets.

2) Decentralized Training:

- Decentralized training takes this concept further by distributing the entire training process across a network of nodes. This not only improves privacy but also makes the training process more resilient to failures and reduces the dependence on any single point of failure.

3) Blockchain Integration:

- Some researchers are exploring the integration of blockchain technology with decentralized learning to enhance security, transparency, and traceability. This could lead to new models of AI development where contributions from various stakeholders are recorded and rewarded in a decentralized manner.

6. Domain-Specific LLMs

As LLMs become more widespread, there is a growing interest in developing models that are specialized for specific domains, such as healthcare, law, or finance.

1) Fine-Tuned Models:

- While general-purpose LLMs like GPT-3 are powerful, they may not always provide the best performance for specialized tasks. Fine-tuning general models on domain-specific data can create more accurate and reliable models for particular industries or applications.

2) Custom Architectures:

- In some cases, entirely new architectures may be developed to meet the unique needs of certain domains. For example, healthcare LLMs might integrate medical ontologies and databases to improve their understanding of complex medical terminology and relationships.

3) Ethical and Regulatory Considerations:

- Domain-specific LLMs will need to adhere to the ethical and regulatory standards of their respective fields. For instance, medical LLMs must comply with healthcare regulations such as HIPAA, while legal LLMs need to ensure accuracy and fairness in their outputs.

7. Energy Efficiency and Green AI

The environmental impact of training large models has become a growing concern. Future LLM architectures will likely focus more on energy efficiency and sustainability.

1) Green AI Initiatives:

- Green AI refers to the development of AI models and techniques that are designed to be energy-efficient and environmentally friendly. This includes optimizing algorithms to reduce the energy required for training and inference and exploring alternative hardware solutions that consume less power.

2) Carbon Offsetting and Renewable Energy:

- Companies and research institutions are increasingly considering carbon offsetting measures and the use of renewable energy sources to power AI training. Future LLMs may incorporate these considerations into their design and deployment strategies, helping to reduce the overall carbon footprint of AI development.

3) Efficient Algorithms:

- Research into more efficient algorithms, such as those that reduce the need for multiple passes over data or that compress models without significant loss of accuracy, will play a key role in making LLMs more sustainable.

The future of LLM architectures is full of exciting possibilities. As researchers and developers continue to innovate, we can expect to see models that are not only more powerful and versatile but also more efficient, ethical, and adaptable to the evolving needs of society. Whether through advances in multimodal learning, continuous adaptation, or ethical AI, the next generation of LLMs will likely reshape how we interact with technology and apply it across various domains.

In the following chapters, we'll dive deeper into practical techniques for building, optimizing, and deploying LLMs, keeping these future trends in mind as we develop models that are both cutting-edge and responsible.

Chapter 3: The Mathematics Behind LLMs

3.1 Linear Algebra for LLMs

Linear algebra is a fundamental mathematical tool that underpins much of the work involved in developing and understanding Large Language Models (LLMs). While it may seem abstract at first, linear algebra provides the framework for many of the operations that LLMs perform, from handling word embeddings to processing data through layers of a neural network. In this section, we'll break down the key concepts of linear algebra that are most relevant to LLMs, making these ideas accessible and applicable to your work with these models.

Vectors and Matrices: The Building Blocks

At the core of linear algebra are vectors and matrices, which are essentially collections of numbers that represent data in a structured way.

1. **Vectors:**

- A vector is a one-dimensional array of numbers. In the context of LLMs, vectors are often used to represent words as numerical entities. For example, a word embedding is a vector that captures the meaning of a word by mapping it into a continuous vector space. Each word in your vocabulary is associated with a vector, where similar words have vectors that are close to each other in this space.
- **Example:** If you have an embedding for the word "cat," it might look something like this: $[0.2, -0.1, 0.5, 0.3]$. This is a 4-dimensional vector, but in practice, these vectors often have hundreds of dimensions to capture complex meanings.

2. **Matrices:**

- A matrix is a two-dimensional array of numbers, essentially a collection of vectors. Matrices are used extensively in LLMs, for example, to store the weights of connections between layers in a neural network or to perform transformations on word embeddings.
- **Example:** Consider a matrix W that transforms an input vector x into an output vector y. If x is a word embedding, W might be a weight matrix that is learned during training to optimize the model's predictions.

Matrix Multiplication: Core to Neural Networks

Matrix multiplication is a key operation in neural networks, including those used in LLMs. Understanding how to multiply matrices is crucial because it forms the basis of how data is processed through the layers of a model.

1. **How It Works:**

- Matrix multiplication involves taking the dot product of rows from the first matrix and columns from the second matrix. If you have two matrices, A and B, the product $C = A \times B$ is a new matrix where each element c_{ij} is the dot product of the i-th row of A and the j-th column of B.
- **Example:** If A is a matrix representing the weights of a neural network layer and B is a vector representing an input, the product $A \times B$ gives you the output of that layer, which is then passed to the next layer or transformed by an activation function.

2. **Application in LLMs:**
   - In LLMs, matrices are used to transform word embeddings as they pass through the layers of the model. For instance, the self-attention mechanism in a Transformer model relies heavily on matrix multiplication to calculate attention scores between words in a sequence.

Eigenvectors and Eigenvalues: Understanding Transformations

Eigenvectors and eigenvalues are concepts from linear algebra that help us understand how matrices transform vectors. In the context of LLMs, they can give insights into the properties of these transformations, particularly in understanding how information flows through the model.

1. **Eigenvectors:**
   - An eigenvector of a matrix A is a non-zero vector v such that when A is multiplied by v, the result is a scalar multiple of v. Mathematically, this is expressed as $A \times v = \lambda \times v$, where λ is the eigenvalue corresponding to the eigenvector v.
   - **Example:** In a neural network, certain patterns of input data might align with the eigenvectors of the weight matrices, meaning that the transformation by the matrix scales these patterns rather than changing their direction.
2. **Eigenvalues:**
   - The eigenvalue λ tells you how much the eigenvector is scaled during the transformation. If λ is greater than 1, the vector is stretched; if it's between 0 and 1, the vector is shrunk. Understanding eigenvalues can help in analyzing the stability and behavior of neural networks, particularly in the context of backpropagation and optimization.

Singular Value Decomposition (SVD): Decomposing Matrices

Singular Value Decomposition (SVD) is a powerful tool in linear algebra that allows you to decompose a matrix into three simpler matrices. SVD is widely used in machine learning, including in the training and analysis of LLMs.

1. **What SVD Does:**
   - SVD decomposes a matrix M into three matrices: $M = U\Sigma V^T$, where U and V are orthogonal matrices, and Σ is a diagonal matrix containing the singular values of M. These singular values can give you insights into the properties of the matrix, such as its rank, stability, and the importance of different dimensions.
   - **Application in LLMs:** SVD can be used in tasks like dimensionality reduction, where you want to reduce the number of dimensions in your data without losing too much information. This is important in LLMs, where managing the size and complexity of data is crucial.

Norms: Measuring the Size of Vectors and Matrices

Norms are a way of measuring the size or length of vectors and matrices. They play an important role in LLMs, particularly in the context of optimization and regularization.

1. **Vector Norms:**
   - The most common vector norm is the Euclidean norm, also known as the $L2$ norm, which measures the length of a vector. For a vector $v = [v_1, v_2, \ldots, v_n]$, the $L2$ norm is given by $\|v\|_2 = \sqrt{v_1^2 + v_2^2 + \cdots + v_n^2}$. This norm is often used in optimization to penalize large weights, helping to prevent overfitting.
   - **Example:** During training, a regularization term might be added to the loss function that includes the $L2$ norm of the weights, encouraging the model to keep the weights small and generalize better to new data.
2. **Matrix Norms:**
   - Matrix norms extend the concept of vector norms to matrices. The Frobenius norm is one of the most commonly used matrix norms, which is the square root of the sum of the absolute squares of its elements. Matrix norms are useful for understanding the stability and sensitivity of linear transformations, which are critical in the training and deployment of LLMs.

Projections: Mapping Data into Subspaces

Projections are used to map data from a higher-dimensional space into a lower-dimensional subspace. This concept is central to many techniques in machine learning, including principal component analysis (PCA) and word embeddings.

1. **How Projections Work:**
   - A projection of a vector v onto a subspace defined by a vector u is the shadow of v on u. Mathematically, the projection of v onto u is given by $\text{proj}_u(v) = \frac{v \cdot u}{u \cdot u} u$. This operation is used to reduce the dimensionality of data while preserving as much relevant information as possible.
   - **Application in LLMs:** Projections are used in techniques like PCA to reduce the dimensionality of word embeddings or other high-dimensional data, making it easier to work with and interpret the data without losing significant information.

Why Linear Algebra Matters for LLMs

Linear algebra is not just a theoretical tool; it is deeply embedded in the practical workings of LLMs. From representing and manipulating word embeddings to understanding the transformations that occur within a neural network, linear algebra provides the mathematical foundation for these operations.

By understanding the key concepts of vectors, matrices, matrix multiplication, eigenvectors, SVD, norms, and projections, you gain the tools needed to work effectively with LLMs. Whether you're training a model, fine-tuning it for specific tasks, or analyzing its behavior, linear algebra will be at the heart of these processes.

In the next section, we'll build on this foundation by exploring how probability and statistics play a role in language modeling, helping to further demystify the mathematics behind LLMs.

3.2 Probability and Statistics in Language Modeling

Probability and statistics are fundamental to the functioning of Large Language Models (LLMs). These models rely heavily on probabilistic methods to understand and generate human language, making concepts from these fields essential for anyone working with LLMs. In this section, we'll cover the key ideas in probability and statistics that are directly applicable to language modeling, helping you understand how LLMs predict words, phrases, and sentences.

1. Probability Distributions: The Basis of Language Prediction

At the heart of LLMs is the concept of probability distributions. A probability distribution assigns a likelihood to each possible outcome in a set of events. In language modeling, these outcomes are typically words or sequences of words.

1. **Discrete Probability Distributions:**
    - In the context of language modeling, a discrete probability distribution might describe the likelihood of each word in a vocabulary given the previous words in a sentence. For example, given the phrase "The cat sat on the," the model assigns probabilities to words like "mat," "floor," and "sofa" based on their likelihood of appearing next.
    - **Example:** If the word "mat" has a probability of 0.7, "floor" has a probability of 0.2, and "sofa" has a probability of 0.1, the model is most likely to predict "mat" as the next word.

2. **Conditional Probability:**

   - Conditional probability is the probability of an event occurring given that another event has occurred. In language models, this is often expressed as $P(w_n|w_1, w_2, \ldots, w_{n-1})$, the probability of the word w_n given the preceding words $w_1, w_2, \ldots, w_{n-1}$.
   - **Application:** This concept is fundamental to the functioning of LLMs, as they are trained to maximize the likelihood of sequences of words by predicting each word based on its context.

2. N-grams and Markov Assumptions

Before the advent of neural networks, simpler models like n-grams were used to estimate the probabilities of word sequences. These models are based on the Markov assumption, which states that the probability of a word depends only on a fixed number of preceding words.

1. **N-grams:**

   - An n-gram is a sequence of n words. For example, in a bigram model (where $n = 2$), the probability of each word depends only on the one word that precedes it. Trigram models (where $n = 3$) consider the two preceding words, and so on.
   - **Example:** In a trigram model, the probability of the word "mat" in the phrase "The cat sat on the" would be calculated based on the preceding words "on the."

2. **Markov Chains:**

   - Markov chains are models that transition from one state to another based on certain probabilities. In the context of language modeling, each state represents a word, and the transitions between states represent the likelihood of one word following another. Markov models assume that the probability of a word depends only on a fixed number of preceding words, which simplifies the modeling process but limits the model's ability to capture long-range dependencies.
   - **Limitations:** While n-grams and Markov models are simpler and computationally less expensive, they struggle with capturing the full context of language, especially when the relevant context spans more words than the model can consider.

3. Bayesian Inference and Language Models

Bayesian inference is a method of statistical inference in which Bayes' theorem is used to update the probability of a hypothesis as more evidence becomes available. In LLMs, Bayesian methods are often used to incorporate prior knowledge into the model.

1. **Bayes' Theorem:**
   - Bayes' theorem relates the conditional and marginal probabilities of random events. It is expressed as:
     $$P(H|E) = \frac{P(E|H) \times P(H)}{P(E)}$$
     where H is the hypothesis, E is the evidence, $P(H|E)$ is the posterior probability of the hypothesis given the evidence, $P(E|H)$ is the likelihood, $P(H)$ is the prior probability of the hypothesis, and $P(E)$ is the marginal likelihood.
   - **Application in LLMs:** Bayes' theorem can be used in language models to update the probability of a word or phrase based on new information. For example, if a model has a prior belief that "mat" is a likely word to follow "sat on the," encountering additional evidence that supports this belief would increase the probability assigned to "mat."

2. **Bayesian Language Models:**
   - Bayesian approaches in language modeling allow for the incorporation of prior knowledge and can be useful in scenarios where data is sparse or when integrating information from multiple sources. These models are particularly useful in tasks like machine translation, where prior knowledge about language pairs can improve translation accuracy.

4. Statistical Estimation: Maximum Likelihood and Maximum A Posteriori

Statistical estimation involves estimating the parameters of a probability distribution based on observed data. Two common methods used in LLMs are Maximum Likelihood Estimation (MLE) and Maximum A Posteriori (MAP) estimation.

1. **Maximum Likelihood Estimation (MLE):**
    - MLE is a method of estimating the parameters of a model by finding the parameter values that maximize the likelihood of the observed data. In language modeling, this involves choosing the parameters that make the observed sequence of words most probable.
    - **Example:** When training an LLM, the goal is to adjust the model's parameters so that the likelihood of the training data—represented as a sequence of words—is maximized.

2. **Maximum A Posteriori (MAP) Estimation:**
    - MAP estimation is similar to MLE but incorporates prior knowledge into the estimation process. It involves maximizing the posterior distribution, which combines the likelihood of the data with a prior distribution over the parameters.
    - **Application:** MAP is particularly useful when you have prior information about the parameters or when you need to regularize the model to prevent overfitting.

5. Entropy and Cross-Entropy: Measuring Uncertainty

Entropy is a concept from information theory that measures the uncertainty or randomness in a probability distribution. In the context of LLMs, entropy can be used to quantify how uncertain a model is about its predictions.

1. **Entropy**:
   - The entropy H of a probability distribution is defined as:

$$H(X) = -\sum_{i} P(x_i) \log P(x_i)$$

     where $P(x_i)$ is the probability of the i-th outcome. Higher entropy indicates greater uncertainty, while lower entropy suggests more confidence in the model's predictions.
   - **Application**: In language modeling, entropy can be used to assess the confidence of the model in predicting the next word. A model with lower entropy is more certain about its predictions, which is often a sign of better performance.

2. **Cross-Entropy**:
   - Cross-entropy is a measure of the difference between two probability distributions. It is often used as a loss function in training LLMs, where the goal is to minimize the cross-entropy between the predicted distribution and the true distribution (represented by the actual words in the training data).
   - **Example**: When training an LLM, the cross-entropy loss quantifies how far off the model's predictions are from the actual words in the dataset. By minimizing this loss, the model becomes better at predicting the correct words.

6. Sampling and Monte Carlo Methods

Sampling techniques and Monte Carlo methods are often used in LLMs to approximate complex probability distributions, especially when exact computation is infeasible.

1. **Sampling from Distributions:**

   - In LLMs, sampling is often used to generate text. For instance, once the model has predicted a probability distribution over the next word, it can sample from this distribution to generate the next word in a sequence. Different sampling strategies, such as greedy sampling, beam search, or top-k sampling, can lead to different text outputs.
   - **Example:** Greedy sampling always picks the word with the highest probability, which can lead to repetitive or less creative outputs. In contrast, top-k sampling limits the choices to the top k most probable words, adding variety and creativity to the generated text.

2. **Monte Carlo Methods:**

   - Monte Carlo methods involve using random sampling to approximate complex integrals or probability distributions. In LLMs, these methods can be used to estimate the expected values of certain quantities, such as the likelihood of a word sequence, when exact computation is too complex.
   - **Application:** Monte Carlo methods are useful in scenarios where the model needs to evaluate the likelihood of many possible outcomes or when performing tasks like Bayesian inference in language modeling.

Why Probability and Statistics Matter for LLMs

Probability and statistics provide the mathematical foundation for LLMs, enabling them to make predictions about language that are grounded in probabilistic reasoning. By understanding these concepts, you can better grasp how LLMs generate and understand text, and you'll be better equipped to train, fine-tune, and evaluate these models.

In the next section, we'll delve into calculus and optimization techniques, which are essential for training LLMs and ensuring that they converge to solutions that generalize well to new data. These mathematical tools will further deepen your understanding of the inner workings of LLMs and how they achieve their impressive results.

3.3 Calculus and Optimization Techniques

Calculus and optimization techniques are essential tools in the training and fine-tuning of Large Language Models (LLMs). These mathematical concepts help us understand how models learn, how to adjust them for better performance, and how to ensure they converge on solutions that generalize well to new data. In this section, we'll cover the key ideas in calculus and optimization that are most relevant to working with LLMs.

1. Derivatives: Understanding Change

Derivatives are a core concept in calculus, representing the rate of change of a function with respect to one of its variables. In the context of LLMs, derivatives help us understand how small changes in the model's parameters affect the model's predictions.

1. **Partial Derivatives:**
   - A partial derivative is the derivative of a function with respect to one variable while holding the other variables constant. In LLMs, the loss function is typically a function of many parameters (the weights and biases of the model), and we use partial derivatives to understand how each individual parameter affects the loss.
   - **Example:** If L is the loss function and w_i is a specific weight in the model, the partial derivative $\frac{\partial L}{\partial w_i}$ tells us how much the loss will increase or decrease if we slightly change w_i. This information is crucial for adjusting the model's parameters during training.

2. **Gradients:**
   - The gradient is a vector of partial derivatives, representing the direction and rate of the steepest ascent or descent in a multi-dimensional space. In LLMs, the gradient of the loss function with respect to all the model's parameters tells us how to adjust the parameters to minimize the loss.
   - **Application:** During training, we compute the gradient of the loss with respect to the model's parameters and use this information to update the parameters in a way that reduces the loss, moving the model closer to an optimal solution.

2. Gradient Descent: The Workhorse of Optimization

Gradient descent is the primary optimization algorithm used to train LLMs. It's a method for finding the minimum of a function by iteratively moving in the direction of the negative gradient.

1. **Basic Gradient Descent:**
    - In each iteration of gradient descent, the model's parameters are updated by subtracting a fraction (the learning rate) of the gradient of the loss function with respect to those parameters. Mathematically, this update rule can be written as:
    $$w_{new} = w_{old} - \eta \cdot \nabla L(w_{old})$$
    where η is the learning rate and $\nabla L(w_{old})$ is the gradient of the loss function with respect to the parameters.
    - **Example:** If the gradient at a particular point is $\nabla L = [2, -3]$ and the learning rate is 0.01, the parameters would be updated by moving in the direction opposite to the gradient, resulting in a decrease in the loss.

2. **Learning Rate:**
    - The learning rate is a crucial hyperparameter in gradient descent. A learning rate that is too high can cause the model to overshoot the optimal solution, while a learning rate that is too low can lead to slow convergence or getting stuck in local minima.
    - **Tuning the Learning Rate:** Various techniques, such as learning rate schedules or adaptive learning rates (as used in algorithms like Adam), can help dynamically adjust the learning rate during training for better performance.

3. Advanced Optimization Techniques

While basic gradient descent works well in many scenarios, advanced techniques are often needed to handle the complexities of training LLMs. These techniques help improve convergence speed, stability, and the model's ability to generalize.

1. **Stochastic Gradient Descent (SGD):**
   - Stochastic Gradient Descent is a variation of gradient descent where the gradient is estimated using only a small batch of data rather than the entire dataset. This introduces some randomness into the optimization process, which can help escape local minima and improve convergence speed.
   - **Application:** SGD is particularly useful in large-scale training, where computing the gradient using the entire dataset at each step would be computationally expensive. By using mini-batches, SGD makes training more efficient.

2. **Momentum:**
   - Momentum is an extension of gradient descent that helps accelerate convergence by considering the past gradients in the update rule. Instead of updating the parameters based solely on the current gradient, momentum adds a fraction of the previous update to the current update. This helps smooth out the updates and can lead to faster convergence.
   - **Mathematical Formulation:** The update rule with momentum can be written as:

$$v_{new} = \beta \cdot v_{old} + \eta \cdot \nabla L(w)$$

$$w_{new} = w_{old} - v_{new}$$

   where β is the momentum coefficient, typically a value close to 1.

3. **Adam Optimizer:**
   - Adam (Adaptive Moment Estimation) is an optimization algorithm that combines the benefits of both momentum and adaptive learning rates. It adjusts the learning rate for each parameter individually based on the first and second moments of the gradients, which helps to achieve faster and more stable convergence.
   - **Why Adam is Popular:** Adam's ability to adaptively adjust the learning rates makes it well-suited for training LLMs, where different parameters may require different learning rates. It's widely used in practice due to its robustness and efficiency.

4. **Second-Order Methods**:
   - Second-order optimization methods, like Newton's method, use second-order derivatives (Hessian matrices) to adjust the step size in gradient descent. These methods can be more accurate than first-order methods (like gradient descent) but are computationally expensive and less commonly used for large-scale models like LLMs.
   - **Hessian-Free Optimization**: In some cases, approximations to the Hessian matrix are used to reduce computational costs, allowing for more efficient second-order optimization. However, these methods are generally more complex and used in specific scenarios where they offer significant benefits.

4. Backpropagation: Calculus in Action

Backpropagation is the algorithm used to compute the gradients of the loss function with respect to each of the model's parameters. It's the key to making gradient descent work in neural networks, including LLMs.

1. **Chain Rule**:
   - Backpropagation relies on the chain rule of calculus, which allows us to compute the derivative of a composite function. In the context of neural networks, the loss function is a composite function of all the layers' activations, weights, and biases.
   - **Example**: If a network has two layers with activation functions f and g, and the loss function L, the derivative of the loss with respect to the weights in the first layer involves applying the chain rule to differentiate $L(f(g(x)))$ with respect to these weights.

2. **Forward and Backward Passes**:
   - During the forward pass, the input data is passed through the network, and the activations are computed at each layer. The loss is then calculated based on the network's predictions. During the backward pass, the gradients are computed starting from the output layer and moving back through the network to the input layer.
   - **Weight Updates**: After the gradients are computed, the model's weights are updated using gradient descent or one of its variants, completing the backpropagation step.

5. Optimization Challenges: Local Minima and Saddle Points

Training LLMs involves navigating a complex loss landscape with many local minima and saddle points. Understanding these challenges is crucial for effectively optimizing LLMs.

1. **Local Minima:**
   - Local minima are points in the loss landscape where the loss is lower than in the surrounding area, but not necessarily the lowest possible. Gradient descent can get stuck in local minima, leading to suboptimal solutions.
   - **Strategies to Avoid Local Minima:** Techniques like using a lower learning rate, adding noise to the gradient (as in SGD), or employing momentum can help the model escape local minima.

2. **Saddle Points:**
   - Saddle points are points in the loss landscape where the gradient is zero, but the point is not a minimum. These points can slow down convergence because the gradient does not provide a clear direction for moving toward a minimum.
   - **Dealing with Saddle Points:** The use of momentum, adaptive learning rates, and techniques like batch normalization can help the model move past saddle points more efficiently.

Why Calculus and Optimization Matter for LLMs

Calculus and optimization are the mathematical engines driving the training of LLMs. By understanding these concepts, you gain the ability to fine-tune your models, improve their performance, and ensure they converge to solutions that generalize well. Whether you're adjusting learning rates, choosing the right optimization algorithm, or diagnosing training issues, these mathematical tools are essential for building and refining LLMs.

In the next section, we'll explore the attention mechanisms that play a crucial role in the effectiveness of Transformer models, giving you a deeper understanding of how LLMs focus on relevant parts of the input to generate accurate and contextually appropriate outputs.

3.4 Understanding Attention Mechanisms

Attention mechanisms are one of the key innovations that have transformed how modern language models, particularly Transformers, process and generate text. By allowing models to focus on specific parts of the input data, attention mechanisms enable more efficient and accurate handling of complex language tasks. In this section, we'll break down the mathematics behind attention mechanisms, making them accessible and understandable.

1. The Core Idea of Attention

The fundamental concept of attention in neural networks is to selectively focus on certain parts of the input while processing it, much like how humans pay attention to relevant information while ignoring the rest.

1. **Why Attention Matters:**
    - In traditional sequence models, such as Recurrent Neural Networks (RNNs), each word in a sentence is processed sequentially, with a fixed amount of "attention" given to each word. This can be limiting, especially when the context needed to understand a word is far from the word itself in the sequence. Attention mechanisms address this limitation by allowing the model to dynamically allocate focus to different parts of the input, depending on what is most relevant at each step.

2. **Self-Attention:**
   - Self-attention, a specific type of attention mechanism, enables a model to consider all words in a sentence simultaneously and weigh their importance relative to each other. This is a core component of the Transformer architecture and is what makes it so powerful for handling long-range dependencies in text.
   - **Example:** If the model is processing the sentence "The cat sat on the mat because it was tired," self-attention allows it to recognize that "it" refers to "the cat," even though these words are separated by several other words.

2. The Mathematics of Self-Attention

Understanding the mathematics of self-attention is key to grasping how it functions within a model like a Transformer. The process can be broken down into several steps, each involving linear algebra and vector operations.

1. **Input Representation:**
   - Each word in the input sequence is first represented as a vector (an embedding) that captures its meaning in a high-dimensional space. Suppose the input sequence consists of n words, each represented by a d-dimensional vector. This sequence can be represented as a matrix X of size $n \times d$, where each row corresponds to the embedding of a word.

2. **Query, Key, and Value Vectors:**
   - The core of the self-attention mechanism involves three key components: queries Q, keys K, and values V. These are all derived from the input matrix X through linear transformations:

   $$Q = XW_Q, \quad K = XW_K, \quad V = XW_V$$

   where W_Q, W_K, and W_V are weight matrices that are learned during training. The sizes of these matrices are typically $d \times d_k$, $d \times d_k$, and $d \times d_v$ respectively, where d_k and d_v are the dimensions of the queries/keys and values, which can differ from d.

3. **Attention Scores:**

   - The attention scores are calculated by taking the dot product of the query vectors with the key vectors, followed by scaling and applying the softmax function:

   $$\text{Attention}(Q, K, V) = \text{softmax}\left(\frac{QK^T}{\sqrt{d_k}}\right)V$$

     - **Dot Product:** The dot product QK^T produces a matrix of size $n \times n$, where each entry represents the attention score between two words in the input sequence.
     - **Scaling:** The division by $\sqrt{d_k}$ is a normalization step that prevents the dot products from becoming too large, which could otherwise lead to very small gradients during training.
     - **Softmax:** The softmax function converts the attention scores into probabilities, ensuring that they sum to 1 for each word in the sequence. These probabilities determine how much attention each word should receive from each other word.

4. **Weighted Sum of Values:**

   - The final step in the self-attention mechanism is to compute a weighted sum of the value vectors V, where the weights are the attention probabilities obtained from the softmax. This produces a new set of vectors that represent the input sequence, with each word now imbued with contextual information from the entire sequence.

3. Multi-Head Attention: Enhancing Self-Attention

While the basic self-attention mechanism is powerful, Transformers go a step further by using multi-head attention, which allows the model to focus on different aspects of the input simultaneously.

1. **How Multi-Head Attention Works:**
   - Instead of performing self-attention once, multi-head attention splits the queries, keys, and values into multiple smaller sets and applies self-attention to each set independently. Each of these sets is known as a "head."
   - **Parallel Attention Heads:** If there are h heads, the original d-dimensional input is split into h different d_h-dimensional subspaces, where $d_h = d/h$. The self-attention mechanism is applied independently in each subspace.
   - **Concatenation:** The outputs of the h attention heads are then concatenated and linearly transformed to produce the final output. This allows the model to capture a richer set of relationships within the input data.

2. **Advantages of Multi-Head Attention:**
   - **Diverse Focus:** Different heads can learn to focus on different types of relationships within the data, such as short-term dependencies, long-term dependencies, or syntactic structure. This makes the model more flexible and powerful.
   - **Improved Generalization:** By considering multiple aspects of the input simultaneously, multi-head attention helps the model generalize better across different tasks and datasets.

4. Attention in Practice: Key Applications

Attention mechanisms have been widely adopted in various NLP tasks due to their ability to capture complex dependencies in data.

1. **Machine Translation:**
   - In machine translation, attention mechanisms help the model focus on the relevant parts of the source sentence while generating each word in the target sentence. This allows for more accurate and contextually appropriate translations, especially in long sentences where the context of a word might be far removed from the word itself.

2. **Text Summarization:**
    - In text summarization, attention mechanisms enable the model to identify and emphasize the most important parts of the input text while generating a concise summary. This results in summaries that are not only shorter but also more informative and focused on the key points.

3. **Question Answering:**
    - In question-answering systems, attention mechanisms help the model locate the most relevant parts of a text passage that can answer a given question. This allows the model to provide accurate and contextually relevant answers, even when the answer is not explicitly stated in the text.

5. The Impact of Attention Mechanisms

Attention mechanisms have fundamentally changed how we approach NLP tasks, making models like Transformers incredibly effective at understanding and generating human language. By enabling models to focus dynamically on relevant information, attention mechanisms allow for better handling of long-range dependencies, more accurate predictions, and greater flexibility in processing diverse types of input data.

Understanding the mathematics behind attention mechanisms gives you insight into why models like BERT, GPT, and T5 perform so well and how you can leverage these mechanisms in your own work with LLMs.

In the next section, we'll explore regularization techniques that help prevent overfitting in LLMs, ensuring that your models generalize well to new data and maintain high performance across a range of tasks.

3.5 Regularization Techniques to Prevent Overfitting

When training Large Language Models (LLMs), one of the biggest challenges is ensuring that the model generalizes well to new, unseen data. Overfitting occurs when a model learns the training data too well, capturing noise and specific patterns that do not generalize beyond that data. Regularization techniques are essential tools to prevent overfitting and ensure that your model performs well on real-world tasks. In this section, we'll discuss the most effective regularization techniques used in training LLMs.

1. L2 Regularization (Ridge Regression)

L2 regularization, also known as ridge regression or weight decay, is one of the most common techniques used to prevent overfitting. It works by adding a penalty to the loss function based on the sum of the squared values of the model's parameters.

1. **How L2 Regularization Works:**
   - In L2 regularization, the loss function L is modified to include an additional term that penalizes large weights. The new loss function can be expressed as:

     $$L_{new} = L + \lambda \sum_i w_i^2$$

     where λ is the regularization parameter, and w_i are the weights of the model. This penalty term discourages the model from assigning too much importance to any one feature, which helps prevent overfitting.
   - **Example:** If your LLM starts assigning excessively large weights to specific words or phrases in the training data, L2 regularization will reduce these weights, leading to a model that is more robust and generalizable.

2. **Choosing the Regularization Parameter λ:**
   - The value of λ controls the strength of the regularization. A higher λ leads to stronger regularization, which can prevent overfitting but may also cause underfitting if set too high. It's crucial to choose an appropriate λ through techniques like cross-validation.

2. L1 Regularization (Lasso Regression)

L1 regularization, also known as lasso regression, is another popular technique that adds a penalty based on the absolute values of the model's parameters. Unlike L2 regularization, L1 regularization can lead to sparse models where some weights are exactly zero.

1. **How L1 Regularization Works:**
   - In L1 regularization, the loss function is modified to include a term that penalizes the sum of the absolute values of the weights:

     $$L_{new} = L + \lambda \sum_i |w_i|$$

     This penalty encourages the model to set some weights to zero, effectively selecting a subset of features and ignoring the rest.
   - **Example:** L1 regularization can be particularly useful when you want to identify the most important features (e.g., specific words or phrases) in a large dataset. By pushing some weights to zero, L1 regularization simplifies the model and reduces the risk of overfitting.

2. **Sparse Representations:**
   - One of the key benefits of L1 regularization is that it leads to sparse models. This means that many parameters are exactly zero, which can simplify the model and make it more interpretable. In the context of LLMs, this can help in identifying the most relevant words or features that contribute to the model's predictions.

3. Dropout: Reducing Overfitting by Randomly Disabling Neurons

Dropout is a widely used regularization technique in neural networks, including LLMs. It involves randomly "dropping out" a fraction of the neurons in a layer during each training iteration, which prevents the model from becoming overly reliant on any single neuron.

1. **How Dropout Works:**
   - During training, dropout randomly sets a fraction of the neurons' outputs to zero in each forward pass. This forces the model to learn more robust features that are not dependent on any one neuron.
   - **Example:** If you apply dropout with a rate of 0.5, half of the neurons in a given layer are randomly disabled during each training iteration. This randomness helps prevent the model from memorizing the training data, thereby reducing overfitting.

2. **Applying Dropout in Practice:**
   - Dropout is typically applied to the fully connected layers in a neural network, but it can also be used in other layers. The dropout rate (the fraction of neurons to drop) is a hyperparameter that needs to be carefully chosen—too high a rate can lead to underfitting, while too low a rate may not sufficiently prevent overfitting.

3. **Inference Mode:**
   - During inference (when the model is making predictions on new data), dropout is not applied. Instead, the full network is used, but the outputs are scaled by the dropout rate to account for the missing neurons during training. This ensures that the model's predictions are consistent with the way it was trained.

4. Early Stopping: Preventing Overtraining

Early stopping is a simple but effective regularization technique where training is halted as soon as the model's performance on a validation set stops improving.

1. **How Early Stopping Works:**
    - During training, the model's performance is monitored on a separate validation set after each epoch (a complete pass through the training data). If the performance on the validation set starts to degrade while the performance on the training set continues to improve, it indicates that the model is beginning to overfit.
    - **Example:** If you notice that the validation loss stops decreasing and starts increasing after a certain number of epochs, early stopping will halt the training at the point where the validation loss was lowest, preserving the model state that is most likely to generalize well.

2. **Implementing Early Stopping:**
    - To implement early stopping, you typically specify a patience parameter, which determines how many epochs to wait after the last improvement before stopping the training. This allows the model to continue training for a few more epochs in case the performance improves again.

5. Data Augmentation: Increasing Data Diversity

Data augmentation is a technique that involves generating additional training data by applying various transformations to the existing data. While it's more commonly used in image processing, it can also be applied to text data in the context of LLMs.

1. **How Data Augmentation Works:**
   - In the context of text, data augmentation can involve techniques like synonym replacement, random insertion, or back-translation, where a sentence is translated to another language and then back to the original language. These techniques create new training examples that are similar to the original data but introduce enough variation to prevent the model from overfitting.
   - **Example:** If your training data includes the sentence "The cat sat on the mat," data augmentation might generate variations like "The feline sat on the mat" or "The cat sat on the rug," increasing the diversity of the training data.

2. **Benefits of Data Augmentation:**
   - By increasing the diversity of the training data, data augmentation helps the model learn more generalizable patterns, reducing the risk of overfitting. It's particularly useful when the available training data is limited or when the model is prone to memorizing specific examples.

6. Regularization in the Context of LLMs

When working with LLMs, regularization techniques are crucial for ensuring that the models do not overfit, especially given the vast amounts of data and the complexity of these models. Combining multiple regularization techniques is often necessary to achieve the best performance.

1. **Combining Techniques:**
   - It's common practice to combine L2 regularization, dropout, and early stopping in the training process. Each technique addresses overfitting from a different angle, and together, they provide a robust defense against it.
   - **Example:** You might use L2 regularization to control the magnitude of the weights, apply dropout to introduce randomness in the training process, and implement early stopping to prevent the model from training too long.

2. **Regularization and Model Complexity:**

   - The need for regularization increases with the complexity of the model. LLMs, with their large number of parameters, are particularly susceptible to overfitting, making regularization an essential part of the training process. Ensuring that your model remains generalizable to new data is key to its success in real-world applications.

Regularization techniques are vital for preventing overfitting in LLMs, helping to ensure that your models perform well not just on the training data but also on unseen data. By understanding and applying techniques like L2 and L1 regularization, dropout, early stopping, and data augmentation, you can build more robust models that generalize better and are more effective in real-world tasks.

In the next section, we'll dive into gradient descent and its variants, exploring how these optimization algorithms work to minimize the loss function and improve the performance of your LLMs.

3.6 Gradient Descent and its Variants in Training LLMs

Gradient descent is the cornerstone of optimization techniques used in training Large Language Models (LLMs). It's the method by which models learn from data, adjusting their parameters iteratively to minimize a loss function. However, the basic gradient descent algorithm has limitations, especially when dealing with the complexity and scale of LLMs. To address these challenges, several variants of gradient descent have been developed, each designed to improve convergence speed, stability, and efficiency. In this section, we'll explore the fundamental concept of gradient descent and delve into its most important variants.

1. Gradient Descent: The Basics

Gradient descent is an iterative optimization algorithm used to minimize a function by moving step-by-step in the direction of the steepest descent, as defined by the negative of the gradient.

1. **The Gradient:**
   - The gradient of a function represents the direction of the steepest increase of the function. For a loss function $L(\theta)$ dependent on model parameters θ, the gradient $\nabla L(\theta)$ points in the direction of the steepest ascent. Gradient descent updates the parameters in the opposite direction to minimize the loss:

   $$\theta_{new} = \theta_{old} - \eta \cdot \nabla L(\theta_{old})$$

   where η is the learning rate.

2. **Choosing the Learning Rate:**
   - The learning rate η determines the size of the steps taken towards the minimum. If η is too large, the algorithm might overshoot the minimum, leading to divergence. If η is too small, convergence might be very slow, requiring many iterations to reach the minimum.

2. Stochastic Gradient Descent (SGD)

Stochastic Gradient Descent is a variant of gradient descent that updates the model parameters more frequently, making it more efficient and often faster in practice.

1. **How SGD Works:**

 - Instead of computing the gradient based on the entire dataset, which can be computationally expensive, SGD updates the parameters using the gradient computed from a single data point (or a small batch of data). This introduces noise into the optimization process but allows for faster iterations:
$$\theta_{new} = \theta_{old} - \eta \cdot \nabla L(\theta_{old}; x_i)$$
where x_i is a single training example.

2. **Advantages of SGD:**

 - **Efficiency:** SGD is more computationally efficient than full-batch gradient descent, especially for large datasets.
 - **Escaping Local Minima:** The noise introduced by using a single example can help the algorithm escape local minima and find a better overall solution.

3. **Challenges with SGD:**

 - **Convergence:** The noisy updates can make convergence more difficult, potentially causing the algorithm to oscillate around the minimum rather than settling smoothly. This issue can be mitigated by gradually decreasing the learning rate.

3. Mini-Batch Gradient Descent

Mini-batch gradient descent is a compromise between full-batch gradient descent and SGD, combining their advantages while mitigating some of their drawbacks.

1. **How Mini-Batch Gradient Descent Works:**
   - In mini-batch gradient descent, the gradient is computed using a small, random subset (mini-batch) of the training data. The model parameters are updated based on this mini-batch:
   $$\theta_{new} = \theta_{old} - \eta \cdot \nabla L(\theta_{old}; X_{batch})$$
   where X_{batch} is a mini-batch of the training data.

2. **Advantages:**
   - **Balanced Updates:** Mini-batch gradient descent provides a balance between the noisy updates of SGD and the stability of full-batch gradient descent. It reduces the variance of the parameter updates, leading to more stable convergence.
   - **Parallelism:** Mini-batches can be processed in parallel, making this method more suitable for large-scale distributed training.

3. **Typical Batch Sizes:**
   - The choice of batch size depends on the specific problem and the computational resources available. Common batch sizes range from 32 to 256, but this can vary widely depending on the model and dataset.

4. Momentum-Based Gradient Descent

Momentum is a technique that helps accelerate gradient descent, especially in scenarios where the loss surface has high curvature, flat regions, or noisy gradients.

1. **How Momentum Works:**
    - Momentum introduces a term that accumulates the past gradients, effectively giving the optimizer "inertia" to keep moving in the same direction:

$$v_{new} = \beta \cdot v_{old} + \eta \cdot \nabla L(\theta_{old})$$

$$\theta_{new} = \theta_{old} - v_{new}$$

where v is the velocity vector, and β is the momentum coefficient, typically set to a value like 0.9.

2. **Advantages:**
    - **Faster Convergence:** Momentum can significantly accelerate convergence, particularly in deep neural networks, by helping to smooth out the path towards the minimum and avoiding the oscillations that can occur with plain gradient descent.

3. **Challenges:**
    - **Tuning:** The momentum coefficient β needs to be carefully tuned to ensure that the algorithm converges smoothly without overshooting.

5. Adaptive Gradient Algorithms

Several adaptive gradient algorithms have been developed to adjust the learning rate for each parameter individually, making the optimization process more efficient and robust.

1. **AdaGrad:**
    - AdaGrad adjusts the learning rate based on the history of gradients for each parameter, making larger adjustments for parameters that have been updated less frequently:

$$\theta_{new} = \theta_{old} - \frac{\eta}{\sqrt{G + \epsilon}} \cdot \nabla L(\theta_{old})$$

where G is a diagonal matrix containing the sum of squares of the past gradients, and ϵ is a small constant to prevent division by zero.

2. **RMSprop:**

   - RMSprop is similar to AdaGrad but with a key difference: it uses an exponentially decaying average of the squared gradients rather than the sum, which helps prevent the learning rate from decaying too much:

$$v_{new} = \gamma \cdot v_{old} + (1 - \gamma) \cdot \nabla L(\theta_{old})^2$$

$$\theta_{new} = \theta_{old} - \frac{\eta}{\sqrt{v_{new} + \epsilon}} \cdot \nabla L(\theta_{old})$$

   where γ is the decay rate, typically set to 0.9.

3. **Adam (Adaptive Moment Estimation):**

   - Adam combines the ideas of momentum and RMSprop, keeping track of both the mean and the variance of the gradients:

$$m_{new} = \beta_1 \cdot m_{old} + (1 - \beta_1) \cdot \nabla L(\theta_{old})$$

$$v_{new} = \beta_2 \cdot v_{old} + (1 - \beta_2) \cdot \nabla L(\theta_{old})^2$$

$$\theta_{new} = \theta_{old} - \frac{\eta \cdot m_{new}}{\sqrt{v_{new}} + \epsilon}$$

   where m is the first moment (mean of the gradients), v is the second moment (uncentered variance), and β_1, β_2 are typically set to 0.9 and 0.999, respectively.

4. **Advantages of Adam:**

   - **Adaptivity:** Adam adjusts learning rates for each parameter individually, making it highly effective for dealing with sparse gradients and different types of data.
   - **Robustness:** Adam is robust and works well across a wide range of problems, making it a popular choice for training LLMs.

6. Advanced Techniques: Hybrid and Customized Algorithms

In addition to these standard variants, researchers often use hybrid or customized optimization algorithms that combine multiple techniques to achieve better performance.

1. **Nesterov Accelerated Gradient (NAG):**

   - NAG is a variation of momentum that anticipates the change in the gradient, leading to more accurate updates:

$$v_{new} = \beta \cdot v_{old} + \eta \cdot \nabla L(\theta_{old} - \beta \cdot v_{old})$$

$$\theta_{new} = \theta_{old} - v_{new}$$

   - **Advantage:** NAG often converges faster and more reliably than standard momentum.

2. **Learning Rate Schedules:**

   - Instead of using a fixed learning rate, many training processes employ a learning rate schedule that decreases the learning rate over time, helping the model to fine-tune its parameters as it approaches the minimum.
   - **Common Schedules:** Common learning rate schedules include step decay, exponential decay, and cosine annealing.

3. **Hyperparameter Tuning:**

   - Finding the best hyperparameters (learning rate, batch size, momentum coefficient, etc.) is crucial for effective training. Techniques like grid search, random search, and Bayesian optimization are often used to automate this process and find the optimal configuration.

Why Gradient Descent Variants Matter for LLMs

The choice of optimization algorithm can significantly impact the performance and convergence of LLMs. Understanding the different variants of gradient descent allows you to select the most appropriate method for your specific problem, leading to faster training times, better model performance, and more stable convergence. Whether you're training a small model or a massive LLM, these optimization techniques are essential tools in your toolkit.

In the next chapter, we'll explore practical strategies for fine-tuning and deploying LLMs, building on the mathematical foundations we've covered to create models that are not only powerful but also efficient and ready for real-world applications.

II

Part II: Practical Implementation of LLMs

Chapter 4: Data Collection and Preprocessing

4.1 Sourcing High-Quality Data for LLM Training

High-quality data is the lifeblood of any Large Language Model (LLM). The effectiveness and accuracy of an LLM largely depend on the quality, diversity, and relevance of the data it's trained on. In this section, we'll discuss how to source high-quality data for training LLMs, ensuring that your model has the best possible foundation for learning and generating meaningful language.

1. The Importance of High-Quality Data

When training LLMs, the data you use directly impacts the model's ability to understand and generate text. High-quality data leads to a more accurate, reliable, and versatile model, while poor-quality data can introduce biases, errors, and limitations.

1. **Accuracy:** The more accurate the data, the better the model can learn the nuances of language, leading to outputs that are contextually appropriate and semantically correct.
2. **Diversity:** A diverse dataset helps the model generalize across different contexts, languages, dialects, and domains. This is crucial for

creating a model that can handle a wide range of tasks.

3. **Relevance:** The data should be relevant to the specific tasks you want your model to perform. Irrelevant data can dilute the model's learning, making it less effective in the areas that matter most.

2. Sources of High-Quality Data

There are several sources from which you can gather data for training LLMs. Each source has its advantages and potential drawbacks, depending on the nature of your project.

1) Public Datasets:

- **Open-Source Datasets:** There are numerous open-source datasets available for NLP tasks, such as the Common Crawl dataset, Wikipedia dumps, and news articles. These datasets are valuable for training general-purpose language models because they cover a wide range of topics and writing styles.
- **Advantages:** Public datasets are often large and diverse, making them ideal for training robust models. They are also relatively easy to access and use, with many available in preprocessed formats.
- **Challenges:** Public datasets may include noise, outdated information, or biased content. Careful curation and preprocessing are necessary to ensure the data is of high quality.

2) Proprietary Datasets:

- **Company Data:** Companies often have access to proprietary data, such as customer support transcripts, product reviews, or internal documents. This data can be invaluable for training models that are specific to a particular domain or industry.
- **Advantages:** Proprietary data is typically more relevant and specific to the tasks you want to perform. It can provide a competitive edge

by enabling the model to understand industry-specific language and context.

- **Challenges:** Access to proprietary data may be restricted due to privacy concerns, legal agreements, or data protection regulations. It's essential to ensure that data collection and usage comply with relevant laws and ethical standards.

3) Web Scraping:

- **Automated Data Collection:** Web scraping involves using automated tools to collect data from websites. This method can be used to gather large volumes of text data from various online sources, such as blogs, forums, news sites, and social media platforms.
- **Advantages:** Web scraping allows for the collection of up-to-date, real-world data from diverse sources. It's particularly useful for gathering data on niche topics or emerging trends.
- **Challenges:** Web scraping can raise ethical and legal issues, particularly if the content is copyrighted or if the website's terms of service prohibit scraping. Additionally, scraped data often requires extensive cleaning and preprocessing to remove noise, duplicates, and irrelevant content.

4) Crowdsourcing:

- **Human-Labeled Data:** Crowdsourcing platforms like Amazon Mechanical Turk allow you to collect human-labeled data, which can be especially useful for tasks that require specific annotations, such as sentiment analysis, entity recognition, or content moderation.
- **Advantages:** Crowdsourcing provides access to a large pool of annotators, enabling the collection of custom-labeled data at scale. This data can improve the accuracy and relevance of your model, particularly for specialized tasks.
- **Challenges:** The quality of crowdsourced data can vary depending

on the skill and attention of the annotators. It's important to implement quality control measures, such as using gold-standard data for verification or incorporating consensus methods.

3. Evaluating Data Quality

Before using a dataset for training, it's crucial to evaluate its quality. High-quality data should be accurate, diverse, relevant, and free from bias as much as possible.

1) Data Accuracy:

- **Verification:** Cross-check the data against reliable sources to ensure its accuracy. This is especially important for factual content, where inaccuracies can lead to incorrect model predictions.
- **Consistency:** Ensure that the data is consistent in terms of formatting, labeling, and content. Inconsistent data can confuse the model and lead to poor performance.

2) Diversity and Coverage:

- **Topic Variety:** The dataset should cover a wide range of topics and writing styles, ensuring that the model can generalize across different contexts. This is particularly important for general-purpose models.
- **Demographic Representation:** The data should represent diverse demographics to avoid bias. For example, a dataset that primarily includes text from a single demographic group may lead to a model that performs poorly on text from other groups.

3) Relevance to the Task:

- **Domain-Specific Data:** If you're training a model for a specific domain, such as legal or medical language, ensure that the dataset includes relevant content. General-purpose data might not be sufficient for specialized tasks.

- **Task-Specific Labels:** For supervised learning tasks, the data should include accurate and relevant labels that align with the task objectives. Poor labeling can mislead the model and degrade its performance.

4) Bias and Ethical Considerations:

- **Bias Detection:** Analyze the dataset for potential biases that could be introduced into the model. This includes examining the distribution of demographic groups, the presence of stereotypes, and the representation of diverse perspectives.
- **Ethical Sourcing:** Ensure that the data is collected and used in an ethical manner, respecting privacy, consent, and intellectual property rights. This is particularly important when dealing with sensitive or proprietary data.

4. Curating and Cleaning the Data

Once you have sourced the data, the next step is to curate and clean it. This process involves removing duplicates, filtering out noise, and ensuring that the data is well-structured and ready for model training.

1) Deduplication:

- **Removing Redundancy:** Duplicate data can skew the model's learning, making it overly sensitive to certain patterns. Use deduplication techniques to identify and remove redundant content from the dataset.

2) Noise Reduction:

- **Filtering Irrelevant Content:** Remove irrelevant content, such as advertisements, boilerplate text, and HTML tags. This helps ensure that the model focuses on meaningful language data during training.

- **Handling Outliers:** Identify and handle outliers that could distort the model's learning process. This might involve removing or down-weighting data points that are significantly different from the rest of the dataset.

3) Normalization:

- **Standardizing Data:** Normalize the text to ensure consistency in case, punctuation, and formatting. For example, converting all text to lowercase and standardizing abbreviations can help the model process the data more effectively.
- **Tokenization:** Break the text into tokens (words, subwords, or characters) that the model can process. Tokenization is a critical step in preparing text data for training, and it should be done carefully to preserve the meaning and structure of the content.

5. Building a Diverse and Robust Dataset

To train an effective LLM, aim to build a dataset that is both diverse and robust. This means including a wide range of sources, covering different topics, styles, and demographics, and ensuring that the data is clean, accurate, and relevant.

1) Combining Multiple Sources:

- **Integrating Data:** Combine data from multiple sources, such as public datasets, proprietary data, and scraped content, to create a comprehensive training set. This helps the model learn from a broad spectrum of language patterns and contexts.

2) Ensuring Balance:

- **Balancing the Data:** Ensure that the dataset is balanced in terms of topics, genres, and demographic representation. An imbalanced dataset can lead to a biased model that performs well on some types of content but poorly on others.

3) Iterative Refinement:

- **Continuous Improvement:** Regularly update and refine the dataset as new data becomes available or as the model's requirements evolve. This helps maintain the model's relevance and performance over time.

Sourcing high-quality data is the first and arguably the most critical step in training a successful LLM. By carefully selecting, evaluating, and curating your data, you lay a strong foundation for building a model that is accurate, versatile, and capable of performing well across a range of tasks. In the next sections, we'll delve into the preprocessing techniques that prepare this data for training, ensuring that it's optimized for the model's learning process.

4.2 Text Preprocessing Techniques: Tokenization, Stemming, Lemmatization

Before training a Large Language Model (LLM), the raw text data must undergo several preprocessing steps to transform it into a format that the model can effectively learn from. These steps help normalize the data, reduce complexity, and ensure consistency, making it easier for the model to identify patterns and relationships within the text. In this section, we'll cover some of the most essential text preprocessing techniques, including tokenization, stemming, and lemmatization.

1. Tokenization: Breaking Text into Manageable Pieces

Tokenization is the process of splitting text into smaller units, called tokens. These tokens can be words, subwords, or even characters, depending on the granularity needed for the model. Tokenization is a critical step because it transforms a stream of text into discrete elements that the model can process.

1) Word Tokenization:

- **What It Is:** Word tokenization splits the text into individual words. For example, the sentence "The quick brown fox" would be tokenized into ["The", "quick", "brown", "fox"].
- **Advantages:** Word tokenization is straightforward and preserves the meaning of the text. It's commonly used in models that rely on a vocabulary of whole words.
- **Challenges:** Word tokenization can struggle with out-of-vocabulary (OOV) words, such as rare words, misspellings, or new words not included in the model's vocabulary. It also doesn't handle compound words or word variations well.

2) Subword Tokenization:

- **What It Is:** Subword tokenization breaks words down into smaller units, such as prefixes, suffixes, or even individual characters. Techniques like Byte-Pair Encoding (BPE) or WordPiece are often used.
- **Example:** The word "unhappiness" might be tokenized into ["un", "happiness"], or even ["un", "##happy", "##ness"] in a WordPiece model.
- **Advantages:** Subword tokenization reduces the OOV problem by breaking down words into smaller, reusable components. It's particularly useful in languages with rich morphology or in models that need to handle a vast vocabulary.

- **Challenges:** Subword tokenization can result in longer sequences of tokens, which may increase the computational load and make the model harder to interpret.

3) Character Tokenization:

- **What It Is:** Character tokenization breaks text down to the level of individual characters. For example, "cat" would be tokenized into ["c", "a", "t"].
- **Advantages:** This method completely eliminates the OOV issue since every word is composed of characters. It's also useful in tasks where the model needs to learn fine-grained linguistic features, such as in certain NLP tasks or when working with languages that don't use spaces between words.
- **Challenges:** Character tokenization results in very long sequences, which can make training more computationally expensive and potentially lead to overfitting if not managed carefully.

2. Stemming: Reducing Words to Their Root Forms

Stemming is a technique used to reduce words to their base or root form, often by chopping off prefixes or suffixes. This helps group together different forms of a word so that they can be analyzed as a single entity.

1) How Stemming Works:

- **Basic Principle:** Stemming algorithms, like the Porter Stemmer or Snowball Stemmer, apply a set of rules to strip affixes from words, thereby reducing them to a common base form. For instance, "running," "runner," and "ran" might all be reduced to "run."
- **Advantages:** Stemming helps in reducing the dimensionality of the text data, making it easier for the model to identify and learn from patterns across different word forms.

- **Challenges:** Stemming is a crude method that often produces non-linguistic root forms. For example, "studies" might be stemmed to "studi," which is not a valid word. This can sometimes lead to a loss of meaning or introduce ambiguity.

2) Use Cases for Stemming:

- **Search Engines:** Stemming is widely used in search engines to match queries with documents, even if different word forms are used. For example, a search for "running" might also return results containing "runner" or "ran."
- **Basic NLP Tasks:** In simpler NLP tasks, where the exact form of a word is less important, stemming can be an effective way to reduce the complexity of the text data.

3. Lemmatization: Mapping Words to Their Canonical Forms

Lemmatization is similar to stemming but more sophisticated. It reduces words to their canonical or dictionary form (lemma) based on their meaning and context, rather than just chopping off affixes.

1) How Lemmatization Works:

- **Linguistic Basis:** Lemmatization relies on understanding the context and part of speech of a word to reduce it to its lemma. For example, "better" might be lemmatized to "good," and "ran" to "run," depending on the sentence.
- **Advantages:** Lemmatization typically produces more meaningful and accurate base forms than stemming, as it considers the grammatical context of the word. This leads to better consistency in the data and can improve model performance.
- **Challenges:** Lemmatization is more computationally intensive than stemming and requires access to detailed linguistic resources like

dictionaries or morphological analyzers. It may also introduce complexities when handling different languages or dialects.

2) Use Cases for Lemmatization:

- **Text Analysis:** Lemmatization is particularly useful in tasks where the exact meaning of words matters, such as sentiment analysis, machine translation, or text summarization.
- **Advanced NLP Applications:** For more complex NLP applications, where understanding the precise meaning and usage of words is crucial, lemmatization offers significant advantages over stemming.

4. Choosing the Right Technique for Your Model

The choice between tokenization, stemming, and lemmatization—or a combination of these—depends on the specific requirements of your model and the nature of the text data.

1) Task-Specific Considerations:

- **For Text Classification:** If you're working on a text classification task where the exact form of words is less important, stemming might be sufficient to reduce noise and improve efficiency.
- **For Language Models:** If your model needs to generate or translate text, lemmatization might be a better choice to preserve the semantic integrity of the words.

2) Balancing Complexity and Performance:

- **Computational Resources:** Consider the trade-off between computational cost and performance. While lemmatization provides better accuracy, it's also more resource-intensive. In contrast, stemming and basic tokenization are faster but may compromise on the quality of the preprocessing.

- **Data Characteristics:** The nature of your dataset—such as the language, domain, and amount of available data—can also influence which techniques are most appropriate. For example, highly inflected languages may benefit more from lemmatization.

Text preprocessing is a critical step in preparing data for training LLMs. By applying techniques like tokenization, stemming, and lemmatization, you can transform raw text into a structured format that enhances the model's ability to learn and perform well. Understanding these preprocessing methods allows you to make informed decisions that align with the goals of your project, ensuring that your LLM is trained on clean, consistent, and meaningful data.

In the following sections, we'll discuss how to handle imbalanced datasets, manage noise and outliers, and apply data augmentation techniques to further refine the quality of your training data. These steps will help you build a robust dataset that supports the development of high-performance

4.3 Handling Imbalanced Datasets

Imbalanced datasets are a common challenge in training Large Language Models (LLMs) and other machine learning models. When the distribution of classes or categories in your dataset is skewed, it can lead to biased models that perform poorly on underrepresented classes. In this section, we'll discuss strategies to effectively handle imbalanced datasets, ensuring that your model learns to treat all classes fairly and makes accurate predictions across the board.

1. Understanding the Impact of Imbalanced Datasets

When training data is imbalanced, the model may become biased toward the majority class, because it encounters these examples more frequently. This can lead to several issues:

1) Biased Predictions:

- The model may tend to predict the majority class more often, simply because it has seen more examples of it. This can result in high accuracy but poor performance on minority classes.
- **Example:** In a sentiment analysis model, if the training data contains 90% positive reviews and 10% negative reviews, the model might overwhelmingly predict "positive," even when presented with a negative review.

2) Poor Generalization:

- Imbalanced datasets can cause the model to generalize poorly, especially on the minority class. This is because the model doesn't learn enough about the minority class to make accurate predictions.
- **Impact:** Poor generalization can be particularly problematic in critical applications, such as medical diagnosis or fraud detection, where correctly identifying the minority class is crucial.

3) Misleading Performance Metrics:

- Common evaluation metrics like accuracy can be misleading when applied to imbalanced datasets. A model that always predicts the majority class could achieve high accuracy, despite failing to correctly identify any instances of the minority class.
- **Need for Better Metrics:** Precision, recall, F1 score, and area under the ROC curve (AUC-ROC) are more informative metrics when dealing

with imbalanced data, as they provide a better understanding of the model's performance on each class.

2. Strategies for Handling Imbalanced Datasets

Several techniques can help address the challenges posed by imbalanced datasets. These strategies can be broadly categorized into data-level and algorithm-level approaches.

Data-Level Approaches

1) Resampling Techniques:

- **Oversampling:** This technique involves increasing the number of instances in the minority class by duplicating existing examples or generating synthetic ones. A popular method for synthetic data generation is SMOTE (Synthetic Minority Over-sampling Technique), which creates new examples by interpolating between existing ones.
- **Example:** If your dataset has 100 positive reviews and 10 negative reviews, you could apply SMOTE to create additional synthetic negative reviews, balancing the dataset.
- **Undersampling:** In contrast, undersampling reduces the number of instances in the majority class to match the minority class. This approach can help balance the dataset but risks losing valuable information from the majority class.
- **Example:** Reducing the majority class size to match the minority class can make the dataset more balanced, but careful consideration is needed to avoid discarding important data.

2) Data Augmentation:

- **Text Augmentation:** Techniques such as paraphrasing, synonym replacement, and back-translation can be used to generate more examples for the minority class. These methods help increase the diversity and size of the minority class without simply duplicating existing examples.

- **Example:** In a dataset with few examples of a particular sentiment, you might create additional examples by rephrasing sentences while preserving their original meaning.

3) Creating Balanced Subsets:

- **Balanced Sampling:** When training, you can create balanced batches or subsets of data that contain an equal number of examples from each class. This approach ensures that the model sees a balanced representation of each class during training.
- **Application:** Balanced batches can be particularly effective in mini-batch gradient descent, where each batch is used to update the model's parameters. This helps prevent the model from becoming biased toward the majority class.

Algorithm-Level Approaches

1) Adjusting Class Weights:

- **Weighted Loss Functions:** By assigning higher weights to the minority class in the loss function, you can penalize the model more for misclassifying minority class examples. This encourages the model to pay more attention to the minority class during training.
- **Implementation:** Many machine learning frameworks allow you to specify class weights directly. For example, in a binary classification problem with class imbalance, you might set the weight for the minority class to be higher than that for the majority class.

2) Cost-Sensitive Learning:

- **Custom Loss Functions:** In some cases, you might design a custom loss function that directly incorporates the cost of misclassifying different classes. This approach can be tailored to specific applications where the cost of errors varies between classes.

- **Example:** In fraud detection, the cost of missing a fraudulent transaction is much higher than the cost of a false positive. A cost-sensitive loss function would reflect this, encouraging the model to be more cautious about predicting "non-fraud."

3) Ensemble Methods:

- **Boosting and Bagging:** Ensemble methods like AdaBoost, Gradient Boosting, and Random Forests can be adapted to handle imbalanced data by focusing on hard-to-classify examples or by combining the predictions of multiple models to improve overall accuracy.
- **Advantages:** These methods are particularly effective in dealing with imbalanced datasets because they can combine the strengths of different models and reduce the risk of overfitting to the majority class.

3. Evaluating Models on Imbalanced Datasets

When working with imbalanced datasets, it's crucial to use appropriate evaluation metrics that reflect the model's performance across all classes.

1. **Precision, Recall, and F1 Score:**
   - **Precision:** Measures the proportion of true positive predictions among all positive predictions made by the model. It's particularly important when the cost of false positives is high.
     - **Formula:** $\text{Precision} = \frac{\text{True Positives}}{\text{True Positives} + \text{False Positives}}$
   - **Recall:** Measures the proportion of true positive predictions among all actual positives. It's crucial when missing true positives is more costly than having false positives.
     - **Formula:** $\text{Recall} = \frac{\text{True Positives}}{\text{True Positives} + \text{False Negatives}}$
   - **F1 Score:** The harmonic mean of precision and recall, providing a single metric that balances the trade-off between the two.
     - **Formula:** $\text{F1 Score} = 2 \times \frac{\text{Precision} \times \text{Recall}}{\text{Precision} + \text{Recall}}$

2. **Confusion Matrix:**
   - A confusion matrix provides a detailed breakdown of the model's performance across all classes, showing the true positives, true negatives, false positives, and false negatives for each class. This allows for a more nuanced understanding of where the model is performing well and where it's struggling.

3. **AUC-ROC Curve:**
   - The Area Under the Receiver Operating Characteristic Curve (AUC-ROC) is a popular metric for evaluating models on imbalanced datasets. It plots the true positive rate against the false positive rate, providing insight into the trade-offs between sensitivity and specificity.
     - **Higher AUC:** A higher AUC indicates better model performance, particularly in distinguishing between the majority and minority classes.

Handling imbalanced datasets is crucial for building robust and fair LLMs that perform well across all classes. By using a combination of data-level and algorithm-level techniques, you can mitigate the effects of class imbalance and ensure that your model learns to treat each class appropriately. With the right strategies, you can improve the accuracy, fairness, and reliability of your LLM, making it more effective in real-world applications.

In the next section, we'll delve into dealing with noise and outliers in data, further refining the preprocessing pipeline to enhance the quality of the training data and the performance of the model.

4.4 Dealing with Noise and Outliers in Data

In the process of collecting and preparing data for training Large Language Models (LLMs), you'll inevitably encounter noise and outliers. Noise refers to irrelevant or erroneous data, while outliers are data points that significantly differ from the rest of the dataset. Both can negatively impact the performance of your model by introducing inaccuracies or bias. In this section, we'll discuss strategies for identifying and handling noise and outliers to ensure that your training data is clean, reliable, and conducive to building effective LLMs.

1. Understanding Noise and Outliers

Before diving into methods for dealing with noise and outliers, it's important to understand what these terms mean in the context of text data.

1) Noise in Text Data:

- **What It Is:** Noise in text data includes irrelevant or incorrect information that doesn't contribute to the learning process. Examples include typos, grammatical errors, irrelevant text (like advertisements or HTML tags), and poorly formatted data.
- **Impact on Models:** Noise can confuse the model, leading it to learn patterns that don't generalize well to new data. This can result in poor performance, especially in tasks requiring precision, such as text classification or sentiment analysis.

2) Outliers in Text Data:

- **What It Is:** Outliers are data points that deviate significantly from the norm. In text data, this could be sentences or documents that are vastly different in content, style, or length compared to the majority of the dataset.
- **Impact on Models:** Outliers can skew the model's understanding of the data, leading to biased predictions or overfitting. For example, if your dataset mostly consists of short sentences but includes a few extremely long ones, the model might struggle to generalize across different lengths.

2. Identifying Noise and Outliers

The first step in dealing with noise and outliers is identifying them within your dataset. Several techniques can help with this process.

1) Manual Inspection:

- **What It Is:** Manually reviewing a subset of your data can provide insights into the types of noise and outliers present. This approach is particularly useful for understanding the nature of the dataset and identifying common issues.
- **Advantages:** Manual inspection allows for a deep understanding of the dataset, making it easier to design automated processes for handling noise and outliers.
- **Challenges:** It's time-consuming and may not be feasible for very large datasets. However, it can be supplemented with automated methods.

2) Statistical Methods:

- **Z-Score and IQR:** For quantitative features (like sentence length, word frequency, etc.), you can use statistical methods such as Z-scores or the Interquartile Range (IQR) to identify outliers. A Z-score indicates how many standard deviations a data point is from the mean, while the IQR identifies data points that fall outside the typical range.

- **Advantages:** These methods are effective for detecting outliers in numerical data, such as the length of text or the frequency of specific words.
- **Challenges:** Text data is inherently qualitative, so these methods are most useful for numerical representations of text features.

3) Clustering and Anomaly Detection:

- **Clustering:** By grouping similar data points together using clustering algorithms (like K-means or DBSCAN), you can identify data points that don't fit well into any cluster, flagging them as potential outliers.
- **Anomaly Detection:** Algorithms specifically designed for anomaly detection, such as Isolation Forests or One-Class SVM, can help identify unusual data points based on their features.
- **Advantages:** These methods are scalable and can handle large datasets, making them suitable for automated detection of outliers.
- **Challenges:** They require careful tuning and may produce false positives, identifying normal data points as outliers.

4) Natural Language Processing (NLP) Techniques:

- **Language Models:** Pre-trained language models can be used to identify noisy or outlying text by scoring how well each sentence fits the learned language patterns. Sentences with unusually low scores might be considered noise or outliers.
- **Text Similarity:** By measuring the similarity between text samples using techniques like cosine similarity or BERT embeddings, you can identify text that deviates significantly from the norm.
- **Advantages:** These methods leverage the power of modern NLP techniques to detect subtle inconsistencies in the data.

- **Challenges:** They require computational resources and may be complex to implement.

3. Handling Noise in Text Data

Once you've identified noise in your dataset, the next step is to clean the data. Here are some common techniques for handling noisy text data.

1) Text Normalization:

- **Lowercasing:** Convert all text to lowercase to ensure consistency, especially when dealing with case-insensitive tasks.
- **Removing Punctuation:** Remove unnecessary punctuation marks that don't contribute to the meaning of the text.
- **Spell Checking:** Correct spelling errors using automated spell-check tools or dictionaries to reduce noise caused by typos.

2) Filtering Irrelevant Content:

- **Removing Stop Words:** Stop words (like "and," "the," "is") are common words that may not contribute significant meaning in many NLP tasks. Removing them can reduce noise and improve model performance.
- **HTML Tags and Metadata:** For web-scraped data, remove HTML tags, boilerplate text, and metadata that aren't useful for model training.
- **Irrelevant Text:** Filter out irrelevant sections of text, such as advertisements or unrelated topics, that could distract the model from learning the relevant patterns.

3) Handling Inconsistent Formatting:

- **Normalization:** Standardize formats, such as dates, numbers, and abbreviations, to ensure consistency across the dataset.

- **Tokenization:** Use tokenization techniques to break text into meaningful units while handling inconsistencies in spacing or punctuation.

4. Handling Outliers in Text Data

Dealing with outliers involves deciding whether to remove them, adjust them, or keep them based on their impact on the model.

1) Removing Outliers:

- **Extreme Cases:** If outliers are extreme and irrelevant to the task, removing them from the dataset can help improve model performance and prevent overfitting.
- **Rare Cases:** However, consider the context—if outliers represent rare but important cases (like rare medical conditions in a healthcare dataset), removing them might lead to a biased model that underperforms on these critical examples.

2) Adjusting Outliers:

- **Truncation:** For text data, this might involve truncating excessively long sentences or documents to bring them more in line with the rest of the dataset.
- **Normalization:** Adjusting outliers by transforming them to fit within a reasonable range can help reduce their impact while retaining their informational value.

3) Retaining Outliers:

- **Value in Outliers:** In some cases, outliers might represent valuable information, such as edge cases or novel examples that the model should learn from. Carefully evaluate whether outliers contribute positively to the model's learning.

- **Balancing Impact:** If you choose to retain outliers, consider balancing their impact by using techniques like weighted loss functions or creating synthetic examples to balance the dataset.

5. Evaluating the Impact of Cleaning

After cleaning your dataset, it's important to evaluate the impact of your changes on the model's performance.

1) Before-and-After Comparison:

- **Model Metrics:** Train the model on the dataset before and after cleaning to compare key metrics like accuracy, precision, recall, and F1 score. This will help you assess whether your cleaning process has improved the quality of the data and the model's performance.
- **Error Analysis:** Perform error analysis to understand how the cleaning process has affected specific types of predictions. This can reveal whether the model is better at handling edge cases or if certain errors have been reduced.

2) Iterative Refinement:

- **Continuous Improvement:** Data cleaning is often an iterative process. Use feedback from the model's performance to refine your cleaning methods, making further adjustments as necessary to optimize the dataset.

Dealing with noise and outliers is a crucial step in preparing high-quality data for LLM training. By carefully identifying and handling these issues, you can ensure that your model learns from clean, relevant, and representative data, leading to better performance and more reliable outcomes. In the next section, we'll explore data augmentation techniques that can further enhance your dataset, providing the variety and richness needed to train robust and versatile LLMs.

4.5 Large-Scale Data Augmentation Techniques

Data augmentation is a powerful technique used to increase the size and diversity of a dataset without the need for additional data collection. In the context of training Large Language Models (LLMs), data augmentation helps create more robust and generalizable models by exposing them to a wider variety of inputs. This section will cover several large-scale data augmentation techniques that can be applied to text data, enhancing the training process and improving model performance.

1. The Importance of Data Augmentation

Data augmentation helps address several challenges in training LLMs:

1) Improving Generalization:

- By increasing the diversity of training data, augmentation helps the model generalize better to new, unseen data. This is especially important for LLMs, which need to handle a wide range of language patterns and contexts.

2) Mitigating Overfitting:

- Augmentation introduces variations in the training data, reducing the risk of overfitting to the original dataset. This ensures that the model learns broader language patterns rather than memorizing specific examples.

3) Handling Data Scarcity:

- In cases where collecting large amounts of data is difficult or expensive, augmentation allows you to artificially expand the dataset, providing the model with more examples to learn from.

2. Basic Text Augmentation Techniques

Several basic techniques can be applied to augment text data, each introducing different types of variability into the dataset.

1) Synonym Replacement:

- **What It Is:** Synonym replacement involves randomly replacing words in the text with their synonyms, creating new variations of the sentence.
- **Example:** The sentence "The cat sat on the mat" might be augmented to "The feline sat on the mat" or "The cat rested on the mat."
- **Advantages:** This method is simple to implement and helps increase lexical diversity in the dataset.
- **Challenges:** Care must be taken to ensure that the replacements do not alter the meaning of the text or introduce unnatural language.

2) Back-Translation:

- **What It Is:** Back-translation involves translating a sentence into another language and then translating it back to the original language. This often results in a paraphrased version of the original sentence.
- **Example:** The sentence "The cat sat on the mat" might be translated to French as "Le chat était assis sur le tapis" and then back to English as "The cat was sitting on the rug."
- **Advantages:** Back-translation preserves the original meaning while introducing variations in structure and wording.
- **Challenges:** The quality of the back-translation depends on the accuracy of the translation models. Poor translations can introduce

errors or distort the original meaning.

3) Random Insertion and Deletion:

- **Random Insertion:** This technique involves inserting random words (usually from a predefined list of relevant words) into a sentence to create new variations.
- **Example:** "The cat sat on the mat" might become "The happy cat sat on the mat."
- **Random Deletion:** Randomly removing words from a sentence can also create variations.
- **Example:** "The cat sat on the mat" might become "Cat sat on the mat."
- **Advantages:** These techniques introduce variety and can help the model learn to handle incomplete or noisy input.
- **Challenges:** Random insertion or deletion can sometimes create unnatural sentences or alter the meaning in unintended ways.

4) Shuffling Words or Phrases:

- **What It Is:** Shuffling involves randomly rearranging words or phrases within a sentence while maintaining grammatical correctness.
- **Example:** "The cat sat on the mat" might be shuffled to "On the mat, the cat sat."
- **Advantages:** This method helps the model learn to recognize meaning in different word orders, which is particularly useful in languages with flexible syntax.
- **Challenges:** Care is needed to ensure that the shuffling doesn't result in nonsensical or grammatically incorrect sentences.

3. Advanced Data Augmentation Techniques

In addition to basic methods, more advanced techniques can be used to generate large-scale variations in text data.

1) Contextual Embeddings for Augmentation:

- **What It Is:** This technique leverages pre-trained language models (like BERT or GPT) to generate contextually appropriate variations of sentences. The model can replace words with similar ones based on the context or generate entire sentences that are semantically similar to the original.
- **Example:** Given the sentence "The cat sat on the mat," a model might generate "The kitten was resting on the rug" as an augmentation.
- **Advantages:** Contextual embeddings ensure that the augmented text remains meaningful and contextually appropriate, leading to higher-quality data.
- **Challenges:** This method requires access to powerful pre-trained models and can be computationally expensive.

2) Mixup Augmentation:

- **What It Is:** Mixup is a technique where two or more examples are combined to create a new synthetic example. This is done by interpolating between the input sentences and their corresponding labels.
- **Example:** Mixing "The cat sat on the mat" and "The dog barked loudly" could generate a sentence like "The cat barked on the mat," with a corresponding interpolated label.
- **Advantages:** Mixup increases the diversity of the dataset and helps regularize the model by introducing more challenging examples.
- **Challenges:** The resulting sentences might be unrealistic or nonsensical, so this technique is typically used in tasks where the exact wording

is less critical.

3) Generative Models for Data Augmentation:

- **What It Is:** Generative models, such as GPT-3 or VAEs (Variational Autoencoders), can be used to generate entirely new sentences based on the distribution of the training data. These models can create synthetic text that closely resembles the original data, providing a rich source of augmentation.
- **Example:** A generative model trained on a corpus of news articles could generate new articles or headlines that are similar in style and content to the original data.
- **Advantages:** This technique can produce a vast amount of diverse, high-quality data, which is particularly useful for training large models.
- **Challenges:** Generative models require significant computational resources and may generate content that is off-topic or irrelevant, necessitating additional filtering.

4. Scaling Data Augmentation for Large Datasets

When working with large datasets, it's important to scale your augmentation techniques efficiently. Here are some strategies:

1) Parallel Processing:

- **What It Is:** Use parallel processing to apply augmentation techniques to large datasets simultaneously. This can be done using distributed computing frameworks like Apache Spark or Dask.
- **Advantages:** Parallel processing significantly speeds up the augmentation process, making it feasible to augment large-scale datasets.
- **Challenges:** Implementing parallel processing requires careful management of resources and can be complex to set up.

2) Batch Augmentation:

- **What It Is:** Instead of augmenting the entire dataset at once, apply augmentation techniques in batches, processing smaller chunks of data sequentially.
- **Advantages:** Batch augmentation reduces memory overhead and allows for more manageable processing of large datasets.
- **Challenges:** Batch processing can be slower overall and may require careful management to ensure that the entire dataset is augmented consistently.

3) On-the-Fly Augmentation:

- **What It Is:** Apply augmentation techniques dynamically during training, generating augmented data in real-time as the model is trained. This can be done using data generators that apply transformations to each batch before it's fed to the model.
- **Advantages:** On-the-fly augmentation reduces storage requirements and ensures that the model sees a different augmented version of the data with each epoch.
- **Challenges:** This approach increases the computational load during training and may slow down the training process.

5. Evaluating the Impact of Data Augmentation

After applying data augmentation, it's essential to evaluate its impact on the model's performance.

1) Performance Metrics:

- **Evaluation:** Compare key metrics such as accuracy, precision, recall, and F1 score before and after augmentation to assess whether the augmented data has improved the model's performance.

- **Overfitting Check:** Ensure that the model's performance on the validation set improves, which indicates better generalization. If the model's performance only improves on the training set, this could be a sign of overfitting.

2) Error Analysis:

- **Detailed Analysis:** Perform error analysis to understand how the augmented data has affected the model's ability to handle edge cases, ambiguous inputs, or minority classes. This can reveal whether the augmentation has helped the model become more robust.

3) Iterative Refinement:

- **Continuous Improvement:** Data augmentation is often an iterative process. Based on the evaluation results, refine your augmentation techniques, tweak parameters, and continue to experiment until the desired level of performance is achieved.

Large-scale data augmentation is a vital tool in the training of LLMs, helping to increase data diversity, improve generalization, and mitigate overfitting. By applying a range of augmentation techniques, from basic methods like synonym replacement to advanced techniques using generative models, you can create a richer and more varied dataset that enhances your model's learning. In the next section, we'll address the ethical considerations involved in data collection and augmentation, ensuring that your processes align with best practices and legal standards.

4.6 Ethical Considerations in Data Collection

When collecting data for training Large Language Models (LLMs), it's essential to consider the ethical implications of your practices. The data you collect not only shapes the performance and capabilities of your model but also has broader impacts on society. In this section, we'll discuss key ethical considerations to keep in mind during data collection, ensuring that your practices align with responsible AI development and respect for individuals and communities.

1. Informed Consent and Privacy

One of the most fundamental ethical principles in data collection is respecting the privacy and consent of the individuals whose data is being used.

1) Informed Consent:

- **What It Means:** Informed consent involves ensuring that individuals are fully aware of how their data will be collected, used, and shared, and that they voluntarily agree to these terms.
- **Best Practices:** When collecting data, especially from platforms like social media or surveys, make sure that users have given explicit consent for their data to be used for AI training. This includes clear communication about how the data will be used and the potential implications.
- **Challenges:** Obtaining informed consent can be difficult when dealing with large-scale data from public sources, where individuals may not be aware that their data is being used. In such cases, it's important to consider whether the data is truly public and whether its use respects the spirit of informed consent.

2) Data Anonymization:

- **Purpose:** Anonymization involves removing personally identifiable information (PII) from the data to protect individuals' privacy. This includes names, addresses, phone numbers, and any other data that could be traced back to an individual.
- **Best Practices:** Apply robust anonymization techniques that go beyond simple removal of names, such as masking or transforming data to prevent re-identification. Always consider the potential for indirect identifiers that could be used to piece together someone's identity.
- **Challenges:** Complete anonymization is difficult to achieve, especially with complex datasets where various data points could be combined to re-identify individuals. Regular audits and updates to anonymization techniques are necessary to maintain privacy protection.

2. Bias and Fairness in Data Collection

Bias in data can lead to unfair or discriminatory outcomes when models are deployed. Ensuring fairness requires careful consideration of how data is collected and used.

1) Understanding Bias:

- **Types of Bias:** Bias in datasets can take many forms, including selection bias (where certain groups are over- or under-represented), label bias (where the labeling process introduces subjective judgments), and confirmation bias (where data collection methods reinforce existing beliefs).
- **Impact:** If a model is trained on biased data, it is likely to produce biased predictions, which can perpetuate or even exacerbate inequalities. For example, a model trained on data that underrepresents certain demographic groups may perform poorly for those groups.

2) Mitigating Bias:

- **Diverse Data Sources:** Collect data from a wide range of sources to ensure that different perspectives and experiences are represented. This includes considering demographic diversity in terms of age, gender, race, socioeconomic status, and geographic location.
- **Balanced Datasets:** Where possible, ensure that your dataset is balanced and representative of the population it's meant to serve. This may involve oversampling minority groups or using data augmentation techniques to increase representation.
- **Bias Audits:** Regularly audit your data for potential biases, and apply corrections where necessary. This might include re-weighting certain data points, adjusting labels, or removing biased data entirely.

3) Transparency and Accountability:

- **Documenting Data Sources:** Keep detailed records of where your data comes from, how it was collected, and any steps taken to address bias. This transparency helps in identifying and addressing biases that may emerge later.
- **Ethical Review:** Consider implementing an ethical review process for data collection, involving stakeholders who can assess the potential impacts and fairness of your practices. This helps ensure accountability and promotes ethical decision-making.

3. Intellectual Property and Legal Compliance

Respecting intellectual property rights and adhering to legal requirements is crucial when collecting data for LLM training.

1) Copyright Considerations:

- **What It Means:** Many data sources, such as books, articles, and online content, are protected by copyright. Using copyrighted material without permission can lead to legal issues and ethical concerns.

- **Best Practices:** Ensure that you have the legal right to use the data you collect. This might involve obtaining licenses, using public domain data, or relying on data sources that explicitly allow for their use in AI training under open licenses.
- **Challenges:** It's not always clear whether certain data can be used, especially in cases where the boundaries of copyright law are ambiguous. When in doubt, seek legal advice or opt for more clearly permissible data sources.

2) Compliance with Data Protection Laws:

- **Relevant Laws:** Different regions have different laws governing data protection, such as the General Data Protection Regulation (GDPR) in the European Union or the California Consumer Privacy Act (CCPA) in the United States. These laws regulate how personal data can be collected, stored, and used.
- **Best Practices:** Ensure compliance with all relevant data protection laws by understanding the requirements in the regions where your data collection occurs. This includes adhering to principles like data minimization, purpose limitation, and ensuring individuals' rights to access and delete their data.
- **Challenges:** Navigating the complexities of international data protection laws can be challenging, especially when collecting data from multiple regions. It's important to stay informed about legal developments and seek legal counsel when necessary.

4. Ethical Use of Public Data

Publicly available data presents unique ethical challenges, even when it's legally accessible.

1) Respecting Contextual Integrity:

- **What It Means:** Just because data is publicly accessible doesn't mean it's ethical to use it for any purpose. Contextual integrity refers to respecting the context in which the data was originally shared. For example, social media posts shared within a specific community might not be intended for broad public consumption or commercial use.
- **Best Practices:** Consider the original context of the data and whether its use in LLM training respects the intentions of the data creators. When in doubt, avoid using data that could be perceived as violating the privacy or trust of individuals.
- **Challenges:** It's often difficult to determine the original context or intended audience for public data, especially when dealing with large-scale datasets scraped from the web. Erring on the side of caution and seeking guidance on ethical data use is advisable.

2) Impact on Individuals and Communities:

- **Potential Harm:** Using public data in ways that individuals didn't anticipate can lead to unintended consequences, such as reinforcing stereotypes, exposing private information, or causing psychological harm.
- **Best Practices:** Assess the potential impact of using public data on the individuals and communities it represents. Consider conducting impact assessments or consulting with representatives from affected communities to understand their concerns.
- **Challenges:** Balancing the benefits of using public data with the need to protect individuals and communities can be complex. Ethical decision-making requires a careful evaluation of the potential risks and benefits.

5. Long-Term Ethical Considerations

The ethical implications of data collection don't end with the dataset. Consider the long-term impacts of your model and the data it was trained on.

1) Model Deployment and Usage:

- **Responsible AI:** Think about how your model will be used and the potential societal impacts. For example, will it be deployed in ways that could disadvantage certain groups? Will it be used in high-stakes environments where accuracy and fairness are critical?
- **Continuous Monitoring:** Even after deployment, continue to monitor the model's performance and impact. This includes being open to feedback and willing to make changes if the model causes harm or produces biased outcomes.

2) Ethical AI Development:

- **Ongoing Reflection:** The field of AI is constantly evolving, and so are the ethical considerations. Stay informed about developments in AI ethics and be prepared to adapt your practices as new challenges and standards emerge.
- **Community Engagement:** Engage with the broader AI and ethics communities to share insights, learn from others, and contribute to the development of best practices. This collaborative approach helps ensure that AI development is aligned with societal values and ethical principles.

Ethical considerations in data collection are critical to building responsible and fair LLMs. By prioritizing informed consent, privacy, fairness, legal compliance, and the ethical use of public data, you can ensure that your data collection practices support the development of models that are not only effective but also aligned with ethical principles. In the next chapter, we'll explore the architectures and frameworks that power LLMs, building on the foundation of high-quality and ethically sourced data.

Chapter 5: Training LLMs from Scratch

5.1 Setting Up the Training Environment: Hardware and Software Requirements

Training a Large Language Model (LLM) from scratch is a resource-intensive task that requires careful planning and the right infrastructure. In this section, we'll cover the hardware and software requirements necessary to set up an effective training environment. Whether you're working on a small-scale project or aiming to train a cutting-edge model, understanding these requirements will help you optimize your setup for both performance and cost-efficiency.

1. Hardware Requirements

The hardware you choose for training LLMs is critical, as it directly impacts the speed, scalability, and feasibility of your project. Here are the key components to consider:

1) GPUs (Graphics Processing Units):

- **Why GPUs Matter:** GPUs are the workhorses of deep learning. Their ability to handle parallel computations makes them ideal for the matrix operations that underpin LLM training.
- **Selecting GPUs:** The choice of GPU will depend on your budget, the size

of the model, and the volume of data. Popular options include NVIDIA's A100, V100, and RTX 3090 GPUs. For cutting-edge performance, the NVIDIA A100 offers exceptional capabilities, especially for large-scale models.

- **Multi-GPU Setup:** For larger models, consider using multiple GPUs to distribute the workload. This setup can significantly reduce training time but requires careful configuration to ensure efficient parallelism.

2) TPUs (Tensor Processing Units):

- **What They Are:** TPUs are specialized hardware accelerators designed by Google specifically for training machine learning models. They offer high performance for tensor operations, which are core to deep learning.
- **When to Use TPUs:** TPUs are particularly useful for large-scale training tasks and can be more cost-effective than GPUs for certain workloads. They are available through Google Cloud and are optimized for TensorFlow, though they also support PyTorch via the XLA compiler.
- **Cloud vs. On-Premises:** Deciding between cloud-based TPUs and on-premises GPUs depends on your specific needs. Cloud TPUs offer scalability and ease of use, while on-premises setups provide more control and potentially lower long-term costs.

3) CPU (Central Processing Unit):

- **Role of CPUs:** While GPUs and TPUs handle most of the heavy lifting during training, CPUs are still essential for managing data loading, preprocessing, and general system tasks.
- **Selecting a CPU:** Choose a CPU with multiple cores and high clock speeds to keep up with the demands of data preprocessing and other non-GPU tasks. Intel Xeon or AMD EPYC processors are common choices in high-performance setups.

4) Memory (RAM):

- **Importance of RAM:** Adequate RAM is necessary to handle the large datasets typically involved in LLM training. RAM is also used to store intermediate results and manage data loading efficiently.
- **Recommended Amount:** For most LLM training tasks, a minimum of 64GB of RAM is recommended, though larger models or datasets might require 128GB or more. The exact amount depends on the size of the dataset and the complexity of the model.

5) Storage:

- **Fast Storage:** Fast storage is crucial for quickly accessing large datasets and storing checkpoints during training. Solid-State Drives (SSDs) are preferred for their speed and reliability.
- **Capacity:** Depending on the size of your dataset and the number of checkpoints you plan to save, storage requirements can vary. For large projects, consider using multi-terabyte SSDs or network-attached storage (NAS) systems.
- **Data Management:** Organize your storage to facilitate quick access to data, backups, and checkpoints. Regularly backing up your work is crucial to prevent data loss.

2. Software Requirements

The software environment is just as important as the hardware when it comes to training LLMs. Here's what you need to consider:

1) Operating System:

- **Linux:** Most deep learning frameworks and tools are optimized for Linux, making it the preferred operating system for LLM training. Ubuntu and CentOS are popular choices.

- **Windows:** While Windows can be used, it may require additional setup and configuration to ensure compatibility with deep learning tools. WSL (Windows Subsystem for Linux) can help bridge this gap by allowing you to run a Linux environment on Windows.

2) Deep Learning Frameworks:

- **TensorFlow:** TensorFlow is a widely used framework that supports both research and production environments. It's particularly well-suited for use with TPUs and offers extensive libraries for LLM training.
- **PyTorch:** PyTorch is another popular deep learning framework, known for its flexibility and ease of use. It has a strong community and is widely used in research, especially in NLP tasks.
- **Choosing a Framework:** The choice between TensorFlow and PyTorch often comes down to personal preference or specific project requirements. Both frameworks offer robust support for LLM training, with extensive documentation and community support.

3) Libraries and Tools:

- **Transformers Library:** The Hugging Face Transformers library is essential for LLM training, offering pre-built models, tokenizers, and tools for fine-tuning and training from scratch.
- **Dataloading and Preprocessing:** Tools like pandas, numpy, and datasets (by Hugging Face) are crucial for handling and preprocessing large text datasets.
- **Distributed Training:** For multi-GPU or TPU setups, libraries like Horovod, PyTorch Distributed, or tf.distribute in TensorFlow enable efficient parallel training.

4) Containerization and Virtualization:

- **Docker:** Docker is widely used for creating consistent and reproducible training environments. It allows you to package your entire software environment, including dependencies, into containers that can be easily deployed across different machines.

- **Kubernetes:** For managing multiple containers across a cluster, Kubernetes provides powerful orchestration capabilities. It's particularly useful in large-scale training environments where multiple jobs need to be managed simultaneously.

5) Version Control and Collaboration:

- **Git:** Using version control systems like Git is essential for managing code, collaborating with team members, and tracking changes. Platforms like GitHub or GitLab integrate well with most development workflows.
- **Experiment Tracking:** Tools like MLflow or Weights & Biases can be used to track experiments, monitor model performance, and manage different training runs. These tools are invaluable for large projects where multiple experiments are run in parallel.

3. Optimizing Your Training Environment

Once you have the hardware and software in place, optimizing your environment can make a significant difference in training efficiency.

1) Efficient Data Pipelines:

- **Data Loading:** Use optimized data pipelines to load and preprocess data in parallel with training. This ensures that your GPUs or TPUs are fully utilized and not idling while waiting for data.
- **Caching:** Implement caching strategies to reduce the need to reload data from disk, especially for large datasets that are used repeatedly.

2) Monitoring and Logging:

- **Real-Time Monitoring:** Tools like nvidia-smi for GPUs or htop for CPUs can provide real-time insights into resource usage, helping you identify bottlenecks and optimize performance.
- **Automated Logging:** Set up automated logging for key metrics such as loss, accuracy, and resource utilization. This allows you to track progress and quickly identify any issues that arise during training.

3) Scalability Considerations:

- **Cloud vs. On-Premises:** If you anticipate scaling your project, consider the pros and cons of cloud-based versus on-premises setups. Cloud platforms offer easy scalability but may incur higher long-term costs, while on-premises setups require significant upfront investment but offer more control.
- **Resource Allocation:** For distributed training, ensure that resources are allocated efficiently. This includes managing GPU memory, balancing workloads across devices, and minimizing communication overhead between nodes.

Setting up the right training environment is crucial for successfully training LLMs from scratch. By carefully selecting the appropriate hardware and software, and optimizing your setup for efficiency and scalability, you can ensure that your model training process runs smoothly and effectively. In the next section, we'll delve into distributed training techniques, exploring how to scale your setup across multiple GPUs or TPUs to handle even the most demanding LLM projects.

5.2 Distributed Training: Multi-GPU and TPU Setup

Training Large Language Models (LLMs) from scratch often requires substantial computational resources, especially when dealing with large datasets and complex architectures. Distributed training, which involves spreading the workload across multiple GPUs or TPUs, is essential for speeding up the training process and handling models of significant size. In this section, we'll discuss the practical aspects of setting up distributed training environments, focusing on both multi-GPU and TPU configurations.

1. Why Distributed Training is Necessary

When training LLMs, the size of the model and the amount of data can quickly overwhelm a single GPU or TPU. Distributed training allows you to:

1. **Scale Up:** By distributing the training across multiple devices, you can handle larger models and datasets that would be impossible to process on a single machine.
2. **Speed Up:** Parallelizing the workload reduces the overall training time, enabling faster iteration and experimentation.
3. **Efficient Resource Utilization:** Distributed setups make better use of available hardware, reducing idle time and ensuring that all resources contribute to the training process.

2. Setting Up Multi-GPU Training

Multi-GPU training involves splitting the workload across several GPUs, which can be on a single machine or spread across multiple machines. Here's how to get started:

1) Data Parallelism:

- **What It Is:** In data parallelism, the model is replicated across each GPU, and the data is split into batches that are processed independently by each GPU. After processing, the gradients are averaged, and the model parameters are updated synchronously across all GPUs.

- **Implementation:** Most deep learning frameworks, including TensorFlow and PyTorch, support data parallelism out of the box. In PyTorch, for example, you can use the DataParallel or DistributedDataParallel modules to easily implement this approach.
- **Challenges:** Data parallelism requires efficient communication between GPUs to synchronize updates, which can introduce overhead, particularly with large models.

2) Model Parallelism:

- **What It Is:** In model parallelism, different parts of the model are split across different GPUs. This is useful when the model is too large to fit into the memory of a single GPU.
- **Implementation:** Model parallelism is more complex to implement than data parallelism. It requires careful partitioning of the model and coordination between GPUs. Frameworks like PyTorch and TensorFlow provide lower-level APIs for implementing model parallelism.
- **Challenges:** The main challenge with model parallelism is balancing the workload across GPUs and minimizing the communication overhead between them.

3) Hybrid Parallelism:

- **Combining Data and Model Parallelism:** In some cases, combining data and model parallelism can yield the best results. This approach involves splitting both the model and the data across multiple GPUs, maximizing the use of resources and enabling the training of extremely large models.
- **Implementation:** Hybrid parallelism requires a more sophisticated setup and careful tuning to ensure that the workload is evenly distributed and that communication overhead is minimized.

4) Optimizing Multi-GPU Training:

- **Efficient Data Loading:** Use data loaders that can feed data to each GPU in parallel to avoid bottlenecks. Pre-fetching data and using pinned memory can help improve data transfer speeds.
- **Gradient Accumulation:** If GPU memory is a constraint, gradient accumulation allows you to simulate larger batch sizes by accumulating gradients over several smaller batches before updating the model parameters.
- **Mixed Precision Training:** By using mixed precision (combining 16-bit and 32-bit floating-point computations), you can reduce memory usage and increase training speed without sacrificing accuracy. Both TensorFlow and PyTorch offer built-in support for mixed precision training.

3. Setting Up TPU Training

TPUs are specialized hardware designed by Google to accelerate machine learning workloads, particularly for TensorFlow. They are highly efficient for LLM training and offer a different set of tools and approaches compared to GPUs.

1) Understanding TPU Architecture:

- **What TPUs Offer:** TPUs are designed to handle tensor operations more efficiently than GPUs, which makes them ideal for training large models like LLMs. TPUs are available in various configurations, including TPU v2, v3, and the more recent TPU v4, each offering different levels of performance.
- **TPU Pods:** For large-scale training, TPU Pods combine multiple TPU devices into a single, powerful distributed system. TPU Pods allow you to train models that are orders of magnitude larger than what a single TPU can handle.

2) Setting Up TPU Training:

- **Google Cloud Platform (GCP):** TPUs are primarily available through GCP, where you can easily set up and manage your training environment. GCP provides pre-configured environments optimized for TPU usage.
- **Using TensorFlow with TPUs:** TensorFlow is natively optimized for TPUs. By using the tf.distribute.TPUStrategy API, you can distribute your model training across multiple TPU cores with minimal code changes.
- **XLA Compiler:** The XLA (Accelerated Linear Algebra) compiler further optimizes TensorFlow code to run efficiently on TPUs, automatically handling low-level optimizations and ensuring that your model takes full advantage of TPU hardware.

3) Optimizing TPU Training:

- **Batch Size:** TPUs can handle much larger batch sizes than GPUs, thanks to their efficient memory architecture. Increasing the batch size can significantly speed up training, but it may require adjustments to the learning rate.
- **Dynamic Padding:** To maximize TPU efficiency, use dynamic padding to ensure that each input batch is the same size. This reduces the amount of wasted computation and speeds up processing.
- **Monitoring TPU Utilization:** GCP provides tools for monitoring TPU utilization, which helps you identify bottlenecks and optimize your setup. Ensure that your input pipeline is fast enough to keep the TPUs fully utilized.

4. Common Challenges and Best Practices

Distributed training can introduce new challenges that need to be addressed to ensure smooth operation:

1) Synchronization Issues:

- **Gradients and Parameters:** Synchronizing gradients and parameters across devices is critical. Any delays or mismatches can cause issues such as gradient staleness, which affects model convergence.
- **Solution:** Use built-in synchronization tools provided by your framework, such as torch.distributed in PyTorch or tf.distribute in TensorFlow. These tools ensure that gradients are properly averaged and parameters are updated consistently across devices.

2) Communication Overhead:

- **Impact:** As the number of GPUs or TPUs increases, the amount of data that needs to be communicated between devices can create a bottleneck.
- **Solution:** Reduce communication overhead by optimizing the way data is partitioned and ensuring that network bandwidth is sufficient. Techniques like gradient compression and communication overlap can also help.

3) Resource Management:

- **Balancing Load:** Ensuring that all devices are fully utilized can be challenging, especially in heterogeneous environments where devices have different capabilities.
- **Solution:** Monitor resource usage closely and use tools like Kubernetes or GCP's AI Platform to manage and scale resources dynamically.

4) Debugging Distributed Systems:

- **Complexity:** Debugging issues in a distributed environment can be more complex than in a single-device setup, due to the added layers of synchronization and communication.
- **Solution:** Use logging and monitoring tools that are designed for distributed systems. Both TensorFlow and PyTorch offer detailed

logging capabilities, and tools like TensorBoard or Weights & Biases provide visualization and tracking that can help identify issues.

Distributed training using multi-GPU or TPU setups is essential for training Large Language Models efficiently and effectively. By understanding the hardware and software requirements, implementing best practices, and addressing common challenges, you can set up a robust distributed training environment that scales with your needs. In the next section, we'll discuss hyperparameter tuning, another critical aspect of optimizing LLM training to achieve the best possible performance.

5.3 Hyperparameter Tuning for Optimal Performance

Hyperparameter tuning is a crucial step in training Large Language Models (LLMs) from scratch. The right set of hyperparameters can significantly improve model performance, reduce training time, and ensure that your model generalizes well to new data. However, finding the optimal configuration can be challenging due to the vast number of possible combinations and the computational cost involved. In this section, we'll explore key hyperparameters to tune, effective strategies for tuning them, and practical tips for managing the process efficiently.

1. Key Hyperparameters in LLM Training

Understanding the impact of different hyperparameters on your model is the first step toward effective tuning. Here are the most important hyperparameters to consider:

1) Learning Rate:

- **What It Is:** The learning rate determines the size of the steps taken during gradient descent. It controls how quickly or slowly the model learns from the data.

- **Impact:** A learning rate that is too high can cause the model to overshoot the optimal solution, leading to divergence. A rate that is too low can result in slow convergence and potentially getting stuck in local minima.
- **Tuning Tips:** Start with a moderate learning rate and adjust based on initial training performance. Learning rate schedules, such as cosine annealing or exponential decay, can help maintain a balance between fast convergence and stability.

2) Batch Size:

- **What It Is:** Batch size refers to the number of training examples processed in one iteration before the model's parameters are updated.
- **Impact:** Larger batch sizes can make training faster by utilizing parallelism but might require a lower learning rate to avoid instability. Smaller batch sizes provide more frequent updates but can lead to noisier gradients.
- **Tuning Tips:** Experiment with different batch sizes in relation to your available hardware. Use gradient accumulation if memory constraints prevent using larger batches.

3) Number of Layers and Hidden Units:

- **What It Is:** The architecture of the model, including the number of layers and the number of hidden units (neurons) per layer, directly affects its capacity and complexity.
- **Impact:** More layers and hidden units can enable the model to capture more complex patterns but also increase the risk of overfitting and require more computational resources.
- **Tuning Tips:** Start with a proven architecture for your task (e.g., a standard transformer setup) and adjust based on performance. Use regularization techniques to combat overfitting when increasing

model capacity.

4) Dropout Rate:

- **What It Is:** Dropout is a regularization technique where a fraction of the neurons is randomly "dropped" during training, preventing the model from becoming too dependent on any one neuron.
- **Impact:** A higher dropout rate can reduce overfitting but may also slow down learning if too much information is discarded. A lower rate might not provide enough regularization.
- **Tuning Tips:** Common dropout rates range from 0.1 to 0.5. Start with a moderate rate and adjust based on the model's tendency to overfit.

5) Weight Decay:

- **What It Is:** Weight decay, also known as L2 regularization, adds a penalty to the loss function based on the size of the model weights, encouraging smaller weights and reducing overfitting.
- **Impact:** Proper weight decay can help improve generalization, but if set too high, it may overly constrain the model, preventing it from learning complex patterns.
- **Tuning Tips:** Typical values for weight decay range from 1e-5 to 1e-2. Experiment with different values to find a balance between regularization and model flexibility.

6) Learning Rate Schedulers:

- **What It Is:** Learning rate schedulers automatically adjust the learning rate during training based on predefined rules or the training progress.
- **Impact:** Dynamic adjustment of the learning rate can lead to more stable training and better convergence, particularly in later stages of training.
- **Tuning Tips:** Popular schedulers include cosine annealing, exponen-

tial decay, and step decay. Choose one that fits your training dynamics and adjust its parameters (e.g., decay rate or steps) based on the model's performance.

2. Strategies for Hyperparameter Tuning

Given the high dimensionality of the hyperparameter space, finding the optimal set requires a systematic approach. Here are some common strategies:

1) Grid Search:

- **What It Is:** Grid search involves manually specifying a grid of hyperparameter values to explore. The model is trained and evaluated for each combination of parameters.
- **Advantages:** Grid search is straightforward and guarantees that all combinations are tested, which can be useful for smaller models or datasets.
- **Challenges:** It becomes computationally expensive as the number of hyperparameters and values increases, making it impractical for large-scale models.

2) Random Search:

- **What It Is:** Random search samples hyperparameter values randomly from a specified distribution. This approach explores a broader range of the hyperparameter space without testing every combination.
- **Advantages:** Random search is more efficient than grid search, often finding good hyperparameter combinations with fewer trials.
- **Challenges:** Since it's random, there's no guarantee of finding the best combination, and some areas of the hyperparameter space may be underexplored.

3) Bayesian Optimization:

- **What It Is:** Bayesian optimization uses a probabilistic model to predict the performance of different hyperparameter combinations, focusing on the most promising areas of the hyperparameter space.
- **Advantages:** It's more efficient than grid or random search, often finding optimal or near-optimal configurations with fewer evaluations.
- **Challenges:** Bayesian optimization can be complex to implement and may require more sophisticated tooling, such as Optuna or HyperOpt.

4) Successive Halving and Hyperband:

- **What It Is:** These are adaptive resource allocation methods that start by evaluating many hyperparameter configurations with a small budget (e.g., few epochs), progressively allocating more resources to the best-performing configurations.
- **Advantages:** These methods are efficient for large-scale hyperparameter tuning, allowing you to test more configurations while focusing resources on the most promising ones.
- **Challenges:** Requires careful management of resources and may need tuning of its own parameters (like initial budgets and reduction rates).

3. Practical Tips for Hyperparameter Tuning

Hyperparameter tuning can be resource-intensive, so it's important to approach it strategically:

1) Start with Defaults:

- Begin with default or commonly used values for hyperparameters. This provides a baseline that you can improve upon as you understand how each parameter affects the model's performance.

2) Use Smaller Models or Subsets of Data:

- When tuning hyperparameters, especially in the early stages, consider using a smaller version of your model or a subset of the data. This allows for faster experimentation and quicker feedback on how changes affect performance.

3) Focus on the Most Impactful Parameters:

- Not all hyperparameters have the same impact on performance. Prioritize tuning those that are known to have the most significant effect, such as the learning rate and batch size.

4) Automate the Process:

- Tools like Optuna, Ray Tune, or HyperOpt can automate hyperparameter tuning, allowing you to scale the process across multiple machines or GPUs. Automation helps manage the complexity and can significantly reduce the time required to find optimal configurations.

5) Track Experiments:

- Use experiment tracking tools like Weights & Biases, MLflow, or TensorBoard to log hyperparameters, metrics, and outcomes. This helps keep track of what has been tested and the results, making it easier to iterate and improve.

6) Balance Performance and Cost:

- Consider the trade-off between model performance and the computational cost of hyperparameter tuning. In some cases, a slightly less optimal set of hyperparameters that requires less training time might be preferable, especially in production environments.

4. Evaluating the Impact of Hyperparameter Tuning

Once you've conducted hyperparameter tuning, it's crucial to evaluate its impact:

1) Comparison with Baseline:

- Compare the performance of your tuned model with the baseline model (using default parameters). This helps quantify the improvements gained through tuning.

2) Cross-Validation:

- Use cross-validation to ensure that the hyperparameter settings generalize well across different subsets of the data. This reduces the risk of overfitting to a specific training set.

3) Check for Overfitting:

- Monitor for signs of overfitting, such as a significant gap between training and validation performance. If overfitting occurs, consider adjusting regularization parameters, dropout rates, or simplifying the model.

4) Continuous Tuning:

- Hyperparameter tuning isn't a one-time task. As you iterate on your model or collect more data, revisit the tuning process to ensure that your model continues to perform optimally.

Hyperparameter tuning is an essential part of training LLMs, allowing you to fine-tune your model for optimal performance. By understanding the key hyperparameters, employing effective tuning strategies, and following best practices, you can significantly enhance the capabilities of your model. In the next section, we'll explore common pitfalls in LLM training and how to address them, ensuring a smooth and efficient training process.

5.4 Addressing Common Training Pitfalls

Training Large Language Models (LLMs) from scratch is a complex task that can present a variety of challenges, even for experienced practitioners. From unexpected model behavior to resource management issues, understanding and addressing common pitfalls can save you significant time and effort. In this section, we'll explore some of the most frequent problems that arise during training and provide practical solutions to overcome them.

1. Overfitting and Underfitting

Balancing overfitting and underfitting is crucial in model training. Overfitting occurs when the model performs well on training data but poorly on unseen data, while underfitting happens when the model fails to capture the underlying patterns in the data.

1) Recognizing Overfitting:

- **Symptoms:** A significant gap between training and validation performance, where the model performs much better on the training set.
- **Solutions:**
- **Regularization:** Apply techniques like L2 regularization (weight decay) or dropout to prevent the model from relying too heavily on any single feature.
- **Data Augmentation:** Increase the diversity of your training data through augmentation, which can help the model generalize better.
- **Early Stopping:** Monitor the validation loss and stop training when it

begins to increase, indicating that the model is starting to overfit.

2) Recognizing Underfitting:

- **Symptoms:** Poor performance on both training and validation sets, indicating that the model is too simple to capture the data's complexity.
- **Solutions:**
- **Increase Model Complexity:** Add more layers or increase the number of hidden units to give the model more capacity to learn complex patterns.
- **Tune Hyperparameters:** Adjust hyperparameters such as the learning rate, batch size, and dropout rate to improve learning.
- **More Training Data:** Sometimes, the model needs more data to learn effectively. If possible, expand your dataset.

2. Exploding and Vanishing Gradients

Exploding and vanishing gradients are common issues in training deep neural networks, where gradients either become too large or too small, disrupting the learning process.

1) Vanishing Gradients:

- **Symptoms:** Slow or stalled training progress, particularly in deeper layers of the model, where gradients shrink as they are backpropagated.
- **Solutions:**
- **Use Proper Initialization:** Initialize weights using techniques like Xavier or He initialization, which help maintain gradient flow through the network.
- **Gradient Clipping:** Set a threshold for gradients to prevent them from becoming too small, ensuring they remain in a range that allows

effective learning.

- **Activation Functions:** Choose activation functions that mitigate vanishing gradients, such as ReLU (Rectified Linear Unit) or its variants like Leaky ReLU.

2) Exploding Gradients:

- **Symptoms:** Rapidly increasing loss values, leading to NaN (Not a Number) errors or instability in the model's predictions.
- **Solutions:**
- **Gradient Clipping:** Apply gradient clipping to prevent gradients from becoming excessively large, which can destabilize training.
- **Learning Rate Adjustment:** Lower the learning rate to reduce the size of parameter updates, helping to stabilize the training process.
- **Batch Normalization:** Incorporate batch normalization layers to stabilize the distribution of activations, which can help manage gradient magnitudes.

3. Imbalanced Data Issues

Imbalanced datasets can lead to biased models that perform well on the majority class but poorly on the minority class.

1) Recognizing Imbalanced Data:

- **Symptoms:** High accuracy but poor performance metrics (like precision, recall, or F1 score) for the minority class.
- **Solutions:**
- **Resampling Techniques:** Use oversampling for the minority class or undersampling for the majority class to balance the dataset.
- **Class Weights:** Adjust the loss function to penalize misclassifications of the minority class more heavily, encouraging the model to pay more attention to it.

- **Data Augmentation:** Generate synthetic examples for the minority class using techniques like SMOTE (Synthetic Minority Over-sampling Technique).

4. Computational Resource Constraints

Training LLMs requires significant computational resources, and managing these resources effectively is crucial for a successful training run.

1) Running Out of Memory:

- **Symptoms:** Out-of-memory (OOM) errors during training, particularly with large models or batch sizes.
- **Solutions:**
- **Reduce Batch Size:** Lower the batch size to fit the model within the available memory. Use gradient accumulation to maintain an effective larger batch size.
- **Use Mixed Precision:** Mixed precision training reduces memory usage by using 16-bit floats instead of 32-bit, which can allow larger models or batch sizes to fit into memory.
- **Model Pruning:** Simplify the model by pruning unnecessary layers or parameters, reducing the overall memory footprint.

2) Long Training Times:

- **Symptoms:** Prolonged training durations that make experimentation and iteration difficult.
- **Solutions:**
- **Distributed Training:** Utilize multiple GPUs or TPUs to parallelize the workload and reduce overall training time.
- **Efficient Data Pipelines:** Optimize data loading and preprocessing to ensure that GPUs are not idling while waiting for data. Prefetching and parallel data loading can help.

- **Checkpoints and Resume:** Regularly save checkpoints during training so you can resume from the last point in case of interruptions, avoiding the need to restart from scratch.

5. Debugging Training Issues

Debugging issues that arise during training can be challenging but is essential for identifying and resolving problems quickly.

1) Inconsistent Results:

- **Symptoms:** Variability in training outcomes, where the model's performance differs significantly between runs.
- **Solutions:**
- **Seed Randomness:** Set random seeds for reproducibility. This ensures that your model's initialization and data shuffling are consistent across runs.
- **Monitor Data Pipeline:** Verify that the data pipeline is functioning correctly and that the data is being fed into the model as expected. Look out for issues like data corruption or incorrect preprocessing.

2) Training Instability:

- **Symptoms:** Fluctuating loss values, NaN errors, or sudden drops in performance during training.
- **Solutions:**
- **Gradient Clipping:** Apply gradient clipping to prevent instabilities caused by excessively large gradients.
- **Learning Rate Warmup:** Implement a learning rate warmup phase, gradually increasing the learning rate at the beginning of training to stabilize the initial learning process.
- **Log and Analyze:** Use logging tools to monitor training metrics closely. Detailed logs can help you pinpoint where and why instability occurs,

allowing you to take corrective action.

Training LLMs is a complex process, but understanding and addressing common pitfalls can significantly improve your chances of success. By proactively managing issues like overfitting, gradient problems, imbalanced data, and resource constraints, you can create a more stable and effective training environment. In the next section, we'll discuss monitoring and logging practices that will help you keep track of your training process, ensuring that you can quickly identify and address any issues that arise.

5.5 Monitoring and Logging During Training

Monitoring and logging are critical aspects of training Large Language Models (LLMs). These practices help you track progress, diagnose issues, and make informed decisions during the training process. Without proper monitoring and logging, you might miss important signals that indicate whether your model is learning effectively, whether the training process is stable, and whether resources are being used efficiently. In this section, we'll explore best practices for monitoring and logging during LLM training, ensuring that you can keep your training process on track and respond quickly to any issues that arise.

1. The Importance of Monitoring and Logging

Monitoring and logging serve several key purposes during LLM training:

1) Tracking Model Performance:

- **What It Means:** Regularly measuring key metrics like loss, accuracy, precision, recall, and other relevant performance indicators helps you understand how well your model is learning and whether it's

improving over time.
- **Impact:** Continuous tracking allows you to identify trends and patterns that indicate the model's progress. It also helps you detect when the model might be overfitting, underfitting, or encountering other training issues.

2) Detecting Training Instabilities:

- **What It Means:** Monitoring the stability of the training process, including checking for anomalies like NaN values, sudden spikes in loss, or oscillations in key metrics, is crucial for maintaining a smooth training process.
- **Impact:** Early detection of instabilities allows you to intervene quickly, adjusting hyperparameters, modifying the learning rate, or implementing other corrective measures to keep the training on course.

3) Resource Management:

- **What It Means:** Keeping an eye on the utilization of computational resources such as GPU/TPU usage, memory consumption, and data loading efficiency ensures that you're making the most of your available hardware.
- **Impact:** Efficient resource management helps minimize training time and costs while maximizing throughput, particularly in distributed training environments.

2. Tools for Monitoring and Logging

Several tools are available to help you monitor and log your training process effectively. Here are some of the most widely used options:

1) TensorBoard:

- **What It Is:** TensorBoard is a visualization toolkit that provides a suite of visualizations and dashboards for monitoring metrics, viewing model graphs, and analyzing training data.
- **How to Use It:** TensorBoard can be easily integrated into TensorFlow and PyTorch training scripts. By logging metrics, you can visualize them in real-time, making it easier to track progress and diagnose issues.
- **Key Features:** TensorBoard offers a range of features, including scalar plots for tracking metrics over time, histograms for analyzing model weights and activations, and graph visualizations for understanding the model architecture.

2) Weights & Biases:

- **What It Is:** Weights & Biases (W&B) is a comprehensive experiment tracking tool that integrates with most deep learning frameworks, providing extensive logging, visualization, and collaboration features.
- **How to Use It:** W&B allows you to log metrics, track hyperparameters, compare different runs, and even collaborate with team members by sharing dashboards and reports.
- **Key Features:** W&B offers advanced features like hyperparameter sweeps, automated alerts, and integrations with cloud platforms, making it a powerful tool for managing large-scale experiments.

3) MLflow:

- **What It Is:** MLflow is an open-source platform for managing the machine learning lifecycle, including experiment tracking, model management, and deployment.
- **How to Use It:** MLflow's tracking component allows you to log metrics, parameters, and artifacts during training. It also provides an interface for comparing different runs and visualizing results.
- **Key Features:** MLflow's versatility and integration with various frame-

works and tools make it a valuable option for tracking experiments and managing models throughout their lifecycle.

4) Custom Logging with Python:

- **What It Is:** For more tailored logging needs, you can implement custom logging solutions using Python's built-in logging library. This approach allows for greater flexibility in how you capture and store logs.
- **How to Use It:** Set up logging in your training script to capture key events, metrics, and other relevant information. Logs can be written to files, databases, or other storage solutions for later analysis.
- **Key Features:** Custom logging provides the ability to capture specific information that may not be available through standard tools, allowing for a more granular understanding of the training process.

3. Key Metrics to Monitor

To effectively monitor your LLM training, focus on the following key metrics:

1) Training and Validation Loss:

- **What It Tells You:** The training loss indicates how well the model is fitting the training data, while the validation loss reflects its performance on unseen data. Monitoring both helps you detect overfitting or underfitting.
- **Best Practices:** Track these losses over time and compare them. A widening gap between training and validation loss often signals overfitting.

2) Accuracy, Precision, Recall, and F1 Score:

- **What It Tells You:** These metrics provide a more detailed understanding of model performance, especially in classification tasks. They help assess how well the model distinguishes between classes.
- **Best Practices:** Monitor these metrics throughout training, particularly after each epoch or batch, to ensure that the model is improving and not favoring any particular class.

3) Learning Rate:

- **What It Tells You:** The learning rate influences the speed and stability of training. Monitoring the learning rate, especially if using a learning rate scheduler, helps ensure that the model is learning efficiently.
- **Best Practices:** Visualize the learning rate alongside loss and accuracy to assess whether changes in the learning rate correspond to improvements or issues in training.

4) Gradient Norms:

- **What It Tells You:** The gradient norms indicate the magnitude of the gradients during backpropagation. Large gradients can lead to instability (exploding gradients), while very small gradients may slow down learning (vanishing gradients).
- **Best Practices:** Keep an eye on the gradient norms to detect any signs of instability early on. Implement gradient clipping if necessary to maintain control.

5) Resource Utilization:

- **What It Tells You:** Monitoring CPU, GPU, and memory usage helps ensure that your resources are being used efficiently and that there are no bottlenecks in the data pipeline.
- **Best Practices:** Use tools like nvidia-smi for GPU monitoring and system monitoring tools like htop for CPUs to track resource usage in

real-time. Address any issues such as underutilized GPUs or memory leaks promptly.

4. Implementing Alerts and Automation

To stay informed about the training process without constantly monitoring it manually, consider setting up automated alerts and triggers:

1) Automated Alerts:

- **How They Work:** Alerts can be set up to notify you when certain thresholds are crossed, such as a sudden spike in loss, NaN values, or when a specific metric reaches a predefined value.
- **Tools to Use:** Weights & Biases and MLflow both offer integrations for setting up automated alerts. You can also use custom scripts to send notifications via email, Slack, or other channels.
- **Best Practices:** Configure alerts for critical metrics that require immediate attention. This ensures that you can intervene quickly if something goes wrong.

2) Automated Checkpoints:

- **How They Work:** Saving model checkpoints at regular intervals allows you to resume training from the last saved state in case of interruptions. Checkpoints also serve as a backup in case you want to revert to an earlier state of the model.
- **Tools to Use:** Both TensorFlow and PyTorch offer built-in support for checkpointing. Customize the frequency and conditions under which checkpoints are saved, based on your training process.
- **Best Practices:** Set checkpoints to save at the end of each epoch or after a significant improvement in performance. Ensure that checkpoints are stored reliably, especially in distributed training environments.

5. Analyzing Logs and Visualizations

Regularly reviewing logs and visualizations is crucial for understanding how the training process is progressing:

1) Log Analysis:

- **How to Do It:** Periodically review logs to identify patterns, anomalies, or trends that might not be immediately apparent in real-time monitoring. Logs can also help diagnose issues after training has completed.
- **Best Practices:** Organize logs in a structured way, making it easy to search and filter for specific events or metrics. Use log analysis tools to automate the detection of common issues.

2) Visualizations:

- **How to Use Them:** Visualizations provide an intuitive way to understand the training process, track progress, and compare different experiments. Use tools like TensorBoard or W&B to create visual representations of metrics over time.
- **Best Practices:** Customize your dashboards to focus on the most critical metrics. Regularly review these visualizations to make data-driven decisions about training adjustments.

Monitoring and logging are essential practices for successful LLM training. By effectively tracking key metrics, utilizing the right tools, and setting up automated alerts, you can ensure that your training process remains on track and that any issues are quickly identified and resolved. In the final section of this chapter, we'll dive into a case study that walks through the process of training a GPT-like model from scratch, applying the principles and techniques discussed throughout the chapter.

5.6 Case Study: Training a GPT-like Model from Scratch

In this case study, we'll walk through the process of training a GPT-like model from scratch, applying the principles and techniques discussed in this chapter. This example will help you understand how to set up the training environment, configure distributed training, tune hyperparameters, monitor progress, and address common issues. By the end, you'll have a practical understanding of what it takes to train a powerful language model, even if you're starting with a blank slate.

1. Defining the Project Goals

Before diving into the technical setup, it's important to clearly define the goals of the project:

1. **Objective:** Train a GPT-like model capable of generating coherent and contextually relevant text based on a given prompt. The model should be able to handle a variety of topics and generate text that mimics human-like writing.
2. **Dataset:** We'll use a large corpus of English text, such as Wikipedia articles, books, and open-domain conversational datasets. The dataset should be diverse enough to cover a wide range of topics and writing styles.
3. **Model Architecture:** The model will follow the GPT (Generative Pre-trained Transformer) architecture, which uses a stack of transformer decoder layers. We'll configure the model with 12 layers, 12 attention heads, and a hidden size of 768, similar to GPT-2's smaller variant.
4. **Performance Metrics:** Key metrics to monitor include training and validation loss, perplexity, and text generation quality. We'll also track resource utilization to ensure efficient use of hardware.

2. Setting Up the Training Environment

With the project goals in place, the next step is to set up the training environment:

1) Hardware:

- **GPUs:** We'll use a multi-GPU setup with 4 NVIDIA A100 GPUs. This setup provides enough computational power to handle the large dataset and complex model architecture.
- **Storage:** A fast SSD with at least 2TB of storage is required to store the dataset and model checkpoints. Additionally, we'll set up a network-attached storage (NAS) system for backing up data.
- **Memory:** 128GB of RAM will ensure smooth data loading and preprocessing, especially when working with large batches.

2) Software:

- **Operating System:** Ubuntu 20.04 LTS, a stable and widely supported Linux distribution that works well with deep learning frameworks.
- **Deep Learning Framework:** PyTorch will be used for model implementation and training. PyTorch is chosen for its flexibility and ease of use, especially when experimenting with different model architectures.
- **Tools and Libraries:** We'll use the Hugging Face Transformers library to streamline the implementation of the GPT architecture. Additionally, tools like datasets for data loading, numpy for numerical operations, and torch.distributed for distributed training will be essential.

3) Environment Configuration:

- **Docker:** We'll use Docker to create a consistent and reproducible environment. The Docker image will include all necessary dependencies, including PyTorch, CUDA drivers, and the required Python libraries.

- **Version Control:** Git will be used to manage the project's codebase, ensuring that changes are tracked and collaboration is seamless.

3. Data Preparation

With the environment set up, the next step is to prepare the dataset:

1) Data Collection:

- **Sources:** We'll collect text data from a variety of sources, including the English Wikipedia, Project Gutenberg books, and open-domain conversational datasets. The data will be downloaded and stored on the SSD.
- **Preprocessing:** The raw text will be tokenized using the Byte-Pair Encoding (BPE) method, which efficiently handles rare words and out-of-vocabulary tokens. The Hugging Face tokenizers library will be used to implement BPE.
- **Data Splitting:** The dataset will be split into training (80%), validation (10%), and test (10%) sets to ensure that the model's performance can be accurately evaluated.

2) Data Augmentation:

- **Augmentation Techniques:** To increase the diversity of the training data, we'll apply techniques like synonym replacement and back-translation. This helps the model generalize better and improve its text generation capabilities.
- **Batching:** The data will be organized into batches of 64 samples each. Batch sizes may be adjusted based on GPU memory constraints and training speed.

4. Model Training

With the data prepared, we can now begin the training process:

1) Distributed Training Setup:

- **Data Parallelism:** We'll use PyTorch's DistributedDataParallel module to distribute the model across the 4 GPUs. Each GPU will process a different portion of the batch in parallel, with gradients synchronized across devices after each update.
- **Gradient Accumulation:** To effectively utilize the GPUs and manage memory, we'll implement gradient accumulation. This allows us to simulate a larger batch size by accumulating gradients over several smaller batches before updating the model parameters.

2) Hyperparameter Tuning:

- **Initial Hyperparameters:** We'll start with a learning rate of 3e-5, a batch size of 64, and a dropout rate of 0.1. These values are chosen based on common settings for similar models.
- **Tuning Process:** Using random search, we'll experiment with different learning rates, batch sizes, and dropout rates to find the combination that yields the best performance on the validation set.
- **Learning Rate Scheduling:** A cosine annealing scheduler will be used to gradually decrease the learning rate over time, helping the model converge smoothly.

3) Monitoring and Logging:

- **TensorBoard Integration:** We'll log key metrics like training and validation loss, perplexity, and learning rate to TensorBoard. This allows us to monitor the training process in real-time and make adjustments as needed.

- **Checkpointing:** Model checkpoints will be saved after each epoch to ensure that we can resume training in case of interruptions. The best-performing checkpoint, based on validation loss, will be used for final evaluation.

5. Evaluation and Fine-Tuning

After the initial training phase, the model will be evaluated and fine-tuned:

1) Evaluation Metrics:

- **Perplexity:** We'll calculate perplexity on the validation and test sets to assess how well the model predicts the next word in a sequence. Lower perplexity indicates better performance.
- **Human Evaluation:** Generated text samples will be manually reviewed to evaluate coherence, relevance, and creativity. This qualitative assessment complements the quantitative metrics.

2) Fine-Tuning:

- **Task-Specific Fine-Tuning:** Depending on the target application, we may fine-tune the model on a specific dataset, such as a customer support dataset for a chatbot application.
- **Hyperparameter Adjustments:** During fine-tuning, we'll revisit hyperparameters like learning rate and batch size, as these may need to be adjusted for the new task.

6. Conclusion and Lessons Learned

After completing the training and fine-tuning process, we'll review the outcomes:

1) Model Performance:

- **Summary of Results:** We'll summarize the model's performance on both the validation and test sets, discussing how well it met the initial project goals.
- **Comparison with Benchmarks:** The model's performance will be compared with existing GPT-like models to gauge its relative effectiveness.

2) Challenges and Solutions:

- **Key Challenges:** We'll highlight the main challenges encountered during the project, such as managing resource constraints, tuning hyperparameters, and ensuring data quality.
- **Solutions:** For each challenge, we'll discuss the solutions implemented and their effectiveness, providing insights that can be applied to future projects.

3) Next Steps:

- **Future Work:** Based on the case study results, we'll outline potential next steps, such as scaling the model to larger architectures, experimenting with different datasets, or deploying the model in a real-world application.

This case study demonstrates the full process of training a GPT-like model from scratch, highlighting the importance of careful planning, rigorous testing, and continuous monitoring. By following these steps, you can successfully train and deploy powerful language models that are tailored to your specific needs and applications.

Chapter 6: Fine-Tuning Pre-trained Models

6.1 Introduction to Transfer Learning

Transfer learning has revolutionized the field of natural language processing (NLP) by allowing us to leverage pre-trained models for a wide range of tasks. Instead of training a model from scratch—which is often resource-intensive and time-consuming—transfer learning enables us to start with a model that has already learned a lot about language from vast amounts of text. This foundational knowledge can then be fine-tuned to perform specific tasks, such as sentiment analysis, text classification, or question-answering.

1. What is Transfer Learning?

Transfer learning involves taking a model that has been pre-trained on a large, general-purpose dataset and adapting it to a specific task or domain. The pre-trained model acts as a starting point, providing a strong foundation that can be fine-tuned to meet the needs of your particular application.

1) Pre-trained Models:

- These are models that have been trained on large corpora, such as Wikipedia, Common Crawl, or large datasets like the BookCorpus. The training process typically involves learning to predict the next word in a sentence (language modeling) or filling in the blanks in a text (masked language modeling).
- Popular pre-trained models include BERT (Bidirectional Encoder Representations from Transformers), GPT (Generative Pre-trained Transformer), and T5 (Text-To-Text Transfer Transformer).

2) Fine-Tuning:

- Fine-tuning involves continuing the training of the pre-trained model on a smaller, task-specific dataset. During this process, the model adapts its learned representations to better suit the specific task at hand.
- For example, a pre-trained BERT model can be fine-tuned on a dataset of movie reviews to perform sentiment analysis, where it learns to classify reviews as positive or negative.

3) Why Transfer Learning is Effective:

- **Efficiency:** Transfer learning significantly reduces the computational resources and time required to train a model. Since the model starts with pre-learned knowledge, it only needs to learn the nuances of the specific task, rather than starting from scratch.
- **Performance:** Pre-trained models often achieve higher performance on specific tasks because they have already learned a broad range of language patterns and features that are useful across different domains.

2. The Importance of Pre-trained Models in NLP

The introduction of pre-trained models in NLP has been a game-changer. These models serve as a universal backbone for many NLP tasks, providing the following benefits:

1) Rich Representations:

- Pre-trained models learn complex language representations, including syntax, semantics, and contextual information. These representations are transferable, meaning they can be applied to a variety of downstream tasks with minimal adjustments.

2) Handling Limited Data:

- Many NLP tasks suffer from a lack of large labeled datasets. Transfer learning allows models to perform well even with limited data by leveraging the knowledge gained from large pre-training datasets. This is especially useful in specialized domains like legal or medical text, where labeled data is scarce.

3) Accelerated Research and Development:

- The availability of pre-trained models has accelerated progress in NLP research and application development. Researchers and developers can now focus on fine-tuning and applying models to specific problems without the overhead of training large models from scratch.

3. How Transfer Learning Works in Practice

In practice, transfer learning in NLP typically involves the following steps:

1) Choosing a Pre-trained Model:

- The first step is selecting a pre-trained model that is well-suited to the task at hand. This decision is based on factors such as the model's architecture, the type of data it was trained on, and the specific needs of your task.

2) Preparing the Data:

- Next, you need to prepare a task-specific dataset. This dataset should be labeled according to the task (e.g., sentiment labels for sentiment analysis) and formatted appropriately for the model.

3) Fine-Tuning:

- Fine-tuning involves training the pre-trained model on your specific dataset. This process typically requires adjusting the learning rate and potentially freezing some of the model's layers to prevent overfitting.

4) Evaluation:

- After fine-tuning, the model is evaluated on a validation set to ensure that it performs well on the task. Additional adjustments to hyperparameters may be necessary to optimize performance.

4. Advantages and Considerations of Transfer Learning

While transfer learning offers many advantages, there are also some considerations to keep in mind:

1) Advantages:

- **Reduced Training Time:** Fine-tuning a pre-trained model is much faster than training from scratch, making it accessible even to those with limited computational resources.

- **Improved Performance:** Leveraging a model that has already learned a wide range of linguistic features often leads to better performance on specific tasks, especially in low-data scenarios.
- **Versatility:** Pre-trained models are versatile and can be adapted to a wide variety of tasks, from text classification to language generation.

2) Considerations:

- **Model Size:** Many pre-trained models are large and require significant computational resources for fine-tuning and inference. It's important to consider whether your infrastructure can handle the model size.
- **Domain Mismatch:** If the domain of your task is significantly different from the data used to pre-train the model, additional fine-tuning or even re-training on domain-specific data may be necessary.
- **Overfitting:** There's a risk of overfitting when fine-tuning, especially if the task-specific dataset is small. Techniques like layer freezing and careful learning rate scheduling can help mitigate this risk.

Transfer learning has transformed NLP by enabling more efficient and effective use of pre-trained models. It allows you to build powerful models for specific tasks without the need for extensive computational resources or vast amounts of data. In the following sections, we'll delve deeper into selecting the right pre-trained model, fine-tuning techniques, and strategies for adapting models to specific domains, ensuring that you can make the most of transfer learning in your projects.

6.2 Selecting the Right Pre-trained Model

Choosing the right pre-trained model is a critical step in fine-tuning for specific NLP tasks. With numerous models available, each with its own strengths and specializations, selecting the most appropriate one can significantly impact your project's success. In this section, we'll discuss the key factors to consider when selecting a pre-trained model and provide guidance on making an informed choice.

1. Understanding Your Task Requirements

The first step in selecting a pre-trained model is to clearly understand the requirements of your task:

1) Task Type:

- **Classification:** If your task involves categorizing text into predefined categories (e.g., sentiment analysis, spam detection), models like BERT or RoBERTa are well-suited because of their ability to generate rich contextual embeddings.
- **Text Generation:** For tasks like text completion, machine translation, or dialogue generation, GPT or T5 models are more appropriate, as they are designed to generate coherent sequences of text.
- **Named Entity Recognition (NER):** Models like BERT and its variants excel in identifying and classifying entities within text due to their strong understanding of contextual relationships.

2) Domain Specificity:

- **General vs. Domain-Specific:** Consider whether your task requires general language understanding or if it's specialized in a particular domain like medical, legal, or scientific text. While models like BERT are general-purpose, domain-specific models such as BioBERT (for biomedical text) or LegalBERT (for legal documents) can offer better performance in specialized tasks.

3) Resource Availability:

- **Computational Resources:** Some pre-trained models are extremely large (e.g., GPT-3) and require significant computational power for fine-tuning and inference. Ensure that you have the necessary hardware (e.g., GPUs or TPUs) to handle the model efficiently.
- **Training Data:** If you have a large amount of task-specific data, you can afford to fine-tune larger models for potentially better performance. However, if your dataset is small, a smaller or more specialized model might be more appropriate to avoid overfitting.

2. Popular Pre-trained Models and Their Use Cases

Here's a look at some of the most popular pre-trained models and their typical use cases:

1) BERT (Bidirectional Encoder Representations from Transformers):

- **Overview:** BERT is designed to understand the context of a word based on both its left and right surroundings, making it highly effective for tasks requiring deep language understanding.
- **Best For:** Text classification, NER, question answering, and any task where understanding context is critical.
- **Variants:** RoBERTa (a robustly optimized version of BERT), DistilBERT (a smaller, faster version), and domain-specific versions like BioBERT.

2) GPT (Generative Pre-trained Transformer):

- **Overview:** GPT is focused on generating coherent text based on a given input prompt, making it ideal for generative tasks.
- **Best For:** Text generation, dialogue systems, and creative writing.
- **Variants:** GPT-2 and GPT-3, which differ mainly in size and capabilities, with GPT-3 being the most powerful but also the most resource-intensive.

3) T5 (Text-To-Text Transfer Transformer):

- **Overview:** T5 treats every NLP task as a text-to-text problem, allowing it to be flexible across a wide range of tasks.
- **Best For:** Tasks like text summarization, translation, and any application where input text needs to be transformed into output text.
- **Variants:** T5's model size ranges from small to 11 billion parameters, with the smaller versions being more manageable for resource-constrained environments.

4) XLNet:

- **Overview:** XLNet combines the strengths of BERT and autoregressive models like GPT, making it highly versatile and capable of handling a range of NLP tasks.
- **Best For:** Tasks where capturing long-range dependencies in text is important, such as text classification, question answering, and sequence tagging.

5) ALBERT (A Lite BERT):

- **Overview:** ALBERT is a lighter, faster variant of BERT, designed to reduce memory consumption and improve training speed without sacrificing much in terms of performance.
- **Best For:** Scenarios where computational efficiency is important, particularly when dealing with large-scale tasks on limited hardware.

3. Evaluating Model Performance and Suitability

Once you've identified potential models, it's important to evaluate their performance and suitability for your specific task:

1) Pre-trained Model Benchmarks:

- **Task-Specific Benchmarks:** Look for benchmarks or research papers that report the performance of these models on tasks similar to yours. This can give you a good idea of how well a model might perform out of the box.
- **Community Feedback:** Explore community forums, GitHub repositories, and machine learning platforms like Hugging Face's Model Hub to see how others have applied these models to similar tasks. User feedback and shared code can be invaluable in making your decision.

2) Model Size and Complexity:

- **Model Parameters:** Larger models tend to perform better on complex tasks but require more resources. Consider whether the marginal performance gain is worth the additional computational cost.
- **Inference Speed:** If your application requires real-time or low-latency processing, the inference speed of the model becomes crucial. Smaller models like DistilBERT or MobileBERT might be more appropriate in such cases.

3) Transferability:

- **Domain Adaptability:** Some models are better at transferring their learned representations to different domains. For instance, while GPT is excellent for generating text in general domains, domain-specific models like SciBERT (for scientific text) might be more effective for specialized tasks.
- **Ease of Fine-Tuning:** Consider the ease with which a model can be fine-tuned. Some models, like BERT, have well-documented fine-tuning procedures and community support, making them easier to adapt to new tasks.

4. Making the Final Selection

With all these factors in mind, you can make a well-informed decision:

1) Pilot Testing:

- Before fully committing to a model, it's often useful to conduct a pilot test. Fine-tune a smaller version of the model on a subset of your data to gauge its performance and resource requirements.

2) Cost-Benefit Analysis:

- Weigh the performance benefits of the model against its resource requirements and implementation complexity. Sometimes a slightly less powerful model that is easier to deploy and fine-tune might be the better choice overall.

3) Scalability Considerations:

- If you anticipate scaling your application, consider how the model will perform with larger datasets or in production environments. Some models scale better than others, both in terms of training and inference.

Selecting the right pre-trained model is a crucial step in the fine-tuning process. By carefully considering your task requirements, evaluating model performance, and conducting pilot tests, you can choose a model that will give you the best balance of performance, efficiency, and ease of use. In the next section, we'll dive into specific fine-tuning techniques, such as layer freezing and learning rate scheduling, to help you get the most out of your chosen model.

6.3 Fine-Tuning Techniques: Layer Freezing, Learning Rate Schedulers

Fine-tuning a pre-trained model is a delicate process that involves making adjustments to adapt the model to your specific task. Two of the most important techniques in this process are layer freezing and learning rate scheduling. These techniques help control how the model learns, ensuring that it adapts effectively without overfitting or forgetting what it has already learned. In this section, we'll explore these techniques in detail, explaining how and when to apply them to achieve the best results.

1. Layer Freezing

Layer freezing is a technique used to control which parts of a pre-trained model are updated during fine-tuning. By freezing certain layers, you prevent them from being modified, allowing the model to retain the general language knowledge it has already acquired.

1) Why Layer Freezing is Useful:

- **Preserving Learned Knowledge:** The lower layers of a pre-trained model usually capture fundamental language patterns and structures, which are broadly applicable across different tasks. Freezing these layers helps preserve this general knowledge while fine-tuning the higher layers to adapt to your specific task.
- **Reducing Overfitting:** If your task-specific dataset is small, there's a risk that the model might overfit to the new data, losing some of its generalization capabilities. Freezing layers can reduce this risk by limiting the number of parameters that are updated during training.

2) How to Implement Layer Freezing:

- **Choosing Which Layers to Freeze:** Typically, the lower layers (closer to the input) are frozen because they capture general features, while the higher layers (closer to the output) are fine-tuned. For example, in a 12-layer transformer model like BERT, you might freeze the first 6 layers and fine-tune the remaining layers.

- **Freezing Layers in Practice:** In frameworks like PyTorch and TensorFlow, you can easily freeze layers by setting their parameters' requires_grad attribute to False. This prevents the optimizer from updating these layers during backpropagation.
- **Gradual Unfreezing:** In some cases, you might start by freezing most layers and gradually unfreeze them as training progresses. This allows the model to adapt slowly, giving it time to learn task-specific patterns without forgetting the general knowledge.

3) When to Use Layer Freezing:

- **Small Datasets:** When you have a limited amount of task-specific data, freezing layers helps prevent the model from overfitting and maintains the general features learned during pre-training.
- **Resource Constraints:** Freezing layers can also reduce the computational load during fine-tuning, as fewer parameters need to be updated. This is useful when working with limited computational resources.

2. Learning Rate Schedulers

The learning rate is one of the most important hyperparameters in any training process, and its value can significantly affect the model's ability to learn effectively. Learning rate schedulers dynamically adjust the learning rate during training, helping to improve convergence and prevent issues like overshooting or getting stuck in local minima.

1) Why Learning Rate Scheduling is Important:

- **Balancing Speed and Stability:** A high learning rate can speed up training but may cause the model to miss optimal solutions. A low learning rate ensures more precise updates but can slow down training. Scheduling helps balance these factors by adjusting the learning rate as training progresses.

- **Avoiding Overfitting:** Towards the end of training, reducing the learning rate can help fine-tune the model more precisely, avoiding large updates that could lead to overfitting.

2) Common Learning Rate Schedulers:

- **Step Decay:** The learning rate is reduced by a factor (e.g., halved) at specific intervals or epochs. This approach is simple and works well for tasks where the model needs more time to converge as training progresses.
- **Exponential Decay:** The learning rate decreases exponentially over time, providing a smoother reduction than step decay. This method is useful when a gradual reduction in learning rate is desired throughout the training process.
- **Cosine Annealing:** The learning rate follows a cosine curve, gradually reducing and then occasionally increasing it again. This method is particularly effective in avoiding local minima and encouraging the model to explore more diverse solutions.
- **Warmup Scheduler:** The learning rate starts low and gradually increases during the initial training epochs, then follows a standard scheduler like step decay or exponential decay. Warmup schedulers are useful in preventing instability during the early stages of training.

3) Implementing Learning Rate Schedulers:

- **Choosing a Scheduler:** The choice of scheduler depends on the task, model, and dataset. For example, cosine annealing is often used in conjunction with large models and datasets, while step decay might be preferred in smaller or more straightforward tasks.

- **Configuring the Scheduler:** Most frameworks, including PyTorch and TensorFlow, provide built-in learning rate schedulers that are easy to configure. You'll need to set parameters such as the initial learning rate, decay rate, and the schedule (e.g., how often the learning rate should change).
- **Monitoring and Adjusting:** It's important to monitor the model's performance during training to see how it responds to the learning rate adjustments. If the model isn't converging well, you might need to tweak the scheduler's parameters or choose a different scheduling strategy.

4) When to Use Learning Rate Schedulers:

- **Complex Tasks:** When training on complex tasks or with large models, a dynamic learning rate is often necessary to achieve optimal performance.
- **Extended Training Periods:** For models that require long training periods, using a scheduler can help ensure that the learning rate remains appropriate throughout the process, preventing issues like overshooting or stagnation.

3. Combining Layer Freezing and Learning Rate Scheduling

These two techniques can be highly effective when used together:

1. **Initial Phase:** Start with most layers frozen and use a learning rate scheduler with a warmup period. This allows the model to adapt gently to the new task.
2. **Mid-Phase:** Gradually unfreeze layers and continue to adjust the learning rate as the model begins to converge. This helps fine-tune the model without losing its pre-trained knowledge.
3. **Final Phase:** As the model approaches convergence, reduce the learning rate significantly and unfreeze all layers. This allows

the model to fine-tune all parameters, ensuring the best possible performance on the task.

Layer freezing and learning rate scheduling are powerful techniques for fine-tuning pre-trained models. By carefully controlling which parts of the model are updated and how quickly they learn, you can tailor the model to your specific task while preserving its general language understanding. In the next section, we'll explore strategies for adapting pre-trained models to specific domains, further enhancing their performance in specialized applications.

6.4 Domain Adaptation Strategies

Fine-tuning a pre-trained model on a specific task is often just the beginning. When the task involves specialized content—like medical texts, legal documents, or financial reports—it's crucial to adapt the model to that particular domain. Domain adaptation enhances the model's performance by making it more familiar with the terminology, style, and context specific to the domain. In this section, we'll discuss effective strategies for domain adaptation and how to apply them to ensure your model is well-suited to specialized tasks.

1. Understanding Domain Adaptation

Domain adaptation refers to the process of tailoring a pre-trained model to perform better on data that comes from a specific domain or field. While general pre-trained models like BERT or GPT-3 are trained on diverse datasets covering various topics, they might not perform optimally on specialized texts due to differences in vocabulary, syntax, and semantic usage.

1) Why Domain Adaptation is Important:

- **Terminology:** Specialized domains often use jargon or technical terms that aren't common in general corpora. Without adaptation, the model may misinterpret these terms or fail to understand their context.
- **Contextual Relevance:** In certain fields, the meaning of words and phrases can change depending on the context. For example, the term "deposition" has a different meaning in legal contexts compared to geological contexts.
- **Improved Performance:** Adapting the model to the specific language and structure of the domain can lead to better accuracy, relevance, and reliability in task performance.

2. Data Collection for Domain Adaptation

The first step in domain adaptation is gathering a suitable dataset that represents the domain you're targeting:

1) Identifying Relevant Data Sources:

- **Domain-Specific Corpora:** Look for existing datasets that are tailored to your domain. For example, PubMed is a rich source of biomedical texts, while arXiv provides scientific papers across various disciplines.
- **Company or Organization Data:** Internal documents, reports, or communication logs can be valuable sources of domain-specific data. Ensure you have the right to use this data and that it's properly anonymized if necessary.
- **Web Scraping:** If publicly available domain-specific data is sparse, consider web scraping as a method to collect relevant content. Be mindful of legal and ethical considerations when scraping data.

2) Preparing the Data:

- **Cleaning and Preprocessing:** Raw data often requires cleaning to remove noise, irrelevant information, and inconsistencies. Preprocessing steps like tokenization, stemming, and lemmatization can help standardize the data.
- **Balancing the Dataset:** Ensure that the dataset is balanced in terms of topic coverage and document types to prevent the model from becoming biased toward certain subdomains within your field.
- **Data Augmentation:** If the dataset is small, consider using data augmentation techniques, such as back-translation or synonym replacement, to increase the diversity and volume of training data.

3. Techniques for Domain Adaptation

There are several techniques you can use to adapt a pre-trained model to a specific domain:

1) Fine-Tuning on Domain-Specific Data:

- **What It Is:** Fine-tuning involves continuing the training of the pre-trained model using your domain-specific dataset. This process adjusts the model's weights to better align with the specialized language and context of the domain.
- **How to Implement:** Start with the pre-trained model and fine-tune it using your domain-specific dataset. Depending on the size of your dataset, you might freeze some layers of the model (as discussed in the previous section) to prevent overfitting.

2) Pre-training on Domain-Specific Data:

- **What It Is:** If you have a large domain-specific dataset, you can pre-train the model on this data before fine-tuning it on your specific task. This step helps the model build a strong foundation in the domain's language before adapting to the task.

- **How to Implement:** Begin by pre-training the model on your domain-specific corpus using the same objectives as the original model (e.g., masked language modeling for BERT). After pre-training, fine-tune the model on the task-specific data.

3) Mixed-Domain Training:

- **What It Is:** In mixed-domain training, the model is trained on a combination of general and domain-specific data. This approach helps the model retain its general language understanding while also learning the specifics of the domain.
- **How to Implement:** Create a training schedule that alternates between batches of general and domain-specific data. This ensures that the model doesn't lose its broad language capabilities while adapting to the domain.

4) Knowledge Distillation:

- **What It Is:** Knowledge distillation involves transferring knowledge from a larger, domain-adapted model (teacher) to a smaller, more efficient model (student). This approach is useful when you need a domain-adapted model that is lightweight and suitable for deployment in resource-constrained environments.
- **How to Implement:** Train the student model to mimic the outputs of the teacher model on a domain-specific dataset. This process typically involves using a loss function that penalizes differences between the teacher's and student's predictions.

4. Evaluating Domain Adaptation

After adapting the model to your domain, it's essential to evaluate its performance to ensure that the adaptation has been successful:

1) Domain-Specific Evaluation Metrics:

- **Task-Specific Metrics:** Depending on your task, evaluate the model using metrics such as accuracy, F1 score, precision, recall, or BLEU score. These metrics should reflect the model's ability to handle domain-specific content effectively.
- **Human Evaluation:** For tasks involving text generation or complex reasoning, consider having domain experts review the model's output. This qualitative feedback can provide insights into the model's understanding and relevance within the domain.

2) Cross-Domain Generalization:

- **Why It Matters:** Even after domain adaptation, it's important to ensure that the model doesn't lose its ability to generalize to broader contexts. Test the model on general datasets to check whether it still performs adequately outside the specialized domain.
- **How to Assess:** Use a mix of domain-specific and general datasets for evaluation. Compare the performance across these datasets to identify any trade-offs between domain specificity and generalization.

3) Continuous Monitoring and Updating:

- **Ongoing Adaptation:** Domains evolve, and so should your model. Regularly update the model with new data and re-evaluate its performance to ensure it remains relevant and effective.
- **Retraining:** Depending on the results of your evaluations, consider periodic retraining or additional fine-tuning to keep the model up-to-date with the latest domain knowledge.

Domain adaptation is a crucial step in fine-tuning pre-trained models, particularly when working with specialized content. By carefully collecting and preparing domain-specific data, applying targeted adaptation techniques, and thoroughly evaluating the model's performance, you can create a model that excels in your specific field. In the next section, we'll focus on how to evaluate the performance of your fine-tuned models to ensure they meet the desired criteria for your tasks.

6.5 Evaluating the Performance of Fine-Tuned Models

Once you've fine-tuned your pre-trained model, the next step is to evaluate its performance to ensure that it meets the desired criteria for your specific task. Proper evaluation is critical for understanding how well your model generalizes to new data, how effectively it has adapted to your domain, and whether it is ready for deployment. In this section, we'll cover the key aspects of evaluating fine-tuned models, including selecting the right metrics, understanding the results, and iterating based on the evaluation.

1. Selecting the Right Evaluation Metrics

The first step in evaluating a fine-tuned model is to choose the right metrics that align with your task's goals. Different tasks require different metrics, so it's important to select the ones that best reflect your model's performance.

1) Classification Tasks:

- **Accuracy:** Measures the proportion of correct predictions out of the total predictions. Accuracy is a good general-purpose metric but can be misleading if your data is imbalanced.
- **Precision, Recall, and F1 Score:** These metrics provide a more nuanced view of performance, especially in cases of class imbalance.
- **Precision:** The proportion of true positive predictions out of all positive predictions. High precision means fewer false positives.

- **Recall:** The proportion of true positive predictions out of all actual positives. High recall means fewer false negatives.
- **F1 Score:** The harmonic mean of precision and recall, offering a balance between the two.

2) Regression Tasks:

- **Mean Absolute Error (MAE):** Measures the average magnitude of errors in predictions without considering their direction. It's a straightforward metric for understanding prediction accuracy.
- **Mean Squared Error (MSE):** Similar to MAE but squares the error before averaging, which penalizes larger errors more heavily. MSE is useful when you want to prioritize reducing larger errors.
- **R-squared (R^2):** Indicates how well the predictions fit the actual data, with 1 indicating a perfect fit. It's useful for understanding the overall fit of your model.

3) Sequence-to-Sequence Tasks (e.g., Translation, Summarization):

- **BLEU Score:** Measures the similarity between the machine-generated text and reference text, commonly used in machine translation.
- **ROUGE Score:** Compares the overlap of n-grams between the generated and reference texts, often used for summarization tasks.
- **Perplexity:** Common in language modeling, perplexity measures how well the model predicts a sequence of words. Lower perplexity indicates better predictive performance.

4) Named Entity Recognition (NER) and Similar Tasks:

- **Exact Match Ratio:** Measures the proportion of entities correctly predicted by the model compared to the true entities.
- **Intersection Over Union (IoU):** A metric often used in object detection and NER, IoU measures the overlap between the predicted entities and

the true entities.

2. Evaluating Model Generalization

Generalization refers to the model's ability to perform well on new, unseen data. To ensure your model isn't just memorizing the training data but is truly learning the underlying patterns, it's crucial to evaluate its generalization performance.

1) Validation and Test Sets:

- **Validation Set:** After training on the training set, the model's performance is evaluated on a validation set, which helps tune hyperparameters and make decisions about model improvements.
- **Test Set:** The final evaluation is done on a test set, which the model has never seen during training or validation. This gives you a true measure of how the model will perform in the real world.

2) Cross-Validation:

- **What It Is:** Cross-validation involves splitting your data into multiple folds and training the model on different combinations of these folds. This process helps ensure that your model's performance isn't overly dependent on any particular subset of the data.
- **How to Implement:** Common approaches include k-fold cross-validation, where the data is split into k subsets, and the model is trained and validated k times, each time using a different subset as the validation set.

3) Out-of-Domain Testing:

- **Why It's Important:** To ensure your model's robustness, test it on data that comes from a slightly different distribution than the training data. This could involve using data from a different but related domain or applying slight perturbations to the test data.

- **How to Assess:** Compare the model's performance on in-domain versus out-of-domain data to assess its robustness and generalization capabilities.

3. Understanding and Interpreting Results

Once you have your evaluation metrics, it's important to interpret the results correctly to understand your model's strengths and weaknesses.

1) Metric Trade-offs:

- **Precision vs. Recall:** In some cases, you may need to trade off precision and recall depending on the task's requirements. For example, in a spam detection system, you might prefer high precision to avoid falsely marking legitimate emails as spam, even if it means some spam emails slip through (lower recall).
- **Overfitting Indicators:** A large gap between training and validation performance can indicate overfitting. If your model performs well on the training data but poorly on validation or test data, consider applying regularization techniques or reducing model complexity.

2) Error Analysis:

- **Identifying Weaknesses:** Examine the errors made by the model to identify patterns. For instance, does the model consistently misclassify certain types of data? Understanding these errors can guide further model improvements.
- **Confusion Matrix:** For classification tasks, a confusion matrix shows the breakdown of true positives, false positives, true negatives, and false negatives. This helps you see where the model is making mistakes and which classes are often confused with one another.

3) A/B Testing:

- **What It Is:** A/B testing involves comparing two versions of a model (e.g., with different hyperparameters or fine-tuning strategies) to see which one performs better on a specific task.
- **How to Implement:** Deploy both models and compare their performance on a shared validation or test set. This method is particularly useful when fine-tuning involves making many small adjustments, and you want to systematically compare their impacts.

4. Iterating Based on Evaluation

Evaluation isn't just a final step—it's part of an ongoing process of improving and refining your model.

1) Hyperparameter Tuning:

- Based on the evaluation results, you may need to adjust hyperparameters such as learning rate, batch size, or dropout rate. Small changes in these parameters can lead to significant improvements in model performance.

2) Additional Fine-Tuning:

- If the model isn't performing as well as expected, consider further fine-tuning. This might involve additional training on the domain-specific dataset, adjusting layer freezing strategies, or experimenting with different learning rate schedules.

3) Model Ensembling:

- If individual models are underperforming, consider creating an ensemble of models. Ensembles can often outperform single models by combining their predictions, which can reduce the impact of individual model weaknesses.

4) Deploying the Model:

- Once you're satisfied with the evaluation results, the model can be prepared for deployment. This involves ensuring that the model is optimized for production environments, including considerations for latency, scalability, and robustness.

Evaluating the performance of fine-tuned models is a crucial step in the model development process. By carefully selecting appropriate metrics, understanding and interpreting the results, and iterating based on those insights, you can ensure that your model is not only effective but also robust and reliable for real-world applications. In the final section of this chapter, we'll walk through a real-world example of fine-tuning BERT for sentiment analysis, tying together all the concepts we've covered so far.

6.6 Real-World Example: Fine-Tuning BERT for Sentiment Analysis

In this section, we'll walk through a real-world example of fine-tuning the BERT model for a sentiment analysis task. Sentiment analysis involves classifying text—such as movie reviews, tweets, or customer feedback—into categories like positive, negative, or neutral. BERT, with its strong contextual understanding, is well-suited for this task, making it a popular choice for sentiment analysis projects.

1. Preparing the Dataset

The first step in fine-tuning BERT is to prepare a dataset that's relevant to the sentiment analysis task.

1) Dataset Selection:

- **Example Dataset:** We'll use the IMDb movie reviews dataset, which consists of 50,000 reviews labeled as either positive or negative. This dataset is widely used for sentiment analysis and provides a good mix of different writing styles and sentiments.
- **Data Download:** The dataset can be downloaded directly using libraries like datasets from Hugging Face, which makes it easy to access and preprocess standard datasets.

2) Data Preprocessing:

- **Text Tokenization:** Since BERT uses WordPiece tokenization, the text data needs to be tokenized accordingly. Hugging Face's transformers library provides a BertTokenizer that handles this process efficiently.
- **Padding and Truncation:** BERT has a fixed input size, so each review needs to be padded or truncated to a consistent length (typically 512 tokens). This ensures that all inputs are of the same size and compatible with the model's architecture.
- **Creating Data Batches:** The dataset is then split into batches for training and validation. Batching allows the model to process multiple reviews at once, which speeds up training and makes better use of computational resources.

2. Fine-Tuning BERT

With the dataset prepared, we can now fine-tune BERT to perform sentiment analysis.

1) Setting Up the Environment:

- **Framework:** We'll use PyTorch along with the Hugging Face transformers library, which simplifies working with BERT and other transformer models. Ensure that you have the necessary libraries installed, including torch, transformers, and datasets.
- **Hardware:** Fine-tuning BERT requires significant computational resources, so it's recommended to use a GPU. If you don't have access to a GPU locally, consider using cloud-based platforms like Google Colab or AWS.

2) Configuring the Model:

- **Model Initialization:** We start by loading the pre-trained BERT model (bert-base-uncased), which has 12 layers, 768 hidden units, and 12 attention heads. This version of BERT is lowercased, meaning all input text is converted to lowercase before tokenization.
- **Adjusting the Output Layer:** Since our task is binary classification (positive vs. negative), we modify the output layer of BERT to have two units, corresponding to the two sentiment classes.

3) Training Process:

- **Optimizer:** We'll use the AdamW optimizer, which is well-suited for fine-tuning transformer models. It incorporates weight decay, which helps prevent overfitting.
- **Learning Rate Scheduling:** A warmup scheduler is applied to gradually increase the learning rate during the first few epochs, followed by a

linear decay. This approach helps stabilize training and leads to better convergence.

- **Training Loop:** The model is trained over several epochs (typically 3 to 5). During each epoch, the model processes the training data in batches, updating its weights to minimize the classification loss (often using cross-entropy loss).

4) Validation and Monitoring:

- **Validation Set:** After each epoch, the model's performance is evaluated on a separate validation set. This helps monitor overfitting and ensures that the model is learning to generalize well to unseen data.
- **Monitoring Metrics:** Key metrics to track include validation accuracy and loss. These metrics provide insight into how well the model is performing on the sentiment analysis task.

3. Evaluating the Fine-Tuned Model

After fine-tuning, the next step is to thoroughly evaluate the model's performance.

1) Test Set Evaluation:

- **Accuracy:** The final model is evaluated on a held-out test set to determine its accuracy. For the IMDb dataset, a well-tuned BERT model typically achieves accuracy above 90%, which indicates strong performance.
- **Precision and Recall:** These metrics are especially important if the data is imbalanced. For instance, if there are more positive reviews than negative ones, precision and recall will give a clearer picture of how well the model handles each class.
- **Confusion Matrix:** A confusion matrix can be generated to see how often the model confuses positive and negative reviews. This helps in

understanding the types of errors the model is making and whether any further adjustments are needed.

2) Error Analysis:

- **Reviewing Misclassifications:** It's valuable to examine the reviews that the model misclassified. Understanding these errors can provide insights into potential model improvements, such as further fine-tuning or adjusting the preprocessing steps.
- **Domain-Specific Considerations:** If the model is intended to be used in a specific domain (e.g., product reviews vs. movie reviews), evaluate its performance on domain-specific test sets to ensure it generalizes well to that context.

4. Deploying the Model

Once satisfied with the model's performance, it's time to deploy it for real-world use.

1) Optimizing for Inference:

- **Model Pruning and Quantization:** To reduce the model size and improve inference speed, techniques like pruning (removing unnecessary weights) and quantization (reducing the precision of model weights) can be applied. These optimizations are particularly useful if the model will be deployed in resource-constrained environments.
- **Serving the Model:** The fine-tuned BERT model can be deployed using platforms like TensorFlow Serving, TorchServe, or directly integrated into an application via REST APIs. Hugging Face's transformers library also provides tools for exporting and serving models efficiently.

2) Monitoring Post-Deployment:

- **Performance Monitoring:** After deployment, continuously monitor the model's performance to ensure it remains accurate over time. This includes checking for data drift (when the input data changes over time) and making sure the model's predictions align with user expectations.
- **Periodic Re-training:** As more data becomes available, periodically re-train the model to keep it up-to-date. This ensures that the model adapts to any changes in the data distribution or user behavior.

Fine-tuning BERT for sentiment analysis is a powerful way to leverage pre-trained models for specific tasks. By carefully preparing the dataset, fine-tuning the model with appropriate techniques, and thoroughly evaluating its performance, you can create a highly effective sentiment analysis tool. This process not only demonstrates the versatility of BERT but also provides a solid foundation for applying similar techniques to other NLP tasks.

III

Part III: Advanced Techniques and Concepts

Chapter 7: Prompt Engineering

7.1 Introduction to Prompting and its Importance

Prompt engineering is an essential technique in working with Large Language Models (LLMs). It involves crafting specific inputs—known as prompts—that guide the model to generate the desired output. The effectiveness of a language model often hinges on the quality and structure of the prompts you use, making prompt engineering a critical skill for anyone looking to leverage LLMs in real-world applications.

1. What is Prompting?

At its core, prompting is simply the process of providing an LLM with an input or question to elicit a response. The way you phrase your prompt can dramatically influence the model's output. For instance, asking a model to summarize an article will yield a different response than asking it to extract key points, even though both prompts are related to content distillation.

- **Example of a Basic Prompt:** If you input the prompt, "Translate the following English sentence into French: 'Hello, how are you?'", the model is clearly instructed on what to do and will likely generate the correct translation.
- **Example of a Complex Prompt:** For more complex tasks, such as "Summarize the key themes of this article and suggest potential

research questions," the prompt must be carefully crafted to ensure the model understands and executes all parts of the request.

2. Why Prompt Engineering is Important

Prompt engineering is crucial because it directly impacts the quality, relevance, and accuracy of the model's output. A well-designed prompt can lead to insightful and useful responses, while a poorly designed one can produce irrelevant or incorrect information.

1) Maximizing Model Utility:

- **Efficient Use of LLMs:** Since LLMs can generate vast amounts of information, the key is guiding them to produce outputs that are both useful and precise. Effective prompts help streamline this process, reducing the time spent refining or correcting outputs.
- **Task-Specific Customization:** Prompts allow you to customize the behavior of a model for specific tasks without needing to retrain it. This makes LLMs versatile tools that can be adapted to a wide range of applications with minimal adjustments.

2) Improving Accuracy and Relevance:

- **Reducing Ambiguity:** Ambiguous prompts can lead to vague or irrelevant answers. Clear, specific prompts reduce this risk, ensuring that the model's responses are aligned with your expectations.
- **Handling Complex Queries:** For tasks that require nuanced understanding, such as generating creative content or performing detailed analysis, prompt engineering helps break down the complexity into manageable instructions that the model can follow.

3) Enhancing User Experience:

- **Natural Interaction:** Well-crafted prompts make interacting with LLMs feel more natural and intuitive. Users are more likely to get the results they need without extensive trial and error, which improves overall satisfaction and productivity.
- **Contextual Awareness:** Effective prompts help the model maintain context, especially in multi-turn interactions where previous responses need to be taken into account. This leads to more coherent and contextually relevant outputs.

3. The Role of Prompt Engineering in Different Applications

Prompt engineering is not a one-size-fits-all approach. Different applications require different types of prompts to achieve optimal results. Here's how prompting plays a role in various scenarios:

1) Content Creation:

- **Writing Assistance:** Prompts can be used to generate blog posts, articles, or creative writing pieces. For example, starting with a prompt like "Write a persuasive article on the benefits of remote work" gives the model a clear direction to follow.
- **Idea Generation:** When you need inspiration, prompts like "List five innovative marketing strategies for small businesses" can help the model generate fresh ideas.

2) Data Analysis:

- **Summarization:** For summarizing large documents, prompts like "Summarize the following research paper in three sentences" guide the model to condense the content effectively.
- **Extraction:** In data extraction tasks, prompts such as "Extract all the dates mentioned in this document" help the model focus on specific information.

3) Customer Support:

- **Automated Responses:** For customer service, prompts like "Provide a polite response to a customer complaint about delayed delivery" help generate appropriate and contextually aware replies.
- **FAQ Generation:** Creating FAQs from a knowledge base can be streamlined with prompts like "Generate five FAQs from this product manual."

Prompt engineering is a powerful technique that enhances the effectiveness of Large Language Models across a wide range of tasks. By understanding the importance of crafting clear, specific, and contextually appropriate prompts, you can unlock the full potential of LLMs and make them valuable tools in your work. In the following sections, we'll dive deeper into different types of prompts and how to tailor them for various applications, helping you become proficient in this essential aspect of working with LLMs.

7.2 Types of Prompts: Zero-shot, Few-shot, and Custom Prompts

When working with Large Language Models (LLMs), the way you structure your prompts can greatly influence the model's performance. There are different types of prompts you can use depending on the task and the level of guidance you want to provide. Understanding the distinctions between zero-shot, few-shot, and custom prompts will help you choose the most effective approach for your specific needs.

1. Zero-shot Prompts

Zero-shot prompting is the simplest form of prompting, where you ask the model to perform a task without providing any examples or prior context. In this approach, the model relies entirely on its pre-existing knowledge and understanding of the task based on the way the prompt is phrased.

1) How Zero-shot Prompts Work:

- **No Examples Provided:** You give the model a clear instruction or question, and it generates a response based purely on its training data. For example, a zero-shot prompt could be, "Translate 'Hello, how are you?' into Spanish."
- **Model's Generalization:** The model must generalize from the prompt alone, which can be effective for straightforward tasks or when the task is well-aligned with the model's training data.

2) When to Use Zero-shot Prompts:

- **Simple Tasks:** Zero-shot prompts are ideal for tasks that are simple or have a clear, unambiguous instruction, such as basic translation, fact retrieval, or summarization.
- **Broad Knowledge Tasks:** Use zero-shot prompts when you expect the model to leverage its broad training, such as asking general knowledge questions or performing common tasks.

3) Advantages and Limitations:

- **Advantages:** Zero-shot prompts are quick and easy to use, requiring no additional data preparation. They work well for tasks that the model is already well-equipped to handle.
- **Limitations:** The lack of examples can lead to less accurate or inconsistent results, especially for more complex or nuanced tasks where

the model's interpretation might vary.

2. Few-shot Prompts

Few-shot prompting provides the model with a few examples within the prompt itself. These examples help the model understand the task better by providing context, which can improve the quality of its response.

1) How Few-shot Prompts Work:

- **Including Examples:** In a few-shot prompt, you include one or more examples that demonstrate the task you want the model to perform. For example, to teach the model to translate phrases, you might prompt, "Translate the following phrases into French: 'Good morning' -> 'Bonjour', 'How are you?' -> 'Comment ça va?'. Now translate: 'What time is it?'."
- **Guiding the Model:** These examples guide the model's understanding of the task, making it more likely to generate a relevant and accurate response.

2) When to Use Few-shot Prompts:

- **Complex or Ambiguous Tasks:** Few-shot prompts are particularly useful for tasks where the model's interpretation could vary or where the task requires a nuanced understanding. For example, creative writing prompts or domain-specific tasks benefit from a few examples to set the tone or context.
- **Task Customization:** If you need the model to follow a specific format or style, few-shot prompting allows you to demonstrate exactly what you're looking for.

3) Advantages and Limitations:

- **Advantages:** Few-shot prompts improve the model's performance by providing clear guidance. They are particularly effective when you need the model to understand the task's subtleties or when working with specialized content.
- **Limitations:** The prompt length can become an issue if you need to include multiple examples, as LLMs have a maximum token limit. Additionally, creating good examples requires some effort and understanding of the task.

3. Custom Prompts

Custom prompts involve tailoring the prompt to your specific task or application, often by combining zero-shot or few-shot techniques with additional context or instructions. This approach is highly flexible and allows for the most precise control over the model's behavior.

1) How Custom Prompts Work:

- **Task-Specific Tailoring:** Custom prompts are designed with the specific task in mind, often including detailed instructions, context, or constraints that the model should follow. For example, a custom prompt for generating a technical summary might look like this: "Summarize the following research paper in two paragraphs, focusing on the methodology and key findings. Avoid any unnecessary technical jargon."
- **Combining Techniques:** You can mix zero-shot and few-shot approaches within a custom prompt, providing examples where needed while also giving specific instructions to guide the model's output.

2) When to Use Custom Prompts:

- **Highly Specific Tasks:** Custom prompts are ideal for tasks that require precise control over the output, such as legal document drafting,

technical writing, or creative content generation.
- **Applications with Constraints:** If your task has specific constraints—like a required format, length, or tone—a custom prompt allows you to incorporate these directly into the model's instructions.

3) Advantages and Limitations:

- **Advantages:** Custom prompts offer the greatest flexibility and control, making them suitable for a wide range of applications. They allow you to fine-tune the model's behavior without needing to retrain it.
- **Limitations:** Crafting effective custom prompts requires a deep understanding of both the task and the model's capabilities. It can be time-consuming to experiment and refine the prompt until it produces the desired output.

Understanding the different types of prompts—zero-shot, few-shot, and custom—is crucial for getting the most out of Large Language Models. Each type has its own strengths and is suited to different types of tasks, from simple queries to complex, highly specific applications. By choosing the right type of prompt for your task, you can significantly improve the quality and relevance of the model's responses. In the next section, we'll explore how to craft effective prompts for various tasks, helping you apply these techniques in practical scenarios.

7.3 Crafting Effective Prompts for Different Tasks

Creating effective prompts is a critical skill when working with Large Language Models (LLMs). The way you frame a prompt can significantly influence the quality of the output, making it essential to tailor prompts carefully to the specific task at hand. In this section, we'll discuss strategies for crafting prompts that are well-suited to a variety of tasks, ensuring that you get the best possible results from your model.

1. Understanding the Task Requirements

Before you start crafting a prompt, it's important to have a clear understanding of the task's requirements. Different tasks will need different levels of specificity and context in the prompt.

1) Task Clarity:

- **Define the Goal:** Clearly define what you want the model to do. Are you asking for a summary, a translation, a creative story, or an answer to a factual question? The clearer your goal, the easier it is to create an effective prompt.
- **Identify the Output Format:** Consider the desired format of the output. Should the model respond with a paragraph, a list, a single sentence, or a code snippet? Specifying this in your prompt helps guide the model toward producing the right type of response.

2) Contextual Needs:

- **Incorporate Relevant Information:** If the task requires specific context—such as a background story or a set of data—make sure to include this information in the prompt. For example, if you're asking for a summary of a meeting, include the key points discussed during that meeting.
- **Avoid Ambiguity:** Be specific about what you want to avoid vague or irrelevant outputs. If there are particular details you don't need, state that in the prompt to prevent the model from focusing on the wrong aspects.

2. Strategies for Different Types of Tasks

Different tasks require different prompting strategies. Below are examples of how to craft prompts for various common tasks.

1) Text Summarization:

- **Prompt Structure:** When asking for a summary, it's important to specify the focus of the summary and any constraints. For instance, "Summarize the following article in three sentences, focusing on the main findings and avoiding any technical jargon."
- **Length Control:** If you need the summary to be of a certain length, make that clear in the prompt. Example: "Summarize this document in no more than 100 words."

2) Creative Writing:

- **Setting the Scene:** For creative tasks like storytelling or content generation, it's useful to set the scene or provide a theme. For example, "Write a short story about a detective solving a mystery in a small town, with a twist ending."
- **Tone and Style:** Specify the tone or style you want, such as "Write a poem in a humorous tone about the first day of school."

3) Question Answering:

- **Direct Questions:** Keep questions straightforward and unambiguous. For example, "What are the main benefits of renewable energy?" This encourages the model to focus on providing a concise, relevant answer.
- **Contextual Questions:** If the answer depends on specific information, include that context in the prompt. Example: "Based on the following text, what are the main challenges in implementing renewable energy solutions?"

4) Code Generation:

- **Specific Instructions:** When asking for code, provide specific instructions about what the code should do. Example: "Write a Python function that takes a list of numbers and returns the list sorted in descending order."
- **Include Examples:** If possible, include an example input and output to guide the model. Example: "Write a function in Python that calculates the factorial of a number. For example, factorial(5) should return 120."

5) Translation:

- **Clarity in Language:** For translation tasks, it's important to clearly specify the languages involved. Example: "Translate the following English sentence into French: 'The weather is nice today.'"
- **Cultural Context:** If the translation needs to consider cultural nuances, include that in the prompt. Example: "Translate the following sentence into Japanese, maintaining a formal tone: 'Please confirm your attendance at the meeting.'"

3. Refining Prompts Through Iteration

Creating effective prompts often requires some trial and error. Start with a basic prompt and refine it based on the outputs you receive.

1) Evaluate the Output:

- **Check for Relevance:** After generating an output, assess whether it meets the task's requirements. If the output is off-target, consider what might be unclear or missing in your prompt.
- **Adjust for Precision:** If the output is too broad or vague, try making the prompt more specific. Add more details or constraints to guide the model toward a more precise answer.

2) Experiment with Variations:

- **Test Different Approaches:** Try different phrasings or structures for your prompt to see which one yields the best results. Sometimes a small change in wording can lead to a significant improvement in the output.
- **Combine Techniques:** For complex tasks, consider combining elements of zero-shot, few-shot, and custom prompts. For example, you might start with a few-shot prompt that includes examples, then refine it with additional instructions to further tailor the output.

3) Gather Feedback:

- **Iterate Based on Feedback:** If you're working on a task with others, gather feedback on the outputs and use it to refine your prompts. This collaborative approach can help you discover more effective ways to phrase your prompts.

Crafting effective prompts is a key skill for getting the most out of Large Language Models. By understanding the specific needs of your task, applying tailored strategies for different types of prompts, and refining your approach through iteration, you can significantly enhance the quality of the model's output. In the next section, we'll dive into prompt tuning, where we'll explore how to optimize prompts for even better performance, taking your prompt engineering skills to the next level.

7.4 Prompt Tuning: Optimizing Prompts for Better Performance

Prompt tuning is the process of refining and optimizing prompts to improve the performance of a Large Language Model (LLM) on specific tasks. While crafting an initial prompt is important, fine-tuning that prompt can make a significant difference in the quality, relevance, and accuracy of the model's responses. In this section, we'll discuss strategies for tuning your prompts, the importance of context, and how to iteratively improve your prompts for optimal results.

1. The Importance of Context in Prompt Tuning

Context plays a crucial role in how an LLM interprets and responds to a prompt. By providing the right context, you can guide the model more effectively, ensuring it understands the task at hand.

1) Embedding Relevant Information:

- **Incorporating Context:** When fine-tuning prompts, ensure that all necessary background information is included. For example, if you're asking the model to analyze a text, include any relevant excerpts or summaries that might influence its response.
- **Clarifying Ambiguities:** If the task could be interpreted in multiple ways, clarify any potential ambiguities within the prompt. This helps the model focus on the correct interpretation and avoids irrelevant or off-target responses.

2) Positioning of Information:

- **Order of Details:** The order in which you present information in a prompt can affect the output. Important details should be placed early in the prompt to ensure they are prioritized in the model's processing.

- **Layering Instructions:** For complex tasks, break down instructions into clear, sequential steps. For instance, if you're asking the model to first analyze and then summarize a text, explicitly separate these instructions within the prompt.

2. Techniques for Optimizing Prompts

Optimizing prompts involves experimenting with different structures, phrasings, and levels of detail to achieve the best possible output. Here are some techniques to consider:

1) Adjusting the Level of Detail:

- **More Specificity:** If the model's responses are too vague, add more specific instructions or examples. For instance, instead of asking, "Summarize this article," you might prompt, "Summarize this article in three sentences, focusing on the key arguments and any data supporting them."
- **Reducing Complexity:** Conversely, if the prompt is too complex or detailed, simplifying it can sometimes lead to better results. For example, a complex prompt like "Discuss the economic, social, and environmental impacts of renewable energy" could be broken into separate prompts for each impact area.

2) Experimenting with Different Phrasings:

- **Rewording Prompts:** Small changes in wording can have a big impact on the model's output. If the initial response isn't quite right, try rephrasing the prompt. For example, instead of saying "What are the benefits of exercise?" you could ask, "List the top five benefits of regular exercise."
- **Using Synonyms:** Sometimes, changing a single word can improve the model's understanding. For instance, replacing "explain" with

"describe" might yield a more detailed response depending on the context.

3) Incorporating Few-shot Examples:

- **Adding Examples:** Few-shot prompting can enhance performance by showing the model exactly what you expect. Provide a few examples within the prompt to demonstrate the desired format or style. For instance, "Here are two examples of product reviews. Now, write a review for the following product: [product details]."
- **Balancing Examples:** Ensure that the examples are representative of the task and don't introduce bias. If the examples vary too much in style or tone, the model might produce inconsistent outputs.

3. Iterative Refinement Process

Prompt tuning is an iterative process. You'll often need to test and refine your prompts multiple times to achieve the best results.

1) Testing Outputs:

- **Initial Testing:** Start by testing the initial prompt and reviewing the outputs. Are the responses aligned with your expectations? Identify areas where the model's response could be improved.
- **Evaluating Consistency:** Test the prompt across different inputs to ensure consistency. A good prompt should yield reliable and relevant results across a range of scenarios.

2) Making Incremental Adjustments:

- **Small Tweaks:** Make small, incremental changes to the prompt and re-test. For example, if the model's responses are too brief, try adding a phrase like "Provide a detailed explanation."

- **Tracking Changes:** Keep track of the changes you make to the prompt and the corresponding outputs. This will help you understand which adjustments lead to improvements and which do not.

3) Finalizing the Prompt:

- **Consolidating Improvements:** Once you've tested and refined the prompt to the point where it consistently produces high-quality outputs, finalize it. Make sure the prompt is clear, concise, and well-aligned with the task's objectives.
- **Documentation:** Document the final version of the prompt and any important observations from the tuning process. This will be useful for future reference or if the prompt needs to be adapted for similar tasks.

4. Common Pitfalls and How to Avoid Them

While tuning prompts, it's important to be aware of common pitfalls that can hinder performance:

1) Overloading the Prompt:

- **Too Much Information:** Including too much detail in a prompt can overwhelm the model and lead to unfocused or incoherent responses. Focus on the most critical information and omit anything that isn't essential to the task.
- **Avoiding Run-On Instructions:** Keep instructions concise and avoid combining too many tasks into a single prompt. If the task is complex, consider breaking it down into multiple, smaller prompts.

2) Neglecting Iterative Testing:

- **Assuming One-Size-Fits-All:** Don't assume that a prompt that works well in one context will work equally well in another. Iterative testing across different scenarios is crucial to ensure robustness.

- **Ignoring Feedback:** Be open to feedback, whether from the model's outputs or from other users. Use this feedback to refine and improve your prompts continuously.

Prompt tuning is a vital part of getting the most out of Large Language Models. By carefully considering context, experimenting with different strategies, and refining your prompts iteratively, you can significantly enhance the performance and reliability of your models. In the next section, we'll explore advanced prompting techniques with practical examples, further expanding your toolkit for effective prompt engineering.

7.5 Advanced Prompting Techniques with Examples

As you become more experienced with prompt engineering, you'll discover a range of advanced techniques that can significantly enhance the performance and versatility of Large Language Models (LLMs). These techniques allow you to tackle more complex tasks, generate higher-quality outputs, and fine-tune the behavior of the model to suit specific needs. In this section, we'll explore some advanced prompting techniques and provide practical examples to help you apply these methods effectively.

1. Chain-of-Thought Prompting

Chain-of-thought prompting involves guiding the model through a step-by-step reasoning process to reach a conclusion. This technique is particularly useful for tasks that require logical reasoning, problem-solving, or complex decision-making.

1) How it Works:

- **Step-by-Step Guidance:** Instead of asking the model for a direct answer, you prompt it to go through the reasoning process step by step. This helps the model break down the task and consider each part before arriving at a final answer.
- **Example:** For a math problem like, "What is the sum of 123 and 456?" instead of directly asking for the answer, you might prompt: "First, add the hundreds digits (1 + 4 = 5). Next, add the tens digits (2 + 5 = 7). Finally, add the ones digits (3 + 6 = 9). Therefore, the sum is 579."

2) When to Use It:

- **Complex Calculations:** When tasks involve multiple steps, such as multi-step arithmetic problems or logical puzzles, chain-of-thought prompting can help ensure that the model doesn't skip any steps.
- **Reasoned Responses:** For tasks where the reasoning behind the answer is as important as the answer itself, this technique ensures the model provides a thorough explanation.

2. Role-Playing and Persona-Based Prompting

Role-playing involves assigning the model a specific role or persona to guide the tone, style, and content of its responses. This technique is useful for creative writing, customer support, or any task where the model's behavior needs to align with a particular character or voice.

1) How it Works:

- **Assigning a Role:** You explicitly tell the model to adopt a particular role or persona. For example, you might prompt, "You are a tech support agent. Help the user troubleshoot their internet connection issue."
- **Example:** For a creative writing task, you might use a prompt like, "You are a detective in a noir-style mystery novel. Describe the scene as you enter the dimly lit room where the crime took place."

2) When to Use It:

- **Customer Support:** In scenarios where consistency in tone and approach is crucial, such as customer service chatbots, assigning a role ensures the model responds in a way that aligns with the brand's voice.
- **Creative Tasks:** When generating content that needs to fit a specific genre or style, persona-based prompting helps the model maintain the desired tone throughout the output.

3. Contextual Few-shot Prompting

Contextual few-shot prompting extends the standard few-shot approach by carefully selecting examples that are highly relevant to the task and context. This technique improves the model's understanding of the task by providing examples that are closely aligned with the desired output.

1) How it Works:

- **Choosing Relevant Examples:** Select examples that are directly related to the specific task or context. These examples should closely mirror the format, tone, and content you expect in the final output.
- **Example:** If you're asking the model to generate marketing copy for a product, you might include examples of successful marketing copy for similar products. For instance, "Here's an example of a product description: [Example 1]. Now, write a description for this new product: [Product details]."

2) When to Use It:

- **Domain-Specific Tasks:** When working on tasks that require domain-specific knowledge, providing contextually relevant examples helps the model generate more accurate and context-appropriate responses.

- **High-Precision Outputs:** For tasks where the quality and relevance of the output are critical, such as legal document drafting or technical writing, contextual few-shot prompting ensures the model aligns closely with the required standards.

4. Iterative Prompting

Iterative prompting involves refining the model's output through multiple rounds of interaction. Instead of expecting the perfect response in one go, you guide the model through a series of prompts to gradually improve the quality of the output.

1) How it Works:

- **Multiple Rounds:** Start with an initial prompt and review the model's output. Based on this output, you provide a follow-up prompt to refine or expand on the response.
- **Example:** If you're generating a complex report, you might begin with, "Provide an overview of the main findings on renewable energy adoption." After receiving the initial response, you might prompt, "Expand on the economic benefits mentioned in the overview, providing specific data points."

2) When to Use It:

- **Complex Content Generation:** For tasks that require detailed, nuanced responses, such as writing reports or developing in-depth analyses, iterative prompting helps ensure all aspects of the task are thoroughly covered.
- **Quality Assurance:** When precision and thoroughness are essential, iterative prompting allows you to guide the model toward the best possible outcome through a series of refinements.

5. Prompt Stacking

Prompt stacking involves combining multiple prompts into a single interaction to achieve more complex outputs. This technique is useful when you want the model to perform several related tasks or consider multiple aspects of a problem simultaneously.

1) How it Works:

- **Combining Prompts:** Create a single prompt that includes multiple instructions or questions, each designed to elicit a specific part of the overall response. For example, "Describe the features of this product, list its advantages, and suggest potential target markets."
- **Example:** For a comprehensive analysis, you might prompt, "First, summarize the key points of this article. Then, provide a critical evaluation of its arguments. Finally, suggest areas for further research based on the conclusions drawn."

2) When to Use It:

- **Comprehensive Tasks:** When a task requires a multifaceted response, such as analyzing a text from different perspectives, prompt stacking helps cover all necessary aspects in one go.
- **Task Sequencing:** For tasks that naturally involve a sequence of steps, such as problem-solving or project planning, prompt stacking ensures that the model addresses each step in order.

Advanced prompting techniques offer powerful tools for getting the most out of Large Language Models. Whether you're guiding the model through complex reasoning with chain-of-thought prompting, tailoring its behavior with role-playing, or refining its output through iterative prompting, these techniques can greatly enhance the quality and relevance of the model's responses. By experimenting with and combining these methods, you can tackle even the most challenging tasks with confidence. In the final section of this chapter, we'll look at case studies that showcase successful applications of these techniques, providing real-world examples of their effectiveness.

7.6 Case Studies: Successful Applications of Prompt Engineering

In this section, we'll explore real-world examples of how prompt engineering has been successfully applied across different domains. These case studies highlight the versatility and impact of effective prompt design, demonstrating how careful crafting of prompts can lead to significant improvements in the performance and usefulness of Large Language Models (LLMs).

Case Study 1: Enhancing Customer Support with Role-Playing Prompts

- **Background:** A tech company wanted to improve the efficiency and consistency of its customer support chatbot. The chatbot needed to handle a wide range of customer inquiries, from technical troubleshooting to product recommendations, all while maintaining a friendly and professional tone.
- **Challenge:** The initial prompts used for the chatbot were too generic, leading to inconsistent responses that varied in tone and clarity. The company needed a way to ensure that the chatbot's responses were both helpful and aligned with the company's brand voice.
- **Solution:** The team implemented role-playing prompts by assigning the chatbot a specific persona: a friendly and knowledgeable tech support agent. They crafted prompts like, "You are a tech support agent. Provide a step-by-step solution for a user who cannot connect

to the Wi-Fi," and, "Recommend a laptop for a user who needs a machine for graphic design and gaming."

- **Outcome:** The role-playing prompts significantly improved the chatbot's performance. Customer satisfaction scores increased as users received more consistent, clear, and helpful responses. The chatbot's responses also became more aligned with the company's brand voice, enhancing the overall customer experience.

Case Study 2: Improving Academic Research Summaries with Chain-of-Thought Prompting

- **Background:** A university research group needed a tool to help generate summaries of complex academic papers. The goal was to create concise yet comprehensive summaries that captured the key points, methodologies, and conclusions of each paper.
- **Challenge:** Initial attempts to generate summaries using simple prompts often resulted in incomplete or superficial summaries. The model struggled to capture the depth and complexity of the research.
- **Solution:** The team applied chain-of-thought prompting to guide the model through the summarization process. Instead of asking for a summary in one step, they used prompts like, "First, identify the research question and hypothesis. Next, describe the methodology used in the study. Then, summarize the key findings, and finally, discuss the implications of the results."
- **Outcome:** The chain-of-thought prompting approach led to much richer and more accurate summaries. The model was able to break down the academic papers into their essential components, resulting in summaries that were both detailed and easy to understand. This approach saved the research group significant time and effort, allowing them to quickly get up to speed on new publications.

Case Study 3: Generating Creative Marketing Content with Iterative Prompting

- **Background:** A marketing agency wanted to use an LLM to generate creative content for social media campaigns. The content needed to be engaging, original, and aligned with the client's brand messaging.
- **Challenge:** The initial content generated by the model was hit-or-miss. Some outputs were on-brand and creative, while others were generic or didn't fully capture the intended message. The agency needed a way to refine the outputs without manually rewriting them.
- **Solution:** The agency used iterative prompting to refine the model's outputs. They started with a basic prompt like, "Write a social media post about the benefits of our new eco-friendly product." After reviewing the initial output, they provided follow-up prompts to improve specific aspects, such as, "Make the tone more playful," or, "Highlight the environmental benefits more strongly."
- **Outcome:** The iterative approach allowed the agency to hone in on the perfect message. By guiding the model through several rounds of refinement, they were able to generate content that was not only creative but also closely aligned with the client's brand. This approach reduced the time spent on content creation and led to more successful campaigns.

Case Study 4: Automating Legal Document Drafting with Custom Prompts

- **Background:** A law firm wanted to automate the drafting of standard legal documents, such as contracts and agreements, to save time and reduce the workload on its legal team.
- **Challenge:** Legal documents require precise language and must adhere to strict formatting and legal standards. Initial attempts to generate these documents using generic prompts led to outputs that were either too vague or not legally sound.

- **Solution:** The firm developed custom prompts tailored to the specific type of document being drafted. For example, they used prompts like, "Draft a standard non-disclosure agreement (NDA) that includes clauses on confidentiality, terms of agreement, and dispute resolution," and, "Generate a contract for a freelance graphic designer, including payment terms, deliverables, and intellectual property rights."
- **Outcome:** The custom prompts enabled the model to generate legally sound and properly formatted documents that met the firm's requirements. The legal team was able to review and finalize the drafts quickly, significantly reducing the time spent on routine document drafting. This allowed the firm to focus more on complex legal matters, improving overall efficiency.

Case Study 5: Enhancing Data Extraction from Scientific Articles with Contextual Few-shot Prompting

- **Background:** A pharmaceutical company needed to extract specific data points from a large volume of scientific articles to support its drug development process. The data included information on clinical trials, dosage levels, and patient outcomes.
- **Challenge:** The articles varied in structure and language, making it difficult for the model to consistently extract the correct information using simple prompts.
- **Solution:** The team implemented contextual few-shot prompting by providing the model with a few examples of correctly extracted data points, such as, "In this trial, 200 mg of the drug was administered daily, and 75% of patients showed improvement in symptoms." These examples were included in the prompt to guide the model's data extraction process.
- **Outcome:** The contextual few-shot prompts significantly improved the accuracy of data extraction. The model became more reliable in identifying and extracting the required information, even across arti-

cles with different structures and terminologies. This improvement helped the company accelerate its research and development efforts by providing faster access to critical data.

These case studies illustrate the power and versatility of prompt engineering across different domains and tasks. By applying techniques like role-playing, chain-of-thought prompting, iterative prompting, custom prompts, and contextual few-shot prompting, you can dramatically enhance the performance of Large Language Models. These examples also demonstrate that with the right prompts, LLMs can be effectively integrated into workflows to save time, improve accuracy, and achieve better outcomes in a wide range of applications.

Chapter 8: Retrieval-Augmented Generation (RAG)

8.1 Understanding Retrieval-Augmented Generation

Retrieval-Augmented Generation (RAG) is a powerful technique that combines the strengths of two distinct approaches in natural language processing: retrieval-based methods and generation-based models. By leveraging both, RAG can generate highly relevant and contextually accurate responses that are grounded in external knowledge sources. This makes it particularly useful for tasks where the model needs to provide detailed, fact-based answers or generate content that is informed by specific, up-to-date information.

1. What is Retrieval-Augmented Generation?

At its core, Retrieval-Augmented Generation is a framework that enhances the capabilities of language models by incorporating a retrieval mechanism that pulls in relevant information from an external knowledge base. Here's how it works:

1) Retrieval Component:

- **Fetching Relevant Information:** Before generating a response, the model first queries an external knowledge base to retrieve the most relevant pieces of information. This knowledge base could be anything from a database of scientific articles to a collection of company documents.

- **Top-K Retrieval:** The model typically retrieves the top-K most relevant documents or snippets based on the query, ensuring that the information fed into the generation process is closely related to the user's request.

2) Generation Component:

- **Informed Response Generation:** Once the relevant information is retrieved, the generation model (often a variant of GPT, BERT, or another transformer-based architecture) uses this data to craft a response. This ensures that the output is not only fluent and coherent but also grounded in real-world data.
- **Contextual Integration:** The generation process seamlessly integrates the retrieved information with the model's own learned knowledge, producing an output that is both contextually aware and factually accurate.

2. Why is RAG Important?

RAG addresses several limitations inherent in standalone retrieval-based or generation-based models:

1) Enhanced Accuracy:

- **Grounded Responses:** Traditional generation models might generate plausible-sounding but inaccurate responses due to their reliance on patterns learned during training. By incorporating real-time data retrieval, RAG models can generate answers that are not only contextually appropriate but also factually correct.

- **Reduced Hallucination:** Language models sometimes "hallucinate," producing information that seems correct but is actually made up. RAG reduces this risk by anchoring the generated content in verifiable sources.

2) Scalability and Flexibility:

- **Domain Adaptability:** RAG models can easily adapt to different domains by swapping out the underlying knowledge base. Whether the task involves legal documents, medical research, or product manuals, RAG can be tailored to provide domain-specific information without needing to retrain the model extensively.
- **Up-to-Date Information:** Because the retrieval component can access and use the latest information from external sources, RAG models are particularly useful in dynamic fields where knowledge is constantly evolving.

3) Improved User Experience:

- **Contextually Rich Interactions:** By pulling in detailed and relevant information, RAG models can enhance user interactions, providing deeper insights and more comprehensive answers. This makes them valuable in applications like customer support, research assistance, and content creation.

3. How Does RAG Work?

To better understand RAG, let's break down its typical workflow:

1) Input Query:

- The process begins with a user input, such as a question or a request for information. This input is the starting point for both the retrieval and generation components.

2) Retrieval Phase:

- The model uses the input query to search an external knowledge base. This search can be conducted using various methods, such as keyword matching, vector search, or more advanced retrieval models that rank documents based on relevance to the query.
- The top-K relevant documents or snippets are then selected to feed into the next phase.

3) Generation Phase:

- With the relevant information at hand, the generation model processes both the user query and the retrieved content to generate a final response. This response is designed to be not only relevant but also coherent and contextually appropriate.

4) Output Response:

- The final output is a response that combines the model's natural language generation capabilities with the factual grounding provided by the retrieved information. This output is then presented to the user.

4. Applications of RAG

RAG has a wide range of applications across different fields:

1) Customer Support:

- RAG can be used to power chatbots and virtual assistants that provide accurate, contextually relevant answers by accessing a company's knowledge base or support documentation.

2) Research Assistance:

- In academic and scientific research, RAG models can help summarize and synthesize information from vast databases of research papers, aiding in literature reviews and data-driven analysis.

3) Content Creation:

- RAG is useful in generating content that requires factual accuracy, such as news articles, technical documentation, and educational materials.

4) Healthcare:

- In the medical field, RAG can assist in providing clinicians with the latest research findings or guidelines, ensuring that medical advice is informed by the most current data.

Retrieval-Augmented Generation represents a significant advancement in the capabilities of language models. By combining the strengths of both retrieval and generation, RAG models are able to produce responses that are not only fluent and coherent but also grounded in real-world data. This makes them invaluable tools in a wide range of applications, from customer support to research and beyond. In the next section, we'll delve into the role of external knowledge bases in RAG, exploring how these systems are built and integrated to maximize the effectiveness of RAG models.

8.2 The Role of External Knowledge Bases in RAG

External knowledge bases play a crucial role in the effectiveness of Retrieval-Augmented Generation (RAG). They act as repositories of information that the model can access to enhance the quality, relevance, and accuracy of the responses it generates. By integrating these knowledge bases, RAG models can provide factually grounded outputs, making them far more reliable and useful in various real-world applications.

1. What is an External Knowledge Base?

An external knowledge base is a structured repository of information that can be queried by a model to retrieve relevant data. These knowledge bases can vary widely in content, structure, and purpose, but they all serve the same fundamental role: providing a source of truth that the model can draw upon to generate informed and accurate responses.

1) Types of Knowledge Bases:

- **Textual Databases:** Collections of documents, articles, or books that cover a broad range of topics. For example, a legal knowledge base might consist of statutes, case law, and legal opinions.
- **Structured Databases:** Databases that store information in a structured format, such as SQL databases, which contain rows and columns of data. These are often used in applications requiring precise data retrieval, like customer databases or inventory systems.
- **Domain-Specific Repositories:** Specialized knowledge bases that focus on a particular field, such as medical journals, scientific research databases, or technical manuals. These are particularly valuable in tasks requiring domain expertise.

2) How Knowledge Bases Are Used in RAG:

- **Retrieval Process:** When a user query is made, the RAG model first retrieves relevant information from the knowledge base. This retrieval is based on the query's content and is aimed at finding the most pertinent data that can inform the model's response.
- **Integration with Generation:** The retrieved information is then fed into the generation component of the model, which uses this data to produce a response that is both contextually appropriate and factually accurate.

2. Importance of External Knowledge Bases in RAG

The inclusion of an external knowledge base in the RAG framework offers several key benefits that enhance the overall performance and utility of the model.

1) Improving Accuracy and Relevance:

- **Fact-Checking:** By grounding the generation process in verified information, knowledge bases help ensure that the responses generated by the model are accurate. This is particularly important in fields like healthcare, finance, or law, where accuracy is critical.
- **Contextual Relevance:** Knowledge bases allow the model to produce responses that are more contextually relevant, drawing on the most pertinent data available. This relevance is essential for providing users with meaningful and actionable information.

2) Enabling Up-to-Date Responses:

- **Dynamic Information:** Unlike static training data, which may become outdated, knowledge bases can be regularly updated to reflect the latest information. This ensures that the model can provide up-to-date answers, especially in fast-changing fields like technology or current events.

- **Real-Time Access:** In some implementations, knowledge bases can be connected to live data sources, enabling real-time information retrieval. This capability is invaluable in scenarios where the most current data is needed, such as breaking news or real-time market analysis.

3) Enhancing Domain-Specific Applications:

- **Tailored Knowledge:** In domain-specific applications, knowledge bases provide the specialized information needed to produce high-quality outputs. For example, in a medical application, a knowledge base containing the latest clinical guidelines and research can help the model generate accurate and relevant medical advice.
- **Supporting Complex Queries:** Knowledge bases allow the model to handle more complex and nuanced queries by providing access to detailed and specific information that might not be readily available in the model's training data.

3. Challenges and Considerations

While external knowledge bases greatly enhance the capabilities of RAG models, they also introduce certain challenges and considerations that need to be addressed.

1) Quality and Reliability of Data:

- **Data Verification:** It's crucial to ensure that the information contained in the knowledge base is accurate and reliable. Poor-quality data can lead to incorrect or misleading outputs, which can be particularly problematic in sensitive areas like healthcare or finance.
- **Source Credibility:** The sources used to populate the knowledge base must be credible and authoritative. This is especially important in applications where the integrity of the information is paramount.

2) Scalability and Maintenance:

- **Data Volume:** Managing large volumes of data in a knowledge base can be challenging. As the knowledge base grows, it may become more difficult to efficiently retrieve relevant information, potentially impacting the model's performance.
- **Regular Updates:** To maintain the accuracy and relevance of the knowledge base, regular updates are necessary. This requires a system for continually ingesting new data, verifying its accuracy, and integrating it into the existing knowledge base.

3) Integration with the RAG Model:

- **Seamless Querying:** The retrieval process must be seamless and efficient, ensuring that the model can quickly access and utilize the most relevant data. This requires careful optimization of the retrieval algorithms and indexing methods used.
- **Handling Ambiguity:** The model must be able to handle ambiguous queries effectively, retrieving the most relevant information even when the query is not entirely clear. This might involve advanced natural language processing techniques to interpret the query accurately.

4. Best Practices for Using External Knowledge Bases in RAG

To maximize the benefits of external knowledge bases in RAG models, consider the following best practices:

1) Curate High-Quality Data:

- Focus on building a knowledge base with data from credible, authoritative sources. Regularly review and update the content to ensure it remains relevant and accurate.

2) Optimize Retrieval Algorithms:

- Invest in developing or selecting efficient retrieval algorithms that can handle large-scale data and return the most relevant results quickly. Consider using advanced techniques like semantic search or vector-based retrieval.

3) Tailor the Knowledge Base to the Task:

- Customize the knowledge base to align with the specific needs of the task at hand. This might involve creating separate knowledge bases for different domains or applications to ensure that the model has access to the most relevant information.

4) Monitor and Maintain the Knowledge Base:

- Establish processes for ongoing monitoring and maintenance of the knowledge base. This includes regularly updating the data, removing outdated or incorrect information, and ensuring that the retrieval process remains efficient as the knowledge base grows.

External knowledge bases are a foundational component of Retrieval-Augmented Generation, providing the information necessary to produce accurate, relevant, and up-to-date responses. By carefully curating, maintaining, and integrating these knowledge bases, you can significantly enhance the performance of RAG models across a wide range of applications. In the next section, we'll explore how to build and integrate knowledge retrieval systems, delving into the technical aspects of making RAG models work effectively with external data sources.

8.3 Building and Integrating Knowledge Retrieval Systems

Building and integrating a knowledge retrieval system is a critical step in setting up a successful Retrieval-Augmented Generation (RAG) framework. This system serves as the backbone for fetching relevant information that the model can use to generate accurate and contextually rich responses. In this section, we'll discuss how to design, build, and integrate knowledge retrieval systems that are efficient, scalable, and tailored to specific tasks.

1. Designing a Knowledge Retrieval System

The design phase involves deciding how your retrieval system will operate, what data it will access, and how it will interact with your RAG model. This phase is crucial for ensuring that the system meets the specific needs of your application.

1) Identifying the Data Sources:

- **Choosing Relevant Data:** Start by identifying the data sources that will populate your knowledge base. These could include databases, document repositories, APIs, or even web-based sources. The choice of data sources should align with the specific needs of your application, whether it's legal documents, research articles, or customer support logs.
- **Data Quality Considerations:** Ensure that the data sources you select are reliable, up-to-date, and relevant to the tasks the model will be performing. High-quality data is essential for generating accurate and trustworthy outputs.

2) Defining the Retrieval Mechanism:

- **Keyword-Based Search:** A basic retrieval mechanism might involve keyword matching, where the system retrieves documents that contain specific keywords from the user query. This approach is straightforward but may not always capture the full context or nuance of the query.

- **Semantic Search:** More advanced systems use semantic search techniques, which go beyond simple keyword matching by understanding the meaning behind the words. This can involve techniques like vector-based search, where queries and documents are represented as vectors in a multidimensional space, allowing the system to retrieve content based on similarity in meaning rather than just keyword matches.
- **Hybrid Approaches:** A combination of keyword and semantic search can be effective, especially when dealing with large, diverse datasets. Hybrid approaches can leverage the strengths of both methods to improve retrieval accuracy.

3) Optimizing for Performance:

- **Indexing:** To ensure fast retrieval times, it's important to index the data effectively. Indexing creates a structured representation of the data that can be searched quickly. Common indexing techniques include inverted indexes for text search or vector indexes for semantic search.
- **Scalability Considerations:** As your knowledge base grows, the retrieval system must scale accordingly. Consider using distributed databases or cloud-based solutions that can handle large volumes of data and queries without a drop in performance.

2. Building the Knowledge Retrieval System

Once the design is in place, the next step is to build the knowledge retrieval system. This involves implementing the components that will fetch, index, and retrieve data as efficiently as possible.

1) Data Ingestion and Indexing:

- **Ingesting Data:** The first step in building the system is to ingest data from your selected sources. This process involves extracting data from its original format, cleaning it to remove noise or irrelevant content, and transforming it into a format suitable for indexing.
- **Indexing the Data:** After ingestion, the data is indexed to enable fast and efficient retrieval. This can involve creating inverted indexes for text-based data or using libraries like FAISS (Facebook AI Similarity Search) for vector-based search. The choice of indexing method should align with the retrieval mechanism defined during the design phase.

2) Implementing the Retrieval Engine:

- **Search Algorithms:** Depending on your retrieval mechanism, you'll need to implement the appropriate search algorithms. For keyword-based systems, this might involve traditional text search algorithms. For semantic search, it could mean implementing or integrating machine learning models that can understand and compare the meanings of different texts.
- **Query Processing:** The retrieval engine needs to process user queries efficiently. This involves parsing the query, possibly expanding it (e.g., with synonyms or related terms), and then searching the index to find the most relevant documents or data points.

3) Integrating with the RAG Model:

- **API Integration:** Typically, the knowledge retrieval system will be integrated with the RAG model through an API. When the model receives a query, it sends a request to the retrieval system, which returns the top-K relevant documents or data snippets. These are then used by the model to generate a response.
- **Real-Time Retrieval:** For applications that require up-to-date infor-

mation, it's important that the retrieval system can operate in real-time, fetching the latest data as queries are made. This requires a well-optimized system that can handle frequent updates to the knowledge base without significant latency.

3. Challenges in Building Knowledge Retrieval Systems

Building an effective knowledge retrieval system comes with its own set of challenges, from handling large datasets to ensuring that retrieval is both fast and accurate.

1) Handling Large-Scale Data:

- **Storage and Retrieval:** Large datasets require efficient storage solutions that support fast retrieval. This might involve using distributed databases or specialized storage formats that allow for quick indexing and retrieval.
- **Data Diversity:** When dealing with diverse data sources, it's important to ensure that the retrieval system can handle different formats and types of data, from structured tables to unstructured text.

2) Ensuring Data Relevance:

- **Precision vs. Recall:** Balancing precision (the relevance of the retrieved documents) and recall (the completeness of the retrieval) is crucial. A system that retrieves too many irrelevant documents (high recall, low precision) can overwhelm the model, while one that misses relevant information (high precision, low recall) can lead to incomplete responses.
- **Relevance Ranking:** Implementing effective ranking algorithms is essential to ensure that the most relevant documents are returned first. This might involve scoring documents based on their relevance to the query and using machine learning models to improve ranking over

time.

3) Maintaining Up-to-Date Information:

- **Regular Updates:** The knowledge base needs to be updated regularly to reflect the latest information. This involves continuously ingesting new data, re-indexing, and ensuring that outdated or irrelevant information is removed.
- **Dynamic Data Sources:** In some cases, the system may need to access dynamic data sources, such as real-time news feeds or APIs. This requires the retrieval system to be flexible and capable of integrating with various data streams.

4. Best Practices for Integration

Integrating the knowledge retrieval system with a RAG model requires careful consideration to ensure smooth operation and high performance.

1) Seamless API Design:

- Ensure that the API between the RAG model and the retrieval system is designed for efficiency. This includes minimizing latency, handling errors gracefully, and supporting asynchronous queries where possible.

2) Monitoring and Logging:

- Implement monitoring tools to track the performance of the retrieval system, including response times, query success rates, and data relevance. Logging is also essential for diagnosing issues and improving the system over time.

3) Iterative Testing and Improvement:

- Continuously test the integration in real-world scenarios, gathering feedback to refine the system. This iterative process helps identify areas for optimization and ensures that the system evolves to meet changing needs.

Building and integrating a knowledge retrieval system is a complex but essential step in implementing an effective Retrieval-Augmented Generation model. By carefully designing, building, and fine-tuning this system, you can ensure that your RAG model has access to the most relevant and accurate information, enabling it to generate high-quality, contextually rich responses. In the next section, we'll discuss how to fine-tune RAG models for specific tasks, further enhancing their performance and applicability across different domains.

8.4 Fine-Tuning RAG Models for Specific Tasks

Fine-tuning Retrieval-Augmented Generation (RAG) models is a crucial step in optimizing their performance for specific tasks. By tailoring the model to the unique requirements of a particular application, you can significantly improve its accuracy, relevance, and overall utility. In this section, we'll discuss the process of fine-tuning RAG models, from selecting the right data to adjusting the model's parameters, and explore how these adjustments can lead to better task-specific outcomes.

1. Understanding the Need for Fine-Tuning

RAG models, by design, are versatile and capable of handling a wide range of tasks. However, to achieve optimal performance in a specific domain or application, fine-tuning is necessary. Fine-tuning involves making targeted adjustments to the model and its retrieval system to better align with the task at hand.

1) Why Fine-Tuning Matters:

- **Task-Specific Accuracy:** General-purpose models may not fully understand the nuances of specialized tasks. Fine-tuning helps the model grasp the specific language, concepts, and contexts relevant to the task.
- **Improved Relevance:** By focusing the model on domain-specific data, fine-tuning ensures that the outputs are more relevant and useful to the end-user, whether it's in healthcare, legal analysis, or customer support.

2) When to Fine-Tune:

- **New Domains:** When deploying a RAG model in a new domain where it hasn't been trained before, fine-tuning is essential to adapt the model to the specific language and content of that domain.
- **Performance Gaps:** If the model's initial performance is lacking in certain areas, fine-tuning can address these gaps by refining the model's understanding of the task.

2. Selecting the Right Data for Fine-Tuning

The success of fine-tuning largely depends on the quality and relevance of the data used. It's important to select data that accurately represents the tasks the model will perform.

1) Curating Task-Specific Data:

- **Domain Relevance:** Ensure that the data you select is directly related to the specific task. For example, if you're fine-tuning a model for medical diagnosis, the data should consist of relevant medical records, case studies, and research papers.
- **Diversity of Examples:** Include a wide range of examples that cover

different aspects of the task. This helps the model generalize better and perform well across various scenarios within the domain.

2) Balancing the Dataset:

- **Avoiding Bias:** When curating your dataset, it's important to avoid biases that could skew the model's performance. Ensure that the data is balanced in terms of topics, perspectives, and sub-domains to prevent the model from overfitting to a narrow set of examples.
- **Quality Over Quantity:** While having a large dataset can be beneficial, the quality of the data is more important. High-quality, accurately labeled data will lead to better fine-tuning outcomes than a larger, less precise dataset.

3. Adjusting the Retrieval System

Fine-tuning isn't just about adjusting the generation model; it also involves refining the retrieval system to ensure that it delivers the most relevant information for the task.

1) Optimizing Retrieval Algorithms:

- **Task-Specific Query Expansion:** Modify the retrieval algorithms to better handle the types of queries expected in your specific task. For instance, in a legal context, you might adjust the algorithm to recognize and prioritize legal terms and phrases.
- **Relevance Scoring:** Adjust the relevance scoring mechanisms to prioritize documents or snippets that are more likely to be useful for the task. This might involve fine-tuning the weights assigned to different features in the retrieval process.

2) Customizing the Knowledge Base:

- **Task-Aligned Content:** Ensure that the knowledge base contains content that aligns with the specific needs of the task. This might involve adding new documents, updating existing ones, or even creating a specialized subset of the knowledge base that focuses on the most relevant content.
- **Dynamic Updates:** For tasks that require up-to-date information, implement a system for regularly updating the knowledge base to reflect the latest developments in the field.

4. Fine-Tuning the Generation Model

The generation component of the RAG model can also be fine-tuned to produce outputs that are more closely aligned with the task's requirements.

1) Adjusting Model Parameters:

- **Learning Rate and Epochs:** Fine-tune the learning rate and the number of training epochs to achieve the best balance between learning new patterns and retaining useful pre-existing knowledge.
- **Layer Freezing:** Depending on the task, you may choose to freeze certain layers of the model to retain general language understanding while fine-tuning only the task-specific layers.

2) Task-Specific Objective Functions:

- **Custom Loss Functions:** Implement custom loss functions that better reflect the objectives of the task. For example, in a sentiment analysis task, you might design a loss function that penalizes misclassification of strong sentiments more heavily than neutral ones.
- **Evaluation Metrics:** Define evaluation metrics that align with the specific goals of the task. These metrics will guide the fine-tuning process and help ensure that the model is improving in the areas that matter most.

5. Iterative Testing and Validation

Fine-tuning is an iterative process that requires continuous testing and validation to ensure that the model is improving.

1) Validation Sets:

- **Task-Specific Validation:** Use a validation set that reflects the actual tasks the model will encounter in deployment. This allows you to monitor the model's performance in a realistic setting and make adjustments as needed.
- **Regular Checkpoints:** Implement regular checkpoints during fine-tuning to evaluate the model's progress. This helps in identifying when the model has reached optimal performance or if further adjustments are needed.

2) A/B Testing:

- **Comparing Versions:** Conduct A/B testing to compare the performance of the fine-tuned model against the original or other versions. This helps ensure that the fine-tuning process is genuinely improving the model's performance for the specific task.

3) User Feedback Integration:

- **Real-World Feedback:** Incorporate feedback from end-users to refine the fine-tuned model further. User feedback can provide insights into how well the model is performing in practice and highlight areas for further improvement.

Fine-tuning RAG models for specific tasks is a powerful way to enhance their effectiveness and ensure they meet the unique demands of particular domains. By carefully selecting the right data, optimizing both the retrieval and generation components, and continuously testing and refining the model, you can achieve significant improvements in performance. In the next section, we'll look at a real-world case study to illustrate how these fine-tuning principles are applied in practice, demonstrating the tangible benefits of a well-tuned RAG model.

8.5 Case Study: Implementing RAG in a Real-World Application

To illustrate the practical application of Retrieval-Augmented Generation (RAG), let's delve into a case study where RAG was successfully implemented to solve a real-world problem. This case study will showcase the steps taken, the challenges encountered, and the outcomes achieved, providing a clear example of how RAG can be leveraged to enhance performance in specific domains.

Background

A multinational pharmaceutical company needed a solution to streamline the process of summarizing and analyzing the latest scientific literature related to new drug developments. The research team was overwhelmed by the sheer volume of new publications and struggled to keep up with the latest findings, which were crucial for informing drug development and regulatory submissions.

The Challenge

The primary challenge was to develop a system that could:

1) Efficiently Retrieve Relevant Documents:

- The system needed to sift through thousands of new scientific papers published each month to identify those most relevant to the company's research.
- It had to prioritize documents based on factors such as relevance to ongoing projects, the credibility of the sources, and the novelty of the findings.

2) Generate Accurate Summaries:

- Once relevant documents were retrieved, the system needed to generate concise summaries that highlighted key findings, methodologies, and implications for drug development.
- These summaries had to be both scientifically accurate and written in a way that could be easily understood by researchers and decision-makers.

3) Integrate with Existing Workflows:

- The solution needed to integrate seamlessly with the company's existing research tools and workflows, allowing researchers to easily access, review, and act on the information generated by the system.

Solution: Implementing a RAG-Based System

To address these challenges, the company implemented a RAG-based system that combined the power of retrieval with the generative capabilities of a state-of-the-art language model.

1) Building the Knowledge Retrieval System:

- **Data Sources:** The system was connected to several external databases and repositories of scientific publications, including PubMed, clinical trial databases, and proprietary research databases maintained by the company.

- **Indexing and Retrieval:** The retrieval system was built using a combination of keyword and semantic search techniques. Documents were indexed using advanced vector-based representations to ensure that the system could quickly and accurately retrieve relevant papers based on the queries posed by the research team.
- **Custom Relevance Scoring:** A custom relevance scoring mechanism was developed to prioritize documents that were most likely to impact the company's drug development projects. This scoring considered factors such as the recency of the publication, the reputation of the journal, and the presence of specific keywords related to ongoing research.

2) Fine-Tuning the Generation Model:

- **Task-Specific Fine-Tuning:** The generative model was fine-tuned using a curated dataset of existing research summaries written by the company's experts. This helped the model learn the specific language, tone, and structure preferred by the research team.
- **Custom Loss Functions:** A custom loss function was employed during fine-tuning to emphasize the accuracy and relevance of the generated summaries, ensuring that the model focused on the most critical aspects of each paper.

3) Integrating with Existing Workflows:

- **API Integration:** The RAG system was integrated with the company's internal research management platform through a well-designed API. This allowed researchers to submit queries directly through the platform and receive summarized outputs within seconds.
- **User Feedback Loop:** A feedback loop was established where researchers could rate the relevance and accuracy of the summaries, providing data that was used to further fine-tune and improve the

system over time.

Challenges and Solutions

Throughout the implementation process, several challenges were encountered, each of which was addressed with targeted solutions:

1) Handling Ambiguous Queries:

- **Challenge:** Researchers sometimes posed queries that were ambiguous or broad, leading to less relevant retrievals.
- **Solution:** The system was enhanced with a query refinement feature that suggested more specific queries based on the initial input, helping users narrow down their requests and improve retrieval accuracy.

2) Balancing Speed and Accuracy:

- **Challenge:** There was a need to balance the speed of retrieval and generation with the accuracy and depth of the summaries.
- **Solution:** The retrieval system was optimized to quickly return a shortlist of highly relevant documents, which were then passed through a more detailed and slower generation process to ensure high-quality summaries.

3) Maintaining Up-to-Date Information:

- **Challenge:** The fast-paced nature of scientific research required the knowledge base to be constantly updated with new publications.
- **Solution:** The system was equipped with an automated ingestion pipeline that regularly updated the knowledge base with the latest data, ensuring that the information used for retrieval was always current.

Outcomes

The implementation of the RAG system led to several notable outcomes:

1) Increased Efficiency:

- Researchers were able to process and review relevant scientific literature much more quickly, freeing up time for deeper analysis and experimental work.
- The time spent on literature review was reduced by approximately 60%, allowing the research team to stay on top of the latest developments without feeling overwhelmed.

2) Improved Decision-Making:

- The concise, accurate summaries generated by the system provided decision-makers with the critical information they needed to make informed choices about drug development priorities.
- The relevance and clarity of the summaries led to better-informed discussions during project meetings and strategy sessions.

3) Higher User Satisfaction:

- Feedback from the research team was overwhelmingly positive, with users particularly appreciating the system's ability to deliver relevant information quickly and in an easy-to-digest format.
- The continuous feedback loop and iterative improvements ensured that the system evolved to better meet the needs of the users over time.

This case study demonstrates the real-world impact that a well-implemented RAG system can have in a specialized domain like pharmaceutical research. By effectively combining retrieval with generation, the company was able to streamline its research processes, enhance decision-making, and improve overall efficiency. The success of this project highlights the potential for RAG models to transform how organizations manage and utilize large volumes of information, providing actionable insights in a fraction of the time it would take using traditional methods. In the final section of this chapter, we'll explore future directions in RAG research, considering how this technology might evolve and what new capabilities could emerge in the coming years.

8.6 Future Directions in RAG Research

Retrieval-Augmented Generation (RAG) is a rapidly evolving field that holds significant promise for advancing the capabilities of AI in real-world applications. As the technology matures, researchers and developers are exploring new ways to enhance the performance, efficiency, and versatility of RAG models. In this section, we'll discuss some of the key areas where RAG research is likely to focus in the coming years, highlighting the innovations that could shape the future of this technology.

1. Enhancing Retrieval Algorithms

One of the primary areas of focus in future RAG research will be the continued improvement of retrieval algorithms. The goal is to make these algorithms more accurate, faster, and better suited to handling diverse and complex queries.

1) Semantic Understanding:

- **Deepening Contextual Awareness:** Future retrieval algorithms are expected to incorporate deeper semantic understanding, allowing them to better grasp the nuances of complex queries. This could involve leveraging more sophisticated language models that can understand context at a deeper level, resulting in more precise retrievals.

- **Contextual Embeddings:** The use of advanced contextual embeddings, which capture the meaning of words in context, will likely become more common. These embeddings will help retrieval systems more accurately match queries with relevant documents, even when the query wording differs significantly from the document text.

2) Real-Time Retrieval:

- **Speed Improvements:** As the demand for real-time information grows, there will be a push to develop retrieval systems that can operate at lightning speed without sacrificing accuracy. This could involve innovations in indexing techniques, distributed computing, and hardware acceleration.
- **Dynamic Updates:** Future systems might also feature dynamic retrieval capabilities, where the knowledge base is continuously updated in real-time, ensuring that the most current information is always available for generation.

2. Integration with Multimodal Data

As AI applications expand beyond text, there will be a growing need to integrate RAG models with multimodal data—data that includes not just text, but also images, audio, video, and more.

1) Multimodal Retrieval:

- **Unified Retrieval Systems:** Researchers are likely to develop unified retrieval systems capable of handling multiple data types simultaneously. For example, a query might retrieve both text documents and related images, which can then be used together in the generation process.
- **Cross-Modal Search:** Future RAG models may incorporate cross-

modal search capabilities, where a text query could retrieve not only relevant text but also images or videos that align with the content, enhancing the richness of the generated output.

2) Generation with Multimodal Inputs:

- **Integrated Outputs:** By integrating multimodal data, RAG models could generate outputs that combine text with other media, such as generating a report that includes both written analysis and relevant charts or images. This would make RAG models more versatile and useful in fields like media production, education, and more.

3. Personalization and Adaptation

Personalization will be a key trend in the future of RAG, with models becoming increasingly adept at adapting their outputs to individual users' needs, preferences, and contexts.

1) User-Centric Retrieval:

- **Personalized Knowledge Bases:** One avenue of research will be the development of personalized knowledge bases that evolve based on a user's past interactions. This could involve models that learn from user feedback and automatically prioritize documents or data that align with the user's interests.
- **Adaptive Retrieval Mechanisms:** Future systems might also include adaptive retrieval mechanisms that adjust how they retrieve information based on user behavior, providing more relevant results over time.

2) Tailored Generation:

- **Context-Aware Outputs:** As models become more aware of the context in which they are being used, they will be able to tailor their outputs more effectively. For instance, a RAG model used in a professional setting might generate more formal responses, while the same model used in a casual setting might adopt a more conversational tone.

- **Learning from Interactions:** By continuously learning from user interactions, RAG models could refine their output generation to better meet individual needs, making them more useful in a wide range of applications, from customer support to personalized learning.

4. Ethical and Responsible AI Development

As RAG models become more powerful, there will be an increased focus on ensuring that these systems are developed and deployed in an ethical and responsible manner.

1) Bias Mitigation:

- **Reducing Bias in Retrieval:** Future research will likely focus on methods to reduce bias in the retrieval process. This could involve developing techniques that ensure a more balanced and fair representation of perspectives in the information retrieved, especially in sensitive domains like healthcare, law, and social media.
- **Fairness in Generation:** Similarly, efforts will be made to ensure that the generation component of RAG models does not perpetuate or amplify biases present in the training data. This might involve incorporating fairness constraints into the model's objective functions or employing post-processing techniques to adjust outputs.

2) Transparency and Explainability:

- **Explaining Retrieval Decisions:** As RAG models are increasingly used in high-stakes environments, there will be a demand for greater transparency in how retrieval decisions are made. Future models might include features that allow users to understand why certain documents were retrieved and how they influenced the final output.

- **User-Controlled Outputs:** Researchers may also develop tools that give users more control over the generation process, allowing them to specify certain constraints or preferences that guide the model's outputs in a way that aligns with ethical considerations.

5. Expanding RAG Applications

The application of RAG models is likely to expand into new areas as the technology continues to evolve, opening up possibilities that were previously unimaginable.

1) Healthcare and Medicine:

- **Clinical Decision Support:** In healthcare, RAG models could become integral to clinical decision support systems, helping doctors quickly access the latest research and guidelines when diagnosing or treating patients. These models could provide real-time, evidence-based recommendations that are tailored to individual patient cases.
- **Medical Research:** RAG could also revolutionize medical research by automating literature reviews, identifying emerging trends in research, and even suggesting new avenues for investigation based on gaps in the existing literature.

2) Education and Learning:

- **Personalized Learning Tools:** In education, RAG models could be used to create personalized learning experiences, where the system retrieves and generates content tailored to a student's current level, learning style, and progress. This could make learning more efficient and engaging, catering to the needs of each individual student.
- **Content Creation and Curation:** RAG could also assist educators in

creating and curating content for courses, generating lecture notes, exam questions, and other educational materials based on the latest research and pedagogical practices.

3) Business and Industry:

- **Knowledge Management:** In business, RAG models could play a key role in knowledge management, helping organizations retrieve and synthesize information from vast internal databases, making it easier for employees to access the information they need to make informed decisions.
- **Customer Support Automation:** RAG could further enhance customer support systems by providing more accurate, contextually relevant responses to customer queries, reducing response times and improving customer satisfaction.

The future of Retrieval-Augmented Generation is full of exciting possibilities. As researchers continue to push the boundaries of what RAG models can do, we can expect to see these systems become even more powerful, versatile, and integral to a wide range of applications. Whether through enhancing retrieval algorithms, integrating multimodal data, personalizing outputs, or ensuring ethical deployment, the ongoing evolution of RAG technology will undoubtedly lead to innovations that transform how we interact with and utilize information. As we look ahead, it's clear that RAG will play a central role in the next generation of AI-driven solutions.

Chapter 9: Model Optimization for Production

9.1 Model Compression Techniques: Quantization, Pruning, and Distillation

As the demand for deploying large language models (LLMs) in production environments grows, one of the key challenges is managing the size and complexity of these models. Large models, while powerful, can be resource-intensive, making them difficult to deploy efficiently in real-world applications. To address this, model compression techniques such as quantization, pruning, and distillation are essential. These methods help reduce the model's size, improve inference speed, and lower the computational resources required, all without significantly sacrificing performance.

1. Quantization

Quantization is a technique that reduces the precision of the model's weights and activations, which in turn decreases the model's size and speeds up inference.

1) How Quantization Works:

- **Lowering Precision:** Most models are trained using 32-bit floating-point numbers (FP32). Quantization involves converting these weights and activations to lower precision, such as 16-bit floating points (FP16) or 8-bit integers (INT8). This reduces the amount of memory needed to store the model and accelerates the computations.
- **Post-Training Quantization:** This is one of the most common approaches, where a trained model is quantized after the training process is complete. It's relatively straightforward and can often be applied without retraining the model.
- **Quantization-Aware Training (QAT):** In QAT, the model is trained with quantization in mind. This approach can lead to better performance compared to post-training quantization, especially for more complex models or when higher accuracy is required.

2) Benefits and Trade-Offs:

- **Improved Efficiency:** Quantization can significantly reduce both the memory footprint and the computational demands of a model, making it more suitable for deployment in resource-constrained environments, such as mobile devices or edge computing.
- **Potential Accuracy Loss:** While quantization can lead to some loss in accuracy, especially when reducing to very low precision (like INT8), the trade-off is often acceptable in scenarios where speed and efficiency are prioritized.

3) Practical Applications:

- **Edge AI:** Quantized models are often used in edge AI applications, where devices like smartphones or IoT sensors require efficient models that can run with limited processing power and memory.
- **Real-Time Systems:** In real-time applications, where latency is critical, quantization helps meet performance requirements by speeding up inference times.

2. Pruning

Pruning is the process of removing parts of the model that are less important, effectively reducing the size of the model while maintaining its overall performance.

1) How Pruning Works:

- **Removing Redundant Parameters:** During the training process, not all weights in a model contribute equally to the final performance. Pruning involves identifying and removing these less significant weights, which can be done at various levels, including individual neurons, layers, or entire blocks of the model.
- **Types of Pruning:**
- **Magnitude-Based Pruning:** This method removes weights that are close to zero, under the assumption that they contribute less to the model's predictions.
- **Structured Pruning:** This involves removing entire neurons or filters, leading to a more structured reduction in model size. Structured pruning is often easier to optimize for hardware implementations.
- **Unstructured Pruning:** Here, individual weights are removed without regard to the overall structure. While it can lead to a smaller model, it may require more sophisticated techniques to optimize the resulting sparse matrix operations.

2) Benefits and Trade-Offs:

- **Smaller Models:** Pruning can dramatically reduce the size of the model, making it easier to deploy in environments with limited storage and computational capacity.
- **Complexity in Implementation:** Pruned models, especially those that undergo unstructured pruning, can be more complex to implement and may require specialized libraries or hardware to fully capitalize

on the size reduction.

3) Practical Applications:

- **Cloud Services:** Pruned models are often used in cloud-based services where scaling is important, and reducing the model size can lead to lower operational costs.
- **Deployments on Legacy Hardware:** Pruning is valuable when deploying models on older or less powerful hardware, where the reduced model size can make the difference between feasible and infeasible deployment.

3. Distillation

Model distillation is a technique where a smaller, simpler model (the "student") is trained to replicate the behavior of a larger, more complex model (the "teacher"). This process results in a model that is much smaller and faster but retains much of the performance of the original.

1) How Distillation Works:

- **Teacher-Student Paradigm:** The large, complex model (teacher) is first trained on a task. The smaller model (student) is then trained using the outputs of the teacher model as labels, in addition to the original training data. This way, the student model learns to mimic the teacher, capturing the most important features and patterns.
- **Soft Targets:** Instead of using hard labels (e.g., true/false), distillation uses the probability distribution (soft targets) provided by the teacher model, which often contains more information about the task than the hard labels alone.

2) Benefits and Trade-Offs:

- **Smaller, Efficient Models:** The main advantage of distillation is that it produces a model that is much smaller and faster while maintaining performance close to that of the larger model.
- **Training Complexity:** Distillation can be more complex and resource-intensive because it requires training two models—the teacher and the student. However, once trained, the student model is much more efficient to deploy.

3) Practical Applications:

- **Deploying AI in Constrained Environments:** Distilled models are ideal for deployment in environments where computational resources are limited, such as mobile applications, embedded systems, or web applications with strict latency requirements.
- **Ensemble Learning:** Distillation can also be used to combine the strengths of multiple models (teacher ensemble) into a single, compact student model, providing a powerful yet efficient solution.

Model compression techniques like quantization, pruning, and distillation are essential tools for making large language models more practical for real-world deployment. By reducing the size and computational demands of these models, you can deploy powerful AI systems in environments where resources are limited, without sacrificing too much in terms of performance. As the need for efficient and scalable AI grows, these techniques will become increasingly important in the development and deployment of large language models across various industries. In the next section, we'll explore how to reduce inference latency, another critical aspect of optimizing models for production use.

9.2 Reducing Inference Latency: Techniques and Best Practices

When deploying large language models (LLMs) in production, one of the most critical factors to consider is inference latency—the time it takes for a model to produce an output after receiving an input. High latency can lead to a poor user experience, especially in applications that require real-time or near-real-time responses, such as chatbots, recommendation systems, and interactive applications. In this section, we'll explore techniques and best practices for reducing inference latency, ensuring that your models can deliver quick and efficient results.

1. Understanding Inference Latency

Inference latency is influenced by several factors, including the size of the model, the computational resources available, and the efficiency of the code and infrastructure used to serve the model. Reducing latency often requires a combination of strategies, each targeting different aspects of the model deployment process.

1) Model Size and Complexity:

- **Impact on Latency:** Larger models with more parameters typically require more computation time, leading to higher latency. This is why model compression techniques like quantization, pruning, and distillation (discussed in the previous section) are often essential first steps in reducing latency.
- **Balancing Size and Performance:** While reducing model size can decrease latency, it's important to find a balance that doesn't overly compromise the model's accuracy or effectiveness.

2) Hardware and Infrastructure:

- **GPU vs. CPU:** Inference latency can vary significantly depending on whether the model is run on a CPU or a GPU. GPUs are generally faster for large-scale matrix operations, which are common in LLMs, making them preferable for reducing latency.
- **Scaling with Hardware:** Using multiple GPUs or specialized hardware like TPUs (Tensor Processing Units) can further reduce latency, particularly for large models or high-throughput applications.

3) Software and Code Optimization:

- **Efficient Code Practices:** Optimizing the code that handles model inference can also play a significant role in reducing latency. This includes minimizing data movement between CPU and GPU, optimizing memory usage, and using efficient data structures.
- **Framework Optimizations:** Leveraging optimized machine learning frameworks, such as TensorFlow, PyTorch, or ONNX Runtime, can provide built-in efficiencies that reduce latency.

2. Techniques for Reducing Inference Latency

There are several specific techniques you can apply to reduce inference latency, each targeting different aspects of the inference process.

1) Batching Inference Requests:

- **How Batching Works:** Batching involves processing multiple inference requests at once rather than one at a time. This can significantly reduce the overhead associated with each individual request, especially when running on GPUs, which excel at parallel processing.
- **Trade-Offs:** While batching can reduce latency per request, it introduces some delay because requests are held in a queue until a full batch is ready. It's important to configure batch sizes and timeout thresholds to strike the right balance between throughput and latency.

2) Asynchronous Processing:

- **Non-Blocking Operations:** Asynchronous processing allows the system to handle multiple tasks concurrently, rather than waiting for one task to complete before starting another. This is particularly useful in scenarios where the model must interact with other services or databases during inference.
- **Implementation:** Asynchronous processing can be implemented using async/await patterns in programming languages like Python, enabling the system to initiate multiple inference requests and handle responses as they become available, rather than processing them sequentially.

3) Model Parallelism and Distributed Inference:

- **Splitting the Model:** For very large models, inference can be parallelized across multiple GPUs or even across different machines. This involves splitting the model into segments, with each segment running on a different GPU or node, and then combining the results to produce the final output.
- **Distributed Systems:** In a distributed inference system, the model is served across multiple machines in a cluster, allowing for high scalability and reduced latency. Frameworks like TensorFlow Serving, TorchServe, and NVIDIA Triton can facilitate distributed inference by managing the distribution and coordination of tasks.

4) Cache Inference Results:

- **Using Caches:** For applications where the same or similar queries are likely to be repeated, caching inference results can drastically reduce latency. When a repeated query is received, the system can return the cached result instantly rather than running the model again.
- **Cache Invalidation:** It's important to implement proper cache invalidation strategies to ensure that outdated or irrelevant results are not

served, which could lead to inaccurate responses.

5) Optimize Model Serving Frameworks:

- **Choosing the Right Framework:** Using optimized model serving frameworks can help reduce latency. Frameworks like TensorFlow Serving, ONNX Runtime, and NVIDIA Triton are designed to efficiently manage inference workloads, offering features like automatic batching, dynamic scaling, and support for mixed-precision inference.
- **Custom Inference Pipelines:** In some cases, building a custom inference pipeline tailored to your specific model and use case can offer additional latency reductions, particularly when integrating with other system components or optimizing for specific hardware.

3. Best Practices for Reducing Inference Latency

In addition to the specific techniques mentioned above, there are several best practices that can help ensure your models operate with minimal latency in production.

1) Profiling and Monitoring:

- **Regular Profiling:** Continuously profile your model and inference pipeline to identify bottlenecks. Tools like TensorBoard, PyTorch Profiler, and NVIDIA Nsight Systems can provide insights into where latency is occurring and how to address it.
- **Monitoring in Production:** Implement monitoring tools to track inference latency in real-time. This helps quickly identify and resolve performance issues as they arise, ensuring consistent low-latency performance.

2) Optimize Data Preprocessing:

- **Efficient Data Handling:** The time it takes to preprocess input data can contribute to overall latency. Ensure that data preprocessing steps are optimized and, where possible, offloaded to the GPU or performed in parallel with other tasks.
- **Data Format:** Use data formats that are efficient to parse and minimize the need for conversions during inference. For example, using serialized formats like Protocol Buffers (Protobuf) or FlatBuffers can reduce preprocessing overhead.

3) Avoid Over-Optimization:

- **Balance Optimization Efforts:** While reducing latency is important, it's crucial not to over-optimize in ways that might degrade model accuracy or make the system difficult to maintain. Aim for a balanced approach that achieves the desired performance without unnecessary complexity.

Reducing inference latency is a key consideration when deploying large language models in production environments. By leveraging techniques like batching, asynchronous processing, model parallelism, and caching, as well as following best practices for profiling, data handling, and optimization, you can ensure that your models deliver fast, responsive outputs that meet the demands of real-time applications. In the next section, we'll discuss strategies for optimizing memory usage, another critical aspect of deploying large models in production environments.

9.3 Memory Optimization for Large Models

Deploying large language models (LLMs) in production environments often presents significant challenges related to memory usage. These models, with their millions or even billions of parameters, can consume vast amounts of memory, making it difficult to deploy them efficiently on available hardware. Effective memory optimization is crucial to ensure that these models can run smoothly in production without overwhelming system resources or leading to costly infrastructure upgrades. In this section, we'll explore techniques and best practices for optimizing memory usage when deploying large models.

1. Understanding Memory Bottlenecks

Before diving into specific optimization techniques, it's important to understand where memory bottlenecks typically occur in the deployment of large models.

1) Model Weights and Parameters:

- **Storage Requirements:** The primary source of memory usage in large models is the storage of model weights and parameters. Each layer in the model contributes to the total memory footprint, and as models grow in size, so too does the demand for memory.
- **Activations During Inference:** In addition to storing model weights, memory is also consumed by activations—the intermediate outputs generated by each layer during inference. These activations need to be stored temporarily as the model processes inputs, adding to the overall memory requirements.

2) Batch Size:

- **Impact on Memory:** The size of the input batch directly affects memory usage. Larger batch sizes require more memory to store the inputs, intermediate activations, and outputs. While larger batches can improve throughput, they can also lead to memory exhaustion, especially in resource-constrained environments.

3) Data Movement:

- **CPU-GPU Transfer:** Moving data between the CPU and GPU can lead to significant memory overhead, particularly if data is transferred inefficiently. Optimizing data movement is crucial to reduce unnecessary memory usage and improve overall performance.

2. Techniques for Memory Optimization

Several techniques can be employed to optimize memory usage when deploying large models. These techniques focus on reducing the memory footprint of the model itself, as well as improving the efficiency of data handling during inference.

1) Model Quantization:

- **Reduced Precision:** As discussed in the section on model compression, quantization involves reducing the precision of model weights from 32-bit floating points (FP32) to 16-bit (FP16) or even 8-bit (INT8). This reduces the amount of memory required to store the model, often with minimal impact on accuracy.
- **Mixed Precision Inference:** Mixed precision inference combines high-precision (FP32) and low-precision (FP16) operations to optimize memory usage without compromising too much on model performance. This approach is particularly effective when deployed on GPUs that support mixed precision, such as NVIDIA's Tensor Cores.

2) Layer and Tensor Offloading:

- **Offloading to CPU:** During inference, certain layers or tensors that are not immediately needed can be offloaded to the CPU, freeing up GPU memory for other operations. This technique can be particularly useful in environments where GPU memory is a limiting factor.

- **Checkpointing:** Also known as gradient checkpointing, this technique involves storing only a subset of activations during forward passes and recomputing them during the backward pass (in training scenarios) to save memory. While this technique is more commonly associated with training, it can be adapted for certain inference scenarios where memory conservation is critical.

3) Memory-Efficient Architectures:

- **Lightweight Models:** Where possible, deploying lighter versions of models, such as MobileNet or EfficientNet, can reduce memory requirements. These architectures are specifically designed to be more memory-efficient while maintaining a high level of performance.
- **Sparse Models:** By pruning less important weights, sparse models reduce the number of active parameters, leading to lower memory usage. Sparsity can be introduced during training or through post-training pruning, as discussed earlier.

4) Memory Mapping and Allocation Optimization:

- **Optimized Memory Allocators:** Using custom memory allocators designed to reduce fragmentation and optimize memory allocation can significantly improve memory efficiency. Libraries such as PyTorch's torch.cuda.memory API allow for fine-tuned control over memory allocation on GPUs.
- **Memory Mapping:** Leveraging memory-mapped files allows the model to access large datasets without loading the entire dataset into memory. This technique is particularly useful for handling large input data that doesn't fit entirely into memory.

5) Reducing Batch Size:

- **Dynamic Batching:** Implementing dynamic batching strategies, where the batch size adjusts based on available memory, can help manage memory usage effectively. While reducing batch size can impact throughput, it's often a necessary trade-off to avoid memory overflows.

- **Gradient Accumulation (For Training):** While primarily used during training, gradient accumulation allows for the use of smaller batch sizes by accumulating gradients over multiple forward passes before performing a backward pass. In inference, a similar concept can be applied to split large input batches into smaller ones to fit within memory constraints.

3. Best Practices for Memory Optimization

In addition to specific techniques, there are several best practices to follow when optimizing memory for large models in production.

1) Profiling and Monitoring:

- **Memory Profiling Tools:** Regularly profile your model's memory usage using tools like NVIDIA's Nsight Systems, PyTorch Profiler, or TensorFlow's memory profiler. These tools can help you identify memory bottlenecks and optimize specific parts of your model or inference pipeline.
- **Real-Time Monitoring:** Implement real-time monitoring of memory usage in production to catch and address memory-related issues before they lead to system failures or degraded performance.

2) Iterative Optimization:

- **Start with Baselines:** Begin by deploying the model without optimizations to establish a baseline for memory usage. Then, iteratively apply optimization techniques, monitoring the impact of each change to ensure that it improves memory efficiency without negatively affecting performance.

- **Balance Memory and Latency:** While optimizing for memory, it's important to consider the impact on inference latency. In some cases, optimizing memory usage can increase latency, so it's important to strike a balance that meets both your memory and performance requirements.

3) Plan for Scalability:

- **Scaling Infrastructure:** Ensure that your deployment infrastructure is scalable, allowing you to add more memory or processing power as needed. Cloud platforms and container orchestration tools like Kubernetes can provide the flexibility to scale memory resources on demand.
- **Future-Proofing:** Consider the potential growth of your model and data over time. Implement memory optimization techniques that not only address current needs but also scale as the model or workload increases.

Optimizing memory usage is a crucial aspect of deploying large language models in production, particularly in environments where resources are constrained. By applying techniques such as quantization, offloading, memory-efficient architectures, and dynamic batching, you can significantly reduce the memory footprint of your models, enabling smoother and more cost-effective deployment. In the next section, we'll explore strategies for efficiently serving LLMs in production, ensuring that your optimized models can deliver high performance at scale.

9.4 Efficient Serving of LLMs in Production

Deploying large language models (LLMs) in production requires careful planning and optimization to ensure they can serve predictions efficiently and reliably. Efficient serving is critical for providing fast, scalable, and cost-effective solutions, particularly when dealing with large models that demand significant computational resources. In this section, we'll cover strategies and best practices for serving LLMs efficiently, ensuring they meet the needs of real-world applications.

1. Choosing the Right Serving Infrastructure

The choice of infrastructure plays a crucial role in the efficient serving of LLMs. Whether you're deploying on-premises, in the cloud, or in a hybrid environment, selecting the right tools and platforms is essential for achieving optimal performance.

1) On-Premises vs. Cloud Deployment:

- **On-Premises:** Deploying LLMs on-premises allows for greater control over hardware and data security but may require significant upfront investment in infrastructure. It's typically suited for organizations with stringent data privacy requirements or those needing custom hardware setups.
- **Cloud Deployment:** Cloud platforms, such as AWS, Google Cloud, and Microsoft Azure, offer scalable resources and managed services tailored for AI workloads. Cloud deployment is ideal for organizations looking for flexibility and scalability without the need for significant capital expenditure.

2) Containerization and Orchestration:

- **Containers:** Containerizing your LLM using Docker or other container technologies allows for consistent deployment across different environments. Containers package the model, dependencies, and runtime environment, ensuring that the model behaves the same in production as it does in testing.

- **Orchestration with Kubernetes:** Kubernetes is a popular choice for managing containerized applications at scale. It automates the deployment, scaling, and management of containers, making it easier to serve LLMs efficiently across multiple nodes.

3) Serverless Architectures:

- **Function-as-a-Service (FaaS):** Serverless architectures, where code runs in response to events and automatically scales, can be highly efficient for serving LLMs. This approach reduces the need to manage infrastructure directly and can be cost-effective for workloads with variable demand.

2. Scaling and Load Balancing

To serve LLMs effectively in production, especially under varying load conditions, it's crucial to implement robust scaling and load-balancing strategies.

1) Horizontal Scaling:

- **Adding More Instances:** Horizontal scaling involves adding more instances of the model to handle increased load. This approach is particularly effective in cloud environments, where resources can be dynamically allocated based on demand.
- **Autoscaling:** Many cloud platforms offer autoscaling features that automatically adjust the number of instances based on predefined metrics such as CPU usage, memory consumption, or request rate. Autoscaling ensures that your LLM deployment can handle traffic

spikes without over-provisioning resources.

2) Load Balancing:

- **Distributing Traffic:** Load balancers distribute incoming requests across multiple model instances, ensuring that no single instance becomes a bottleneck. This distribution helps maintain consistent response times and improves overall reliability.
- **Health Checks:** Implement health checks to monitor the status of each model instance. Load balancers can use these checks to route traffic away from unhealthy instances, ensuring continuous availability and minimizing downtime.

3. Optimizing Model Serving Frameworks

Choosing and optimizing the right model serving framework is key to efficient LLM deployment. These frameworks handle the inference requests and manage interactions with underlying hardware.

1) Model Serving Frameworks:

- **TensorFlow Serving:** TensorFlow Serving is a flexible, high-performance serving system for machine learning models. It's optimized for TensorFlow models but also supports other model types. It offers features like version management, which allows you to serve multiple versions of a model simultaneously.
- **TorchServe:** TorchServe, developed by AWS and Facebook, is designed specifically for PyTorch models. It provides tools for managing and deploying PyTorch models at scale, with support for features like multi-model serving, logging, and metrics.
- **NVIDIA Triton Inference Server:** Triton is designed for high-performance inference, supporting models from various frameworks (TensorFlow, PyTorch, ONNX) and optimized for NVIDIA GPUs. It

offers advanced features like dynamic batching, multi-GPU support, and integration with Kubernetes.

2) Optimizing Inference Pipelines:

- **Batching and Parallelization:** Utilize batching to process multiple requests simultaneously, reducing per-request overhead. Parallelize inference operations across multiple GPUs or nodes to further enhance throughput.
- **Mixed Precision Inference:** For models that support it, use mixed precision (combining FP16 and FP32) to reduce memory usage and improve inference speed without sacrificing accuracy. This is particularly effective when deployed on hardware that supports mixed precision, like NVIDIA Tensor Cores.

3) Latency Optimization:

- **Preloading Models:** To minimize latency, preload models into memory before serving requests. This avoids the delay associated with loading models on demand, ensuring that the system can respond to requests immediately.
- **Caching Inference Results:** Implement caching mechanisms for frequently requested inferences. Caching can significantly reduce response times for repetitive queries, as the model doesn't need to recompute results.

4. Ensuring Reliability and Robustness

Reliability is crucial for production deployments. Implementing strategies to ensure that your LLMs remain robust under various conditions will help maintain a seamless user experience.

1) Monitoring and Logging:

- **Comprehensive Monitoring:** Use monitoring tools to track the performance of your LLM deployment, including metrics like latency, throughput, error rates, and resource utilization. Tools like Prometheus, Grafana, and AWS CloudWatch can provide real-time insights into your system's health.
- **Detailed Logging:** Implement logging at multiple levels (application, framework, system) to capture detailed information about model behavior, request handling, and errors. This data is invaluable for troubleshooting and optimizing your deployment.

2) Fault Tolerance and Redundancy:

- **Redundant Instances:** Deploy multiple instances of your model across different availability zones or regions to protect against localized failures. This redundancy ensures that your service remains available even if one instance or region goes down.
- **Graceful Degradation:** Design your system to degrade gracefully in the event of resource constraints or failures. For example, if full LLM inference becomes too slow, the system could switch to a smaller, faster model to maintain responsiveness.

3) Security Considerations:

- **Data Encryption:** Ensure that all data, both in transit and at rest, is encrypted to protect against unauthorized access. Use secure protocols (e.g., HTTPS, SSL/TLS) for communication between clients and the serving infrastructure.
- **Access Control:** Implement strict access controls to limit who can deploy, modify, or interact with the model in production. Role-based access control (RBAC) and identity and access management (IAM) tools can help enforce these controls.

Efficiently serving large language models in production requires a combination of the right infrastructure, robust scaling and load-balancing strategies, optimized model serving frameworks, and a focus on reliability and security. By carefully considering each of these aspects, you can ensure that your LLMs are not only powerful but also scalable, responsive, and secure, providing a solid foundation for a wide range of real-world applications. In the next section, we'll explore a case study that demonstrates the optimization of GPT for real-time applications, highlighting the practical application of the strategies discussed so far.

9.5 Case Study: Optimizing GPT for Real-Time Applications

Optimizing a large language model like GPT for real-time applications presents a unique set of challenges. These models, while powerful, are typically resource-intensive, making them difficult to deploy in scenarios where low latency and high throughput are critical. In this case study, we'll explore how a team successfully optimized GPT for a real-time customer support application, focusing on the strategies used to meet strict performance requirements.

Background

A tech company wanted to enhance its customer support platform by integrating a GPT-based chatbot capable of handling complex queries in real-time. The primary goal was to provide instant, accurate responses to customer inquiries, improving user satisfaction and reducing the workload on human agents.

Challenges:

- **Low Latency Requirement:** The application required response times of under 200 milliseconds to maintain a smooth and responsive user experience.
- **Scalability:** The system needed to handle thousands of concurrent users without degrading performance.
- **Resource Constraints:** The solution had to be cost-effective, minimizing the need for expensive hardware upgrades.

Initial Deployment and Challenges

The team initially deployed a standard GPT model on a cloud-based GPU instance. While the model performed well in terms of accuracy, it quickly became clear that the inference latency was too high, averaging around 500 milliseconds per request. Additionally, the system struggled to maintain performance as the number of concurrent users increased, leading to slower response times and occasional timeouts.

Key Issues Identified:

- **High Latency:** The default setup couldn't meet the required sub-200ms response time.
- **Resource Utilization:** The model's large memory footprint and computational demands led to inefficient use of available GPU resources.
- **Scalability Issues:** The system could not scale effectively to handle peak traffic, leading to bottlenecks and degraded user experience.

Optimization Strategies Implemented

To address these issues, the team employed a combination of optimization techniques, focusing on reducing latency, improving scalability, and optimizing resource usage.

1) Model Compression and Quantization:

- **Quantization:** The first step was to apply post-training quantization, reducing the model's weights from 32-bit floating points (FP32) to 16-bit (FP16). This resulted in a significant reduction in memory usage and computational load, without a noticeable impact on model accuracy.
- **Pruning:** The team also pruned the model by removing less important neurons and layers, which helped reduce the model size further. This was done carefully to ensure that the model's ability to generate coherent and contextually appropriate responses was not compromised.

2) Batching and Parallelization:

- **Dynamic Batching:** Implementing dynamic batching allowed the system to process multiple requests simultaneously, reducing the per-request overhead. This approach significantly improved throughput and reduced overall latency.
- **Parallel Inference:** The model was deployed across multiple GPUs, with parallel inference enabling the system to handle a higher volume of requests. This also allowed the load to be distributed more evenly across available resources, preventing any single GPU from becoming a bottleneck.

3) Infrastructure Optimization:

- **Edge Computing:** To reduce latency further, the team deployed parts of the system closer to the end-users using edge computing resources. By handling some pre-processing tasks at the edge, they were able to reduce the amount of data sent to the centralized model, speeding up the overall process.
- **Autoscaling:** The cloud infrastructure was configured to automatically scale based on real-time demand. During peak hours, additional instances were spun up to handle the increased load, and during off-

peak times, the system scaled down to save costs.

4) Efficient Serving with Triton Inference Server:

- **Using NVIDIA Triton:** The team transitioned to using the NVIDIA Triton Inference Server, which is designed for high-performance inference at scale. Triton's support for dynamic batching, model versioning, and GPU optimization helped reduce latency and improve overall efficiency.
- **Multi-Model Serving:** Triton also allowed the team to serve multiple versions of the model, including a lightweight version for handling less complex queries and the full model for more challenging tasks. This tiered approach helped balance resource usage and maintain fast response times.

Results and Outcomes

After implementing these optimizations, the team saw significant improvements in both latency and scalability:

- **Latency Reduction:** The average inference latency dropped from 500 milliseconds to under 150 milliseconds, comfortably meeting the sub-200ms target. This improvement was crucial for maintaining a smooth and responsive user experience.
- **Scalability:** The system was able to handle a 5x increase in concurrent users without any noticeable degradation in performance. The combination of dynamic batching, parallel inference, and autoscaling allowed the platform to scale efficiently with demand.
- **Cost Efficiency:** By optimizing resource usage through model compression, quantization, and autoscaling, the team was able to reduce the overall cost of deployment. The use of edge computing also minimized the need for expensive centralized infrastructure.

User Impact:

- **Improved User Satisfaction:** With faster, more reliable responses, customer satisfaction ratings improved significantly. Users appreciated the immediate and accurate support provided by the GPT-powered chatbot.
- **Reduced Workload on Human Agents:** The optimized system effectively handled a large volume of routine queries, freeing up human agents to focus on more complex issues that required personal attention.

This case study demonstrates how optimizing a large language model like GPT for real-time applications requires a multifaceted approach. By combining model compression, efficient batching and parallelization, infrastructure optimization, and the use of advanced serving frameworks, it's possible to deploy LLMs that meet strict performance requirements while remaining scalable and cost-effective. These strategies can be applied across various industries where real-time interaction with AI is critical, ensuring that large models can deliver on their potential in practical, production environments.

9.6 Tools and Frameworks for Model Optimization

Optimizing large language models (LLMs) for production requires not only a solid understanding of various techniques but also the right tools and frameworks to implement these optimizations effectively. In this section, we'll explore some of the most widely used tools and frameworks that can help streamline the process of optimizing and deploying LLMs in production environments. These tools cover a range of needs, from model compression to serving and monitoring, ensuring that your models are both efficient and scalable.

1. Model Compression Tools

Model compression is essential for reducing the size and computational requirements of LLMs without sacrificing too much accuracy. Here are some key tools that can help you achieve this:

1) TensorFlow Model Optimization Toolkit:

- **Overview:** TensorFlow's Model Optimization Toolkit provides a suite of techniques for model compression, including quantization, pruning, and clustering. It integrates seamlessly with TensorFlow models and allows for both post-training and quantization-aware training.
- **Use Cases:** Ideal for developers using TensorFlow who want to reduce model size and improve performance on resource-constrained devices.

2) PyTorch Model Pruning:

- **Overview:** PyTorch offers built-in support for model pruning through its torch.nn.utils.prune module. This allows developers to prune model weights based on various criteria, such as magnitude or sparsity, making it easier to reduce model size and improve efficiency.
- **Use Cases:** Useful for PyTorch users who need to implement structured or unstructured pruning in their models.

3) Open Neural Network Exchange (ONNX):

- **Overview:** ONNX is an open-source format for representing machine learning models that supports interoperability between different frameworks, including TensorFlow, PyTorch, and others. ONNX provides tools for optimizing models through techniques like quantization and can significantly reduce model size and inference latency.
- **Use Cases:** Suitable for developers working across multiple frameworks who need a common format for model optimization and deploy-

ment.

2. Inference Serving Frameworks

Efficient serving of LLMs requires robust frameworks that can handle high throughput, low latency, and scalability. Here are some leading frameworks that cater to these needs:

1) TensorFlow Serving:

- **Overview:** TensorFlow Serving is a flexible, high-performance serving system specifically designed for deploying machine learning models in production environments. It supports TensorFlow models natively and offers features like versioning, batching, and A/B testing.
- **Use Cases:** Best for TensorFlow users looking for a well-integrated, scalable serving solution with support for real-time inference.

2) TorchServe:

- **Overview:** TorchServe, a collaboration between AWS and Facebook, is a model-serving framework tailored for PyTorch models. It provides easy-to-use APIs, multi-model serving capabilities, and extensive logging and metrics support.
- **Use Cases:** Ideal for deploying PyTorch models in production with minimal overhead and extensive customization options.

3) NVIDIA Triton Inference Server:

- **Overview:** NVIDIA Triton is a versatile inference server that supports multiple frameworks, including TensorFlow, PyTorch, ONNX, and more. It's optimized for deployment on NVIDIA GPUs and offers advanced features like dynamic batching, concurrent model execution, and multi-GPU support.

- **Use Cases:** Perfect for high-performance applications that require the efficient deployment of models across multiple GPUs, particularly in environments with heavy AI workloads.

3. Profiling and Monitoring Tools

Optimizing models for production is not a one-time task—it requires continuous monitoring and profiling to ensure that performance remains optimal. Here are some tools that can help you track and optimize your models in real-time:

1) NVIDIA Nsight Systems:

- **Overview:** NVIDIA Nsight Systems is a comprehensive tool for profiling applications running on NVIDIA GPUs. It provides detailed insights into GPU utilization, memory usage, and kernel execution times, helping you identify bottlenecks and optimize performance.
- **Use Cases:** Essential for developers running models on NVIDIA GPUs who need to optimize performance at a granular level.

2) Prometheus and Grafana:

- **Overview:** Prometheus is an open-source monitoring system that collects metrics from your applications and infrastructure, while Grafana is a powerful visualization tool that allows you to create dashboards based on those metrics. Together, they provide a robust solution for monitoring the health and performance of your deployed models.
- **Use Cases:** Useful for any production environment where ongoing monitoring of model performance, resource utilization, and system health is required.

3) TensorBoard:

- **Overview:** TensorBoard is a visualization toolkit that comes with TensorFlow but can also be used with other frameworks. It provides real-time visualizations of metrics like loss, accuracy, and model graphs, making it easier to debug and optimize models during and after training.
- **Use Cases:** Best suited for developers who want to monitor training progress, compare model versions, and analyze performance metrics in a visually intuitive way.

4. Orchestration and Deployment Tools

Efficiently deploying and managing models at scale often requires sophisticated orchestration and deployment tools. Here are some key options:

1) Kubernetes:

- **Overview:** Kubernetes is an open-source container orchestration platform that automates the deployment, scaling, and management of containerized applications. It's widely used for deploying machine learning models in production, especially when combined with tools like TensorFlow Serving or Triton.
- **Use Cases:** Ideal for large-scale deployments where models need to be managed across multiple nodes, with automatic scaling and failover support.

2) Kubeflow:

- **Overview:** Kubeflow is a machine learning toolkit for Kubernetes that streamlines the deployment and management of ML workflows. It integrates with popular frameworks and tools, providing a unified platform for deploying, serving, and monitoring models at scale.
- **Use Cases:** Best for organizations that need to manage complex ML pipelines and deployments within a Kubernetes environment.

3) AWS SageMaker:

- **Overview:** AWS SageMaker is a fully managed service that provides every tool needed to build, train, and deploy machine learning models at scale. It includes features for model training, hyperparameter tuning, model hosting, and monitoring, all within the AWS ecosystem.
- **Use Cases:** Ideal for teams that prefer an end-to-end managed service for deploying ML models, particularly within AWS infrastructure.

Choosing the right tools and frameworks is essential for successfully optimizing and deploying large language models in production. Whether you're compressing models to fit within resource constraints, serving them efficiently to handle high traffic, or monitoring their performance in real-time, the tools and frameworks discussed here provide a comprehensive toolkit to meet your needs. By leveraging these resources, you can ensure that your models are not only powerful but also efficient, scalable, and reliable, ready to deliver on the demands of real-world applications.

Chapter 10: Debugging and Troubleshooting LLMs

10.1 Common Issues in LLM Training and Deployment

Training and deploying large language models (LLMs) can be a complex process, with various challenges that can arise at different stages. Understanding the common issues that typically occur during LLM training and deployment is crucial for efficiently diagnosing problems and ensuring smooth operation. In this section, we'll explore some of the most frequent challenges faced by practitioners and provide insights into how to recognize and address them.

1. Training Instability

Training large language models is often an unpredictable process, with instability being a common issue. This instability can manifest in several ways, including sudden spikes in loss, divergence of the model, or failure to converge.

1) Vanishing and Exploding Gradients:

- **The Issue:** Vanishing gradients occur when the gradients used to update the model's weights become very small, effectively stalling learning. Exploding gradients, on the other hand, cause the model's parameters to grow uncontrollably, leading to numerical instability.

- **Signs:** Symptoms include unusually slow training progress (in the case of vanishing gradients) or sudden, large changes in loss (in the case of exploding gradients).
- **Solution:** Implement techniques like gradient clipping to prevent gradients from exploding, and use appropriate initialization methods (e.g., Xavier or He initialization) to mitigate vanishing gradients.

2) Learning Rate Problems:

- **The Issue:** Choosing an inappropriate learning rate is a common pitfall. A learning rate that's too high can cause the model to overshoot minima, leading to erratic training behavior, while a learning rate that's too low can result in slow convergence.
- **Signs:** Look for loss that fluctuates wildly or decreases very slowly. This can indicate that the learning rate needs adjustment.
- **Solution:** Use learning rate schedulers to dynamically adjust the learning rate during training, starting with a higher rate and gradually decreasing it as training progresses. Techniques like warmup phases can also help stabilize training in the initial stages.

3) Overfitting:

- **The Issue:** Overfitting occurs when the model performs well on the training data but fails to generalize to new, unseen data. This is particularly problematic with LLMs, which have a high capacity to memorize training data.
- **Signs:** If your model shows a large gap between training and validation loss, or if it performs poorly on validation or test sets while doing well on training data, overfitting is likely.
- **Solution:** Apply regularization techniques such as dropout, weight decay, or data augmentation. Also, consider reducing the complexity

of the model or using techniques like early stopping to prevent overfitting.

2. Data Quality and Preprocessing Issues

Data quality and preprocessing play a critical role in the performance of LLMs. Poor quality data or improper preprocessing can lead to significant issues, ranging from biased outputs to outright failure of the model to learn effectively.

1) Noisy or Inconsistent Data:

- **The Issue:** LLMs trained on noisy or inconsistent data may learn incorrect patterns, leading to poor generalization and unreliable outputs. Noise can include irrelevant information, mislabeled data, or inconsistent formatting.
- **Signs:** Symptoms include erratic or unexpected model behavior, such as generating nonsensical outputs or failing to perform well on tasks the data should have prepared it for.
- **Solution:** Clean and preprocess your data thoroughly before training. This includes normalizing text, removing duplicates, correcting errors, and ensuring consistent formatting. Techniques like data augmentation can help to create more robust models by exposing them to a wider variety of inputs.

2) Bias in Training Data:

- **The Issue:** Bias in training data can lead to biased models, which may produce outputs that are unfair or discriminatory. This is a significant concern, particularly when deploying models in sensitive applications like hiring, law enforcement, or healthcare.
- **Signs:** Look for systematic errors in the model's predictions that correlate with specific demographics or input characteristics, indicating

potential bias.

- **Solution:** Analyze your training data for bias before training, and apply techniques like balanced sampling or synthetic data generation to mitigate these biases. Post-training, fairness metrics can help assess the model's behavior and identify any biased outcomes.

3) Tokenization Errors:

- **The Issue:** Tokenization is the process of breaking down text into tokens that the model can process. Incorrect or inconsistent tokenization can lead to poor model performance, particularly if the model misinterprets important tokens or phrases.
- **Signs:** Poor performance on tasks requiring a nuanced understanding of language, such as sentiment analysis or named entity recognition, can indicate tokenization issues.
- **Solution:** Use a tokenizer that is well-suited to your language model and data. Ensure that your tokenization process is consistent across training and inference. For custom vocabularies, carefully design and test the tokenizer to avoid errors.

3. Deployment Challenges

Once trained, deploying LLMs comes with its own set of challenges. These issues often revolve around performance, scalability, and ensuring that the model operates as expected in a production environment.

1) Latency and Throughput Issues:

- **The Issue:** LLMs can be computationally intensive, leading to high inference latency and low throughput. This can be particularly problematic in applications where real-time or near-real-time responses are required.
- **Signs:** High response times during inference, or the inability to handle

expected traffic volumes, indicate latency and throughput issues.
- **Solution:** Optimize the model by using techniques like quantization, pruning, or distillation. Implement caching mechanisms, efficient batching, and, where possible, deploy models on hardware that's optimized for machine learning tasks, such as GPUs or TPUs.

2) Scalability Problems:

- **The Issue:** As user demand grows, the system must scale to handle increasing loads without degrading performance. Poorly designed systems may struggle to scale, leading to slow response times, downtime, or failures.
- **Signs:** Inability to handle peak traffic, frequent timeouts, or crashes under load are signs of scalability problems.
- **Solution:** Use cloud-based solutions that support auto-scaling, implement load balancing to distribute traffic evenly across servers, and consider deploying smaller, more efficient model versions for handling less complex queries.

3) Model Drift:

- **The Issue:** Over time, the performance of LLMs can degrade as the data distribution they encounter in the real world drifts from the data they were trained on. This can lead to a decrease in accuracy and reliability.
- **Signs:** A gradual decline in model performance over time, particularly on new data or in changing environments, is indicative of model drift.
- **Solution:** Regularly retrain your model using updated data that reflects the current environment. Implement monitoring tools to detect performance drops and set up a feedback loop to incorporate new data into your training process.

Addressing common issues in LLM training and deployment requires a proactive approach, from careful data preprocessing to thoughtful deployment strategies. By being aware of these potential pitfalls and understanding how to identify and resolve them, you can build and deploy LLMs that are robust, efficient, and capable of performing reliably in production environments. In the next section, we'll delve into specific techniques for identifying and resolving bugs in LLMs, ensuring that your models operate as expected in a variety of conditions.

10.2 Techniques for Identifying and Resolving Bugs

Debugging large language models (LLMs) can be a challenging process due to their complexity and the vast amount of data they process. However, with the right techniques, you can systematically identify and resolve bugs that arise during training, deployment, or inference. This section covers effective methods for diagnosing and fixing issues in LLMs, helping you maintain reliable and high-performing models.

1. Systematic Debugging Approach

A structured approach to debugging is essential for efficiently identifying and resolving issues. This process involves breaking down the problem, isolating the cause, and applying targeted fixes.

1) Reproduce the Issue:

- **Understand the Problem:** The first step in debugging is to reproduce the issue consistently. Whether it's a training failure, unexpected output during inference, or performance degradation, being able to replicate the problem is crucial for understanding its nature.
- **Use Consistent Inputs:** Ensure that you're using consistent inputs and configurations when reproducing the issue. This helps rule out external factors and focuses your investigation on the model and code.

2) Isolate the Cause:

- **Component Testing:** Break down your model into individual components (e.g., data preprocessing, specific layers, inference pipeline) and test them independently. This can help you identify whether the issue lies within a specific part of the model or a broader system interaction.
- **Simplify the Model:** Simplify your model by removing or disabling certain features or layers. If the problem disappears when certain components are removed, it's likely that the issue resides within those components.

3) Examine the Data Flow:

- **Trace Inputs and Outputs:** Follow the data as it moves through the model to ensure it's being processed as expected. Check intermediate outputs at various stages to identify where the data may be getting distorted or mishandled.
- **Validate Assumptions:** Verify that all assumptions about the data and model behavior are correct. This includes ensuring that inputs are properly preprocessed, data types are consistent, and the model's architecture is as intended.

2. Debugging Training Issues

Training large language models involves handling a variety of challenges, from convergence problems to overfitting. Here are some specific techniques for debugging issues that occur during training.

1) Monitoring Loss Curves:

- **Identify Patterns:** Loss curves provide valuable insights into how your model is learning. Look for patterns like stagnation (where the loss plateaus), divergence (where the loss increases), or instability (where the loss fluctuates wildly). These patterns can help you pinpoint issues such as learning rate problems, inappropriate initialization, or data issues.

- **Cross-Validation:** Use cross-validation to ensure that your model is not overfitting or underfitting. A significant difference between training and validation loss often indicates that the model is not generalizing well, which might require adjustments to the model complexity or regularization techniques.

2) Gradient Checks:

- **Check for Anomalies:** Gradients play a crucial role in training by guiding the optimization process. If gradients are too small (vanishing gradients) or too large (exploding gradients), it can lead to training failure. Regularly inspect the gradients to ensure they are within reasonable ranges.
- **Gradient Clipping:** If you detect exploding gradients, implement gradient clipping to cap the gradients at a specific threshold. This helps stabilize training and prevent the model from diverging.

3) Hyperparameter Tuning:

- **Learning Rate Adjustments:** The learning rate is one of the most critical hyperparameters. If the model is not converging, experiment with different learning rates. Use techniques like learning rate schedules or adaptive learning rates to fine-tune this parameter dynamically.
- **Batch Size and Momentum:** Other hyperparameters, such as batch size and momentum, also impact training stability. Try different configurations to find the optimal balance that allows the model to learn effectively without introducing noise or instability.

3. Debugging Inference and Deployment Issues

Once the model is trained, issues may still arise during deployment or inference, particularly in production environments. These problems often relate to performance, accuracy, or unexpected behavior.

1) Model Output Analysis:

- **Check for Consistency:** Ensure that the model's outputs are consistent with expectations. Inconsistent or illogical outputs may indicate issues with the inference pipeline, such as incorrect data preprocessing, model versioning errors, or bugs in the post-processing logic.
- **Compare Against Benchmarks:** Benchmark your model's outputs against a known, reliable model or dataset. Discrepancies can help you identify if the issue lies with the model itself or with the deployment setup.

2) Latency and Throughput Monitoring:

- **Profiling Tools:** Use profiling tools to monitor latency and throughput during inference. Tools like NVIDIA Nsight, TensorFlow Profiler, or PyTorch Profiler can help you identify bottlenecks in the model or the serving infrastructure.
- **Optimize Inference Pipeline:** If latency is high, consider optimizing the inference pipeline by using techniques like batch processing, caching, or deploying the model on hardware optimized for inference, such as GPUs or TPUs.

3) Version Control and Rollbacks:

- **Track Model Versions:** Keep detailed records of model versions, including changes in hyperparameters, training data, and code. If a new version of the model introduces issues, being able to roll back to a previous, stable version is crucial.

- **Test in Staging Environments:** Before deploying a new model version to production, thoroughly test it in a staging environment that closely mirrors the production setup. This helps catch any deployment-specific bugs that might not appear during development or testing.

4. Tools and Best Practices for Debugging

Leveraging the right tools and adhering to best practices can significantly streamline the debugging process.

1) Integrated Development Environments (IDEs):

- **Debugging Features:** Use IDEs like PyCharm, Visual Studio Code, or Jupyter Notebooks, which offer robust debugging tools such as breakpoints, variable inspection, and step-by-step execution. These features make it easier to identify where and why a problem is occurring in your code.
- **Code Versioning:** Implement version control using tools like Git to track changes to your model and codebase. This not only helps in debugging but also ensures that you can revert to previous versions if needed.

2) Logging and Monitoring:

- **Detailed Logging:** Implement comprehensive logging throughout your model pipeline, including data preprocessing, model training, and inference stages. Logs provide a detailed record of the model's behavior, making it easier to identify and diagnose issues.
- **Real-Time Monitoring:** Set up real-time monitoring for your production models. Tools like Prometheus, Grafana, and ELK Stack (Elasticsearch, Logstash, and Kibana) can help you monitor metrics such as response times, error rates, and resource utilization, allowing

for quick identification of issues.

3) Collaborative Debugging:

- **Pair Programming:** Collaborate with peers through pair programming or code reviews to identify bugs that you might have missed. A fresh perspective can often lead to quicker problem resolution.
- **Community Resources:** Don't hesitate to leverage community resources such as forums, Stack Overflow, or GitHub issues. Many common problems have already been encountered and solved by others, so searching for existing solutions can save you time and effort.

Debugging large language models requires a systematic approach, a deep understanding of both the model and its environment, and the right set of tools and practices. By reproducing issues, isolating their causes, and applying targeted solutions, you can effectively resolve bugs and ensure that your models perform reliably in production. In the next section, we'll focus on identifying and addressing performance bottlenecks, another critical aspect of maintaining high-performing LLMs.

10.3 Performance Bottlenecks and How to Address Them

Performance bottlenecks can significantly impact the efficiency and usability of large language models (LLMs) in production. These bottlenecks can occur during training, deployment, or inference, and they often lead to slower processing times, increased costs, and degraded user experiences. In this section, we'll discuss common sources of performance bottlenecks in LLMs and provide strategies for identifying and addressing them.

1. Identifying Performance Bottlenecks

The first step in addressing performance bottlenecks is identifying where they occur. Bottlenecks can manifest in various ways, including increased latency, higher computational costs, or reduced throughput.

1) Profiling and Monitoring Tools:

- **Use Profiling Tools:** Profiling tools like NVIDIA Nsight, TensorBoard, and PyTorch Profiler allow you to monitor your model's performance in real-time. These tools provide insights into GPU/CPU utilization, memory usage, and the time taken by different operations, helping you pinpoint exactly where the bottlenecks are.
- **Monitor Metrics:** Regularly monitor key performance metrics such as inference latency, training time per epoch, and resource utilization (CPU, GPU, memory). Significant deviations from expected values can indicate bottlenecks.

2) Analyzing Logs and Performance Data:

- **Review Logs:** Detailed logs can reveal patterns that suggest performance issues. For instance, frequent garbage collection events might indicate memory leaks, while repeated timeouts could point to network-related bottlenecks.
- **Compare with Benchmarks:** Compare your model's performance against known benchmarks or past performance data. A decline in performance can signal the onset of a bottleneck.

3) Simulate High Load Conditions:

- **Stress Testing:** Simulate high load conditions to see how your model and infrastructure handle increased demand. Stress testing can reveal scalability issues and help you identify potential bottlenecks before they impact production.

2. Common Sources of Performance Bottlenecks

Several factors can contribute to performance bottlenecks in LLMs. Understanding these sources can help you focus your optimization efforts where they will have the most impact.

1) Inefficient Data Handling:

- **Data Loading and Preprocessing:** Slow data loading and preprocessing can become significant bottlenecks, especially with large datasets. If the model is waiting for data, it leads to underutilized computational resources.
- **Solution:** Use data pipelines that support parallel data loading and preprocessing. Tools like TensorFlow's tf.data API or PyTorch's DataLoader with multiple workers can help speed up these processes. Additionally, prefetching data into memory can reduce wait times during training and inference.

2) Model Complexity:

- **Excessive Model Size:** Large models with millions or billions of parameters require significant computational power and memory. This can lead to longer inference times and increased latency.
- **Solution:** Consider model compression techniques such as pruning, quantization, and distillation. These methods reduce the model's size and complexity without significantly sacrificing performance. Additionally, evaluate whether the full complexity of the model is necessary for the task at hand—sometimes, a smaller, more efficient model can achieve similar results with fewer resources.

3) Hardware Limitations:

- **Underpowered Hardware:** Running complex models on hardware that doesn't meet the required specifications can lead to significant bottlenecks. For instance, using CPUs instead of GPUs or TPUs for inference can drastically increase latency.
- **Solution:** Deploy your models on hardware optimized for AI workloads. GPUs and TPUs are designed for high-throughput, parallel processing, making them ideal for serving LLMs. Ensure that your hardware is sufficient to handle the model's requirements, especially during peak loads.

4) Inefficient Code and Model Architecture:

- **Suboptimal Code:** Inefficient coding practices, such as redundant calculations, excessive data copying, or poorly optimized algorithms, can introduce performance bottlenecks.
- **Solution:** Review and optimize your code for performance. Utilize vectorized operations, minimize data transfers between CPU and GPU, and remove any unnecessary computations. Additionally, consider optimizing the model's architecture by using techniques like layer fusion, where compatible layers are merged to reduce computational overhead.

5) Network Latency:

- **Distributed Systems:** In systems where the model is distributed across multiple nodes or relies on remote data sources, network latency can become a bottleneck, particularly if data needs to be transferred frequently.
- **Solution:** Minimize data transfers by keeping as much computation local as possible. Use techniques like model parallelism or edge computing to distribute workloads effectively, reducing the reliance on network bandwidth. Additionally, optimize network configurations and use low-latency connections for critical operations.

3. Strategies for Addressing Performance Bottlenecks

Once you've identified the sources of performance bottlenecks, the next step is to implement strategies to mitigate or eliminate them.

1) Optimize Data Pipelines:

- **Batch Processing:** Use batch processing to group multiple inputs into a single operation. This reduces the per-operation overhead and improves throughput, especially during inference.
- **Asynchronous Data Loading:** Implement asynchronous data loading and processing to ensure that the model is always receiving data without waiting. This can be achieved using tools like TensorFlow's tf.data or PyTorch's DataLoader with async I/O.

2) Leverage Mixed Precision and Quantization:

- **Mixed Precision Training:** Mixed precision training uses both 16-bit and 32-bit floating-point operations, reducing memory usage and speeding up computation. This is particularly effective on GPUs with Tensor Cores that are optimized for mixed precision.
- **Post-Training Quantization:** Apply quantization techniques after training to reduce the model's memory footprint and increase inference speed, especially in resource-constrained environments.

3) Parallelism and Distributed Computing:

- **Model Parallelism:** Distribute different parts of the model across multiple GPUs or nodes to parallelize computations. This can reduce the overall computation time and improve scalability.
- **Data Parallelism:** Implement data parallelism by splitting the input data across multiple devices, allowing the model to process different batches simultaneously. This approach is particularly effective in

distributed training environments.

4) Improve Model Serving Efficiency:

- **Caching:** Implement caching strategies to store and reuse frequently requested inferences. This reduces the need for the model to repeatedly process the same inputs, saving time and computational resources.
- **Dynamic Batching:** Use dynamic batching to group incoming requests into batches in real-time, optimizing GPU utilization and reducing latency.

4. Best Practices for Continuous Performance Monitoring

Addressing performance bottlenecks is not a one-time task; it requires ongoing monitoring and optimization to ensure that your models continue to perform well in production.

1) Regular Profiling and Benchmarking:

- **Scheduled Profiling:** Regularly profile your models and infrastructure to identify potential bottlenecks early. This should be part of your ongoing maintenance routine, especially after deploying updates or scaling the system.
- **Benchmarking:** Continuously benchmark your models against key performance indicators (KPIs) such as latency, throughput, and accuracy. This helps maintain performance standards and provides a baseline for comparison when making changes.

2) Adaptive Resource Management:

- **Autoscaling:** Implement autoscaling mechanisms that automatically adjust the number of resources based on real-time demand. This ensures that your system remains responsive under varying loads without over-provisioning resources.

- **Resource Allocation:** Dynamically allocate resources based on current needs, prioritizing critical tasks and scaling down non-essential processes during peak times.

3) Feedback Loops:

- **Monitor and Adapt:** Set up feedback loops to continuously monitor performance metrics and adapt the system accordingly. Use tools like Prometheus, Grafana, and ELK Stack for real-time monitoring and alerting.
- **User Feedback:** Incorporate user feedback to identify areas where performance improvements can have the most impact. Understanding how users interact with the system can provide valuable insights for optimization.

Performance bottlenecks can hinder the effectiveness of large language models, especially in production environments where speed and efficiency are critical. By systematically identifying and addressing these bottlenecks—whether they arise from data handling, model complexity, hardware limitations, or inefficient code—you can ensure that your LLMs deliver optimal performance. In the next section, we'll explore how to handle edge cases in LLM applications, ensuring that your models can gracefully manage unusual or unexpected inputs.

10.4 Handling Edge Cases in LLM Applications

Edge cases are those rare or unexpected scenarios that a model might encounter in production, which it wasn't specifically trained or optimized for. While large language models (LLMs) are powerful and versatile, they can still struggle with these unusual inputs, leading to errors, unintended behavior, or even failures. Effectively handling edge cases is crucial for building robust and reliable AI systems. In this section, we'll explore strategies for identifying, managing, and mitigating edge cases in LLM applications.

1. Understanding Edge Cases

Edge cases in LLMs can arise from a variety of sources, including atypical input data, unexpected combinations of input features, or interactions that the model was not designed to handle. These cases can lead to degraded performance, incorrect outputs, or failures that impact the user experience.

1) Types of Edge Cases:

- **Unseen or Uncommon Inputs:** Inputs that are rare in the training data, such as obscure language, dialects, or domain-specific jargon.
- **Ambiguous Queries:** Inputs that are open to multiple interpretations, where the model might choose the wrong context or meaning.
- **Out-of-Distribution Inputs:** Inputs that differ significantly from the training data, such as foreign languages or completely new topics.
- **Complex Combinations:** Inputs that involve complex relationships or dependencies that the model may not have adequately learned during training.

2) Why Edge Cases Matter:

- **Impact on Reliability:** Failing to handle edge cases can lead to a loss of trust in the AI system, especially in critical applications like healthcare, finance, or customer support.
- **User Experience:** Poor handling of edge cases can frustrate users, especially if the model provides nonsensical or irrelevant responses.

2. Strategies for Identifying Edge Cases

The first step in managing edge cases is identifying them effectively. This can be done through a combination of data analysis, user feedback, and stress testing.

1) Data Analysis:

- **Analyze Error Patterns:** Review errors and unexpected outputs in your model's performance to identify common characteristics of edge cases. Look for patterns in failed predictions or inconsistent behavior.
- **Diversity Audits:** Conduct audits on your training and test datasets to ensure they include a wide range of inputs. Identify any gaps where certain types of inputs or scenarios are underrepresented.

2) User Feedback and Monitoring:

- **Gather User Feedback:** Encourage users to report instances where the model's response was incorrect or inadequate. This direct feedback can help you identify edge cases that occur in real-world usage.
- **Monitoring Systems:** Implement monitoring tools that track the types of inputs your model receives in production. Look for anomalies or unexpected distributions that might indicate edge cases.

3) Stress Testing and Adversarial Testing:

- **Stress Testing:** Push your model to its limits by feeding it challenging inputs that are likely to trigger edge cases. This could include very long inputs, inputs with ambiguous context, or highly technical language.
- **Adversarial Testing:** Use adversarial testing techniques to deliberately create inputs designed to confuse or mislead the model. This helps in identifying weaknesses and areas where the model might be vulnerable to edge cases.

3. Techniques for Managing Edge Cases

Once edge cases have been identified, the next step is to develop strategies to handle them effectively.

1) Data Augmentation:

- **Expand Training Data:** Augment your training data with examples of identified edge cases. This can involve collecting additional data or generating synthetic data that represents the edge cases.
- **Diverse Datasets:** Use diverse datasets during training that include a wide range of scenarios and input types. This helps the model generalize better to edge cases.

2) Specialized Models and Fine-Tuning:

- **Domain-Specific Fine-Tuning:** Fine-tune your model on domain-specific data to improve its performance on edge cases that are relevant to that domain. For example, a medical chatbot could be fine-tuned on medical literature to handle rare medical terms or conditions.
- **Ensemble Models:** Use an ensemble of specialized models, each trained to handle different types of edge cases. The outputs of these models can be combined or selected based on the input type.

3) Fallback Mechanisms:

- **Rule-Based Systems:** Implement rule-based systems as a fallback for when the model encounters inputs it's unsure about. These rules can handle straightforward tasks or provide default responses when the model's confidence is low.
- **Human-in-the-Loop:** For critical applications, consider involving human operators who can review and correct the model's outputs in edge cases. This ensures accuracy while still leveraging the speed and

scalability of the model.

4) Confidence Scoring and Thresholding:

- **Confidence Scores:** Implement confidence scoring to assess how certain the model is about its predictions. For low-confidence predictions, the system can trigger alternative actions, such as requesting clarification from the user or escalating to a human operator.
- **Thresholding:** Set confidence thresholds that determine when the model should rely on its predictions versus when it should defer to a fallback mechanism.

4. Mitigating the Impact of Edge Cases

While it may not be possible to eliminate all edge cases, you can mitigate their impact through careful design and robust system architecture.

1) User Communication:

- **Transparent Feedback:** Clearly communicate to users when the model is uncertain or has provided a fallback response. Transparency helps manage user expectations and maintains trust in the system.
- **Requesting Clarification:** Encourage users to provide additional context or clarify their queries when the model struggles with edge cases. This can improve the model's performance and reduce frustration.

2) Continuous Learning:

- **Iterative Improvement:** Use the data collected from edge cases to iteratively improve the model. Regular updates based on real-world usage data help the model adapt to new and unforeseen scenarios.
- **Retraining on Edge Cases:** Regularly retrain your model on edge case data to ensure it stays current with the types of inputs it's likely to

encounter in production.

3) Monitoring and Alerting:

- **Real-Time Monitoring:** Continuously monitor the model's performance, particularly in scenarios known to involve edge cases. Set up alerts for when the model encounters inputs that fall outside normal operating conditions.
- **Feedback Loops:** Establish feedback loops that allow edge case data to be quickly incorporated into future model updates, ensuring the model evolves with changing inputs and user needs.

Handling edge cases effectively is key to deploying robust and reliable LLMs in production. By identifying potential edge cases through data analysis, user feedback, and testing, and by implementing strategies such as data augmentation, specialized models, and fallback mechanisms, you can significantly improve your model's ability to manage these scenarios. In the next section, we'll delve into logging and monitoring practices that further enhance your ability to troubleshoot and maintain high-performing models in production.

10.5 Logging and Monitoring for Effective Troubleshooting

Effective logging and monitoring are essential components of maintaining and troubleshooting large language models (LLMs) in production. These practices not only help in diagnosing issues when they arise but also in proactively identifying potential problems before they impact users. In this section, we'll discuss the best practices for setting up logging and monitoring systems that enable you to keep your LLMs running smoothly and efficiently.

1. The Importance of Logging and Monitoring

Logging and monitoring serve as the eyes and ears of your production system. They provide visibility into the behavior of your LLMs, allowing you to track performance, detect anomalies, and diagnose problems in real-time.

1) Logging:

- **Detailed Record-Keeping:** Logs capture detailed records of events, errors, and system operations. They are invaluable for understanding the sequence of actions leading up to an issue, making it easier to pinpoint the root cause.
- **Post-Mortem Analysis:** Logs are crucial for post-mortem analysis after an incident. They help you reconstruct the events that led to a failure, ensuring that similar issues can be prevented in the future.

2) Monitoring:

- **Real-Time Insight:** Monitoring provides real-time insight into the health and performance of your LLMs. It helps you detect issues as they occur, enabling you to take swift corrective action.
- **Trend Analysis:** Over time, monitoring data can be used to identify trends in performance, resource usage, and user behavior, allowing you to optimize your system proactively.

2. Best Practices for Setting Up Logging

To make the most of logging, it's important to implement best practices that ensure your logs are comprehensive, useful, and easy to interpret.

1) Log Everything Relevant:

- **Errors and Exceptions:** Always log errors and exceptions with as much detail as possible, including stack traces, input data, and the specific operation that failed. This information is crucial for diagnosing and fixing issues.
- **Model Outputs and Decisions:** Log the model's outputs, including confidence scores and any decisions made during inference. This helps in understanding how the model arrived at a particular conclusion, which is useful for debugging and optimization.
- **System Events:** Log key system events such as model deployments, updates, and scaling actions. This provides context when reviewing logs and helps correlate system changes with performance issues.

2) Use Structured Logging:

- **JSON or XML Formats:** Use structured logging formats like JSON or XML to ensure that logs are machine-readable and easily searchable. Structured logs allow you to query and filter logs based on specific fields, making it easier to find relevant information.
- **Consistent Log Levels:** Implement consistent log levels (e.g., DEBUG, INFO, WARN, ERROR) across your system. This ensures that you can easily filter logs by severity and focus on the most critical issues.

3) Centralize Logs:

- **Log Aggregation Tools:** Use log aggregation tools like Elasticsearch, Logstash, and Kibana (ELK Stack), or cloud-based solutions like AWS CloudWatch or Google Cloud Logging, to centralize and manage your logs. Centralized logging makes it easier to search, analyze, and visualize logs from different parts of your system.
- **Retention Policies:** Implement log retention policies to manage the storage of logs efficiently. Determine how long logs should be kept based on their relevance and importance, and automate the archival or deletion of older logs.

4) Anonymize and Secure Logs:

- **Data Privacy:** Ensure that logs do not contain sensitive information, especially when working with user data. Anonymize or mask personal data to comply with data privacy regulations.
- **Secure Access:** Restrict access to logs to authorized personnel only, and ensure that logs are stored securely to prevent unauthorized access or tampering.

3. Best Practices for Setting Up Monitoring

Monitoring systems need to be well-designed to provide timely and actionable insights into the performance and health of your LLMs.

1) Key Metrics to Monitor:

- **Performance Metrics:** Monitor key performance metrics such as latency, throughput, and error rates. These metrics give you a real-time view of how well your model is performing and can indicate potential issues before they escalate.
- **Resource Utilization:** Track resource utilization, including CPU, GPU, memory, and disk usage. Monitoring these metrics helps ensure that your infrastructure is not overburdened and that resources are being used efficiently.
- **Model-Specific Metrics:** Implement model-specific metrics such as inference times, confidence scores, and prediction accuracy. These metrics provide insights into the model's behavior and can help identify when retraining or fine-tuning is needed.

2) Alerting and Notifications:

- **Threshold-Based Alerts:** Set up threshold-based alerts that notify you when metrics exceed predefined limits (e.g., latency exceeds 200ms, error rate exceeds 5%). Alerts should be configured to notify the appropriate team members via email, SMS, or messaging apps like Slack.

- **Anomaly Detection:** Implement anomaly detection algorithms that can identify unusual patterns or deviations in your metrics. These systems can automatically flag potential issues that might not be caught by simple threshold-based alerts.

3) Visual Dashboards:

- **Real-Time Dashboards:** Use monitoring tools like Grafana, Prometheus, or Datadog to create real-time dashboards that visualize key metrics. Dashboards should be easy to interpret and provide a comprehensive view of your system's health at a glance.
- **Custom Views:** Create custom views that focus on specific aspects of your system, such as model performance, infrastructure health, or user interaction metrics. Custom views allow different teams to focus on the metrics most relevant to their roles.

4) Automated Remediation:

- **Self-Healing Systems:** Implement automated remediation processes that can address certain issues without human intervention. For example, automatically scaling resources when utilization is high or restarting services when error rates spike.
- **Escalation Policies:** Define escalation policies that determine how alerts are handled. For example, if an alert is not acknowledged within a certain time frame, it can be escalated to a higher level of management.

4. Using Logs and Monitoring Data for Troubleshooting

Logs and monitoring data are invaluable for troubleshooting issues in production. Here's how to leverage this data effectively.

1) Correlate Logs and Metrics:

- **Cross-Reference Data:** When an issue arises, cross-reference logs with monitoring data to identify correlations. For example, a spike in latency might correlate with a specific error logged during that time, helping you trace the problem to its source.
- **Timeline Analysis:** Use timeline analysis to understand the sequence of events leading up to an issue. By analyzing the timing of logs and metric changes, you can often pinpoint the exact moment when things started to go wrong.

2) Root Cause Analysis:

- **Drill Down:** Use the information from logs and monitoring to drill down into specific components or operations that might be causing issues. Detailed logs can help you understand the context of a failure, while monitoring data can show the impact of that failure on overall performance.
- **Iterative Investigation:** Troubleshooting often requires an iterative approach. Start with the most likely causes based on your logs and metrics, and methodically rule out potential issues until you identify the root cause.

3) Post-Incident Reviews:

- **Conduct Post-Mortems:** After resolving an issue, conduct a post-mortem review to analyze what went wrong, how it was fixed, and what can be done to prevent similar issues in the future. Logs and monitoring data should be central to this review process.

- **Continuous Improvement:** Use insights gained from post-incident reviews to improve your logging and monitoring systems. This might include adding new metrics, refining alerts, or adjusting log verbosity.

Effective logging and monitoring are essential for maintaining the health and performance of large language models in production. By implementing best practices for logging, monitoring, and using this data to troubleshoot issues, you can ensure that your LLMs operate reliably and efficiently. In the next section, we'll look at a case study that demonstrates how these principles can be applied to debug a faulty language model in a real-world scenario.

10.6 Case Study: Debugging a Faulty Language Model

In this case study, we'll walk through a real-world scenario where a large language model (LLM) exhibited unexpected behavior in production. We'll examine the steps taken to diagnose the problem, identify the root cause, and implement a solution. This case study highlights the importance of systematic debugging, effective logging, and continuous monitoring in maintaining robust LLM deployments.

Background

A company deployed a GPT-based chatbot to handle customer inquiries on their e-commerce platform. The chatbot was trained on a large dataset of customer service interactions and had been performing well during initial testing. However, shortly after going live, users began reporting issues with the chatbot's responses. Some responses were irrelevant to the questions asked, while others were outright incorrect. These issues led to a poor user experience and a drop in customer satisfaction.

Step 1: Reproducing the Issue

The first step in debugging the faulty language model was to reproduce the issues reported by users. The team reviewed the logs and identified several instances where the chatbot provided incorrect or irrelevant answers.

1) Logs Analysis:

- **Patterns in Errors:** The team noticed that the errors occurred more frequently during certain types of queries, particularly those involving product recommendations and order status updates.
- **Consistency:** The issues were consistent across different users, indicating a systemic problem rather than isolated incidents.

2) Reproducing in a Test Environment:

- **Test Queries:** The team recreated the problematic queries in a test environment to observe the chatbot's behavior under controlled conditions. The same issues were reproduced, confirming that the problem was with the model rather than external factors like network latency or user input errors.

Step 2: Isolating the Cause

With the issue successfully reproduced, the next step was to isolate the cause. The team focused on narrowing down the potential sources of the problem.

1) Model Output Analysis:

- **Reviewing Outputs:** The team reviewed the chatbot's outputs in response to the problematic queries. They noticed that the model often failed to pick up on key contextual clues, leading to irrelevant or incorrect responses.

- **Confidence Scores:** By analyzing the confidence scores associated with the chatbot's responses, the team found that the model was overly confident in its incorrect answers, suggesting an issue with the model's training or inference process.

2) Data Pipeline Inspection:

- **Preprocessing Pipeline:** The team inspected the data preprocessing pipeline to ensure that inputs were being correctly formatted and tokenized before being fed into the model. They discovered that certain special characters and emojis were not being properly handled, leading to garbled inputs.
- **Training Data Review:** A review of the training data revealed that it contained inconsistencies, such as duplicate entries and mislabeled examples. These issues likely contributed to the model's poor performance on specific query types.

3) Infrastructure and Deployment Check:

- **Version Control:** The team checked whether the correct model version was deployed and found that an older, less fine-tuned version had been mistakenly deployed during an update.
- **Resource Utilization:** They also examined the server logs and noticed that the model was occasionally running into memory constraints, leading to incomplete processing of certain inputs.

Step 3: Implementing the Solution

After identifying the root causes—data preprocessing issues, inconsistent training data, deployment of an outdated model version, and resource constraints—the team implemented a series of fixes.

1) Fixing Data Preprocessing:

- **Improved Tokenization:** The team updated the preprocessing pipeline to handle special characters and emojis correctly, ensuring that inputs were clean and consistent.
- **Data Cleaning:** They cleaned the training data to remove duplicates, correct mislabeled examples, and add more diverse examples related to the problematic query types.

2) Model Update and Re-Deployment:

- **Retraining the Model:** The model was retrained using the cleaned and improved dataset. Additional fine-tuning was performed to address specific weaknesses identified during the debugging process.
- **Correct Model Version:** The correct, fine-tuned model version was deployed, replacing the older version that had caused issues.

3) Infrastructure Improvements:

- **Resource Allocation:** The team increased the allocated memory for the model's deployment environment to prevent resource constraints from affecting performance.
- **Monitoring Enhancements:** They also updated the monitoring system to include alerts for memory usage and model version mismatches, ensuring that similar issues would be detected and addressed promptly in the future.

Step 4: Validation and Post-Mortem

With the fixes in place, the team conducted extensive testing to validate the effectiveness of the solutions and to ensure that the chatbot was performing as expected.

1) Testing and Validation:

- **Test Suite:** A comprehensive test suite was used to validate the chatbot's responses across a wide range of queries, including those that had previously caused issues.
- **User Feedback:** The team also monitored user interactions closely after the update, gathering feedback to confirm that the issues were resolved.

2) Post-Mortem Analysis:

- **Root Cause Documentation:** The team documented the root causes of the problem, the steps taken to resolve it, and the lessons learned. This documentation was shared with the broader development and operations teams to prevent similar issues in the future.
- **Process Improvements:** Based on the post-mortem analysis, the team implemented several process improvements, including stricter version control procedures, more rigorous data validation steps, and enhanced monitoring capabilities.

This case study illustrates the importance of a systematic approach to debugging and troubleshooting LLMs. By carefully reproducing the issue, isolating the cause, implementing targeted solutions, and validating the results, the team was able to restore the chatbot's functionality and improve its performance. The lessons learned from this process also led to long-term improvements in how the team manages and monitors LLM deployments, ensuring greater reliability and user satisfaction in the future.

IV

Part IV: Deployment and Scaling

Chapter 11: Production-Ready LLMs

11.1 Preparing LLMs for Deployment

Deploying large language models (LLMs) into production environments is a critical step that requires careful preparation. The transition from development to production involves ensuring that the model is robust, efficient, and capable of operating reliably under real-world conditions. In this section, we'll cover the essential steps to prepare LLMs for deployment, focusing on aspects like testing, optimization, and ensuring that the model is ready to meet the demands of production use.

1. Finalizing the Model

Before deployment, it's important to ensure that the model is finalized and performs well across the key metrics that matter most for your application.

1) Evaluation and Validation:

- **Performance Metrics:** Thoroughly evaluate the model's performance using the metrics most relevant to your use case, such as accuracy, F1 score, or BLEU score. Ensure that the model meets or exceeds the benchmarks you've set during development.
- **Generalization Testing:** Validate the model's ability to generalize to new data by testing it on a separate validation or test set that was not

used during training. This helps ensure that the model will perform well on unseen inputs once deployed.

2) Stress Testing:

- **Edge Cases:** Conduct stress tests by feeding the model challenging or unusual inputs that it might encounter in production. This helps identify potential weaknesses or areas where the model might fail.
- **Scalability Testing:** Simulate high-load conditions to test how the model handles increased traffic. This is particularly important if the model will be used in a high-traffic environment.

3) Model Optimization:

- **Compression Techniques:** Apply model compression techniques such as pruning, quantization, or distillation to reduce the model's size and computational requirements. This helps ensure that the model can operate efficiently in production, especially on resource-constrained environments.
- **Latency Optimization:** Optimize the model for low-latency inference by fine-tuning its architecture or implementing more efficient algorithms. This is crucial for applications where real-time or near-real-time responses are required.

2. Preparing the Infrastructure

The infrastructure supporting your LLM deployment plays a crucial role in ensuring that the model runs efficiently and reliably. Proper preparation of the infrastructure is essential for a smooth deployment.

1) Choosing the Right Environment:

- **Cloud vs. On-Premises:** Decide whether to deploy the model in a cloud environment (e.g., AWS, Google Cloud, Azure) or on-premises. Cloud environments offer scalability and flexibility, while on-premises deployments may provide better control and security for sensitive data.

- **Hardware Considerations:** Ensure that the hardware used for deployment, whether it's CPUs, GPUs, or TPUs, is sufficient to handle the model's computational needs. Consider using specialized AI hardware for optimized performance.

2) Containerization and Orchestration:

- **Containerization:** Package the model and its dependencies into a container (e.g., using Docker) to ensure consistency across different environments. Containers make it easier to deploy, scale, and manage the model in production.
- **Orchestration with Kubernetes:** Use orchestration tools like Kubernetes to manage containerized deployments, automate scaling, and handle failovers. Kubernetes is particularly useful for managing large-scale deployments with multiple instances of the model.

3) Security and Compliance:

- **Data Privacy:** Implement measures to protect user data and ensure compliance with data privacy regulations such as GDPR or HIPAA. This might include encryption of data in transit and at rest, as well as access controls to sensitive information.
- **Access Control:** Restrict access to the deployed model and its infrastructure using role-based access control (RBAC) or similar mechanisms. Ensure that only authorized personnel can make changes to the model or its environment.

3. Deployment Strategy

Choosing the right deployment strategy is key to minimizing downtime and ensuring a smooth transition from development to production.

1) Gradual Rollout:

- **Canary Deployment:** Start with a canary deployment, where the new model is gradually rolled out to a small subset of users. Monitor its performance and gather feedback before fully scaling it to all users. This approach helps catch any issues early and minimizes the impact of potential failures.
- **Blue-Green Deployment:** Consider using a blue-green deployment strategy, where the new version of the model (blue) is deployed alongside the current version (green). Traffic is gradually shifted from green to blue, allowing for a seamless transition and easy rollback if issues arise.

2) Monitoring and Alerts:

- **Real-Time Monitoring:** Set up real-time monitoring of key performance indicators (KPIs) such as latency, error rates, and resource utilization. This allows you to detect and respond to issues quickly.
- **Alerts and Notifications:** Configure alerts for critical metrics so that your team is immediately notified of any issues that could affect the model's performance or availability.

3) Fallback Mechanisms:

- **Fallback Models:** Implement fallback mechanisms, such as using a simpler or previously validated model in case the primary model fails. This ensures continuity of service even if the new model encounters issues.

- **Graceful Degradation:** Design your system to degrade gracefully under heavy load or when facing unexpected issues, such as by reducing the complexity of outputs or limiting certain features to maintain overall stability.

4. Documentation and Knowledge Transfer

Clear documentation and effective knowledge transfer are essential for ensuring that your team is equipped to manage and maintain the deployed model.

1) Comprehensive Documentation:

- **Model Documentation:** Document the model's architecture, training process, hyperparameters, and performance metrics. Include details about any optimizations applied and the rationale behind key design decisions.
- **Deployment Guide:** Provide a detailed deployment guide that covers the steps required to deploy the model, the infrastructure setup, and any specific configurations needed for the production environment.

2) Training and Support:

- **Team Training:** Ensure that the operations team is trained on how to manage and monitor the deployed model. This includes understanding the model's dependencies, how to respond to alerts, and how to roll back to previous versions if necessary.
- **Ongoing Support:** Establish a support plan for addressing any issues that arise post-deployment. This might include setting up a dedicated support channel, regular check-ins, and a process for handling escalations.

Preparing an LLM for deployment requires careful planning and attention to detail. By finalizing and optimizing the model, preparing the infrastructure, choosing the right deployment strategy, and ensuring thorough documentation and knowledge transfer, you can significantly increase the likelihood of a successful deployment. In the following sections, we'll delve deeper into ensuring robustness and reliability in production, as well as the strategies for scaling LLMs to handle large-scale workloads.

11.2 Ensuring Robustness and Reliability in Production

Deploying large language models (LLMs) in production requires not just preparing the model for deployment but also ensuring that it operates reliably and robustly under various conditions. In this section, we'll cover key strategies to maintain the performance and reliability of LLMs once they're in production, helping you avoid downtime and ensure a positive user experience.

1. Building Robustness into the Model

Ensuring robustness starts with the model itself. A robust model can handle a wide range of inputs, manage edge cases gracefully, and continue to perform well under different conditions.

1) Diverse Training Data:

- **Data Diversity:** Train your model on a diverse dataset that includes a wide range of inputs and scenarios. This helps the model generalize better to real-world data and reduces the likelihood of encountering inputs it cannot handle.
- **Augmenting Data:** Use data augmentation techniques to create variations of the training data, exposing the model to different types of noise, context, and ambiguity. This helps the model become more

resilient to variations it might encounter in production.

2) Error Handling Mechanisms:

- **Graceful Degradation:** Implement mechanisms that allow the model to degrade gracefully when it encounters inputs it struggles with. For instance, the model can fall back to simpler responses or trigger predefined error-handling workflows rather than failing outright.
- **Fallback Logic:** Incorporate fallback logic that kicks in when the model's confidence in its output is low. This could involve using a simpler model for certain tasks or providing users with options to clarify their queries.

3) Regularization Techniques:

- **Overfitting Prevention:** Use regularization techniques like dropout, weight decay, or early stopping during training to prevent overfitting. A model that is overfitted to the training data is less likely to perform well on unseen production data, especially in edge cases.
- **Continuous Evaluation:** Regularly evaluate the model on a validation set that includes new and evolving data. This helps ensure that the model continues to generalize well over time and adapts to changes in the data distribution.

2. Implementing Redundancy and Failover Strategies

In production, it's important to anticipate potential failures and have strategies in place to maintain service continuity.

1) Redundant Deployments:

- **Multiple Instances:** Deploy multiple instances of the model across different servers or regions. This ensures that if one instance fails, others can take over, minimizing downtime and ensuring high availability.

- **Load Balancing:** Use load balancers to distribute traffic evenly across multiple model instances. This not only improves performance by preventing any single instance from becoming a bottleneck but also provides a fallback if one instance fails.

2) Failover Mechanisms:

- **Automated Failover:** Implement automated failover mechanisms that detect when a model instance is down and reroute traffic to another instance. This helps maintain uninterrupted service in case of unexpected failures.
- **Hot Standby Models:** Maintain hot standby models—instances that are preloaded and ready to take over if the primary model fails. This reduces the switchover time and ensures that service continues without noticeable disruption.

3) Data Backup and Recovery:

- **Regular Backups:** Regularly back up critical data, including model versions, training datasets, and configuration files. In the event of a failure, having up-to-date backups ensures that you can quickly restore the system to a working state.
- **Disaster Recovery Plan:** Develop and test a disaster recovery plan that outlines the steps to be taken in the event of a major failure, such as a data center outage or significant data corruption. This plan should include how to restore data, redeploy models, and resume operations with minimal impact.

3. Continuous Monitoring and Health Checks

Maintaining robustness and reliability in production requires continuous monitoring of the model's performance and health.

1) Health Checks:

- **Automated Health Checks:** Implement automated health checks that regularly test the model's functionality and responsiveness. These checks can include simple queries to verify that the model is operational and more complex tests to ensure it's performing correctly.
- **Service-Level Indicators (SLIs):** Define and monitor SLIs, such as uptime, response time, and error rates, to ensure that the model meets the required service levels. These indicators help you quickly detect and respond to issues before they impact users.

2) Performance Monitoring:

- **Real-Time Monitoring:** Set up real-time monitoring to track key performance metrics such as latency, throughput, and resource utilization. Use dashboards and alerts to keep the team informed of the model's status and any emerging issues.
- **Long-Term Trend Analysis:** Analyze performance trends over time to identify any gradual degradation in performance, such as increasing latency or error rates. Early detection of such trends allows you to take corrective action before they lead to significant problems.

3) User Feedback Loop:

- **Feedback Integration:** Integrate user feedback into your monitoring system to capture issues that may not be detected by automated checks. Encourage users to report problems and provide a simple mechanism for them to do so.

- **Continuous Improvement:** Use the feedback to continuously improve the model's performance. This might involve retraining the model on new data, adjusting its architecture, or fine-tuning its parameters based on real-world usage.

4. Planning for Scalability

Robustness and reliability also depend on the model's ability to scale as demand increases.

1) Horizontal Scaling:

- **Auto-Scaling:** Implement auto-scaling to automatically adjust the number of model instances based on current demand. This ensures that the system can handle peak loads without performance degradation.
- **Load Testing:** Conduct load testing to determine how well the model scales with increasing traffic. Use the results to fine-tune the auto-scaling parameters and ensure that the system remains responsive under heavy load.

2) Vertical Scaling:

- **Resource Optimization:** Optimize resource usage by ensuring that the model is efficiently using available CPU, GPU, and memory resources. This can involve tuning the model's configuration, optimizing its code, or deploying it on more powerful hardware as needed.
- **Scaling Strategies:** Develop strategies for scaling up the system to handle larger models or more complex workloads. This might involve upgrading hardware, optimizing the deployment architecture, or leveraging distributed computing resources.

Ensuring robustness and reliability in production is essential for maintaining the performance and availability of large language models. By building robustness into the model, implementing redundancy and failover strategies, continuously monitoring performance, and planning for scalability, you can create a production environment where your LLMs operate reliably and deliver consistent results. In the next section, we'll discuss how to set up Continuous Integration and Continuous Deployment (CI/CD) pipelines specifically tailored for LLMs, further enhancing your ability to manage and deploy these models effectively in production.

11.3 Continuous Integration and Continuous Deployment (CI/CD) for LLMs

Incorporating Continuous Integration and Continuous Deployment (CI/CD) practices into the development and deployment pipeline of large language models (LLMs) is essential for maintaining agility, consistency, and reliability. CI/CD helps automate the process of testing, building, and deploying models, ensuring that new updates are smoothly and safely integrated into production. In this section, we'll explore how to set up an effective CI/CD pipeline for LLMs, focusing on best practices and the unique challenges posed by these models.

1. Understanding CI/CD for LLMs

CI/CD is a set of practices that automates the integration and deployment of code changes. For LLMs, these practices are extended to include not only the code but also the data, models, and configurations that are integral to their performance.

1) Continuous Integration (CI):

- **Automated Testing:** CI involves automatically testing changes to the model, data pipeline, or codebase to ensure that they do not introduce errors or degrade performance. This includes unit tests, integration tests, and model-specific tests like accuracy and latency benchmarks.

- **Version Control Integration:** CI is tightly integrated with version control systems (e.g., Git), where every change is automatically tested in an isolated environment before being merged into the main branch.

2) Continuous Deployment (CD):

- **Automated Deployment:** CD automates the process of deploying new versions of the model to production after they pass all tests. This reduces manual intervention and speeds up the deployment process, enabling faster iteration and response to changes in data or requirements.
- **Rollback Mechanisms:** CD pipelines include mechanisms for automatically rolling back to a previous version if the new deployment encounters issues in production. This ensures that service continuity is maintained even when problems arise.

2. Setting Up a CI/CD Pipeline for LLMs

Implementing a CI/CD pipeline for LLMs involves several steps, each tailored to the specific needs of large-scale models and their associated infrastructure.

1) Version Control and Branching Strategy:

- **Version Control:** Use a robust version control system like Git to manage changes to the codebase, model configurations, and even data preprocessing scripts. Every change should be tracked, reviewed, and documented.
- **Branching Strategy:** Adopt a branching strategy such as Gitflow or trunk-based development to manage feature development, hotfixes,

and model updates. Feature branches allow for isolated development, while the main branch remains stable and ready for deployment.

2) Automated Testing:

- **Unit and Integration Tests:** Write unit tests for individual components of the model (e.g., preprocessing functions, data loaders) and integration tests to ensure that all parts of the system work together as expected. These tests should run automatically whenever a change is pushed to the repository.
- **Model-Specific Tests:** Implement tests that evaluate the model's performance on key metrics such as accuracy, F1 score, and inference latency. Set thresholds for these metrics to ensure that new changes do not degrade the model's performance.
- **Data Validation:** Include data validation steps in the CI pipeline to check for issues like data drift, missing values, or inconsistencies in the input data. This is crucial for maintaining the quality of the data that the model relies on.

3) Build and Packaging:

- **Model Packaging:** Package the model and its dependencies into a container (e.g., using Docker) to ensure that it can be consistently deployed across different environments. The container should include everything needed to run the model, including the runtime environment, libraries, and configuration files.
- **Dependency Management:** Use tools like pip or conda to manage the dependencies of your model. Ensure that all dependencies are explicitly defined and versioned to avoid conflicts during deployment.

4) Deployment Automation:

- **Automated Deployments:** Set up the CD pipeline to automatically

deploy the model to the production environment after it passes all tests. Use tools like Jenkins, GitLab CI, or CircleCI to orchestrate the deployment process.
- **Environment Configuration:** Automate the configuration of different environments (e.g., development, staging, production) to ensure consistency across deployments. Use infrastructure-as-code tools like Terraform or Ansible to manage environment configurations.

5) Monitoring and Rollback:

- **Deployment Monitoring:** Implement monitoring tools to track the performance of the model after deployment. Key metrics such as latency, error rates, and resource usage should be continuously monitored to detect any issues early.
- **Rollback Strategy:** Configure the CD pipeline with rollback capabilities to revert to the previous model version if the new deployment causes problems. Rollbacks should be automated and trigger based on predefined criteria, such as a significant drop in performance or a spike in errors.

3. Challenges and Considerations

While CI/CD offers many benefits, implementing these practices for LLMs comes with its own set of challenges. Here's how to address them:

1) Large Model Sizes:

- **Handling Large Models:** LLMs can be very large, making them difficult to test and deploy. Use model compression techniques like quantization and pruning to reduce model size and optimize the CI/CD pipeline for handling large files.
- **Storage and Transfer:** Efficiently manage storage and transfer of large models by using distributed storage solutions (e.g., AWS S3) and

parallel data transfer protocols to reduce deployment time.

2) Complex Dependencies:

- **Dependency Management:** LLMs often depend on a wide range of libraries and frameworks, which can complicate the build process. Use virtual environments or containers to isolate dependencies and ensure that they are consistent across environments.
- **Compatibility Issues:** Regularly test the compatibility of dependencies, especially after updates to the underlying frameworks (e.g., TensorFlow, PyTorch). Automated tests should include checks for compatibility to catch issues early.

3) Data Handling:

- **Data Versioning:** Versioning data is as important as versioning code for LLMs. Use data versioning tools like DVC or Delta Lake to track changes in data and ensure reproducibility.
- **Privacy and Security:** Ensure that sensitive data used for training or testing is handled securely in the CI/CD pipeline. Implement encryption and access controls to protect data during transfer and storage.

4. Best Practices for CI/CD in LLMs

To maximize the effectiveness of your CI/CD pipeline for LLMs, consider the following best practices:

1) Incremental Updates:

- **Small, Incremental Changes:** Aim for small, incremental updates to the model and codebase. This makes it easier to identify the cause of issues when they arise and reduces the risk of introducing bugs or performance regressions.

- **Feature Flags:** Use feature flags to gradually roll out new features or model versions. This allows you to control the exposure of new changes and quickly roll back if needed.

2) Continuous Learning:

- **Regular Retraining:** Set up the CI/CD pipeline to include regular retraining of the model with new data. This helps the model stay up-to-date and improves its performance over time.
- **Feedback Loops:** Incorporate feedback loops from production into the CI/CD process. Use real-world data to refine the model and adjust the pipeline based on user feedback and observed performance.

3) Collaborative Development:

- **Cross-Team Collaboration:** Encourage collaboration between data scientists, engineers, and operations teams in developing and maintaining the CI/CD pipeline. A collaborative approach ensures that the pipeline meets the needs of all stakeholders and operates smoothly.
- **Documentation and Training:** Document the CI/CD process and provide training to all team members involved. This ensures that everyone understands the pipeline and can contribute to its maintenance and improvement.

Implementing CI/CD for large language models is crucial for maintaining a high level of agility, reliability, and performance in production environments. By automating testing, building, and deployment processes, you can ensure that updates to your models are smoothly integrated and that potential issues are caught early. As you develop your CI/CD pipeline, consider the unique challenges of LLMs, such as their size and complexity, and adopt best practices to address these challenges effectively. In the next section, we'll explore strategies for scaling LLMs to handle large-scale workloads, ensuring that your models can meet the demands of production environments.

11.4 Scaling LLMs to Handle Large-Scale Workloads

As large language models (LLMs) become an integral part of many applications, scaling them to handle increasing workloads is crucial. Whether your LLM is supporting millions of users, processing massive amounts of data, or delivering real-time responses, effective scaling ensures that the model remains performant and reliable. In this section, we'll explore strategies for scaling LLMs, focusing on both horizontal and vertical scaling, as well as techniques for optimizing performance under heavy load.

1. Horizontal Scaling

Horizontal scaling involves adding more instances of the model to handle increased traffic. This approach allows you to distribute the workload across multiple servers, improving both performance and fault tolerance.

1) Load Balancing:

- **Traffic Distribution:** Implement load balancers to evenly distribute incoming requests across multiple instances of the model. This prevents any single instance from becoming a bottleneck and ensures that traffic spikes are managed efficiently.
- **Health Checks:** Configure health checks on your load balancers to monitor the status of each model instance. If an instance becomes unresponsive or fails, the load balancer can automatically route traffic to healthy instances, maintaining service continuity.

2) Auto-Scaling:

- **Dynamic Scaling:** Set up auto-scaling rules that automatically add or remove model instances based on real-time demand. This ensures that the system can handle peak traffic periods without over-provisioning resources during quieter times.
- **Scaling Policies:** Define scaling policies based on key metrics like CPU usage, memory utilization, or request latency. These policies trigger scaling actions when thresholds are met, allowing the system to adapt to changing workloads.

3) Session Management:

- **Stateful vs. Stateless Sessions:** Design your LLM to handle stateless sessions where possible, allowing any instance to process a request without needing session-specific information. For stateful sessions, consider using a distributed cache or database to store session data that can be accessed by any instance.

2. Vertical Scaling

Vertical scaling involves increasing the resources (e.g., CPU, memory, GPU) of a single instance of the model. This can be an effective way to enhance performance, especially for tasks that require significant computational power.

1) Optimizing Hardware:

- **GPU and TPU Utilization:** Deploy your LLM on hardware optimized for AI workloads, such as GPUs or TPUs. These processors are designed for parallel processing, making them ideal for handling the intensive computations required by LLMs.
- **Memory Considerations:** Ensure that your model instances have sufficient memory to handle large inputs and complex operations without swapping to disk, which can severely degrade performance.

2) Resource Allocation:

- **Priority Allocation:** Allocate more resources to critical processes within the LLM's workflow, such as inference or real-time data processing. This ensures that the most important tasks are prioritized under heavy load.
- **Efficient Resource Usage:** Optimize the model and its environment to make the most efficient use of available resources. Techniques like mixed precision training, model pruning, and quantization can reduce resource consumption without significantly impacting performance.

3) Upgrading Infrastructure:

- **Hardware Upgrades:** As demand grows, consider upgrading your infrastructure to more powerful machines. This might involve moving to a newer generation of GPUs or increasing the number of cores and memory available to each instance.
- **Network Optimization:** Ensure that your network infrastructure can handle the increased data flow associated with scaling. This includes optimizing data transfer rates, reducing latency, and ensuring that your network topology supports high throughput.

3. Data and Model Optimization

Scaling isn't just about adding more hardware; it also involves optimizing the model and data pipelines to handle large-scale workloads efficiently.

1) Data Sharding and Partitioning:

- **Sharding Databases:** If your LLM relies on large databases, consider sharding the database across multiple servers. Sharding divides the data into smaller, more manageable pieces, each hosted on a separate server, which can reduce query times and improve performance.

- **Partitioning Data Pipelines:** Partition data processing tasks across multiple workers or servers to parallelize operations. This can be particularly useful for batch processing large datasets or streaming data in real time.

2) Model Compression Techniques:

- **Pruning:** Reduce the size of the model by removing unnecessary weights and connections. Pruning can help decrease inference time and resource consumption, making it easier to scale the model across multiple instances.
- **Quantization:** Convert the model's parameters from floating-point to lower-precision formats like int8. Quantization reduces the model's memory footprint and computational requirements, which can improve performance in scaled environments.

3) Caching and Precomputation:

- **Result Caching:** Cache frequently requested results to reduce the load on the model. This is particularly effective in scenarios where the same queries are processed repeatedly, such as in recommendation systems or FAQ bots.
- **Precomputation:** Precompute complex operations or intermediate results that can be reused across multiple requests. This reduces the computational load during inference and speeds up response times.

4. Managing Latency and Throughput

As you scale your LLM, it's important to manage latency and ensure that the system can handle high throughput without degrading performance.

1) Batch Processing:

- **Batch Inference:** Process multiple requests in batches rather than one at a time. Batch processing can significantly reduce inference time per request by taking advantage of parallel processing capabilities in GPUs or TPUs.
- **Dynamic Batching:** Implement dynamic batching, where requests are grouped into batches in real-time based on the current load. This ensures that batching benefits are realized even during varying traffic levels.

2) Asynchronous Processing:

- **Async Inference:** Use asynchronous processing to handle requests without blocking other operations. This allows the system to start processing new requests while previous ones are still being handled, improving overall throughput.
- **Queue Management:** Implement request queuing with priority handling to ensure that high-priority requests are processed promptly, while lower-priority tasks can be deferred or batched.

3) Latency Optimization:

- **Edge Computing:** Deploy LLM instances closer to users by using edge computing. This reduces the distance data needs to travel, lowering latency and improving response times, especially for real-time applications.
- **Network Optimization:** Optimize network routes and reduce bottlenecks by using content delivery networks (CDNs) and optimizing data transfer protocols. Ensuring a low-latency network connection is crucial for maintaining high performance at scale.

5. Monitoring and Scaling Automation

Scaling effectively requires continuous monitoring and automation to adapt to changing workloads.

1) Real-Time Monitoring:

- **Performance Metrics:** Continuously monitor key metrics like CPU/GPU utilization, memory usage, request latency, and error rates. Use these metrics to identify when scaling actions are needed.
- **Alerting Systems:** Set up alerts for critical thresholds to ensure that your team is notified immediately when scaling issues arise, allowing for rapid response.

2) Automated Scaling Decisions:

- **Auto-Scaling Policies:** Implement policies that automatically adjust the number of model instances based on current load, ensuring that the system scales up during peak times and scales down to save resources during quieter periods.
- **Predictive Scaling:** Use machine learning models to predict traffic patterns and preemptively scale resources in anticipation of high demand. This approach helps avoid delays and ensures that resources are available when needed.

3) Feedback Loops:

- **Continuous Improvement:** Use data from monitoring and scaling activities to continuously refine your scaling strategy. Regularly review and adjust scaling policies based on observed performance and changes in workload patterns.

Scaling large language models to handle large-scale workloads is a complex but essential task to ensure that your applications remain performant and reliable as demand grows. By implementing both horizontal and vertical scaling strategies, optimizing data and model performance, managing latency, and automating scaling decisions, you can create a robust system capable of meeting the demands of any workload. In the next section, we'll discuss how to effectively monitor and maintain LLMs post-deployment, ensuring that they continue to operate smoothly in production environments.

11.5 Monitoring and Maintenance Post-Deployment

Once a large language model (LLM) is deployed in production, the work doesn't stop there. Continuous monitoring and maintenance are essential to ensure that the model continues to perform optimally, adapts to new challenges, and remains aligned with user needs. In this section, we'll discuss best practices for monitoring LLMs post-deployment and strategies for ongoing maintenance to keep the model running smoothly.

1. The Importance of Monitoring

Monitoring is critical for detecting issues early, understanding how the model performs under real-world conditions, and ensuring that it meets performance and reliability goals.

1) Real-Time Monitoring:

- **Key Metrics:** Continuously monitor key performance metrics such as latency, throughput, error rates, and resource utilization (CPU, GPU, memory). These metrics provide a real-time view of the model's health and can help detect issues before they impact users.
- **User Interaction Metrics:** Track how users interact with the model,

including response accuracy, user satisfaction, and engagement levels. This data can provide insights into how well the model is serving its intended purpose.

2) Anomaly Detection:

- **Automated Alerts:** Set up automated alerts for anomalies in performance metrics. For example, a sudden increase in latency or error rates should trigger an alert, allowing your team to investigate and address the issue promptly.
- **Trend Analysis:** Regularly analyze trends in the collected metrics to identify gradual changes that could indicate emerging issues. For instance, a slow but steady increase in resource usage might signal a memory leak or inefficiency that needs to be addressed.

3) Logging and Traceability:

- **Detailed Logging:** Implement comprehensive logging to capture every request, response, and internal process. Logs should include details about input data, model decisions, and any errors or exceptions that occur.
- **Traceability:** Ensure that all logs and metrics are traceable back to specific model versions, configurations, and deployments. This makes it easier to pinpoint when and where issues arise, facilitating quicker diagnosis and resolution.

2. Regular Maintenance and Updates

Ongoing maintenance is essential to keep the LLM up-to-date, secure, and performing well over time. This includes both technical updates and continuous learning to adapt to new data and evolving user needs.

1) Model Retraining:

- **Continuous Learning:** Set up a process for regularly retraining the model with new data to keep it current. This is particularly important in dynamic environments where the underlying data changes over time, such as in news, social media, or customer interactions.
- **Data Monitoring:** Monitor the quality and relevance of the data used for retraining. Ensure that the data is representative of the current environment and that any biases or inaccuracies are addressed before retraining.

2) Performance Tuning:

- **Hyperparameter Optimization:** Periodically revisit the model's hyperparameters to ensure they are still optimal. As data evolves, what worked best initially may need adjustment to maintain performance.
- **Resource Optimization:** Review and optimize the resources allocated to the model. For instance, you may find opportunities to reduce memory usage or improve inference speed with more efficient code or hardware.

3) Security and Compliance:

- **Security Updates:** Keep the infrastructure and software up-to-date with the latest security patches. This includes the underlying operating system, libraries, and frameworks used by the LLM.
- **Compliance Checks:** Ensure that the model and its data handling processes continue to comply with relevant regulations (e.g., GDPR, HIPAA). As laws and regulations evolve, your model's deployment and data practices may need adjustment to remain compliant.

3. Handling Model Degradation

Over time, models can experience performance degradation due to changes in data distributions, shifts in user behavior, or evolving requirements. It's important to detect and address these issues early.

1) Monitoring for Degradation:

- **Model Drift:** Watch for signs of model drift, where the model's performance on new data gradually declines. This can happen when the data distribution changes in ways that the model wasn't trained to handle.
- **Performance Benchmarks:** Regularly compare the model's current performance to historical benchmarks. If the model's accuracy, precision, recall, or other key metrics start to decline, it may be time to retrain or fine-tune the model.

2) Retraining Triggers:

- **Scheduled Retraining:** Implement a schedule for regular retraining, even if no issues are immediately apparent. This proactive approach can prevent degradation before it becomes a problem.
- **Performance-Based Retraining:** Set up automated triggers to initiate retraining when performance metrics fall below a certain threshold. This ensures that the model is retrained only when necessary, balancing performance with resource usage.

3) Version Control and Rollbacks:

- **Version Tracking:** Maintain strict version control for all model updates, including retraining, hyperparameter changes, and infrastructure adjustments. This allows you to track changes and their impacts over time.

- **Rollback Mechanisms:** Be prepared to roll back to a previous version of the model if an update introduces issues. Rollbacks should be automated where possible, with minimal disruption to users.

4. User Feedback and Continuous Improvement

User feedback is a valuable resource for improving the LLM's performance and ensuring it continues to meet user needs.

1) Feedback Collection:

- **User Surveys:** Implement surveys or feedback forms to gather user opinions on the model's performance. This direct feedback can highlight areas where the model excels and where it may need improvement.
- **In-App Feedback:** Provide users with a simple way to report issues or suggest improvements directly within the application. This real-time feedback can be invaluable for quick adjustments.

2) Feedback-Driven Updates:

- **Incorporate Feedback:** Use the feedback gathered to guide model updates and retraining efforts. Focus on the areas that users identify as most important, such as improving accuracy, reducing response times, or expanding the model's knowledge base.
- **Iterative Improvement:** Adopt an iterative approach to model improvement, where feedback is continuously incorporated into the development process. This helps ensure that the model evolves in line with user expectations and needs.

3) User Education:

- **Transparent Communication:** Keep users informed about how the

model works, including its limitations and how they can get the best results. Educated users are more likely to provide constructive feedback and have realistic expectations of the model's capabilities.
- **Update Notifications:** Inform users about significant updates or changes to the model. This can include new features, improved accuracy, or other enhancements that directly impact the user experience.

Monitoring and maintenance are ongoing processes that are critical to the long-term success of large language models in production. By setting up robust monitoring systems, performing regular maintenance, addressing performance degradation, and incorporating user feedback, you can ensure that your LLM continues to operate effectively and meet the needs of its users. In the final section of this chapter, we'll explore a case study that demonstrates the challenges and best practices involved in deploying an LLM in a high-traffic environment.

11.6 Case Study: Deploying an LLM in a High-Traffic Environment

Deploying a large language model (LLM) in a high-traffic environment presents unique challenges and requires careful planning to ensure success. This case study explores the deployment of an LLM for a popular e-commerce platform that needed to handle millions of user interactions daily. We'll walk through the key decisions, challenges, and strategies that led to a successful deployment, ensuring the LLM could scale effectively and provide reliable service under heavy load.

Background

The e-commerce platform in question was expanding its use of AI to improve customer support, personalize product recommendations, and enhance the overall user experience. The LLM was designed to power a chatbot that could handle customer queries, recommend products, and assist with order tracking, among other tasks. With millions of users visiting the platform daily, the LLM needed to operate at scale, delivering fast and accurate responses without compromising on performance.

1. Preparing for High Traffic

The first step in the deployment process was preparing the LLM to handle high traffic. This involved optimizing both the model and the infrastructure to ensure they could scale to meet demand.

1) Load Testing:

- **Simulating Traffic:** Before going live, the team conducted extensive load testing to simulate the expected traffic patterns. This involved generating synthetic traffic that mimicked real user behavior, including peaks during sales events and other high-traffic periods.
- **Identifying Bottlenecks:** The load tests revealed potential bottlenecks in the system, particularly around the model's response times and resource utilization. These insights were critical in guiding further optimizations.

2) Optimization Strategies:

- **Model Pruning and Quantization:** To reduce the model's size and improve inference speed, the team implemented model pruning and quantization techniques. These optimizations helped lower the computational load without sacrificing accuracy.

- **Efficient Serving Frameworks:** The team deployed the model using an optimized serving framework that supported GPU acceleration, enabling faster processing of large batches of requests.

3) Auto-Scaling Setup:

- **Dynamic Scaling:** An auto-scaling strategy was implemented to dynamically adjust the number of model instances based on real-time traffic. This ensured that the system could handle sudden spikes in demand without over-provisioning resources during quieter periods.
- **Pre-Warming Instances:** To minimize latency during traffic surges, the team configured pre-warmed instances that could be quickly brought online when needed. This reduced the time required to scale up during peak traffic.

2. Managing Deployment Challenges

During deployment, several challenges emerged that required immediate attention. These included managing latency, ensuring data consistency, and maintaining service availability during peak loads.

1) Latency Management:

- **Edge Computing:** To reduce latency, the team deployed instances of the LLM closer to users by leveraging edge computing. This approach minimized the distance data had to travel, significantly improving response times, particularly for real-time interactions.
- **Batching and Caching:** The team implemented request batching to process multiple queries simultaneously, reducing the load on the model. Additionally, caching was used for frequently requested responses, further lowering the response time.

2) Data Consistency:

- **Distributed Databases:** The platform relied on a distributed database system to handle user data across multiple regions. Ensuring data consistency was critical, particularly for stateful interactions where the chatbot needed to maintain context across multiple exchanges.
- **Eventual Consistency:** In some cases, the team opted for eventual consistency models where real-time data synchronization wasn't critical. This decision helped reduce the load on the database while maintaining acceptable performance for the majority of use cases.

3) Service Availability:

- **Redundant Deployments:** To ensure high availability, the LLM was deployed across multiple data centers with redundancy built in. In the event of a failure in one data center, traffic could be seamlessly rerouted to another, ensuring uninterrupted service.
- **Circuit Breakers:** The team implemented circuit breakers to temporarily disable certain non-critical features if the system became overloaded. This allowed the core functionalities of the chatbot to remain operational even under extreme load.

3. Monitoring and Iterative Improvements

After deployment, continuous monitoring was essential to ensure the LLM performed as expected and to make iterative improvements based on real-world usage.

1) Real-Time Monitoring:

- **Performance Dashboards:** The team set up real-time dashboards to monitor key metrics such as response times, error rates, and resource utilization. These dashboards provided immediate visibility into the system's health and helped quickly identify any issues.
- **User Feedback Integration:** The platform included a feature for users

to provide feedback on the chatbot's responses. This feedback was integrated into the monitoring system, allowing the team to identify common issues and prioritize improvements.

2) Iterative Tuning:

- **Model Retraining:** Based on the data collected from user interactions, the team periodically retrained the LLM to improve its accuracy and handle new types of queries. This iterative approach ensured that the model remained relevant and effective over time.
- **System Optimization:** The team continuously optimized the system, making adjustments to the auto-scaling thresholds, fine-tuning the caching strategy, and improving the efficiency of the data pipeline.

4. Outcomes and Lessons Learned

The deployment was a success, with the LLM handling millions of interactions daily while maintaining high levels of performance and reliability. The platform saw a significant improvement in user satisfaction, with faster response times and more accurate recommendations.

1) Key Outcomes:

- **Improved User Experience:** Users reported higher satisfaction with the platform's customer service, noting faster response times and more relevant product recommendations.
- **Scalability Achieved:** The system scaled effectively to handle traffic spikes, including during major sales events, without experiencing downtime or significant performance degradation.

2) Lessons Learned:

- **Proactive Optimization:** Early and thorough optimization of the model and infrastructure was key to handling high traffic. Techniques like pruning, quantization, and edge computing played a critical role in reducing latency and improving scalability.

- **Continuous Monitoring is Essential:** Real-time monitoring allowed the team to quickly identify and address issues, ensuring that the LLM remained reliable under all conditions. Continuous monitoring also enabled the team to make data-driven decisions for further improvements.
- **User-Centric Iteration:** Incorporating user feedback into the monitoring and improvement process helped keep the LLM aligned with user needs, leading to better overall performance and user satisfaction.

Deploying an LLM in a high-traffic environment requires careful planning, robust infrastructure, and continuous monitoring. By implementing proactive optimization strategies, managing deployment challenges effectively, and iterating based on real-world data, the team successfully delivered a scalable, reliable, and user-friendly AI solution. This case study highlights the importance of a holistic approach to deployment, where technical excellence is combined with a deep understanding of user needs and behavior.

Chapter 12: Security and Ethical Considerations

12.1 Ensuring Data Privacy and Security in LLM Deployments

Deploying large language models (LLMs) in production environments comes with significant responsibilities, particularly around ensuring data privacy and security. Given the sensitivity of the data that LLMs often handle, from personal information to proprietary business data, safeguarding this information is paramount. This section will cover key strategies and best practices for maintaining data privacy and security in LLM deployments, helping you protect user data and comply with relevant regulations.

1. Data Privacy Considerations

Protecting the privacy of the data processed by LLMs is a crucial concern, particularly in the context of increasing regulatory scrutiny and user awareness.

1) Data Minimization:

- **Collect Only What's Necessary:** One of the fundamental principles of data privacy is data minimization—collecting only the data necessary for the model to perform its tasks. This reduces the risk of handling sensitive information unnecessarily and limits the potential impact of a data breach.

- **Anonymization and Pseudonymization:** Where possible, anonymize or pseudonymize data before it is processed by the LLM. Anonymization removes personally identifiable information (PII), making it impossible to link data back to an individual. Pseudonymization replaces PII with a placeholder, which can be reversed only with additional information stored separately.

2) User Consent and Transparency:

- **Informed Consent:** Ensure that users are fully informed about what data is being collected, how it will be used, and who will have access to it. Obtaining explicit consent is crucial, especially when dealing with sensitive data.
- **Transparent Practices:** Be transparent about the data handling practices employed in your LLM deployment. Clearly communicate the measures taken to protect user privacy, including data anonymization, encryption, and access controls.

3) Data Retention Policies:

- **Limit Data Retention:** Implement strict data retention policies that define how long data will be stored and when it will be deleted. Retaining data only as long as necessary reduces the risk of exposure in the event of a breach.
- **Regular Audits:** Conduct regular audits to ensure that data is being retained and deleted according to your policies. These audits help maintain compliance with data protection regulations and reinforce good data hygiene practices.

2. Security Best Practices

Ensuring the security of LLM deployments involves protecting the model, the data it processes, and the infrastructure on which it runs. The following best practices are essential for maintaining a secure deployment environment.

1) Data Encryption:

- **Encryption in Transit:** Encrypt data as it travels between users and the model, and between different components of the system. Transport Layer Security (TLS) is commonly used to secure data in transit, preventing interception and tampering.
- **Encryption at Rest:** Store data securely by encrypting it at rest. This protects sensitive information from unauthorized access, even if physical storage devices are compromised.

2) Access Control:

- **Role-Based Access Control (RBAC):** Implement RBAC to ensure that only authorized personnel have access to the model, data, and related infrastructure. Access should be granted based on the principle of least privilege, where users are given only the access they need to perform their tasks.
- **Multi-Factor Authentication (MFA):** Use MFA to add an additional layer of security for accessing critical systems and data. MFA reduces the risk of unauthorized access by requiring more than just a password.

3) Secure Model Deployment:

- **Containerization and Isolation:** Deploy the model in a containerized environment (e.g., Docker) to isolate it from other parts of the system. This containment limits the potential impact of a breach or compromise in one part of the system.

- **Regular Patching and Updates:** Keep the model and its dependencies up-to-date with the latest security patches. Regularly updating the software reduces vulnerabilities that could be exploited by attackers.

4) Monitoring and Incident Response:

- **Security Monitoring:** Continuously monitor the deployment environment for signs of suspicious activity, such as unauthorized access attempts or unusual data transfers. Tools like intrusion detection systems (IDS) and security information and event management (SIEM) systems can help detect and respond to threats.
- **Incident Response Plan:** Develop and maintain an incident response plan that outlines the steps to be taken in the event of a security breach. This plan should include procedures for containing the breach, assessing the impact, notifying affected parties, and restoring normal operations.

3. Compliance with Data Protection Regulations

In addition to implementing best practices for data privacy and security, it's essential to ensure that your LLM deployment complies with relevant data protection regulations. Failure to do so can result in significant legal and financial consequences.

1) Understanding Regulatory Requirements:

- **GDPR, CCPA, and HIPAA:** Familiarize yourself with the regulations that apply to your LLM deployment, such as the General Data Protection Regulation (GDPR) in Europe, the California Consumer Privacy Act (CCPA) in the United States, and the Health Insurance Portability and Accountability Act (HIPAA) for healthcare data.
- **Global Considerations:** If your deployment serves users in multiple

regions, you'll need to ensure compliance with the data protection regulations of each jurisdiction. This might involve implementing region-specific data handling practices and obtaining the necessary legal permissions.

2) Data Subject Rights:

- **Right to Access and Erasure:** Ensure that your system can comply with data subject rights, such as the right to access personal data and the right to request its erasure. These rights are enshrined in regulations like GDPR and require that you have processes in place to respond to such requests in a timely manner.
- **Data Portability:** Provide users with the ability to download their data in a commonly used, machine-readable format. This is another requirement under regulations like GDPR, and it's important to have the necessary infrastructure in place to fulfill these requests.

3) Documentation and Accountability:

- **Compliance Documentation:** Maintain detailed documentation of your data privacy and security practices, including data handling procedures, access controls, and incident response plans. This documentation should be readily available for internal audits and external inspections.
- **Accountability Measures:** Implement accountability measures to ensure that all team members involved in the LLM deployment are aware of their responsibilities regarding data privacy and security. Regular training sessions and compliance checks can help reinforce these practices.

Ensuring data privacy and security in LLM deployments is a complex but essential task that requires careful planning and execution. By implementing best practices for data encryption, access control, and monitoring, as well as staying compliant with relevant regulations, you can protect sensitive information and maintain user trust. As LLMs continue to be integrated into more applications, the importance of robust data privacy and security measures will only grow. In the next section, we'll explore techniques and tools for mitigating bias in LLMs, another critical aspect of deploying these models responsibly.

12.2 Mitigating Bias in LLMs: Techniques and Tools

Bias in large language models (LLMs) is a significant concern, as these models often learn from vast amounts of data that reflect the biases present in society. If not properly addressed, biased outputs can lead to unfair or harmful consequences, especially when LLMs are deployed in sensitive applications like hiring, healthcare, or customer service. In this section, we'll explore techniques and tools to mitigate bias in LLMs, helping ensure that these models operate fairly and equitably.

1. Understanding Bias in LLMs

Before addressing bias, it's important to understand how it manifests in LLMs. Bias can enter a model through various channels, from the training data to the design of the model itself.

1) Sources of Bias:

- **Training Data:** LLMs are trained on large datasets, often scraped from the web. These datasets can contain biased language, stereotypes, and unbalanced representations of different groups, which the model may learn and reproduce.
- **Model Architecture:** The design of the model and the algorithms used to train it can also introduce or amplify biases. For instance, if a model is optimized solely for accuracy without considering fairness, it may

inadvertently favor outcomes that reflect existing biases.

2) Types of Bias:

- **Representation Bias:** This occurs when certain groups are underrepresented or misrepresented in the training data, leading the model to perform poorly for those groups.
- **Associative Bias:** This type of bias arises when the model learns associations between certain words or concepts that reflect stereotypes (e.g., associating certain professions with a specific gender).
- **Outcome Bias:** Outcome bias occurs when the decisions or predictions made by the model systematically disadvantage certain groups (e.g., lower accuracy for one demographic compared to another).

2. Techniques for Mitigating Bias

There are several strategies that can be employed during the development and deployment of LLMs to mitigate bias. These techniques focus on the data, the model, and the evaluation process.

1) Data-Centric Techniques:

- **Balanced Datasets:** Ensure that the training dataset is balanced in terms of representation. This involves including sufficient examples of different demographic groups, perspectives, and contexts to avoid skewing the model's learning.
- **Bias Detection in Data:** Use tools to analyze the training data for bias before it's used to train the model. Techniques like word frequency analysis, topic modeling, and clustering can help identify biased patterns or imbalances.
- **Data Augmentation:** Augment the dataset with additional examples that counteract identified biases. For example, if the dataset overrepresents certain demographics, you can add more data representing

underrepresented groups to balance the training process.

2) Model-Centric Techniques:

- **Bias-Regularization:** Implement regularization techniques that penalize the model for producing biased outputs. This could involve adding a fairness constraint to the loss function during training, which forces the model to minimize bias while optimizing for accuracy.
- **Adversarial Debiasing:** Train the model using adversarial techniques where a secondary model attempts to detect bias in the primary model's outputs. The primary model is trained to perform well while also avoiding detection by the adversary, thus reducing bias.
- **Fair Representation Learning:** Modify the model's architecture to learn fair representations of the data. This might involve encoding inputs in a way that removes sensitive attributes like gender or race, ensuring that the model's predictions are not influenced by these factors.

3) Evaluation and Post-Processing:

- **Fairness Metrics:** Evaluate the model using fairness metrics in addition to traditional performance metrics. Common fairness metrics include demographic parity, equalized odds, and disparate impact, which help measure how the model's performance varies across different groups.
- **Bias Detection in Outputs:** After the model is deployed, regularly analyze its outputs for bias. This can involve testing the model with scenarios specifically designed to reveal biased behavior or using automated tools to flag potentially biased outputs.
- **Post-Processing Adjustments:** Implement post-processing techniques to adjust the model's outputs after they are generated. For example, you can re-rank or filter the model's predictions to ensure they meet fairness criteria before being presented to users.

3. Tools for Bias Mitigation

Several tools and frameworks have been developed to help detect, analyze, and mitigate bias in LLMs. These tools can be integrated into the development pipeline to ensure that bias is addressed at every stage.

1) AI Fairness 360 (AIF360):

- **Overview:** AIF360 is an open-source toolkit developed by IBM that provides metrics to test for bias and algorithms to mitigate it. It supports a range of bias mitigation techniques, including reweighting, resampling, and adversarial debiasing.
- **Integration:** AIF360 can be integrated into your model training and evaluation pipeline to continuously monitor and reduce bias.

2) Fairlearn:

- **Overview:** Fairlearn is a Python library developed by Microsoft that focuses on assessing and improving fairness in machine learning models. It provides tools to evaluate model fairness and offers algorithms for mitigating bias.
- **Features:** Fairlearn includes functionality for measuring disparities in model performance across different groups and allows for the implementation of fairness constraints during model training.

3) The What-If Tool:

- **Overview:** The What-If Tool, developed by Google, is an interactive tool that allows you to explore model behavior and assess fairness. It enables you to simulate different scenarios, test the impact of various changes, and visualize how the model performs across different subsets of data.
- **Application:** The What-If Tool is particularly useful for identifying

bias in a model's predictions and exploring how changes to the model or data affect its fairness.

4. Continuous Bias Mitigation

Bias mitigation is not a one-time task but an ongoing process that requires continuous attention throughout the lifecycle of the LLM.

1) Regular Audits:

- **Periodic Reviews:** Conduct regular audits of the model's performance and fairness. This includes retraining the model with updated data, reassessing fairness metrics, and making necessary adjustments to maintain or improve fairness over time.
- **External Audits:** Consider involving third-party auditors to review the model's fairness and bias mitigation practices. External audits provide an objective assessment and can help build trust with users and stakeholders.

2) User Feedback and Iteration:

- **Incorporate Feedback:** Collect user feedback on the model's outputs, particularly in cases where users perceive bias or unfair treatment. Use this feedback to refine the model and address any issues that are identified.
- **Iterative Improvements:** Continuously improve the model by iterating on its design, data, and algorithms. As societal norms and expectations evolve, so too should the model's approach to fairness and bias mitigation.

3) Ethical Considerations:

- **Transparency:** Be transparent with users about the steps taken to mitigate bias in the LLM. Explain the techniques used, the challenges faced, and the results of fairness evaluations. Transparency builds trust and allows users to understand how the model operates.

- **Accountability:** Hold the development team accountable for the model's fairness. This might involve setting specific goals for bias reduction, tracking progress, and ensuring that bias mitigation remains a priority throughout the development and deployment process.

Mitigating bias in large language models is a complex but essential task that requires a multifaceted approach. By addressing bias in the data, model, and evaluation processes, and by leveraging tools designed for bias detection and mitigation, you can significantly reduce the risk of biased outcomes. Continuous monitoring and iterative improvements are crucial to ensuring that the model remains fair and equitable over time. In the next section, we will delve into the broader ethical implications of deploying LLMs in production, exploring how these powerful tools can be used responsibly and ethically.

12.3 Ethical Implications of LLMs in Production

Deploying large language models (LLMs) in production environments opens up a world of possibilities, but it also comes with significant ethical responsibilities. As LLMs increasingly influence decision-making processes, interact with users, and shape the information landscape, it's crucial to consider the ethical implications of their deployment. In this section, we'll discuss the key ethical concerns associated with LLMs and offer guidance on how to address these issues responsibly.

1. The Power and Responsibility of LLMs

LLMs are powerful tools capable of processing vast amounts of information and generating human-like text. This power comes with the responsibility to ensure that their use aligns with ethical standards.

1) Influence on Decision-Making:

- **Human Impact:** LLMs are often used in applications that directly affect people's lives, such as hiring processes, legal decisions, and healthcare recommendations. Ensuring that these models operate fairly and without bias is essential to prevent harm.
- **Accountability:** When LLMs are used to make decisions, it's important to establish clear accountability. Organizations must be transparent about how decisions are made and who is responsible for the outcomes, particularly when automated systems are involved.

2) Misinformation and Misdirection:

- **Content Generation:** LLMs can generate convincing text, which can be used for both beneficial and harmful purposes. One of the most pressing ethical concerns is the potential for these models to spread misinformation, whether intentionally or unintentionally.
- **Manipulation:** There is also a risk that LLMs could be used to manipulate public opinion or deceive users by producing misleading or biased content. This raises ethical questions about the deployment of LLMs in sensitive areas like news, politics, and social media.

2. Ensuring Fairness and Avoiding Harm

Ethical considerations extend beyond the technical performance of LLMs to the broader impact they have on society. Ensuring fairness and minimizing harm are key priorities.

1) Fair Access and Representation:

- **Equitable Deployment:** Consider how the deployment of LLMs might impact different groups. For example, if an LLM is used in customer service, does it perform equally well for all users, regardless of language, dialect, or cultural background?
- **Representation of Diverse Voices:** LLMs trained on biased datasets may reinforce existing inequalities by marginalizing certain voices or perspectives. It's important to address these issues by ensuring that training data is diverse and representative of the populations the model will serve.

2) Preventing Harm:

- **Avoiding Negative Consequences:** Consider the potential negative consequences of deploying an LLM. For example, in applications like mental health support or legal advice, incorrect or insensitive responses could cause real harm to users.
- **Human Oversight:** In high-stakes applications, it's essential to include human oversight in the decision-making process. This helps mitigate the risk of harm by ensuring that critical decisions are reviewed by qualified professionals.

3. Transparency and Trust

Building trust with users is essential for the ethical deployment of LLMs. Transparency about how these models work and the decisions they make is a key factor in earning and maintaining that trust.

1) Explainability:

- **Understanding Model Decisions:** LLMs are often viewed as "black boxes" because their decision-making processes can be difficult to interpret. However, it's important to provide explanations for the model's outputs, particularly in applications where users rely on the model's decisions.

- **User Education:** Educating users about how the LLM works, including its limitations and the factors that influence its outputs, can help build trust. This transparency allows users to make informed decisions about how to interact with the model.

2) Disclosure of Use:

- **Transparency in Applications:** Clearly disclose when and how LLMs are being used, especially in contexts where users might not expect automated systems to be involved. For example, users should know if they are interacting with a chatbot powered by an LLM rather than a human.
- **Algorithmic Accountability:** Organizations should be accountable for the algorithms they deploy. This includes being transparent about the data used to train the model, the objectives of the model, and any steps taken to mitigate bias or ensure fairness.

4. Long-Term Ethical Considerations

As LLMs continue to evolve and become more integrated into society, it's important to think about the long-term ethical implications of their use.

1) Sustainability and Resource Use:

- **Environmental Impact:** Training and deploying LLMs require significant computational resources, which can have a substantial environmental impact. Consider the sustainability of deploying large-scale models and explore ways to reduce their carbon footprint.
- **Efficiency Improvements:** Optimize the model and its deployment to minimize resource use without compromising performance. This

could involve using smaller, more efficient models where possible or investing in renewable energy sources for data centers.

2) Ethical AI Development:

- **Inclusive Development Processes:** Involve diverse stakeholders in the development and deployment of LLMs, including ethicists, sociologists, and representatives from affected communities. This ensures that a broad range of perspectives is considered in decision-making.
- **Proactive Ethical Considerations:** Anticipate potential ethical dilemmas that could arise as LLMs become more advanced and pervasive. Develop policies and frameworks to address these challenges proactively rather than reacting to issues after they emerge.

The ethical implications of deploying LLMs in production are far-reaching and complex. As these models become more powerful and widely used, it's essential to consider their impact on individuals and society as a whole. By ensuring fairness, transparency, and accountability, and by engaging with ethical considerations at every stage of development and deployment, organizations can harness the benefits of LLMs while minimizing potential harms. In the next section, we'll delve into the legal considerations that come into play when deploying LLMs, exploring how to navigate the regulatory landscape and ensure compliance with relevant laws and standards.

12.4 Legal Considerations for Deploying LLMs

Deploying large language models (LLMs) in real-world applications comes with a host of legal considerations that must be carefully navigated to ensure compliance and mitigate risk. As LLMs become more integrated into various industries, understanding the legal landscape surrounding their use is crucial. This section will cover the key legal issues to be aware of when deploying LLMs, including data protection laws, intellectual property concerns, liability issues, and the importance of transparency.

1. Data Protection and Privacy Laws

One of the most pressing legal considerations when deploying LLMs is ensuring compliance with data protection and privacy laws. These laws regulate how personal data is collected, stored, processed, and shared, and failure to comply can result in significant penalties.

1) General Data Protection Regulation (GDPR):

- **Scope and Applicability:** The GDPR is a comprehensive data protection law that applies to organizations operating within the European Union (EU) or dealing with the personal data of EU residents. It imposes strict requirements on how personal data is handled and grants individuals significant rights over their data.
- **Key Requirements:** Under GDPR, organizations must ensure that personal data is processed lawfully, fairly, and transparently. They must also implement appropriate security measures to protect data, obtain explicit consent for data processing when necessary, and provide individuals with the right to access, correct, and delete their data.

2) California Consumer Privacy Act (CCPA):

- **Scope and Applicability:** The CCPA applies to businesses that collect personal data from California residents and meet certain criteria, such as having annual gross revenues over $25 million or deriving a significant portion of their revenue from selling personal data.
- **Key Requirements:** The CCPA grants California residents the right to know what personal data is being collected about them, the right to

request the deletion of their data, and the right to opt-out of the sale of their data. Businesses must also provide clear and transparent privacy policies.

3) Health Insurance Portability and Accountability Act (HIPAA):

- **Scope and Applicability:** HIPAA applies to healthcare providers, health plans, and healthcare clearinghouses in the United States, as well as their business associates. It sets standards for the protection of health information.
- **Key Requirements:** Organizations subject to HIPAA must implement safeguards to protect the privacy and security of protected health information (PHI). This includes limiting access to PHI, ensuring the confidentiality and integrity of data, and providing patients with rights to access and amend their health records.

4) Cross-Border Data Transfers:

- **Legal Considerations:** When deploying LLMs that process data from multiple jurisdictions, organizations must consider the legal implications of cross-border data transfers. Many data protection laws, such as GDPR, impose restrictions on transferring personal data to countries that do not provide an adequate level of data protection.
- **Mechanisms for Compliance:** To comply with these restrictions, organizations may need to implement mechanisms such as Standard Contractual Clauses (SCCs), Binding Corporate Rules (BCRs), or rely on other legal bases for data transfers, such as obtaining explicit consent from data subjects.

2. Intellectual Property (IP) Concerns

The development and deployment of LLMs involve complex intellectual property issues, particularly regarding the ownership and use of the models, data, and outputs.

1) Ownership of Training Data:

- **Legal Considerations:** The data used to train LLMs often comes from a variety of sources, some of which may be subject to copyright or other intellectual property protections. Organizations must ensure that they have the legal right to use the data for training purposes, which may involve obtaining licenses or permissions from data owners.
- **Derivative Works:** When LLMs generate content based on the data they were trained on, questions may arise about whether the output constitutes a derivative work and who holds the rights to it. This can be particularly complex when the training data includes copyrighted material.

2) Model Ownership and Licensing:

- **Ownership Rights:** The ownership of LLMs typically lies with the entity that developed or trained the model. However, when models are trained using third-party platforms or data, the ownership and licensing arrangements can become more complicated.
- **Licensing Agreements:** Organizations may need to enter into licensing agreements to use pre-trained models developed by others or to allow others to use their models. These agreements should clearly define the rights and limitations associated with the use of the models, including any restrictions on commercial use or distribution.

3) Content Generation and IP Infringement:

- **Generated Content:** LLMs can generate content that may inadvertently infringe on intellectual property rights, such as producing text that closely resembles copyrighted material. Organizations deploying LLMs should implement safeguards to prevent and address potential IP infringements.
- **Liability for Infringement:** It's important to consider who bears liability for any IP infringement that occurs as a result of content generated by an LLM. This can be particularly complex when the LLM is integrated into third-party applications or made available as a service.

3. Liability and Accountability

Determining liability and accountability for the actions and outputs of LLMs is another critical legal consideration. As these models are integrated into decision-making processes, the potential for harm or errors increases, raising questions about who is responsible when things go wrong.

1) Product Liability:

- **Legal Frameworks:** In some cases, LLMs may be considered products under existing legal frameworks, which means that product liability laws could apply. This could make the developers, distributors, or deployers of the model liable for any harm caused by defects or failures in the model's performance.
- **Risk Mitigation:** To mitigate liability risks, organizations should ensure that LLMs are thoroughly tested, properly documented, and deployed with appropriate safeguards. This includes providing clear disclaimers about the model's limitations and ensuring that users understand how to use the model safely and effectively.

2) Negligence and Duty of Care:

- **Duty of Care:** Organizations deploying LLMs may have a duty of care to ensure that the model's outputs are accurate, reliable, and free from bias. Failing to meet this duty of care could result in negligence claims if the model causes harm or loss.

- **Human Oversight:** Incorporating human oversight into the decision-making process can help mitigate the risk of negligence. This involves having qualified professionals review and validate the model's outputs, particularly in high-stakes applications such as healthcare, finance, or legal services.

3) Ethical Accountability:

- **Corporate Responsibility:** Beyond legal liability, organizations have an ethical responsibility to ensure that their use of LLMs aligns with broader societal values. This includes taking proactive steps to address bias, protect privacy, and prevent misuse of the technology.
- **Transparency and Reporting:** Maintaining transparency about the use of LLMs, including disclosing any potential risks or limitations, is essential for building trust with users and stakeholders. Organizations should also be prepared to report and address any issues that arise, demonstrating accountability in their use of AI technology.

4. Navigating the Regulatory Landscape

As the use of LLMs grows, so too does the regulatory landscape surrounding their deployment. Staying informed about relevant laws and regulations is essential for ensuring compliance and minimizing legal risk.

1) Emerging Regulations:

- **AI-Specific Legislation:** Governments around the world are increasingly considering AI-specific legislation to address the unique challenges posed by technologies like LLMs. Organizations should stay informed about these developments and be prepared to adapt to new legal requirements.

- **Sector-Specific Regulations:** In addition to general AI regulations, certain sectors may have specific legal requirements related to the use of LLMs. For example, the financial services industry may impose additional rules on the use of AI for decision-making processes that affect consumers.

2) Compliance Strategies:

- **Legal Counsel:** Engaging legal counsel with expertise in AI and data protection is essential for navigating the complex regulatory environment. Legal professionals can help organizations understand their obligations, assess risks, and develop strategies for compliance.
- **Proactive Compliance:** Rather than waiting for regulations to be enacted, organizations should adopt a proactive approach to compliance by implementing best practices for data protection, fairness, transparency, and accountability. This not only helps ensure legal compliance but also builds trust with users and stakeholders.

The legal considerations surrounding the deployment of LLMs are multifaceted and evolving. From data protection and intellectual property to liability and regulatory compliance, organizations must navigate a complex legal landscape to deploy these powerful models responsibly. By staying informed, implementing best practices, and seeking legal guidance, organizations can minimize legal risks while maximizing the benefits of LLMs. In the next section, we will discuss how to build transparent and explainable LLMs, which is crucial for fostering trust and ensuring ethical AI deployment.

12.5 Building Transparent and Explainable LLMs

As large language models (LLMs) become increasingly integrated into critical applications, the need for transparency and explainability has never been more important. Users, stakeholders, and regulators alike demand to know not only what decisions these models make but also how and why they make them. In this section, we'll explore the importance of transparency and explainability in LLMs, along with practical strategies for achieving these goals in your deployments.

1. The Importance of Transparency and Explainability

Transparency and explainability are key to building trust in LLMs. When users understand how a model works and can see the reasoning behind its decisions, they are more likely to trust its outputs and accept its use in decision-making processes.

1) Building Trust:

- **User Confidence:** Transparency helps users feel confident in the model's outputs by providing clear information about how decisions are made. This is particularly important in high-stakes applications like healthcare, finance, and law, where the consequences of errors or biases can be significant.
- **Accountability:** Transparent models allow organizations to be accountable for their AI systems. When the decision-making process is clear, it's easier to identify and correct mistakes, making the system more reliable and fair.

2) Regulatory Compliance:

- **Meeting Legal Requirements:** Many data protection laws, such as GDPR, require organizations to provide explanations for automated decisions, particularly when they significantly affect individuals. Ensuring that your LLMs are transparent and explainable helps meet these legal obligations.

- **Anticipating Future Regulations:** As AI-specific regulations continue to develop, transparency and explainability are likely to become even more critical. By adopting these practices now, organizations can stay ahead of regulatory changes and demonstrate their commitment to ethical AI use.

2. Strategies for Achieving Transparency

Achieving transparency in LLMs involves making the model's processes, data, and decisions visible and understandable to users and stakeholders.

1) Documentation and Communication:

- **Clear Documentation:** Provide comprehensive documentation that explains how the model was developed, including the data sources used, the training process, and any assumptions or biases that may affect the model's outputs. This documentation should be accessible to both technical and non-technical audiences.
- **User Guides:** Develop user guides that explain how to interact with the model, including its strengths, limitations, and potential sources of error. These guides should also provide examples of typical outputs and explain how users can interpret them.

2) Model Transparency:

- **Access to Model Internals:** Where possible, allow users to access information about the model's internals, such as feature importance, attention weights, or decision trees that illustrate how specific outputs are generated. This transparency can help users understand the factors influencing the model's decisions.

- **Open-Source Models:** Consider open-sourcing the model or parts of the codebase to allow external experts to review and critique the model's design. Open-source models foster collaboration and allow the broader community to contribute to improving transparency and fairness.

3) Transparency in Data Use:

- **Data Provenance:** Clearly communicate the sources of the data used to train the model, including any preprocessing steps that were applied. Transparency in data use helps users understand the context in which the model was trained and the potential biases that may arise.
- **Consent and Data Rights:** Ensure that users understand how their data is being used, stored, and processed by the model. Provide clear options for users to give or withdraw consent for data use, and respect their data rights in line with relevant regulations.

3. Techniques for Enhancing Explainability

Explainability goes a step beyond transparency by providing users with insights into why the model made a particular decision. It involves making the model's reasoning process understandable and interpretable.

1) Interpretable Models:

- **Model Simplification:** Where possible, use simpler models or techniques that are inherently interpretable, such as decision trees, linear models, or rule-based systems. These models are easier to explain and understand, making them suitable for applications where interpretability is crucial.
- **Hybrid Approaches:** Combine LLMs with interpretable models that provide explanations for the LLM's outputs. For example, an LLM could generate a prediction, while a simpler model provides a clear

explanation of the factors that led to that prediction.

2) Post-Hoc Explanation Techniques:

- **LIME (Local Interpretable Model-Agnostic Explanations):** LIME is a technique that generates interpretable explanations for individual predictions by approximating the LLM with a simpler model in the vicinity of the prediction. This approach helps users understand the local behavior of the model without needing to interpret the entire model.
- **SHAP (SHapley Additive exPlanations):** SHAP assigns a value to each feature in a model, indicating its contribution to the final prediction. This technique provides a clear and mathematically grounded explanation of how different features influence the model's outputs.

3) Visualizing Model Decisions:

- **Attention Maps:** For models that use attention mechanisms, such as transformers, attention maps can be used to visualize which parts of the input the model focused on when making a decision. These maps help users see the relationships between different parts of the input and the model's output.
- **Decision Paths:** For models that make decisions in a step-by-step manner, such as decision trees or certain neural networks, visualize the decision path taken for a particular input. This path can show users the sequence of decisions that led to the final output.

4. Balancing Explainability with Performance

While explainability is important, it's also crucial to balance it with the model's performance and complexity. In some cases, highly complex models may provide superior performance but at the cost of being less interpretable.

1) Trade-Offs in Model Choice:

- **Performance vs. Interpretability:** Consider the trade-offs between model performance and interpretability when selecting an LLM for deployment. In high-stakes applications where understanding the model's decisions is critical, a more interpretable model may be preferable, even if it sacrifices some accuracy.
- **Context-Specific Decisions:** The need for explainability may vary depending on the context in which the model is used. For example, in medical diagnosis, high explainability is essential, while in certain low-risk applications, a more complex model may be acceptable if it offers better performance.

2) User-Centered Design:

- **Understanding User Needs:** Engage with users and stakeholders to understand their needs and expectations for explainability. This user-centered approach ensures that the explanations provided are relevant, useful, and accessible to the intended audience.
- **Iterative Improvement:** Continuously iterate on the model and its explainability features based on user feedback. This iterative process helps refine the explanations provided and ensures that they meet the evolving needs of users.

Building transparent and explainable LLMs is not just a technical challenge—it's an ethical imperative. By prioritizing transparency and explainability, organizations can foster trust, ensure compliance with legal requirements, and empower users to make informed decisions. The strategies and techniques outlined in this section provide a roadmap for achieving these goals, helping to ensure that LLMs are used responsibly and effectively. In the final section of this chapter, we will examine a case study that illustrates how addressing ethical concerns in a deployed LLM can lead to better outcomes for both the organization and its users.

12.6 Case Study: Addressing Ethical Concerns in a Deployed LLM

When deploying large language models (LLMs) in real-world applications, ethical concerns often arise that require immediate and thoughtful action. This case study examines a scenario where a company deployed an LLM in a customer support chatbot, only to encounter significant ethical challenges. We will explore how the company identified these issues, the steps taken to address them, and the lessons learned from the experience.

Background

The company, a major online retailer, implemented an LLM-powered chatbot to handle customer inquiries. The chatbot was designed to assist with common queries such as order status, return policies, and product recommendations. Initially, the deployment was seen as a success, with the chatbot handling a large volume of interactions and reducing the workload on human support agents. However, within weeks of deployment, users began reporting troubling interactions with the chatbot, raising ethical concerns that needed to be addressed quickly.

1. Identifying Ethical Concerns

Shortly after the chatbot's launch, the company received complaints from customers about biased and inappropriate responses. These issues were highlighted by both direct user feedback and internal monitoring tools.

1) Bias in Responses:

- **User Reports:** Some users reported that the chatbot provided different levels of service based on the perceived demographic details inferred from their names or the language used in their queries. For instance, the chatbot was more likely to suggest higher-priced products to certain users, raising concerns about socioeconomic bias.

- **Internal Analysis:** Upon reviewing the logs, the development team discovered that the chatbot's product recommendations were skewed by biases present in the training data. The data had inadvertently included patterns where certain user groups were historically offered different products, and the model had learned to replicate these patterns.

2) Inappropriate Content:

- **Unexpected Outputs:** In a few instances, the chatbot generated responses that were deemed inappropriate or offensive. These responses were likely due to the model's exposure to unfiltered online text during training, where it had learned from both high-quality and problematic content.
- **Public Backlash:** Some of these inappropriate interactions were shared on social media, leading to public criticism and damage to the company's reputation. This amplified the need for a swift and effective response to the ethical issues.

2. Addressing the Ethical Challenges

The company quickly mobilized a task force to address the ethical concerns, comprising data scientists, ethicists, legal advisors, and customer support representatives. Their approach focused on both immediate fixes and long-term solutions.

1) Immediate Actions:

- **Model Retraining:** The team retrained the model using a more carefully curated dataset that excluded biased and inappropriate content. They also implemented stricter data preprocessing steps to ensure that the training data better reflected the company's ethical standards.

- **Content Filtering:** A content filtering layer was added to the chatbot's pipeline to screen out inappropriate or offensive outputs before they were presented to users. This layer used a combination of rule-based filters and a secondary model trained specifically to detect harmful content.

2) Long-Term Strategies:

- **Bias Audits:** The company established a regular bias audit process, where the model's outputs were reviewed for signs of bias or unfair treatment. These audits involved both automated tools and human reviewers, ensuring a thorough examination of the model's behavior.
- **Transparency and User Education:** To rebuild trust with users, the company increased transparency about how the chatbot operated. They updated the chatbot's interface to include disclaimers about its limitations and provided users with easy access to feedback mechanisms. The company also published a detailed report on the steps taken to address the ethical issues, fostering an open dialogue with their customer base.

3) Incorporating User Feedback:

- **Feedback Loops:** The company implemented robust feedback loops that allowed users to flag problematic responses directly within the chatbot interface. This feedback was then used to continuously improve the model and the content filtering system.
- **User-Centric Improvements:** Based on user feedback, the team made additional adjustments to the chatbot's recommendation algorithms, ensuring that they were more inclusive and fair. For example, the

model was adjusted to provide a more balanced range of product recommendations across different user demographics.

3. Outcomes and Lessons Learned

The company's proactive approach to addressing the ethical concerns led to significant improvements in the chatbot's performance and a gradual rebuilding of user trust.

1) Improved Model Performance:

- **Reduced Bias:** After retraining and implementing bias audits, the chatbot's outputs became more consistent and fair, with fewer instances of biased recommendations. This led to an increase in user satisfaction and a reduction in negative feedback.
- **Safer Interactions:** The content filtering system effectively prevented inappropriate responses, ensuring that the chatbot's interactions remained professional and aligned with the company's values.

2) Restored Reputation:

- **Positive Public Perception:** The company's transparent handling of the ethical issues, coupled with their commitment to continuous improvement, was well-received by the public. Over time, this helped restore the company's reputation and demonstrated their commitment to ethical AI deployment.
- **Industry Leadership:** By openly addressing the challenges they faced, the company positioned itself as a leader in ethical AI practices within their industry. They shared their experience and best practices with other organizations, contributing to the broader discourse on responsible AI deployment.

3) Key Takeaways:

- **Proactive Ethical Oversight:** The case underscored the importance of proactive ethical oversight when deploying LLMs. Regular audits, transparent communication, and robust feedback mechanisms are crucial for identifying and addressing ethical issues before they escalate.
- **Human-In-The-Loop:** Maintaining human oversight in AI systems, especially in high-stakes applications, can help catch issues that automated systems might miss. Human reviewers played a key role in this case by providing context and judgment that the model lacked.
- **Ongoing Monitoring:** Ethical considerations do not end at deployment. Continuous monitoring, user feedback, and model updates are essential for maintaining ethical standards and ensuring that AI systems evolve in a positive direction.

This case study highlights the real-world challenges and responsibilities involved in deploying LLMs. By taking swift and comprehensive action to address ethical concerns, the company not only mitigated immediate risks but also set a precedent for ethical AI deployment. The lessons learned from this experience serve as a valuable guide for any organization looking to deploy LLMs responsibly and sustainably. As we move forward, it's clear that ethical considerations must remain at the forefront of AI development and deployment, ensuring that these powerful tools are used for the benefit of all.

Chapter 13: Integrating LLMs with Business Applications

13.1 LLMs in E-commerce: Use Cases and Best Practices

The e-commerce landscape is continuously evolving, with businesses constantly seeking new ways to improve customer experience, streamline operations, and drive sales. Large Language Models (LLMs) have emerged as powerful tools in this sector, offering capabilities that can transform various aspects of e-commerce. In this section, we'll explore the key use cases for LLMs in e-commerce and discuss best practices for their integration.

1. Personalizing Customer Interactions

Personalization is a critical factor in enhancing the customer experience and driving sales in e-commerce. LLMs can significantly improve personalization by analyzing vast amounts of customer data and generating tailored recommendations.

1) Product Recommendations:

- **Dynamic Recommendations:** LLMs can analyze user behavior, pur-

chase history, and browsing patterns in real-time to generate personalized product recommendations. This helps in presenting customers with items they are more likely to purchase, increasing conversion rates.
- **Contextual Suggestions:** Beyond simple recommendations, LLMs can understand the context of a user's interaction, such as their current search queries or previous purchases, to offer more relevant suggestions. For example, if a customer is browsing winter clothing, the model might recommend complementary items like gloves or scarves.

2) Customized Content:

- **Personalized Emails:** LLMs can generate personalized email content that resonates with individual customers. By analyzing user data, the model can craft messages that highlight products of interest, special offers, or reminders about abandoned carts, all tailored to the recipient's preferences.
- **Dynamic Web Content:** LLMs can also be used to personalize the content displayed on an e-commerce website. For example, returning visitors might see a homepage that highlights products similar to those they previously viewed, or a special promotion targeted to their interests.

2. Enhancing Customer Support

Customer support is a critical aspect of e-commerce, and LLMs can greatly enhance the efficiency and effectiveness of this function.

1) Chatbots and Virtual Assistants:

- **24/7 Support:** LLM-powered chatbots can provide around-the-clock support to customers, handling a wide range of inquiries such as order status, return policies, and product information. This reduces the burden on human agents and ensures that customers receive prompt assistance.

- **Complex Query Resolution:** LLMs are capable of understanding and resolving more complex queries that go beyond basic FAQs. They can handle nuanced questions and provide detailed answers, improving the overall customer support experience.

2) Sentiment Analysis:

- **Understanding Customer Emotions:** LLMs can be used to analyze customer interactions for sentiment, allowing businesses to understand the emotions behind customer inquiries. This helps in identifying dissatisfied customers early and taking proactive steps to resolve their issues.
- **Tailored Responses:** By understanding the sentiment behind a customer's message, LLMs can generate responses that are empathetic and appropriate to the situation, whether it's calming a frustrated customer or reinforcing a positive experience.

3. Streamlining Operations

LLMs can also be leveraged to optimize various operational aspects of an e-commerce business, leading to increased efficiency and cost savings.

1) Inventory Management:

- **Demand Forecasting:** LLMs can analyze sales data, market trends, and external factors (such as seasonality or economic conditions) to forecast demand for products. Accurate demand forecasting helps businesses maintain optimal inventory levels, reducing the risk of overstocking or stockouts.
- **Automated Reordering:** Based on the demand forecasts, LLMs can

trigger automated reordering processes to ensure that popular items are restocked in time. This automation minimizes manual intervention and ensures that the supply chain operates smoothly.

2) Supply Chain Optimization:

- **Route Planning:** For businesses that handle their own logistics, LLMs can optimize delivery routes by analyzing traffic patterns, delivery schedules, and customer locations. This results in faster deliveries and reduced transportation costs.
- **Supplier Communication:** LLMs can automate communication with suppliers, managing order confirmations, shipment tracking, and issue resolution. This helps in maintaining strong supplier relationships and ensures timely replenishment of stock.

4. Best Practices for Integrating LLMs in E-commerce

While the potential of LLMs in e-commerce is vast, successful integration requires careful planning and execution. Here are some best practices to consider:

1) Start with a Clear Use Case:

- **Identify High-Impact Areas:** Focus on areas where LLMs can deliver the most value, whether it's improving customer experience, optimizing operations, or enhancing marketing efforts. Starting with a clear use case ensures that the implementation is targeted and effective.
- **Pilot Projects:** Before full-scale deployment, consider running pilot projects to test the effectiveness of LLMs in specific areas. This allows you to refine the model and approach based on real-world feedback.

2) Data Quality and Management:

- **High-Quality Data:** LLMs rely on large volumes of data to generate accurate and relevant outputs. Ensure that your data is clean, well-organized, and representative of your customer base. Poor-quality data can lead to biased or inaccurate recommendations.
- **Ongoing Data Maintenance:** Continuously update and maintain your data to reflect changes in customer behavior, product offerings, and market conditions. Regular data audits can help identify and correct any issues that may affect model performance.

3) Ethical Considerations:

- **Bias Mitigation:** Be aware of potential biases in your LLMs, particularly in areas like product recommendations and customer interactions. Regularly audit the model's outputs to ensure that it treats all customer segments fairly and without prejudice.
- **Transparency:** Maintain transparency with your customers about how LLMs are being used, especially when it comes to personalized recommendations or automated support. Providing users with insights into the decision-making process can help build trust.

4) Continuous Improvement:

- **Monitor Performance:** Regularly monitor the performance of LLMs in your e-commerce applications. Use metrics such as conversion rates, customer satisfaction scores, and operational efficiency to assess the impact and identify areas for improvement.
- **Iterative Updates:** LLMs should not be a "set it and forget it" solution. Continuously update the model based on new data, emerging trends, and customer feedback to keep it aligned with business goals and market conditions.

LLMs have the potential to revolutionize e-commerce by enhancing personalization, improving customer support, and streamlining operations. By following best practices for integration, businesses can unlock the full potential of these models while ensuring that they operate ethically and effectively. As the e-commerce landscape continues to evolve, LLMs will play an increasingly important role in driving innovation and delivering exceptional customer experiences.

13.2 Integrating LLMs into Customer Service Workflows

Customer service is at the heart of many businesses, and the integration of Large Language Models (LLMs) into customer service workflows has the potential to transform how companies interact with their customers. LLMs can automate responses, enhance customer engagement, and improve the efficiency of support teams. In this section, we'll discuss how to effectively integrate LLMs into customer service workflows and the benefits this can bring to your business.

1. Automating Routine Inquiries

One of the most immediate benefits of integrating LLMs into customer service is their ability to handle routine inquiries. These are the types of questions that are frequently asked and can be easily addressed with standardized responses.

1) Chatbots for First-Line Support:

- **Handling FAQs:** LLM-powered chatbots can be deployed to handle frequently asked questions (FAQs) such as order status, return policies, or product availability. By automating these routine inquiries, businesses can reduce the workload on human agents, allowing them to focus on more complex issues.

- **Instant Responses:** LLMs can provide instant, accurate responses to customer inquiries, improving the overall customer experience. This immediacy is particularly valuable in today's fast-paced environment, where customers expect quick resolutions.

2) Reducing Response Times:

- **24/7 Availability:** Unlike human agents, LLMs can operate around the clock, providing consistent support regardless of the time of day. This ensures that customers receive assistance whenever they need it, without having to wait for business hours.
- **High Volume Handling:** During peak times, such as holidays or promotional periods, LLMs can handle a high volume of inquiries without compromising response times. This scalability helps maintain service quality even during busy periods.

2. Enhancing Customer Engagement

Beyond automating routine tasks, LLMs can be used to enhance customer engagement by providing personalized and context-aware interactions.

1) Personalized Interactions:

- **Understanding Customer Context:** LLMs can analyze a customer's interaction history, preferences, and past behavior to tailor responses that are more relevant and personalized. For example, if a customer frequently purchases a particular type of product, the LLM can suggest related items or promotions.
- **Proactive Engagement:** LLMs can be used to proactively engage with customers based on their activity. For instance, if a customer lingers on a product page without making a purchase, the LLM can initiate a chat to offer assistance or provide additional information.

2) Emotionally Intelligent Responses:

- **Sentiment Analysis:** By incorporating sentiment analysis, LLMs can gauge the emotional tone of a customer's message and adjust their responses accordingly. If a customer is frustrated, the LLM can respond with empathy and offer solutions to alleviate their concerns.
- **Contextual Awareness:** LLMs can understand the context of a conversation and maintain that context throughout the interaction. This allows for more fluid and natural conversations, where the customer doesn't have to repeat themselves or provide the same information multiple times.

3. Supporting Human Agents

While LLMs excel at handling routine tasks, there will always be scenarios where human intervention is necessary. Integrating LLMs into customer service workflows can support human agents by providing them with the tools and information they need to resolve complex issues more effectively.

1) Agent Assist Tools:

- **Real-Time Suggestions:** LLMs can be integrated into agent assist tools that provide real-time suggestions during customer interactions. For example, the LLM might suggest relevant knowledge base articles, possible solutions, or next steps based on the context of the conversation.
- **Response Drafting:** LLMs can draft responses for agents, who can then review and modify them before sending. This reduces the time agents spend crafting replies, allowing them to handle more inquiries in less time.

2) Knowledge Management:

- **Dynamic Knowledge Base:** LLMs can power a dynamic knowledge base that continuously learns from customer interactions. This knowledge base can be used by both LLMs and human agents to find accurate information quickly, improving the quality and speed of support.
- **Training and Onboarding:** New customer service agents can benefit from LLM-powered training tools that simulate real interactions and provide feedback. This accelerates the onboarding process and ensures that agents are well-prepared to handle a variety of customer scenarios.

4. Best Practices for Integrating LLMs into Customer Service

To maximize the benefits of LLM integration in customer service, it's important to follow best practices that ensure smooth implementation and ongoing success.

1) Start with a Clear Scope:

- **Identify Key Use Cases:** Begin by identifying the specific customer service tasks that would benefit most from LLM integration, such as handling FAQs, providing product recommendations, or assisting agents. Focusing on clear use cases helps in creating targeted solutions that deliver tangible benefits.
- **Pilot Programs:** Implement pilot programs to test the LLM's effectiveness in a controlled environment. This allows you to refine the model and address any issues before rolling it out on a larger scale.

2) Maintain Human Oversight:

- **Hybrid Approach:** Combine LLM capabilities with human oversight to ensure that complex or sensitive issues are handled appropriately. For example, LLMs can manage the initial interaction, with the option to escalate the conversation to a human agent if necessary.

- **Continuous Monitoring:** Regularly monitor the LLM's performance and outputs to ensure that it's meeting customer service standards. Adjustments may be needed over time as customer needs evolve and new challenges arise.

3) Ensure Data Privacy and Compliance:

- **Data Handling Policies:** Implement strict data handling policies to ensure that customer data is used responsibly and in compliance with relevant regulations, such as GDPR or CCPA. This is particularly important when dealing with sensitive information in customer interactions.
- **Transparency with Customers:** Be transparent with customers about the use of LLMs in customer service. Clearly communicate when they are interacting with an AI system and provide options for human assistance if preferred.

4) Continuous Improvement:

- **Regular Updates:** Continuously update the LLM based on new data, feedback, and changing business needs. Regular updates ensure that the model remains accurate, relevant, and aligned with customer service goals.
- **User Feedback:** Encourage customers and agents to provide feedback on their experiences with the LLM. Use this feedback to refine the model and improve its performance over time.

Integrating LLMs into customer service workflows can bring significant benefits, from automating routine inquiries to enhancing customer engagement and supporting human agents. By following best practices and maintaining a focus on both customer satisfaction and operational efficiency, businesses can leverage LLMs to create more responsive, personalized, and effective customer service experiences. As LLM technology continues to advance, its role in customer service is likely to expand, offering even greater opportunities for innovation and improvement.

13.3 LLMs in Content Generation and Marketing

Content generation and marketing are critical components of modern business strategies. As businesses strive to engage audiences, create brand awareness, and drive conversions, the demand for high-quality, relevant content has never been greater. Large Language Models (LLMs) offer powerful tools for automating and enhancing these efforts, allowing companies to scale their content production and deliver personalized marketing experiences. In this section, we'll explore how LLMs can be effectively integrated into content generation and marketing workflows.

1. Automating Content Creation

LLMs can significantly streamline the content creation process by generating text that is both coherent and contextually relevant. This automation can be applied across various content types, from blog posts and articles to social media updates and product descriptions.

1) Blog Posts and Articles:

- **Drafting Content:** LLMs can generate drafts of blog posts and articles based on specific topics, keywords, or outlines provided by the user. This allows content creators to focus on refining and personalizing the content rather than starting from scratch.
- **Content Expansion:** If you have a brief or a list of bullet points, LLMs can expand these into full paragraphs, making the content richer and more detailed. This is particularly useful for creating long-form content where depth and thoroughness are required.

2) Product Descriptions:

- **Dynamic Descriptions:** LLMs can generate product descriptions that highlight key features, benefits, and use cases. By feeding the model specific product information, businesses can produce unique descriptions at scale, ensuring consistency across their catalog.
- **SEO Optimization:** LLMs can also be guided to include specific keywords and phrases that improve search engine optimization (SEO), helping product pages rank higher in search results and attract more organic traffic.

3) Social Media Content:

- **Engaging Posts:** LLMs can craft social media posts tailored to different platforms, whether it's a concise tweet, a compelling Facebook update, or an engaging Instagram caption. By analyzing trending topics and audience preferences, LLMs can help create content that resonates with followers.
- **Hashtag Suggestions:** In addition to generating the content itself, LLMs can suggest relevant hashtags that increase the visibility and reach of social media posts, ensuring that they connect with the right audience.

2. Enhancing Content Personalization

Personalized content is more likely to engage audiences and drive conversions. LLMs can be used to create personalized content experiences that cater to the unique preferences and behaviors of individual users.

1) Email Marketing:

- **Tailored Campaigns:** LLMs can generate personalized email content that speaks directly to the recipient's interests, purchase history, or browsing behavior. This could involve recommending products, offering exclusive deals, or providing content that aligns with the user's past interactions with the brand.

- **Subject Line Optimization:** LLMs can also suggest subject lines that are likely to capture the recipient's attention, based on their previous interactions and open rates. By testing different variations, businesses can optimize their email campaigns for higher engagement.

2) Website Personalization:

- **Dynamic Content Blocks:** LLMs can be used to create dynamic content blocks on websites that adapt to the user's behavior in real-time. For example, a returning visitor might see personalized product recommendations or blog posts related to their previous visits.
- **Localized Content:** For businesses operating in multiple regions, LLMs can generate localized content that reflects the cultural nuances, language preferences, and interests of different audiences. This ensures that the content is relevant and engaging, regardless of where the user is located.

3. Streamlining Marketing Operations

Beyond content creation, LLMs can enhance various aspects of marketing operations, from campaign management to performance analysis.

1) Campaign Management:

- **A/B Testing:** LLMs can automate the creation of multiple variations of ad copy, landing pages, or email content for A/B testing. This allows marketers to quickly identify which version performs best and optimize their campaigns accordingly.
- **Content Scheduling:** LLMs can also assist in planning and scheduling content across multiple platforms. By analyzing engagement patterns,

LLMs can suggest optimal posting times and frequency, ensuring that content reaches the audience when they are most active.

2) Performance Analysis:

- **Sentiment Analysis:** LLMs can analyze customer feedback, reviews, and social media interactions to gauge sentiment towards a brand, product, or campaign. This helps marketers understand how their content is being received and make adjustments to improve future efforts.
- **Content Performance Insights:** By examining metrics such as click-through rates, bounce rates, and conversion rates, LLMs can provide insights into which content pieces are driving the most value. This data-driven approach allows marketers to refine their strategies and focus on what works best.

4. Best Practices for Using LLMs in Content Generation and Marketing

To successfully integrate LLMs into your content generation and marketing strategies, it's important to follow best practices that ensure both effectiveness and alignment with your brand's voice.

1) Maintain Brand Consistency:

- **Style Guides:** Provide LLMs with detailed style guides that outline your brand's tone, voice, and messaging guidelines. This helps ensure that the generated content aligns with your brand's identity and resonates with your target audience.
- **Human Review:** While LLMs can generate high-quality content, it's essential to have a human review process in place. Content creators should review, edit, and approve LLM-generated content to ensure it meets quality standards and is free of errors or inappropriate language.

2) Focus on Value-Driven Content:

- **Audience-Centric Approach:** Ensure that the content generated by LLMs is valuable to your audience. Whether it's educational, entertaining, or informative, the content should meet the needs and interests of your target demographic.
- **Avoid Over-Automation:** While automation can save time and resources, it's important not to rely too heavily on LLMs for every aspect of content creation. Balance automation with human creativity to produce content that is both engaging and authentic.

3) Ethical Considerations:

- **Transparency:** Be transparent with your audience about the use of AI in content generation. This builds trust and allows users to understand the role that LLMs play in your content strategy.
- **Bias Mitigation:** Regularly audit the content generated by LLMs to ensure that it is free from bias and aligns with your company's ethical standards. This is particularly important in marketing, where biased content can negatively impact brand perception.

4) Continuous Learning and Improvement:

- **Feedback Loops:** Establish feedback loops that allow you to continuously learn from the performance of LLM-generated content. Use this feedback to refine the model, improve content quality, and better meet the needs of your audience.
- **Stay Updated:** The field of AI and LLMs is rapidly evolving. Stay informed about the latest developments and advancements to ensure that your content generation and marketing strategies remain cutting-edge.

Integrating LLMs into content generation and marketing can unlock new opportunities for scaling content production, personalizing user experiences, and optimizing marketing operations. By following best practices and maintaining a focus on quality, businesses can leverage LLMs to create compelling content that drives engagement and achieves marketing goals. As the capabilities of LLMs continue to expand, their role in content and marketing strategies is likely to grow, offering even greater potential for innovation and impact.

13.4 Enhancing Business Intelligence with LLMs

Business Intelligence (BI) is crucial for organizations seeking to make informed decisions based on data analysis and insights. Traditionally, BI has relied on structured data and statistical methods to provide actionable information. However, with the advent of Large Language Models (LLMs), businesses can now tap into unstructured data, such as text, to gain deeper insights and enhance their decision-making processes. In this section, we'll explore how LLMs can be integrated into BI workflows to unlock new opportunities and drive business success.

1. Analyzing Unstructured Data

One of the key strengths of LLMs is their ability to process and understand unstructured data, such as text from emails, reports, social media, and customer reviews. Integrating LLMs into BI systems allows businesses to analyze this data alongside traditional structured data.

1. **Text Analysis for Sentiment and Trends:**

- **Sentiment Analysis:** LLMs can analyze text data to determine the sentiment expressed by customers, employees, or stakeholders. By aggregating sentiment data, businesses can gauge overall satisfaction, identify potential issues, and respond proactively to negative feedback.

- **Trend Analysis:** By analyzing large volumes of text data, LLMs can identify emerging trends, topics, or concerns within the market. For example, by processing customer feedback, LLMs might reveal a growing demand for a specific product feature or highlight areas where customers are consistently dissatisfied.

1. **Natural Language Queries:**

- **Simplifying Data Access:** LLMs enable natural language querying of BI systems, allowing users to ask questions in plain language rather than relying on complex query languages. For example, a user might ask, "What were our top-selling products last quarter?" and receive a detailed, context-aware response.
- **Enhancing User Engagement:** Natural language queries make BI tools more accessible to non-technical users, encouraging wider adoption across the organization. This democratization of data allows more employees to contribute to data-driven decision-making.

2. Automating Data Insights

LLMs can automate the extraction of insights from data, reducing the time and effort required to analyze complex datasets and generate reports.

1. **Automated Reporting:**

- **Generating Summaries:** LLMs can automatically generate summaries of data reports, highlighting key findings, trends, and anomalies. This allows decision-makers to quickly grasp the most important insights without sifting through pages of detailed data.
- **Custom Reports:** Based on user inputs or recurring needs, LLMs can create custom reports tailored to specific departments or business goals. For example, a sales team might receive a weekly report on sales

performance, while the marketing team gets insights into campaign effectiveness.

1. **Anomaly Detection:**

- **Identifying Outliers:** LLMs can be trained to detect anomalies in data, such as unexpected spikes in sales, drops in website traffic, or unusual customer behavior. Identifying these outliers early allows businesses to investigate potential issues or capitalize on unexpected opportunities.
- **Automated Alerts:** When an anomaly is detected, LLMs can trigger automated alerts to relevant stakeholders, ensuring that issues are addressed promptly. For example, an LLM might notify the IT team if it detects unusual patterns in network traffic, suggesting a potential security threat.

3. Enhancing Predictive Analytics

Predictive analytics involves using historical data to forecast future trends and outcomes. LLMs can enhance predictive analytics by incorporating unstructured data and providing more accurate and nuanced predictions.

1) Incorporating Text Data:

- **Richer Predictions:** By incorporating unstructured text data, such as customer reviews, social media posts, and news articles, LLMs can provide richer and more informed predictions. For instance, analyzing customer sentiment trends can help predict changes in consumer behavior or demand for specific products.
- **Context-Aware Forecasting:** LLMs can understand the context surrounding certain data points, improving the accuracy of predictions. For example, an LLM might recognize that a sudden increase in sales is due to a successful marketing campaign rather than a long-term

trend.

2) Scenario Analysis:

- **What-If Scenarios:** LLMs can generate and analyze "what-if" scenarios based on different variables or assumptions. This allows businesses to explore the potential impact of various strategies or external factors, such as economic changes or new regulations.
- **Decision Support:** By simulating different scenarios, LLMs can help decision-makers understand the potential outcomes of their choices, supporting more informed and strategic decision-making.

4. Best Practices for Integrating LLMs into BI

To fully leverage the power of LLMs in business intelligence, it's essential to follow best practices that ensure effective implementation and use.

1) Data Integration:

- **Unified Data Sources:** Integrate structured and unstructured data sources into a unified BI platform. This allows LLMs to access and analyze all relevant data, providing a more comprehensive view of the business landscape.
- **Data Quality Management:** Ensure that the data used by LLMs is clean, accurate, and up-to-date. Poor data quality can lead to incorrect insights and flawed decision-making.

2) User Training and Adoption:

- **Training Programs:** Provide training for users on how to interact with LLM-powered BI tools, particularly if they are using natural language queries or analyzing unstructured data. This helps users become comfortable with the technology and maximizes its value.

- **Encouraging Adoption:** Promote the use of LLM-enhanced BI tools across the organization by demonstrating their benefits and ease of use. Encourage teams to integrate these tools into their daily workflows to drive data-driven decision-making.

3) Ethical and Responsible Use:

- **Bias Mitigation:** Regularly audit the outputs of LLMs to ensure that they are free from bias and provide fair, accurate insights. This is especially important when LLMs are used to make predictions or influence strategic decisions.
- **Transparency:** Maintain transparency about how LLMs are used within the BI process. Ensure that users understand the limitations of the models and the sources of data being analyzed.

4) Continuous Improvement:

- **Iterative Refinement:** Continuously refine and update the LLM models based on new data, user feedback, and evolving business needs. This iterative approach ensures that the BI tools remain relevant and effective over time.
- **Monitoring and Evaluation:** Regularly monitor the performance of LLM-enhanced BI tools to ensure they are delivering accurate and actionable insights. Use evaluation metrics such as accuracy, user satisfaction, and business impact to assess their effectiveness.

Integrating LLMs into business intelligence offers a powerful way to enhance data analysis, automate insights, and support more informed decision-making. By effectively combining structured and unstructured data, businesses can unlock new opportunities and gain a deeper understanding of their operations, customers, and markets. As LLM technology continues to evolve, its role in business intelligence will likely expand, providing even greater potential for driving business success.

13.5 Case Study: LLM Integration in a Fortune 500 Company

To understand the real-world impact of Large Language Models (LLMs) in business, it's helpful to look at a case study involving a Fortune 500 company that successfully integrated LLMs into its operations. This case study will explore the challenges, strategies, and outcomes of this integration, offering valuable insights into the potential of LLMs in large-scale business environments.

Background

The company in question is a global leader in consumer electronics, known for its innovative products and extensive supply chain. With a presence in over 100 countries and a diverse range of offerings, the company faced the challenge of managing vast amounts of data and maintaining consistent customer engagement across multiple channels.

To address these challenges, the company decided to integrate LLMs into its business processes, focusing on three key areas: customer service, marketing, and supply chain management. The goal was to enhance efficiency, improve customer satisfaction, and drive growth by leveraging the capabilities of LLMs.

1. Customer Service Transformation

The company's customer service department was dealing with high volumes of inquiries, many of which were repetitive and could be automated. The challenge was to reduce the workload on human agents while maintaining a high level of customer satisfaction.

1) Implementation of LLM-Powered Chatbots:

- **Automating Routine Inquiries:** The company deployed LLM-powered chatbots to handle common customer inquiries, such as product information, troubleshooting, and order status. These chatbots were integrated across the company's website, mobile app, and social media platforms, providing 24/7 support.
- **Personalized Customer Interactions:** The LLMs were trained on historical customer interactions and product data, enabling them to provide personalized responses based on the customer's purchase history and preferences. This personalization helped improve the quality of interactions and customer satisfaction.

2) Outcomes:

- **Reduced Response Times:** The implementation of LLM-powered chatbots led to a significant reduction in response times, with most inquiries being resolved instantly. This allowed human agents to focus on more complex issues, improving overall efficiency.
- **Increased Customer Satisfaction:** Customer satisfaction scores improved as a result of faster, more personalized responses. The company also saw a decrease in customer complaints related to wait times and unresolved issues.

2. Enhancing Marketing Strategies

The company's marketing team was tasked with managing campaigns across different regions and customer segments, each with unique needs and preferences. The challenge was to create tailored marketing content that resonated with diverse audiences while maintaining brand consistency.

1) LLM-Driven Content Creation:

- **Automated Content Generation:** The company used LLMs to generate marketing content, including product descriptions, social media posts, and email campaigns. By feeding the models specific guidelines and data, the company was able to produce content that was both engaging and aligned with its brand voice.
- **Localized Marketing Campaigns:** LLMs were also used to create localized content for different regions, taking into account cultural nuances, language preferences, and regional trends. This allowed the company to connect more effectively with its global customer base.

2) Outcomes:

- **Increased Engagement:** The use of LLM-generated content led to higher engagement rates across the company's digital channels. Personalized and localized content resonated more with customers, leading to improved click-through rates and conversions.
- **Cost and Time Efficiency:** By automating content creation, the company was able to reduce the time and resources spent on developing marketing materials. This efficiency enabled the marketing team to launch campaigns faster and at a lower cost.

3. Optimizing Supply Chain Management

The company's supply chain is vast and complex, involving multiple suppliers, manufacturing plants, and distribution centers. The challenge was to improve demand forecasting and inventory management to ensure products were available where and when needed, without overstocking.

1) LLM-Enhanced Demand Forecasting:

- **Analyzing Historical Data:** The company used LLMs to analyze historical sales data, market trends, and external factors (such as economic indicators and seasonality) to forecast demand more accurately. The models could process large volumes of data and identify patterns that traditional methods might miss.

- **Real-Time Inventory Management:** LLMs were integrated into the company's inventory management system to provide real-time insights into stock levels and reorder points. This allowed the company to optimize its inventory, reducing both stockouts and excess inventory.

2) Outcomes:

- **Improved Forecast Accuracy:** The use of LLMs in demand forecasting led to more accurate predictions, which in turn improved the company's ability to meet customer demand without overstocking. This resulted in reduced inventory costs and increased sales.
- **Streamlined Operations:** The integration of LLMs into inventory management helped streamline supply chain operations, reducing delays and improving the overall efficiency of the supply chain.

4. Challenges and Lessons Learned

While the integration of LLMs brought significant benefits, the company also encountered challenges that provided valuable lessons.

1) Data Quality and Integration:

- **Challenge:** One of the key challenges was ensuring that the data used to train the LLMs was clean, accurate, and comprehensive. Inconsistent or incomplete data led to less effective models and unreliable outputs.
- **Lesson Learned:** The company invested in improving its data quality and integration processes, ensuring that all relevant data was available and properly formatted. This step was crucial for the success of the LLMs and highlighted the importance of robust data management practices.

2) Balancing Automation with Human Oversight:

- **Challenge:** While LLMs were effective in automating many tasks, there were instances where human oversight was needed to handle complex or sensitive issues. Striking the right balance between automation and human intervention was essential.
- **Lesson Learned:** The company developed a hybrid approach, where LLMs handled routine tasks and provided support to human agents for more complex inquiries. This approach maximized efficiency while ensuring that human expertise was available when needed.

3) Ethical and Regulatory Considerations:

- **Challenge:** The use of LLMs raised ethical and regulatory concerns, particularly related to data privacy and bias in AI-generated content. Ensuring compliance with regulations and maintaining ethical standards were critical.
- **Lesson Learned:** The company implemented strict ethical guidelines and compliance measures, including regular audits of LLM outputs to ensure they met legal and ethical standards. Transparency with customers about the use of AI also helped build trust.

The integration of LLMs into this Fortune 500 company's operations led to significant improvements in customer service, marketing, and supply chain management. By leveraging the capabilities of LLMs, the company was able to enhance efficiency, improve customer satisfaction, and drive growth. The challenges encountered along the way provided valuable lessons in data management, balancing automation with human oversight, and addressing ethical considerations. This case study demonstrates the transformative potential of LLMs in large-scale business environments and offers a blueprint for other companies looking to harness this technology.

V

Part V: Case Studies and Real-World Applications

Chapter 14: LLMs in Healthcare

14.1 Overview of LLM Applications in Healthcare

The healthcare industry is increasingly turning to advanced technologies to improve patient outcomes, streamline operations, and enhance decision-making processes. Among these technologies, Large Language Models (LLMs) have emerged as powerful tools with the potential to revolutionize various aspects of healthcare. From aiding in medical diagnosis to supporting clinical research, LLMs offer a wide range of applications that can significantly impact the field.

1. Medical Diagnosis and Decision Support

One of the most promising applications of LLMs in healthcare is their ability to assist in medical diagnosis and provide decision support to healthcare professionals.

1) Symptom Analysis and Diagnosis:

- **Patient Interaction:** LLMs can interact with patients through chatbots or virtual assistants to gather information about their symptoms. By analyzing this data, LLMs can suggest potential diagnoses or highlight symptoms that may require further investigation. This helps in triaging patients and ensuring that those with urgent needs receive prompt attention.

- **Clinical Decision Support:** LLMs can assist healthcare providers by analyzing patient data, including electronic health records (EHRs), lab results, and imaging studies. They can suggest possible diagnoses, recommend treatment options, and even highlight relevant clinical guidelines. This support helps clinicians make informed decisions, reducing the risk of diagnostic errors.

2) Personalized Treatment Plans:

- **Tailored Recommendations:** LLMs can analyze a patient's medical history, genetic information, and lifestyle factors to provide personalized treatment recommendations. For instance, they can suggest the most effective medication based on a patient's unique profile or recommend lifestyle changes that could improve health outcomes.
- **Drug Interactions and Contraindications:** By cross-referencing patient data with vast medical databases, LLMs can alert healthcare providers to potential drug interactions or contraindications, ensuring that prescribed treatments are safe and effective.

2. Enhancing Clinical Research

LLMs also play a crucial role in accelerating clinical research by processing large volumes of medical literature, identifying trends, and generating insights that can guide research efforts.

1) Literature Review and Synthesis:

- **Automated Summaries:** LLMs can process thousands of research papers, clinical trial results, and medical reports to generate summaries that highlight key findings, trends, and gaps in the existing knowledge. This capability significantly reduces the time researchers spend on literature reviews, allowing them to focus on experimentation and hypothesis testing.

- **Identifying Research Opportunities:** By analyzing trends in the medical literature, LLMs can identify emerging research opportunities and suggest areas that may benefit from further investigation. This helps researchers stay ahead of the curve and focus on innovative topics that have the potential to make a significant impact.

2) Supporting Clinical Trials:

- **Participant Recruitment:** LLMs can analyze patient records and match potential participants to relevant clinical trials based on their medical history and current health status. This targeted recruitment improves the efficiency of clinical trials and ensures that they are populated with participants who meet the necessary criteria.
- **Data Analysis:** During clinical trials, LLMs can assist in analyzing data in real-time, identifying trends, and suggesting adjustments to the trial protocol if necessary. This helps researchers make informed decisions throughout the trial, improving the quality and reliability of the results.

3. Patient Communication and Education

Effective communication between healthcare providers and patients is essential for successful treatment outcomes. LLMs can enhance this communication by providing patients with accurate, accessible information and supporting healthcare providers in delivering clear explanations.

1) Patient Education:

- **Health Information:** LLMs can generate easy-to-understand explanations of medical conditions, treatment options, and preventive measures tailored to the patient's level of understanding. This empowers patients to take an active role in their healthcare and make informed decisions about their treatment.

- **Medication Adherence:** LLMs can provide reminders and educational content to help patients adhere to their prescribed medication regimens. They can also explain the importance of adherence in a way that resonates with patients, reducing the likelihood of missed doses or incorrect usage.

2) Virtual Health Assistants:

- **24/7 Support:** LLM-powered virtual health assistants can provide patients with around-the-clock support, answering questions about symptoms, medications, and treatment plans. This continuous availability enhances patient care, especially for those who may not have immediate access to healthcare providers.
- **Mental Health Support:** LLMs can also be used in mental health applications, providing patients with tools for managing stress, anxiety, and depression. These models can offer coping strategies, relaxation exercises, and even virtual therapy sessions, making mental health support more accessible.

4. Operational Efficiency in Healthcare Facilities

In addition to supporting clinical activities, LLMs can improve the operational efficiency of healthcare facilities by automating administrative tasks and optimizing resource allocation.

1) Streamlining Administrative Tasks:

- **Documentation and Reporting:** LLMs can assist in generating medical documentation, including patient notes, discharge summaries, and billing reports. By automating these tasks, healthcare providers can spend more time on patient care and less on paperwork.
- **Appointment Scheduling:** LLMs can manage appointment scheduling,

taking into account the availability of healthcare providers, patient preferences, and the urgency of medical conditions. This helps reduce wait times and ensures that patients receive timely care.

2) Resource Management:

- **Predicting Patient Flow:** LLMs can analyze historical data to predict patient flow patterns, helping hospitals and clinics allocate resources more effectively. For example, they can forecast periods of high demand for emergency services or identify trends in patient admissions, allowing healthcare facilities to adjust staffing levels and resource allocation accordingly.
- **Inventory Management:** In healthcare facilities, managing supplies and medications is critical to ensuring uninterrupted patient care. LLMs can optimize inventory management by predicting usage patterns and automating reordering processes, reducing the risk of stockouts or overstocking.

LLMs are poised to transform the healthcare industry by enhancing medical diagnosis, accelerating clinical research, improving patient communication, and increasing operational efficiency. As these models continue to evolve, their applications in healthcare will likely expand, offering even greater potential for improving patient outcomes and advancing medical knowledge. By integrating LLMs into their operations, healthcare providers can harness the power of AI to deliver better care, support innovation, and meet the challenges of a rapidly changing industry.

14.2 Case Study: LLMs in Medical Diagnosis

The potential of Large Language Models (LLMs) in healthcare is vast, but one of the most impactful applications is in the field of medical diagnosis. This case study explores how an LLM was integrated into a healthcare system to assist in diagnosing complex medical conditions, the challenges encountered, and the outcomes achieved. The case study highlights the real-world implications of LLMs in medical practice and provides insights into their role in improving diagnostic accuracy and patient outcomes.

Background

The healthcare facility in this case study is a large, urban hospital with a diverse patient population. The hospital serves as a referral center for complex cases, often receiving patients with rare or difficult-to-diagnose conditions. While the hospital's medical staff includes experienced specialists, the increasing volume of complex cases strained resources and led to longer diagnostic times.

To address these challenges, the hospital decided to integrate an LLM into its diagnostic processes. The goal was to enhance the diagnostic capabilities of clinicians by providing real-time, data-driven insights that could help identify potential diagnoses more quickly and accurately.

Implementation of the LLM

1) Data Integration and Training:

- **Comprehensive Data Input:** The LLM was trained on a vast dataset that included electronic health records (EHRs), medical literature, imaging studies, lab results, and case histories. This diverse data input allowed the model to learn from a wide range of medical scenarios, improving its ability to recognize patterns and suggest diagnoses.

- **Continuous Learning:** The LLM was designed to continuously learn from new data, including the outcomes of previous diagnoses and treatments. This adaptive learning capability enabled the model to refine its predictions over time, becoming more accurate as it processed more cases.

2) Clinical Workflow Integration:

- **Decision Support Tool:** The LLM was integrated into the hospital's EHR system as a decision support tool. Clinicians could input patient symptoms, lab results, and other relevant data into the system, and the LLM would generate a list of potential diagnoses ranked by likelihood.
- **Collaboration with Specialists:** The LLM's outputs were designed to complement, not replace, the expertise of human specialists. The model provided a starting point for diagnosis, which specialists could then review and refine based on their clinical judgment and experience.

Challenges Encountered

1) Data Quality and Consistency:

- **Challenge:** One of the initial challenges was ensuring that the data fed into the LLM was of high quality and consistent across different sources. Variability in how data was recorded, such as differences in terminology or incomplete records, could lead to inaccurate predictions.
- **Solution:** The hospital implemented data standardization protocols to ensure that the information used by the LLM was consistent and reliable. Additionally, efforts were made to improve the completeness of patient records, including encouraging clinicians to document cases more thoroughly.

2) Clinician Acceptance and Trust:

- **Challenge:** There was initial skepticism among some clinicians regarding the reliability of the LLM's suggestions. Concerns were raised about the model's ability to understand the nuances of complex cases and the potential for over-reliance on AI.
- **Solution:** To address these concerns, the hospital conducted training sessions that demonstrated how the LLM could be used as a collaborative tool rather than a replacement for human expertise. Clinicians were encouraged to use the model as a second opinion rather than a definitive answer, fostering a sense of trust in the technology.

3) Ethical and Legal Considerations:

- **Challenge:** The use of LLMs in medical diagnosis raised ethical and legal questions, particularly around accountability in the event of a misdiagnosis. Determining who was responsible—the clinician or the AI—was a significant concern.
- **Solution:** The hospital established clear guidelines that positioned the LLM as a supportive tool rather than a decision-maker. Clinicians retained full responsibility for the final diagnosis and treatment plan, ensuring that human oversight remained central to patient care.

Outcomes and Impact

1) Improved Diagnostic Accuracy:

- **Faster Identification of Rare Conditions:** The LLM proved particularly valuable in diagnosing rare and complex conditions that might not be immediately apparent to human clinicians. By cross-referencing symptoms with a vast database of case histories, the LLM could suggest potential diagnoses that might otherwise have been overlooked.
- **Reduction in Diagnostic Errors:** The use of the LLM as a decision support tool led to a noticeable reduction in diagnostic errors. In cases where the LLM's suggestions aligned with the clinician's ini-

tial assessment, confidence in the diagnosis was strengthened. In instances where the LLM offered alternative diagnoses, it prompted clinicians to reconsider and further investigate, reducing the likelihood of misdiagnosis.

2) Increased Efficiency:

- **Shorter Diagnostic Times:** The integration of the LLM into the diagnostic process significantly reduced the time required to reach a diagnosis. By quickly narrowing down potential conditions, the LLM allowed clinicians to focus on confirming the most likely options, expediting patient care.
- **Optimized Resource Allocation:** With more accurate and faster diagnoses, the hospital was able to optimize its use of resources, including lab tests and imaging studies. This led to cost savings and allowed the hospital to allocate resources more effectively across its patient population.

3) Enhanced Patient Outcomes:

- **Timelier Treatment:** Faster and more accurate diagnoses enabled patients to receive appropriate treatment sooner, improving their overall outcomes. This was particularly important for conditions where early intervention is critical to the success of treatment.
- **Patient Satisfaction:** The use of advanced AI technology also positively impacted patient satisfaction. Patients appreciated the thoroughness of the diagnostic process and felt reassured that their care was being supported by cutting-edge tools.

This case study illustrates the transformative potential of LLMs in medical diagnosis. By integrating an LLM into its diagnostic workflows, the hospital was able to improve accuracy, efficiency, and patient outcomes while addressing the challenges associated with AI adoption in healthcare. The success of this implementation highlights the value of LLMs as a powerful tool in the hands of skilled clinicians, offering a glimpse into the future of AI-assisted healthcare. As LLM technology continues to advance, its role in medical diagnosis and other areas of healthcare is likely to expand, providing even greater opportunities to enhance patient care.

14.3 Ethical Considerations in Healthcare LLMs

As Large Language Models (LLMs) become increasingly integrated into healthcare, they bring with them a host of ethical considerations that must be carefully addressed. These ethical concerns are particularly important given the high stakes involved in medical decision-making, patient privacy, and the potential for bias in AI-driven systems. In this section, we'll explore the key ethical issues associated with the use of LLMs in healthcare and discuss how they can be managed to ensure that these technologies are used responsibly and effectively.

1. Patient Privacy and Data Security

One of the primary ethical concerns in healthcare is the protection of patient privacy. LLMs require vast amounts of data to function effectively, much of which may include sensitive personal health information.

1) Data Privacy:

- **Risk of Data Breaches:** The more data that is stored and processed by LLMs, the greater the risk of data breaches. Unauthorized access to patient data can lead to serious consequences, including identity theft, discrimination, and loss of trust in healthcare providers.
- **Minimizing Data Exposure:** To mitigate these risks, healthcare

organizations must implement robust data protection measures. This includes encrypting data, anonymizing patient records where possible, and ensuring that access to sensitive information is strictly controlled and monitored.

2) Informed Consent:

- **Transparency in Data Usage:** Patients should be fully informed about how their data will be used by LLMs, including what types of data are being collected, how it will be processed, and the purposes for which it will be used. This transparency is crucial in maintaining patient trust.
- **Obtaining Consent:** Before using patient data to train or operate LLMs, healthcare providers must obtain informed consent. Patients should have the option to opt out of having their data used for AI purposes without facing any negative consequences for their care.

2. Bias and Fairness in LLMs

LLMs are only as unbiased as the data they are trained on, and unfortunately, bias in healthcare data is a well-documented issue. This can lead to LLMs perpetuating or even amplifying existing biases, resulting in unfair treatment of certain patient groups.

1) Bias in Training Data:

- **Historical Inequities:** If an LLM is trained on data that reflects historical inequities in healthcare, such as disparities in treatment based on race, gender, or socioeconomic status, the model may produce biased outcomes. For example, an LLM might underdiagnose conditions in minority populations if those groups were underrepresented in the training data.
- **Addressing Bias:** To combat this, it's essential to ensure that the training data for LLMs is as diverse and representative as possible.

This may involve augmenting datasets to include a broader range of patient demographics and conditions or using techniques to reduce bias in the training process.

2) Fairness in AI Decision-Making:

- **Equitable Treatment:** LLMs must be designed and tested to ensure that they provide equitable treatment recommendations for all patients, regardless of their background. Regular audits should be conducted to check for biases in the model's outputs and to make necessary adjustments.
- **Inclusive AI Development:** Engaging a diverse group of stakeholders in the development and deployment of LLMs can help identify and address potential biases. This includes involving ethicists, social scientists, and representatives from underrepresented groups in the AI design process.

3. Accountability and Liability

The use of LLMs in healthcare raises questions about accountability and liability, particularly in cases where AI-driven decisions lead to adverse outcomes.

1) Shared Responsibility:

- **Human Oversight:** While LLMs can provide valuable decision support, the final responsibility for medical decisions should always rest with human clinicians. This ensures that there is accountability and that the complexities of individual cases are fully considered by experienced professionals.
- **Clear Guidelines:** Healthcare organizations must establish clear guidelines outlining the role of LLMs in clinical decision-making. These guidelines should specify when and how LLMs should be used,

and how discrepancies between AI recommendations and clinical judgment should be handled.

2) Legal and Ethical Implications:

- **Liability in AI-Driven Decisions:** If an LLM provides a recommendation that results in harm to a patient, determining liability can be complex. Healthcare providers, AI developers, and organizations must work together to establish legal frameworks that address these issues, ensuring that patients have recourse in the event of malpractice.
- **Ethical Use of AI:** Beyond legal liability, healthcare providers have an ethical obligation to ensure that LLMs are used in a way that prioritizes patient safety and well-being. This includes conducting thorough testing before deploying LLMs in clinical settings and continually monitoring their performance.

4. Transparency and Explainability

LLMs are often referred to as "black boxes" due to the complexity of their decision-making processes, which can be difficult to understand even for experts. In healthcare, this lack of transparency can be problematic, as patients and clinicians need to trust and understand how decisions are being made.

1) Explainable AI:

- **Making AI Decisions Understandable:** Efforts should be made to develop explainable AI (XAI) models that can provide clear, understandable justifications for their recommendations. This transparency is crucial for building trust in AI-driven healthcare tools.
- **Educating Clinicians and Patients:** Clinicians should be educated about how LLMs work and how to interpret their outputs. Patients should also be provided with information about how AI is being used

in their care, in a way that is accessible and easy to understand.

2) Building Trust:

- **Transparency in AI Development:** AI developers should be transparent about the limitations and potential risks of LLMs in healthcare. This includes acknowledging areas where the model's predictions may be less reliable and involving healthcare providers in the development process to ensure that the technology meets clinical needs.
- **Ongoing Communication:** Maintaining open lines of communication between AI developers, healthcare providers, and patients is essential. Regular updates on how LLMs are being used and the outcomes they are achieving can help build and sustain trust in the technology.

5. Ethical Use of LLMs in Research

LLMs offer significant potential in medical research, but their use in this context also raises ethical concerns, particularly regarding the use of patient data and the implications of AI-driven research findings.

1) Ethical Research Practices:

- **Data Usage:** Researchers must ensure that the use of patient data in training LLMs is conducted ethically, with proper consent and consideration of privacy concerns. This includes being transparent about how data will be used and ensuring that research does not exploit vulnerable populations.
- **Impact on Medical Knowledge:** LLMs can potentially uncover new insights from medical data, but researchers must be cautious about how these findings are interpreted and applied. AI-generated research should be subjected to the same rigorous peer review and validation processes as traditional research.

2) Balancing Innovation and Ethics:

- **Promoting Responsible Innovation:** While LLMs can drive significant advancements in healthcare, it's important to balance innovation with ethical considerations. This involves ensuring that new AI applications are developed with a focus on patient welfare and that ethical dilemmas are addressed proactively.
- **Collaborative Ethical Oversight:** Establishing collaborative oversight bodies that include ethicists, AI experts, healthcare providers, and patient representatives can help guide the ethical development and use of LLMs in healthcare research.

The integration of LLMs into healthcare presents exciting opportunities, but it also brings with it significant ethical challenges. Addressing these challenges is essential to ensure that LLMs are used in a way that is safe, fair, and beneficial to all patients. By prioritizing patient privacy, mitigating bias, ensuring accountability, and fostering transparency, healthcare providers and AI developers can work together to harness the potential of LLMs while upholding the highest ethical standards. As the role of LLMs in healthcare continues to grow, ongoing vigilance and a commitment to ethical practices will be key to realizing their full potential in improving patient care.

14.4 Challenges and Opportunities in Healthcare Applications

The integration of Large Language Models (LLMs) in healthcare brings both significant challenges and exciting opportunities. As these advanced AI systems become more embedded in medical practices, understanding and addressing these challenges is crucial to fully realizing their potential. In this section, we'll explore the key challenges that healthcare providers and AI developers face when implementing LLMs, as well as the opportunities that these technologies present for improving patient care and operational efficiency.

1. Challenges in Implementing LLMs in Healthcare

1) Data Quality and Availability:

- **Incomplete or Inconsistent Data:** One of the biggest challenges in using LLMs in healthcare is the quality and availability of data. Electronic Health Records (EHRs) can be incomplete, inconsistent, or contain errors, which can negatively impact the accuracy of LLM predictions. For example, missing patient history details or inconsistent terminology across different healthcare providers can lead to incorrect or biased outcomes.
- **Data Standardization:** Ensuring that data is standardized across different systems and providers is essential but challenging. This requires significant effort in harmonizing data formats, terminologies, and coding systems across various healthcare institutions, which can be resource-intensive and complex.

2) Integration with Existing Healthcare Systems:

- **Compatibility Issues:** Integrating LLMs with existing healthcare infrastructure, such as EHR systems, can be challenging due to compatibility issues. Many healthcare systems are built on legacy technology that may not easily interface with modern AI tools. This can result in costly and time-consuming IT upgrades or custom solutions.

- **Workflow Disruption:** Introducing LLMs into clinical workflows can disrupt established practices. Healthcare providers may need to adjust to new systems and processes, which can create resistance to adoption. Ensuring a smooth transition requires careful planning, training, and change management.

3) Regulatory and Compliance Barriers:

- **Regulatory Approvals:** LLMs used in healthcare must comply with stringent regulatory standards, such as those set by the FDA in the United States or the EMA in Europe. Obtaining approval for AI-based medical tools can be a lengthy and complex process, involving rigorous testing to ensure safety and efficacy.
- **Data Privacy Laws:** Healthcare data is subject to strict privacy regulations, such as HIPAA in the United States or GDPR in Europe. Ensuring that LLMs comply with these regulations while still being effective can be challenging, particularly when dealing with cross-border data transfer and storage.

4) Ethical and Legal Concerns:

- **Bias and Fairness:** As discussed earlier, bias in LLMs is a significant concern in healthcare. Ensuring that these models are fair and do not perpetuate existing healthcare disparities is a major challenge that requires ongoing monitoring and adjustment.
- **Accountability and Liability:** Determining who is responsible when an LLM-driven decision leads to a negative outcome is another legal and ethical challenge. Establishing clear lines of accountability and ensuring that there are adequate safeguards in place to protect patients is crucial.

2. Opportunities for LLMs in Healthcare

1) Enhanced Diagnostic Accuracy:

- **Improved Decision Support:** LLMs have the potential to significantly enhance diagnostic accuracy by providing clinicians with real-time decision support. By analyzing vast amounts of data, including patient records, medical literature, and clinical guidelines, LLMs can offer suggestions that may not be immediately apparent to human clinicians. This can be particularly valuable in diagnosing rare or complex conditions.
- **Early Detection and Prevention:** LLMs can also be used to identify early warning signs of diseases based on subtle patterns in patient data. This capability can lead to earlier interventions and better outcomes for patients, particularly in areas such as oncology, where early detection is critical.

2) Personalized Medicine:

- **Tailored Treatment Plans:** LLMs can analyze individual patient data, including genetic information, lifestyle factors, and medical history, to develop personalized treatment plans. This approach can optimize the effectiveness of treatments, reduce side effects, and improve patient adherence to prescribed therapies.
- **Predictive Analytics:** By leveraging predictive analytics, LLMs can forecast how a patient might respond to different treatments based on similar cases. This allows healthcare providers to make more informed decisions and tailor interventions to the specific needs of each patient.

3) Streamlining Administrative Processes:

- **Automating Routine Tasks:** LLMs can automate many routine administrative tasks, such as filling out forms, scheduling appointments, and managing billing processes. This automation can reduce the administrative burden on healthcare providers, allowing them to focus more on patient care.

- **Optimizing Resource Allocation:** By analyzing data on patient flow, resource usage, and operational efficiency, LLMs can help healthcare facilities optimize resource allocation. This can lead to more efficient use of staff, equipment, and facilities, reducing costs and improving patient care.

4) Advancing Medical Research:

- **Accelerating Drug Discovery:** LLMs can assist in the drug discovery process by analyzing vast amounts of biomedical data to identify potential new drug candidates. This can significantly speed up the research process and bring new treatments to market more quickly.
- **Enhancing Clinical Trials:** LLMs can also improve the efficiency of clinical trials by identifying suitable participants, predicting outcomes, and optimizing trial protocols. This can lead to faster and more accurate results, ultimately benefiting patients.

3. Balancing Challenges and Opportunities

While the challenges of implementing LLMs in healthcare are significant, they are not insurmountable. By carefully addressing these challenges, healthcare providers can unlock the tremendous opportunities that LLMs offer.

1) Collaborative Development:

- **Partnerships:** Healthcare providers, AI developers, regulators, and ethicists should work together to develop LLMs that meet the specific needs of the healthcare industry. Collaborative efforts can lead to the creation of AI tools that are not only effective but also safe, ethical, and compliant with regulations.

- **Continuous Improvement:** The development and deployment of LLMs in healthcare should be seen as an ongoing process. Regular updates, feedback loops, and real-world testing are essential to refine these models and ensure that they continue to meet the evolving needs of healthcare.

2) Investing in Education and Training:

- **Empowering Clinicians:** To maximize the benefits of LLMs, healthcare providers must invest in training programs that help clinicians understand and effectively use these tools. This includes not only technical training but also education on the ethical implications and limitations of AI.
- **Raising Awareness:** Educating patients about the role of LLMs in their care is equally important. Clear communication about how AI is used and its benefits can help build trust and acceptance among patients.

The challenges of integrating LLMs into healthcare are real and complex, but the opportunities they present are equally significant. By addressing issues related to data quality, system integration, regulation, ethics, and clinician training, healthcare providers can harness the power of LLMs to enhance diagnostic accuracy, personalize treatment, streamline operations, and advance medical research. The key to success lies in balancing these challenges with the potential benefits, ensuring that LLMs are used in a way that improves patient care and supports the overall goals of the healthcare system. As the technology continues to evolve, the healthcare industry must remain proactive in addressing these challenges and seizing the opportunities that LLMs offer.

Chapter 15: LLMs in Finance

15.1 Overview of LLM Applications in Finance

The financial industry is one of the most data-driven sectors, relying heavily on timely and accurate information to make critical decisions. Large Language Models (LLMs) are uniquely positioned to revolutionize this industry by processing vast amounts of unstructured data, automating complex tasks, and providing insights that can enhance decision-making. In this section, we'll explore some of the key applications of LLMs in finance and how they are reshaping the landscape of the industry.

1. Enhancing Financial Analysis and Decision-Making

1) Automated Financial Reports:

- **Generating Reports:** LLMs can automate the generation of financial reports by analyzing data from various sources, such as earnings reports, market data, and news articles. This capability allows financial institutions to produce detailed, accurate reports quickly, helping analysts and executives make informed decisions without the delay associated with manual report generation.
- **Summarizing Insights:** By summarizing complex financial data into key insights, LLMs can provide executives with the information they need at a glance. This can include highlighting trends, identifying

potential risks, or pinpointing areas of opportunity, all of which are crucial for strategic planning.

2) Sentiment Analysis and Market Predictions:

- **Analyzing Market Sentiment:** LLMs are adept at processing large volumes of text data, including news articles, social media posts, and analyst opinions. By analyzing the sentiment expressed in these sources, LLMs can gauge market sentiment and predict potential market movements. For example, a sudden increase in negative sentiment around a particular stock might indicate an impending price drop, providing investors with an early warning.
- **Predictive Analytics:** Beyond sentiment analysis, LLMs can also be used for predictive analytics, helping financial professionals forecast market trends and make more informed investment decisions. By analyzing historical data alongside real-time information, LLMs can identify patterns that might not be immediately obvious to human analysts.

2. Risk Management and Compliance

1) Fraud Detection:

- **Identifying Anomalies:** One of the most critical applications of LLMs in finance is in fraud detection. LLMs can analyze transaction data, customer behavior, and other relevant information to identify patterns indicative of fraudulent activity. For example, an LLM might detect unusual spending patterns on a credit card that suggest it has been compromised.
- **Real-Time Monitoring:** LLMs can be deployed to monitor transactions in real-time, flagging suspicious activities as they occur. This allows financial institutions to respond to potential fraud more quickly, minimizing losses and protecting customers.

2) Regulatory Compliance:

- **Automating Compliance Checks:** Financial institutions are subject to extensive regulations that require them to monitor and report on various activities. LLMs can automate many of these compliance tasks, such as monitoring transactions for signs of money laundering or ensuring that trading activities adhere to regulatory guidelines. By automating these processes, LLMs reduce the burden on compliance teams and help ensure that institutions remain in good standing with regulators.
- **Document Review:** LLMs can also assist in reviewing large volumes of regulatory documents, contracts, and other legal texts to ensure compliance. By highlighting relevant clauses and identifying potential risks, LLMs help legal and compliance teams stay ahead of regulatory requirements.

3. Personalized Financial Services

1) Customer Support:

- **Virtual Assistants:** LLMs can power virtual assistants that provide customers with instant support, answering questions about their accounts, providing financial advice, or helping them navigate complex financial products. These assistants can handle a wide range of inquiries, from simple account balance checks to more complex tasks like advising on investment options, all while maintaining a high level of personalization.
- **Improving Customer Experience:** By offering 24/7 support and instant responses, LLMs enhance the customer experience, reducing wait times and providing more personalized service. This not only improves customer satisfaction but also allows financial institutions to handle higher volumes of inquiries without increasing staff.

2) Tailored Financial Advice:

- **Personalized Recommendations:** LLMs can analyze individual customer data, such as spending habits, investment portfolios, and financial goals, to offer personalized financial advice. This could include recommending investment strategies, suggesting savings plans, or identifying opportunities for debt consolidation.
- **Proactive Financial Management:** Beyond reactive advice, LLMs can also take a proactive role in managing finances by alerting customers to potential issues, such as upcoming bill payments or unusual spending patterns. This helps customers stay on top of their finances and avoid common pitfalls, such as overdraft fees or missed payments.

4. Streamlining Operations and Reducing Costs

1) Automating Back-Office Processes:

- **Data Entry and Reconciliation:** LLMs can automate many of the routine tasks that take up significant time in financial institutions, such as data entry, transaction reconciliation, and account management. By automating these processes, financial institutions can reduce errors, speed up operations, and free up staff to focus on more strategic tasks.
- **Reducing Operational Costs:** Automation driven by LLMs can lead to significant cost savings, as institutions can reduce their reliance on manual processes and the associated labor costs. This is particularly valuable in areas such as trade processing, where LLMs can handle large volumes of transactions with greater speed and accuracy than human workers.

2) Enhancing Regulatory Reporting:

- **Automated Reporting:** Financial institutions are required to submit regular reports to regulators, a process that can be time-consuming and prone to errors. LLMs can automate the generation of these reports, ensuring that they are accurate, complete, and submitted on time. This reduces the risk of non-compliance and the associated penalties.

- **Data Validation:** LLMs can also be used to validate the data used in regulatory reporting, identifying inconsistencies or errors before reports are submitted. This further reduces the risk of regulatory issues and enhances the overall accuracy of the reporting process.

LLMs are rapidly transforming the finance industry by enhancing decision-making, improving risk management, personalizing customer services, and streamlining operations. As these models continue to evolve, their impact on finance is likely to grow, offering even greater opportunities for innovation and efficiency. However, the successful integration of LLMs into financial services requires careful consideration of the challenges they present, including data privacy, regulatory compliance, and the need for ongoing monitoring and refinement. By addressing these challenges, financial institutions can harness the full potential of LLMs to drive growth, reduce costs, and deliver better services to their customers.

15.2 Case Study: Fraud Detection with LLMs

Fraud detection is one of the most critical areas where financial institutions can leverage Large Language Models (LLMs) to protect their assets and customers. The ability of LLMs to analyze vast amounts of transaction data, identify patterns, and detect anomalies in real-time makes them a powerful tool in combating fraudulent activities. This case study examines how a major financial institution successfully implemented an LLM-based fraud detection system, the challenges encountered, and the outcomes achieved.

Background

The financial institution in question is a large multinational bank that processes millions of transactions daily. Despite having a robust traditional fraud detection system in place, the bank faced increasing challenges due to the growing sophistication of fraudulent schemes. Traditional rule-based systems were struggling to keep up with the evolving tactics used by fraudsters, resulting in a rise in false positives (legitimate transactions flagged as fraudulent) and false negatives (fraudulent transactions going undetected).

To address these challenges, the bank decided to implement an LLM-based fraud detection system. The goal was to enhance the accuracy of fraud detection while reducing the operational burden on their fraud investigation team.

Implementation of the LLM-Based Fraud Detection System

1) Data Collection and Preparation:

- **Comprehensive Data Integration:** The bank began by integrating data from multiple sources, including transaction histories, customer profiles, behavioral data, and external data such as social media activity and public records. This diverse dataset provided the LLM with a comprehensive view of each customer's behavior and transaction patterns.
- **Anomaly Detection Training:** The LLM was trained to recognize anomalies in transaction patterns by analyzing historical data. The model learned to identify deviations from a customer's usual behavior, such as unusual spending patterns, transactions in locations far from the customer's usual area, or purchases of goods that didn't align with the customer's typical purchasing habits.

2) Model Deployment and Integration:

- **Real-Time Monitoring:** Once trained, the LLM was deployed to monitor transactions in real-time. Every transaction was evaluated by the model, which assigned a risk score based on the likelihood of fraud. Transactions with high-risk scores were flagged for further investigation by the bank's fraud detection team.
- **Integration with Existing Systems:** The LLM was integrated into the bank's existing fraud detection infrastructure. This allowed the LLM to work alongside traditional rule-based systems, providing an additional layer of protection. Transactions flagged by either the LLM or the traditional system were automatically routed to the investigation team for review.

3) Challenges Encountered:

- **Data Privacy Concerns:** One of the main challenges faced during implementation was ensuring compliance with data privacy regulations. The bank had to carefully manage how customer data was used and stored to avoid potential breaches of privacy laws. This required implementing strict data governance policies and ensuring that all data processing was fully compliant with relevant regulations, such as GDPR.
- **Model Calibration:** Initially, the LLM generated a high number of false positives, overwhelming the fraud investigation team with alerts. To address this, the bank fine-tuned the model by adjusting the thresholds for what constituted a "high-risk" transaction and by continuously updating the model with new data to improve its accuracy.

Outcomes and Impact

1) Enhanced Fraud Detection Accuracy:

- **Reduction in False Positives:** After fine-tuning, the LLM-based system significantly reduced the number of false positives. This allowed the fraud investigation team to focus on genuinely suspicious transactions, improving their efficiency and reducing the workload.

- **Detection of Sophisticated Fraud Schemes:** The LLM proved particularly effective at identifying sophisticated fraud schemes that had previously gone undetected. For example, the model was able to recognize patterns associated with "friendly fraud," where legitimate customers dispute transactions they actually made. The LLM's ability to analyze behavioral data alongside transaction data allowed it to identify these cases more accurately.

2) Operational Efficiency:

- **Streamlined Investigation Process:** With fewer false positives to investigate, the fraud team could allocate more resources to investigating high-risk transactions. The LLM's risk scoring system also helped prioritize cases, ensuring that the most critical incidents were addressed first.
- **Cost Savings:** The improved accuracy of the LLM-based system led to significant cost savings for the bank. By reducing the number of false positives, the bank lowered the costs associated with manual investigations and customer service interventions. Additionally, the early detection of fraud reduced the financial losses associated with fraudulent transactions.

3) Customer Experience:

- **Improved Trust and Satisfaction:** The implementation of the LLM-based fraud detection system had a positive impact on customer satisfaction. By reducing the frequency of false positives, customers experienced fewer interruptions in their transactions. Additionally, the bank's ability to detect and prevent fraud more effectively increased customer trust, as they felt more secure knowing their accounts were protected by advanced technology.

- **Seamless Integration:** Customers were largely unaware of the behind-the-scenes changes, as the LLM operated silently in the background. This seamless integration ensured that the enhanced security measures did not disrupt the customer experience.

The case study demonstrates the significant benefits that LLMs can bring to fraud detection in the financial industry. By leveraging the power of LLMs, the bank was able to enhance the accuracy of its fraud detection efforts, reduce operational costs, and improve the overall customer experience. The successful implementation of this system highlights the potential of LLMs to revolutionize fraud detection, providing financial institutions with a powerful tool to combat increasingly sophisticated fraud schemes. As LLM technology continues to advance, it is likely that more financial institutions will adopt similar approaches, further enhancing the security and efficiency of the global financial system.

15.3 Regulatory Compliance and LLMs in Finance

In the highly regulated financial industry, compliance is not just a requirement—it's a cornerstone of trust and stability. Financial institutions must navigate a complex landscape of regulations designed to prevent fraud, money laundering, and other financial crimes. Large Language Models (LLMs) offer a powerful tool for helping institutions meet these regulatory demands by automating and enhancing many compliance-related tasks. However, the use of LLMs in this context also introduces new challenges that must be carefully managed. In this section, we'll explore how LLMs can support regulatory compliance in finance, the benefits they offer, and the challenges they present.

1. Automating Compliance Monitoring

1) Real-Time Transaction Monitoring:

- **Automated Surveillance:** LLMs can be deployed to monitor financial transactions in real-time, identifying activities that may indicate non-compliance with regulatory requirements. For example, LLMs can detect unusual transaction patterns that may suggest money laundering or other illicit activities. By continuously analyzing transaction data, LLMs help institutions stay ahead of potential compliance issues, reducing the risk of regulatory breaches.
- **Risk Scoring:** LLMs can assign risk scores to transactions based on various factors, such as the transaction amount, the parties involved, and the geographical locations. Transactions with higher risk scores can be flagged for further investigation by compliance officers, ensuring that potential issues are addressed promptly.

2) Document Analysis and Reporting:

- **Automating Document Review:** Compliance in finance often involves the review of large volumes of documents, such as contracts, legal agreements, and regulatory filings. LLMs can automate this process by analyzing these documents for compliance-related content. For instance, an LLM can identify clauses that may not meet regulatory standards or flag missing information that is required for compliance.
- **Generating Compliance Reports:** Financial institutions are required to submit regular reports to regulators, detailing their activities and ensuring adherence to legal standards. LLMs can streamline this process by automatically generating these reports, extracting relevant data from various sources, and formatting it according to regulatory requirements. This not only saves time but also reduces the risk of human error in reporting.

2. Enhancing Regulatory Knowledge Management

1) Keeping Up with Regulatory Changes:

- **Continuous Learning:** Financial regulations are constantly evolving, with new rules and guidelines being introduced regularly. LLMs can be used to keep compliance teams up-to-date with these changes by continuously monitoring regulatory updates, legal publications, and industry news. By summarizing and highlighting key changes, LLMs ensure that compliance teams are always informed and prepared to adapt to new requirements.
- **Training and Development:** LLMs can also be used to create and deliver training materials for compliance officers, helping them stay current with the latest regulatory developments. By providing personalized training based on an individual's role and expertise, LLMs can enhance the effectiveness of compliance training programs.

2) Regulatory Intelligence:

- **Analyzing Regulatory Texts:** LLMs can analyze complex regulatory texts, such as new legislation or amendments to existing laws, to extract the key points relevant to the financial institution. This allows compliance teams to quickly understand the implications of new regulations and take the necessary steps to ensure compliance.
- **Cross-Referencing Regulations:** In cases where multiple regulations apply, LLMs can cross-reference these texts to identify potential conflicts or areas where the institution's policies may need to be adjusted. This capability helps institutions navigate the complex web of regulations that often overlap or interact in unexpected ways.

3. Addressing Compliance Challenges with LLMs

1) Data Privacy and Security:

- **Handling Sensitive Data:** While LLMs can greatly enhance compliance efforts, their use also raises concerns about data privacy and security. Financial institutions must ensure that the data used to train and operate LLMs is handled in accordance with data protection laws, such as GDPR in Europe or CCPA in California. This includes implementing robust encryption, access controls, and data anonymization techniques to protect sensitive information.
- **Regulatory Compliance of AI Systems:** In addition to helping institutions comply with financial regulations, LLMs themselves must be compliant with regulations governing the use of AI in finance. This includes ensuring that AI systems are transparent, explainable, and free from bias, as required by emerging AI governance frameworks.

2) Explainability and Accountability:

- **Transparent Decision-Making:** One of the key challenges of using LLMs in compliance is ensuring that their decisions are explainable. Regulators and compliance officers need to understand how an LLM arrived at a particular decision, especially in cases where a transaction is flagged for further investigation. Developing explainable AI (XAI) models that can provide clear justifications for their decisions is crucial for maintaining trust in LLM-driven compliance systems.
- **Accountability in AI-Driven Compliance:** As LLMs take on more significant roles in compliance, questions of accountability become more pressing. Institutions must establish clear guidelines on who is responsible for decisions made by LLMs, particularly in cases where these decisions have legal or financial consequences. This may involve defining the roles of human compliance officers in overseeing and validating AI-driven decisions.

4. Opportunities and Benefits of LLMs in Compliance

1) Efficiency and Cost Savings:

- **Reducing Manual Work:** By automating routine compliance tasks, LLMs free up compliance teams to focus on more strategic activities, such as risk assessment and policy development. This not only improves the efficiency of compliance operations but also reduces the costs associated with manual labor.
- **Scalability:** LLMs enable financial institutions to scale their compliance efforts more easily, allowing them to handle larger volumes of transactions and documents without a corresponding increase in staffing levels. This is particularly valuable for global institutions that must comply with regulations across multiple jurisdictions.

2) Proactive Compliance:

- **Anticipating Regulatory Risks:** LLMs can help institutions move from reactive to proactive compliance by identifying potential risks before they become issues. For example, an LLM might detect patterns in transaction data that suggest emerging compliance risks, allowing the institution to take preventive action before regulators become involved.
- **Continuous Improvement:** By continuously learning from new data and feedback, LLMs can help institutions refine their compliance strategies over time, ensuring that they remain effective in a rapidly changing regulatory environment.

LLMs offer significant potential to enhance regulatory compliance in the financial industry by automating complex tasks, improving the accuracy of compliance monitoring, and enabling more proactive risk management. However, their implementation also introduces new challenges, particularly in the areas of data privacy, explainability, and accountability. To fully realize the benefits of LLMs in compliance, financial institutions must carefully manage these challenges, ensuring that their AI systems are not only effective but also transparent and trustworthy. As regulations continue to evolve, LLMs will play an increasingly important role in helping financial institutions stay compliant, reduce costs, and build trust with regulators and customers alike.

15.4 Challenges and Opportunities in Financial Applications

The integration of Large Language Models (LLMs) into the financial industry offers immense potential for innovation and efficiency, but it also presents a set of unique challenges that must be carefully navigated. As financial institutions increasingly adopt LLMs to enhance operations, improve customer service, and ensure compliance, understanding these challenges and the opportunities they present is crucial for successful implementation. In this section, we'll explore the key challenges and opportunities that arise when deploying LLMs in financial applications.

1. Challenges in Implementing LLMs in Finance

1) Data Quality and Availability:

- **High-Quality Data Requirements:** LLMs require vast amounts of high-quality data to function effectively. In the financial sector, data quality can vary significantly, with discrepancies often arising from incomplete records, outdated information, or inconsistencies across different systems. Ensuring that LLMs have access to accurate and up-to-date data is essential, but it can be a complex and resource-intensive process.
- **Data Silos:** Financial institutions often operate with data stored in

silos, where different departments or branches maintain their own data sets. Integrating these silos into a unified dataset for LLM training and deployment can be challenging, requiring significant coordination and investment in data infrastructure.

2) Regulatory Compliance and Ethical Concerns:

- **Navigating Complex Regulations:** The financial industry is subject to a web of regulations that vary by jurisdiction. Implementing LLMs in a way that complies with these regulations is challenging, particularly when dealing with cross-border data flows and differing legal standards. Institutions must ensure that their LLM deployments meet all relevant regulatory requirements, including those related to data privacy, consumer protection, and financial reporting.
- **Ethical Considerations:** LLMs in finance raise important ethical questions, particularly regarding bias and fairness. There is a risk that LLMs, if not properly managed, could reinforce existing biases in financial decision-making, leading to unfair outcomes for certain groups of customers. Financial institutions must implement robust measures to detect and mitigate bias in LLM outputs, ensuring that these systems operate fairly and ethically.

3) Operational Risks:

- **Model Robustness and Reliability:** LLMs are complex models that can be sensitive to the data they are trained on. There is a risk that LLMs might produce inaccurate or unreliable outputs if they encounter data that is significantly different from what they were trained on. This could lead to incorrect financial decisions or compliance violations, posing significant risks to the institution.
- **Integration with Legacy Systems:** Many financial institutions rely on legacy systems that may not easily integrate with modern LLMs. Ensuring seamless integration between LLMs and these older systems

can be technically challenging and may require substantial investment in IT infrastructure upgrades.

4) Explainability and Trust:

- **Black Box Nature of LLMs:** One of the biggest challenges with LLMs is their "black box" nature, where the decision-making process is not easily interpretable. In finance, where decisions can have significant consequences, it is crucial that LLMs are explainable so that stakeholders can understand how decisions are made. Without this transparency, gaining trust from regulators, customers, and internal teams can be difficult.
- **Building Trust:** For LLMs to be widely accepted in finance, institutions must build trust in these systems. This involves not only making LLMs more transparent but also ensuring that they are reliable, consistent, and aligned with the institution's values and regulatory obligations.

2. Opportunities for LLMs in Finance

1) Enhanced Decision-Making and Efficiency:

- **Data-Driven Insights:** LLMs have the potential to transform decision-making in finance by providing data-driven insights that were previously inaccessible or too time-consuming to analyze. By processing vast amounts of data in real-time, LLMs can help financial institutions identify trends, assess risks, and make more informed decisions quickly.
- **Operational Efficiency:** LLMs can automate many routine tasks in finance, such as document processing, customer support, and compliance checks. This automation can significantly reduce operational costs, increase efficiency, and free up human resources for more strategic activities.

2) Personalized Customer Experiences:

- **Tailored Financial Products:** LLMs enable financial institutions to offer more personalized products and services. By analyzing individual customer data, LLMs can recommend tailored financial products, such as investment portfolios or loan packages, that best meet the needs of each customer. This personalization can enhance customer satisfaction and loyalty.
- **Improved Customer Support:** LLMs can power virtual assistants that provide 24/7 support to customers, answering questions, providing financial advice, and helping them navigate complex products. This level of personalized, on-demand service can greatly improve the customer experience, making financial services more accessible and user-friendly.

3) Proactive Risk Management:

- **Early Risk Detection:** LLMs can enhance risk management by detecting potential issues before they escalate. For example, LLMs can analyze market data and identify early signs of financial instability, allowing institutions to take proactive measures to mitigate risks. This capability is particularly valuable in volatile markets, where timely decision-making is crucial.
- **Fraud Prevention:** LLMs can improve fraud detection by identifying patterns that indicate fraudulent activity, even as fraudsters develop more sophisticated tactics. By continuously learning from new data, LLMs can adapt to emerging threats and provide more robust protection against financial crimes.

4) Innovation in Financial Products and Services:

- **New Business Models:** The insights generated by LLMs can inspire the development of new financial products and services that better meet customer needs. For example, LLMs can identify gaps in the market or untapped customer segments, enabling institutions to innovate and stay ahead of the competition.

- **Expanding Access to Finance:** LLMs can also play a role in expanding access to financial services for underserved populations. By analyzing non-traditional data sources, LLMs can help institutions assess creditworthiness for individuals or businesses that lack a conventional credit history, enabling them to access loans and other financial products.

3. Balancing Challenges and Opportunities

1) Strategic Implementation:

- **Pilot Programs:** Financial institutions can mitigate the risks associated with LLMs by starting with pilot programs. These pilots allow institutions to test LLMs in a controlled environment, identify potential issues, and refine the models before full-scale deployment.
- **Cross-Functional Teams:** Successful implementation of LLMs requires collaboration across different departments, including IT, compliance, legal, and operations. By forming cross-functional teams, institutions can ensure that all aspects of LLM deployment are considered, from technical integration to regulatory compliance.

2) Continuous Learning and Adaptation:

- **Model Updating:** LLMs need to be continuously updated with new data and feedback to remain effective. Institutions should establish processes for regularly retraining their models, incorporating new information, and adjusting parameters to ensure that LLMs continue to deliver accurate and reliable results.
- **Monitoring and Feedback Loops:** Continuous monitoring of LLM performance is essential for identifying issues and opportunities for improvement. By establishing feedback loops, institutions can refine

their models based on real-world outcomes, ensuring that LLMs remain aligned with their strategic goals.

While the challenges of implementing LLMs in finance are significant, the opportunities they present are equally compelling. By enhancing decision-making, improving customer experiences, and enabling proactive risk management, LLMs can transform the financial industry and provide institutions with a competitive edge. However, to fully realize these benefits, financial institutions must carefully manage the challenges related to data quality, regulatory compliance, operational risks, and trust. Through strategic implementation, continuous learning, and a commitment to ethical AI practices, financial institutions can successfully harness the power of LLMs to drive innovation, efficiency, and growth in the evolving financial landscape.

Chapter 16: LLMs in Education

16.1 Overview of LLM Applications in Education

The field of education is undergoing a transformation, driven in part by advancements in technology. Among these, Large Language Models (LLMs) are emerging as powerful tools that can enhance the learning experience, support educators, and provide personalized education at scale. In this section, we'll explore the various applications of LLMs in education, highlighting how these models are being integrated into educational settings to benefit both students and educators.

1. Personalized Learning

1) Tailored Educational Content:

- **Customized Lessons:** One of the most promising applications of LLMs in education is the ability to create personalized learning experiences for students. LLMs can analyze a student's learning history, strengths, and areas for improvement to generate customized lessons that cater to their unique needs. This means that each student can receive instruction that is perfectly suited to their level and pace, making learning more effective and engaging.
- **Adaptive Learning Platforms:** LLMs power adaptive learning platforms that adjust in real-time based on student performance. For

example, if a student struggles with a particular concept, the system can offer additional resources or adjust the difficulty of future exercises to help the student master the material.

2) Intelligent Tutoring Systems:

- **Virtual Tutors:** LLMs enable the creation of intelligent tutoring systems that can provide students with instant, personalized feedback. These virtual tutors can answer questions, explain concepts in different ways, and guide students through complex problems, offering support similar to what they might receive from a human tutor. This accessibility can be particularly valuable in large classrooms or remote learning environments, where individual attention from teachers may be limited.
- **24/7 Availability:** Unlike traditional tutors, LLM-powered tutors are available 24/7, allowing students to learn at their own pace and schedule. This flexibility can be especially beneficial for students with varying learning styles or those who need extra time to grasp certain concepts.

2. Support for Educators

1) Automating Administrative Tasks:

- **Grading and Feedback:** LLMs can help educators by automating time-consuming tasks such as grading and providing feedback on assignments. For instance, LLMs can evaluate written essays, provide constructive comments, and even suggest improvements. This not only saves educators time but also ensures that students receive timely feedback, which is crucial for their learning process.
- **Curriculum Development:** LLMs can assist in the creation of curriculum materials by generating lesson plans, quizzes, and educational resources. Educators can use these AI-generated materials as a

foundation, customizing them further to meet the specific needs of their students.

2) Professional Development and Resources:

- **Ongoing Training:** LLMs can support educators in their professional development by offering personalized training modules and resources. These systems can recommend articles, research papers, and courses that align with an educator's interests or areas where they seek improvement, helping them stay current with the latest educational trends and best practices.
- **Collaborative Tools:** LLMs can also facilitate collaboration among educators by providing platforms where they can share resources, discuss teaching strategies, and work together on projects. This fosters a community of practice where educators can learn from each other and continuously improve their teaching methods.

3. Enhancing Student Engagement

1) Interactive Learning Experiences:

- **Gamification and Simulations:** LLMs can enhance student engagement by powering interactive learning experiences, such as educational games and simulations. These tools make learning more fun and immersive, helping students stay motivated and retain information better. For example, LLMs can generate scenarios in which students must apply their knowledge to solve real-world problems, making the learning process more relevant and exciting.
- **Conversational Learning:** Through natural language processing, LLMs enable conversational learning, where students can interact with the AI as they would with a teacher or peer. This can take the form of asking questions, engaging in debates, or exploring topics in a more dynamic and interactive way, making the learning process more

engaging and personalized.

2) Supporting Diverse Learning Styles:

- **Multimodal Content:** LLMs can cater to different learning styles by generating multimodal content, such as text, audio, and video. For instance, a student who learns better through visual aids can be provided with diagrams and videos, while another who prefers reading can receive text-based explanations. This flexibility ensures that all students, regardless of their preferred learning style, can benefit from the content.
- **Language Support:** LLMs can also provide language support to students who may be learning in a language that is not their first. By offering translations, simplified explanations, and culturally relevant examples, LLMs make education more accessible to a diverse student body.

4. Expanding Access to Education

1) Education for All:

- **Remote and Rural Learning:** LLMs play a crucial role in expanding access to quality education for students in remote or underserved areas. By delivering educational content and tutoring through digital platforms, LLMs help bridge the gap for students who may not have access to traditional schools or qualified teachers. This democratization of education ensures that more students can receive the support they need, regardless of their location.
- **Lifelong Learning:** LLMs support lifelong learning by providing educational resources that are accessible to people of all ages. Whether someone is pursuing a new skill, seeking career advancement, or simply exploring a new interest, LLMs can offer personalized learning experiences that cater to adult learners and professionals alike.

2) Supporting Special Education:

- **Assistive Technologies:** LLMs can enhance special education by powering assistive technologies that support students with disabilities. For example, LLMs can enable voice-to-text and text-to-speech functions, provide explanations in simpler language, or generate visual aids for students with learning difficulties. These tools make education more inclusive, allowing all students to participate and learn at their own pace.
- **Personalized Learning Plans:** For students with specific educational needs, LLMs can help create personalized learning plans that accommodate their unique challenges and strengths. These plans can be regularly updated based on the student's progress, ensuring that they receive the right level of support throughout their education.

LLMs are poised to revolutionize the field of education by offering personalized learning experiences, supporting educators, and expanding access to quality education for all. From enhancing student engagement to automating administrative tasks, the applications of LLMs in education are vast and varied. As these technologies continue to develop, they will play an increasingly important role in shaping the future of learning, making education more effective, inclusive, and accessible. By embracing these innovations, educators and institutions can better meet the diverse needs of their students, preparing them for success in a rapidly changing world.

16.2 Case Study: Personalized Learning with LLMs

Personalized learning is becoming increasingly important in education, as it addresses the unique needs, strengths, and learning styles of individual students. Large Language Models (LLMs) have the potential to revolutionize this aspect of education by offering tailored educational experiences that adapt to each student's pace and preferences. In this case study, we'll explore how a leading educational institution implemented LLM-based personalized learning tools to enhance student outcomes, the challenges they faced, and the results they achieved.

Background

The educational institution in question is a large online learning platform that serves a diverse student population, ranging from K-12 students to adult learners seeking professional development. Despite offering a wide range of courses and resources, the platform faced challenges in delivering personalized learning experiences at scale. Traditional methods of tailoring content to individual learners were time-consuming and often limited to one-on-one tutoring, which was not feasible for the large number of students enrolled.

To address these challenges, the platform decided to implement LLMs to create personalized learning paths for each student. The goal was to enhance student engagement, improve learning outcomes, and provide a more supportive and flexible learning environment.

Implementation of LLM-Based Personalized Learning

1) Data Collection and Analysis:

- **Gathering Student Data:** The first step in implementing personalized learning was to collect data on each student's performance, learning preferences, and engagement levels. This included analyzing quiz results, assignment submissions, time spent on different topics, and interaction with course materials. Additionally, students were asked to complete a survey detailing their learning goals and preferred learning styles.
- **Data-Driven Insights:** Using this data, the LLM analyzed patterns and trends to identify each student's strengths and areas for improvement. For example, if a student consistently struggled with a particular math

concept, the LLM would flag this area for additional practice and review. Conversely, if a student excelled in a topic, the LLM might suggest more advanced materials to keep them challenged.

2) Creating Personalized Learning Paths:

- **Tailored Content Delivery:** Based on the insights gained from the data analysis, the LLM created a personalized learning path for each student. This path included customized lessons, exercises, and assessments that matched the student's current level and learning preferences. For instance, a student who preferred visual learning might receive more video content and interactive diagrams, while a student who preferred reading might be provided with text-based explanations and articles.
- **Adaptive Learning Progression:** The LLM continuously adapted the learning path as the student progressed through the course. If the student demonstrated mastery of a concept, the LLM would adjust the path to introduce more challenging material. Conversely, if the student struggled, the LLM would provide additional resources and support to help them grasp the concept before moving on.

3) Interactive Tutoring and Feedback:

- **Virtual Tutoring Support:** The LLM-powered virtual tutor played a key role in the personalized learning experience. Students could ask the tutor questions at any time and receive instant, personalized responses. The tutor also provided explanations in different formats—such as written explanations, step-by-step walkthroughs, or real-world examples—depending on the student's learning style.
- **Continuous Feedback:** Throughout the learning process, the LLM provided continuous feedback on the student's performance. This feedback was immediate and actionable, helping students understand their mistakes and learn from them. For example, if a student answered a quiz question incorrectly, the LLM would not only indicate

the correct answer but also explain why the student's answer was incorrect, offering tips for improvement.

Challenges Encountered

1) Data Privacy and Security:

- **Protecting Student Information:** One of the primary challenges in implementing LLM-based personalized learning was ensuring the privacy and security of student data. The institution had to navigate complex data protection regulations, such as GDPR, to ensure that all student information was handled securely. This required implementing robust encryption methods, secure data storage practices, and clear consent protocols.
- **Balancing Personalization with Privacy:** While the LLM required detailed student data to deliver personalized learning, there was also a need to balance personalization with privacy. The institution took steps to anonymize and aggregate data wherever possible, ensuring that personalized learning did not come at the cost of student privacy.

2) Ensuring Equitable Access:

- **Addressing Digital Divide:** Another challenge was ensuring that all students, regardless of their socio-economic background, had access to the personalized learning tools. The institution worked to provide students with the necessary hardware, such as laptops and tablets, and offered internet access solutions for students in areas with limited connectivity. Additionally, they provided training for students and parents on how to use the platform effectively.
- **Cultural Sensitivity in Content:** The LLM had to be trained to recognize and respect cultural differences in learning. For example, certain teaching methods or examples that were effective in one cultural context might not resonate in another. The institution worked to

ensure that the content generated by the LLM was culturally sensitive and relevant to students from diverse backgrounds.

Outcomes and Impact

1) Improved Student Engagement:

- **Increased Participation:** The personalized learning paths created by the LLM led to a significant increase in student engagement. Students were more motivated to participate in lessons and complete assignments, as the content was tailored to their interests and learning preferences. The platform saw a notable decrease in dropout rates and an increase in course completion rates.
- **Positive Feedback:** Students and parents alike reported positive experiences with the personalized learning tools. Many students found the tailored content more engaging and easier to understand, while parents appreciated the real-time feedback and support provided by the virtual tutor.

2) Enhanced Learning Outcomes:

- **Academic Performance:** The institution observed a marked improvement in academic performance across the board. Students who used the personalized learning paths consistently outperformed their peers in assessments, demonstrating better comprehension and retention of the material. The adaptive nature of the learning paths ensured that students were always challenged at an appropriate level, helping them achieve mastery in various subjects.
- **Long-Term Benefits:** Beyond immediate academic gains, the personalized learning approach also fostered a deeper love for learning. Students became more independent and self-directed learners, with many expressing increased confidence in their abilities. These long-term benefits extended beyond the classroom, as students developed

critical thinking and problem-solving skills that would serve them well in future academic and professional pursuits.

This case study highlights the transformative potential of LLMs in creating personalized learning experiences. By leveraging data-driven insights and adaptive learning technologies, the institution was able to significantly improve student engagement and academic performance. While challenges related to data privacy and equitable access had to be addressed, the overall impact of the LLM-based personalized learning tools was overwhelmingly positive. As LLM technology continues to evolve, its application in education is likely to expand, offering even greater opportunities to tailor learning experiences to the needs of individual students.

16.3 Ethical and Privacy Concerns in Educational LLMs

As Large Language Models (LLMs) become increasingly integrated into educational settings, it's essential to address the ethical and privacy concerns that accompany their use. While LLMs offer immense potential to personalize learning and improve educational outcomes, their deployment must be handled with care to ensure that students' rights are protected and that the technology is used responsibly. This section will explore the key ethical and privacy issues associated with LLMs in education and discuss strategies for mitigating these concerns.

1. Data Privacy and Security

1) Handling Sensitive Student Data:

- **Data Collection Practices:** LLMs rely on vast amounts of data to provide personalized learning experiences. In educational contexts, this often involves collecting sensitive information about students, such as their academic performance, learning preferences, and even behavioral data. This raises significant privacy concerns, as mishandling such data could lead to breaches of confidentiality or misuse of personal information.

- **Security Measures:** To protect student data, educational institutions must implement robust security measures. This includes encrypting data both in transit and at rest, using secure authentication methods, and ensuring that only authorized personnel have access to sensitive information. Additionally, institutions should regularly audit their data security practices to identify and address potential vulnerabilities.

2) Compliance with Data Protection Regulations:

- **Legal Frameworks:** Educational institutions must comply with data protection regulations such as the General Data Protection Regulation (GDPR) in Europe or the Family Educational Rights and Privacy Act (FERPA) in the United States. These laws govern how student data can be collected, stored, and used, and they impose strict requirements on institutions to protect students' privacy. Compliance with these regulations is not optional; it is a legal obligation that institutions must take seriously.
- **Consent and Transparency:** One of the core principles of data protection is obtaining informed consent from students or their guardians before collecting personal data. Institutions must be transparent about what data is being collected, how it will be used, and who will have access to it. This transparency builds trust with students and their families and ensures that data is collected and used ethically.

2. Bias and Fairness in LLMs

1) Algorithmic Bias:

- **Impact on Student Outcomes:** LLMs are trained on large datasets, which may contain biases present in the real world. If not carefully managed, these biases can be reflected in the outputs of the model, leading to unfair or discriminatory outcomes. For example, an LLM used for grading or assessment might inadvertently favor certain groups of students over others, perpetuating existing inequalities in education.

- **Mitigation Strategies:** To address algorithmic bias, institutions must implement strategies to detect and correct biases in LLMs. This includes using diverse and representative training data, conducting regular bias audits, and incorporating fairness constraints into the model's design. Additionally, involving educators and ethicists in the development and deployment of LLMs can help ensure that these systems are fair and equitable.

2) Equity in Access to LLM-Based Tools:

- **Digital Divide:** While LLMs can enhance learning for many students, there is a risk that they could exacerbate existing inequalities if not everyone has equal access to these tools. Students from low-income families or rural areas may lack the necessary technology or internet access to benefit from LLM-based learning platforms, putting them at a disadvantage.
- **Addressing Access Issues:** To promote equity, institutions should work to ensure that all students have access to the technology needed to use LLM-based educational tools. This might involve providing devices, offering subsidies for internet access, or creating offline versions of educational content. By addressing these access issues, institutions can help ensure that the benefits of LLMs are available to all students, regardless of their socio-economic background.

3. Ethical Use of LLMs in Education

1) Balancing Personalization with Autonomy:

- **Student Agency:** While LLMs can offer highly personalized learning experiences, there is a risk that they could reduce student autonomy by dictating what and how students should learn. Over-reliance on LLM-generated content might limit students' ability to explore topics independently or develop critical thinking skills. It's important to strike a balance between providing personalized guidance and allowing students the freedom to shape their own learning paths.
- **Supporting Educators' Roles:** LLMs should be viewed as tools to support, not replace, educators. Teachers play a crucial role in guiding students, fostering creativity, and providing mentorship—qualities that LLMs cannot replicate. Ethical use of LLMs involves ensuring that these models complement the work of educators, rather than undermining their authority or reducing their interaction with students.

2) Transparency and Explainability:

- **Understanding AI Decisions:** Another ethical concern is the "black box" nature of LLMs, where the decision-making process is not easily understandable. In an educational context, this lack of transparency can be problematic, especially when LLMs are used for assessments or recommendations. Students, parents, and educators need to understand how and why certain decisions are made by the AI.
- **Improving Explainability:** Institutions should prioritize the development and use of explainable AI models, where the rationale behind decisions is clear and understandable. This might involve simplifying model outputs, providing detailed explanations alongside recommendations, or developing user interfaces that make AI-driven decisions more transparent. Ensuring that all stakeholders understand the role

of LLMs in education is key to building trust and ensuring ethical use.

4. Long-Term Ethical Considerations

1) Impact on Educational Equity:

- **Potential for Widening Gaps:** If not carefully managed, the deployment of LLMs in education could inadvertently widen the gap between advantaged and disadvantaged students. Those with better access to technology and resources could benefit more from LLMs, while others might be left behind. This could lead to a future where educational outcomes are even more polarized than they are today.
- **Promoting Inclusive Education:** To counteract this risk, educational institutions must focus on promoting inclusive education. This involves not only providing access to LLMs but also ensuring that these tools are designed and used in ways that actively promote equity. Institutions should continuously evaluate the impact of LLMs on different student groups and make adjustments to ensure that all students have the opportunity to succeed.

2) The Role of Human Educators in the Age of AI:

- **Preserving the Human Element:** As LLMs become more prevalent in education, it's essential to consider the long-term implications for the role of human educators. While AI can enhance and support education, it cannot replace the unique value that teachers bring to the classroom. Human educators provide emotional support, mentorship, and a deep understanding of individual student needs—qualities that are difficult for AI to replicate.
- **Evolving Educational Roles:** The introduction of LLMs may lead to an evolution in the role of educators, where they become more like facilitators or mentors, guiding students in their use of AI tools. This shift will require educators to develop new skills and adapt to a

changing educational landscape, but it also presents an opportunity to enrich the learning experience by combining the strengths of both human and AI-driven instruction.

The integration of LLMs into education presents both significant opportunities and complex ethical challenges. As these technologies become more widespread, it is crucial for educational institutions to address issues related to data privacy, algorithmic bias, and the ethical use of AI in learning environments. By taking a proactive approach to these challenges, institutions can harness the power of LLMs to enhance education while ensuring that students' rights and well-being are protected. Ultimately, the responsible use of LLMs in education will require a careful balance between innovation and ethical considerations, ensuring that these tools are used in ways that benefit all students.

16.4 Challenges and Opportunities in Educational Applications

As Large Language Models (LLMs) continue to make their way into educational settings, they bring both significant challenges and exciting opportunities. These models have the potential to transform education by personalizing learning, enhancing teaching methods, and providing access to resources on a scale never seen before. However, the successful integration of LLMs in education requires careful consideration of the obstacles that could hinder their effectiveness, as well as a strategic approach to maximizing their potential. In this section, we will explore the key challenges and opportunities associated with LLMs in education.

Challenges in Educational Applications

1) Access and Equity Issues

- **Digital Divide:** One of the most pressing challenges in the deployment of LLMs in education is ensuring equitable access to the necessary technology. Many students, particularly those in underprivileged or rural areas, may lack access to the devices and internet connectivity required to benefit from LLM-powered educational tools. This digital divide could exacerbate existing inequalities, leaving some students at a disadvantage.
- **Addressing Disparities:** To tackle these disparities, it's crucial for educational institutions and policymakers to invest in infrastructure that ensures all students have access to the technology they need. This might include providing devices, offering internet subsidies, or creating community access points where students can use LLM-based tools. Additionally, developing offline capabilities or low-bandwidth versions of educational content can help make these tools more accessible.

2) Teacher Training and Acceptance

- **Resistance to Change:** Teachers play a central role in the successful adoption of LLMs in education, but not all educators may be comfortable with or supportive of these new technologies. Some may be concerned about the potential for LLMs to replace their roles, while others may feel unprepared to integrate AI into their teaching practices. This resistance can slow the adoption of LLMs and limit their impact.
- **Professional Development:** To overcome this challenge, it's important to provide teachers with comprehensive training on how to use LLMs effectively. This training should emphasize that LLMs are tools that can enhance, rather than replace, the role of the teacher. Additionally, involving educators in the development and

implementation of LLM-based tools can help build their confidence and ensure that these tools meet the needs of both teachers and students.

3) Content Quality and Relevance

- **Accuracy and Bias:** LLMs generate content based on the data they've been trained on, which means that inaccuracies or biases present in the training data can be reflected in the outputs. In an educational context, this could lead to the dissemination of incorrect information or the reinforcement of stereotypes, which could harm students' learning and development.
- **Content Curation and Monitoring:** To address this issue, educational institutions need to implement rigorous content curation and monitoring processes. This involves regularly reviewing the outputs of LLMs to ensure accuracy and relevance, as well as providing educators with the ability to flag or correct problematic content. Additionally, ongoing efforts to improve the diversity and quality of training data can help reduce the risk of bias and inaccuracies.

4) Ethical Considerations and Student Privacy

- **Data Privacy Concerns:** As discussed in the previous section, the use of LLMs in education raises significant ethical concerns, particularly regarding student privacy. The collection and processing of sensitive student data, such as learning behaviors and academic performance, must be handled with the utmost care to protect students' rights.
- **Developing Ethical Guidelines:** To navigate these ethical challenges, educational institutions should develop clear guidelines for the ethical use of LLMs. These guidelines should address issues such as data privacy, consent, transparency, and the potential for bias. By establishing a strong ethical framework, institutions can ensure that LLMs are used responsibly and in ways that respect students' rights and dignity.

Opportunities in Educational Applications

1) Personalized Learning at Scale

- **Tailored Education for Every Student:** One of the most exciting opportunities presented by LLMs is the ability to deliver personalized learning experiences at scale. LLMs can analyze each student's strengths, weaknesses, and learning preferences to create customized learning paths that adapt in real-time. This level of personalization, which was previously only possible in one-on-one tutoring, can now be made available to all students, regardless of class size.
- **Supporting Diverse Learning Styles:** LLMs can also cater to different learning styles by generating a variety of content formats, such as text, videos, and interactive simulations. This flexibility ensures that every student can engage with the material in a way that suits them best, leading to improved understanding and retention.

2) Enhanced Educational Resources

- **Content Generation and Curation:** LLMs can be powerful tools for generating high-quality educational content, from lesson plans and quizzes to interactive learning modules. This can significantly reduce the time teachers spend on content creation, allowing them to focus more on instruction and student engagement. Moreover, LLMs can assist in curating and updating educational resources, ensuring that students always have access to the most current and relevant information.
- **Language Support:** LLMs can provide language support to students who are learning in a second language or who require additional help with language comprehension. By offering translations, simplified explanations, and multilingual resources, LLMs can make education more inclusive and accessible to a broader range of students.

3) Data-Driven Insights for Educators

- **Real-Time Student Assessment:** LLMs can offer educators real-time insights into student performance, allowing for more responsive and targeted interventions. By analyzing patterns in student data, such as quiz results or engagement levels, LLMs can identify areas where students may need additional support and suggest appropriate resources or strategies.
- **Supporting Differentiated Instruction:** With access to detailed data on student progress, educators can differentiate their instruction more effectively. LLMs can help teachers group students based on their learning needs, provide tailored assignments, and track the effectiveness of different teaching strategies. This data-driven approach can lead to more effective and efficient teaching, ultimately improving student outcomes.

4) Global Collaboration and Resource Sharing

- **Connecting Educators and Learners Worldwide:** LLMs have the potential to break down geographical barriers in education, enabling global collaboration and resource sharing. Educators can connect with peers around the world to exchange best practices, share resources, and collaborate on projects. Similarly, students can access learning materials and experiences from different cultures and regions, enriching their education and broadening their perspectives.
- **Open Educational Resources (OER):** LLMs can play a key role in the development and dissemination of Open Educational Resources (OER). By generating and curating high-quality, openly accessible content, LLMs can help make education more affordable and accessible to students everywhere, regardless of their socio-economic status.

The integration of LLMs into education presents a unique combination of challenges and opportunities. While there are significant hurdles to overcome, including issues related to access, teacher training, content quality, and ethics, the potential benefits are substantial. LLMs can revolutionize education by providing personalized learning experiences, enhancing educational resources, and offering data-driven insights that support more effective teaching and learning.

To fully realize these opportunities, educational institutions must approach the adoption of LLMs with careful planning and a commitment to equity and ethics. By addressing the challenges head-on and embracing the possibilities that LLMs offer, educators and institutions can create a more inclusive, effective, and future-ready educational system.

VI

Part VI: Future of Large Language Models

Chapter 17: Emerging Trends and Technologies

17.1 The Future of Transformer Architectures

The Transformer architecture has been a game-changer in the field of natural language processing (NLP), powering the most advanced Large Language Models (LLMs) today. However, as technology evolves, so too must the architecture that underpins these models. In this section, we'll look at the emerging trends and advancements that are likely to shape the future of Transformer architectures, making them even more powerful, efficient, and versatile.

1. Efficient Transformer Variants

1) Reducing Computational Costs:

- **Sparse Attention Mechanisms:** One of the main challenges with traditional Transformer models is their high computational cost, particularly as the sequence length increases. To address this, researchers are developing sparse attention mechanisms that focus only on the most relevant parts of the input sequence, reducing the amount of computation needed without sacrificing performance. These sparse attention models are likely to become more prevalent, allowing for more efficient processing of longer sequences.

- **Linear Transformers:** Another approach to reducing the computational burden is the development of linear Transformers, which aim to scale the attention mechanism linearly with the input size, rather than quadratically. This innovation could make it feasible to apply Transformer models to much larger datasets and longer text sequences, broadening their applicability across various domains.

2) Optimizing Memory Usage:

- **Memory-Efficient Models:** The memory requirements of Transformer models can be a significant bottleneck, particularly for devices with limited resources, such as mobile phones or edge devices. Future Transformer architectures are likely to incorporate memory-efficient techniques, such as reversible layers and efficient data structures, to reduce memory usage without compromising model performance. This could enable the deployment of powerful LLMs on a wider range of devices, expanding their reach and utility.
- **Checkpointing Strategies:** Checkpointing, where only a subset of activations are stored during the forward pass and recomputed during backpropagation, is another technique gaining traction. By saving memory at the cost of additional computation, checkpointing allows for the training of larger models on the same hardware, pushing the boundaries of what's possible in terms of model size and complexity.

2. Enhanced Interpretability and Explainability

1) Making Transformers More Transparent:

- **Interpretable Attention Mechanisms:** One criticism of Transformer models is their "black box" nature, where it's often unclear how decisions are made. To address this, researchers are developing more interpretable attention mechanisms that provide insights into what the model is focusing on during processing. These enhancements could make it easier for users to understand and trust the outputs of Transformer-based models, particularly in high-stakes applications like healthcare and finance.

- **Visualization Tools:** Alongside improvements in the models themselves, new tools for visualizing and interpreting the outputs of Transformer models are being developed. These tools can help users and developers alike to better understand how the model is processing information, identify potential biases, and make informed decisions about model deployment.

2) Ethical AI and Bias Mitigation:

- **Fairness-Aware Transformers:** As Transformer models are increasingly used in critical applications, there's a growing focus on ensuring that these models are fair and unbiased. Future Transformer architectures are likely to incorporate fairness-aware training techniques that explicitly address biases in the data and the model's outputs. This could involve adjusting attention weights, incorporating fairness constraints, or using adversarial training to mitigate bias.
- **Regular Audits and Monitoring:** To ensure that Transformer models remain fair and unbiased over time, regular audits and continuous monitoring will become standard practice. These audits will involve evaluating the model's outputs for signs of bias and making necessary adjustments to the architecture or training process to correct any issues.

3. Scaling and Specialization

1) Scaling Up:

- **Larger Models with Specialized Hardware:** As the demand for more powerful LLMs grows, so does the need for larger and more complex

Transformer models. Future architectures will likely be designed to take advantage of specialized hardware, such as GPUs and TPUs, as well as emerging technologies like AI accelerators, to efficiently scale up these models. This scaling will allow for the training of LLMs with trillions of parameters, enabling even more sophisticated and nuanced language understanding.

- **Distributed Training Techniques:** To handle the increasing size of Transformer models, distributed training techniques are also advancing. These techniques allow the training process to be spread across multiple machines, reducing the time and resources required. As a result, even the most massive Transformer models can be trained more efficiently, making it possible to explore new frontiers in LLM capabilities.

2) Task-Specific Transformers:

- **Domain-Specific Models:** While general-purpose Transformers like GPT and BERT have proven extremely versatile, there's a growing interest in developing task-specific or domain-specific models. These specialized Transformers are optimized for particular tasks, such as legal document analysis or medical text processing, where they can outperform more general models. This trend towards specialization will likely continue, with more Transformer architectures being tailored to meet the needs of specific industries and applications.
- **Modular Transformer Architectures:** Another emerging trend is the development of modular Transformer architectures, where different components of the model can be customized or swapped out based on the task at hand. This modularity allows for greater flexibility and adaptability, enabling models to be fine-tuned for a wide range of applications without needing to be retrained from scratch.

4. Integrating Transformers with Other Technologies

1) Multi-Modal Transformers:

- **Combining Text with Other Data Types:** The future of Transformer architectures isn't limited to text processing. Multi-modal Transformers, which can process and integrate different types of data (e.g., text, images, audio, and video), are an exciting area of development. These models can generate more comprehensive and contextually aware outputs by understanding and synthesizing information from multiple modalities. This opens up new possibilities for applications such as video summarization, image captioning, and cross-modal retrieval.
- **Real-Time Multi-Modal Interaction:** As these multi-modal Transformers evolve, we can expect to see real-time applications that seamlessly integrate different data types. For example, an educational tool could analyze a student's spoken questions, written assignments, and facial expressions to provide a more personalized and effective learning experience.

2) Transformers in Edge Computing:

- **Bringing AI Closer to the Data Source:** Another significant trend is the integration of Transformer architectures into edge computing environments. This means bringing AI processing closer to the data source, whether it's a mobile device, IoT sensor, or autonomous vehicle. By deploying efficient Transformer models at the edge, it's possible to perform complex language tasks with low latency and reduced reliance on cloud computing. This could be particularly valuable in scenarios where real-time processing is critical, such as in autonomous driving or remote healthcare monitoring.

The future of Transformer architectures is poised to bring about significant advancements in efficiency, scalability, interpretability, and integration with other technologies. As these models continue to evolve, they will not only become more powerful and versatile but also more transparent and fair, making them suitable for a wider range of applications. By staying at the forefront of these emerging trends, developers, researchers, and practitioners can leverage the full potential of Transformers to drive innovation across industries and domains. The next generation of Transformer architectures promises to push the boundaries of what's possible in natural language processing and beyond.

17.2 Multi-modal LLMs: Combining Text with Other Data Types

The development of Large Language Models (LLMs) has primarily focused on processing and generating text. However, the world of data is not limited to text alone—images, audio, video, and other data types all contribute to the rich tapestry of information we interact with daily. The next frontier for LLMs involves integrating these various data types into a cohesive model, leading to what are known as multi-modal LLMs. These models can process and generate content across different modalities, enabling more sophisticated and contextually aware applications. In this section, we'll explore the concept of multi-modal LLMs, their potential applications, and the challenges they present.

1. The Concept of Multi-modal LLMs

1) What Are Multi-modal LLMs?

- **Beyond Text:** Multi-modal LLMs are models designed to process and generate information across multiple data types, such as text, images, audio, and video. Unlike traditional LLMs, which focus exclusively on text, multi-modal models can understand and produce outputs that incorporate different forms of data, leading to a more holistic understanding of content.

- **Integration of Modalities:** These models integrate different modalities by learning how to relate data from one type to another. For example, a multi-modal LLM might generate a descriptive paragraph based on an image or identify key points in a video and summarize them in text. This ability to combine and cross-reference information from different sources enhances the model's contextual understanding and broadens its potential applications.

2) Key Components and Techniques:

- **Cross-Attention Mechanisms:** A crucial element in multi-modal LLMs is the cross-attention mechanism, which allows the model to focus on relevant aspects of different data types simultaneously. For instance, when generating text based on an image, the model can use cross-attention to align specific visual features with corresponding linguistic expressions, ensuring that the generated text accurately reflects the content of the image.
- **Unified Representations:** Another important technique involves creating unified representations that combine information from different modalities into a single, coherent vector space. This allows the model to reason across modalities more effectively, making it possible to perform tasks like captioning an image, generating dialogue based on a video, or answering questions about an audio clip.

2. Applications of Multi-modal LLMs

1) Image and Video Captioning:

- **Automatic Descriptions:** One of the most prominent applications of multi-modal LLMs is in generating captions for images and videos.

These models can analyze visual content and produce accurate, contextually relevant descriptions, making it easier to index and search through large datasets of visual media. This technology has applications in areas such as social media, digital marketing, and accessibility, where descriptive captions can help make content more inclusive for individuals with visual impairments.

- **Interactive Visual Assistants:** Multi-modal LLMs could also power interactive visual assistants that help users navigate visual content. For example, a user could upload a photo and ask the model to describe specific elements within the image or provide more information about what's depicted. In video, these assistants could summarize scenes, highlight key moments, or even generate real-time commentary.

2) Speech and Text Integration:

- **Speech-to-Text and Text-to-Speech:** While speech recognition and synthesis have been around for some time, multi-modal LLMs can take these technologies further by understanding the context of spoken language and generating text that reflects not just the words spoken but also the intent and emotion behind them. This can lead to more natural and engaging voice assistants, where the AI not only transcribes spoken words but also responds in a way that's attuned to the speaker's tone and context.
- **Audio-Visual Learning Tools:** In educational settings, multi-modal LLMs can combine speech and text with visual aids to create richer learning experiences. For instance, a model could generate explanatory text or captions for educational videos, or it could help language learners by providing real-time translations and explanations as they watch foreign-language content.

3) Enhanced Search and Retrieval:

- **Cross-Modal Search Engines:** Traditional search engines are limited to text-based queries and results. However, multi-modal LLMs can enable more advanced search capabilities by allowing users to input queries in one modality (e.g., text) and retrieve results in another (e.g., images or videos). For example, a user could describe an image they're looking for, and the model could retrieve matching visuals from a database, even if the images themselves are not tagged with the exact words used in the query.

- **Content Recommendation:** Multi-modal LLMs can also improve content recommendation systems by considering multiple types of user interactions. For instance, a model could analyze a user's viewing history (videos), reading preferences (text), and music tastes (audio) to suggest content that aligns with their interests across different media platforms.

4) Interactive and Immersive Experiences:

- **Augmented Reality (AR) and Virtual Reality (VR):** Multi-modal LLMs can enhance AR and VR experiences by integrating real-time data from different sources. In AR, a model could overlay text or audio descriptions onto the physical environment, providing users with contextual information about what they see. In VR, multi-modal LLMs could generate dynamic narratives that respond to the user's actions, creating more immersive and interactive experiences.
- **Gaming and Entertainment:** In the gaming industry, multi-modal LLMs can be used to create more responsive and dynamic game environments. For example, a game could use an LLM to generate dialogue based on the player's actions and choices, or to adapt the game world in response to the player's spoken commands. This level of interactivity can make games more engaging and personalized.

3. Challenges and Considerations

1) Data Alignment and Integration:

- **Complexity of Multi-modal Data:** One of the main challenges in developing multi-modal LLMs is aligning and integrating data from different modalities. Text, images, audio, and video all have distinct characteristics and require different processing techniques. Ensuring that these diverse data types are accurately aligned in a model is a complex task that requires sophisticated data preprocessing, training strategies, and model architectures.
- **Data Scarcity:** Another challenge is the scarcity of large, high-quality datasets that combine multiple modalities. While there are many datasets available for individual data types, such as text corpora or image collections, finding or creating datasets that integrate text with images, audio, and video can be difficult. This limits the ability to train and fine-tune multi-modal models effectively.

2) Model Complexity and Resource Requirements:

- **Increased Computational Demands:** Multi-modal LLMs are inherently more complex than their text-only counterparts, requiring greater computational resources for both training and inference. This can make it challenging to deploy these models on a large scale, particularly in environments with limited hardware capabilities.
- **Optimization and Efficiency:** To address these challenges, researchers are exploring ways to optimize multi-modal LLMs for efficiency. This includes developing more efficient model architectures, using sparse attention mechanisms, and leveraging specialized hardware like GPUs and TPUs. Additionally, techniques such as model distillation and pruning can help reduce the computational demands of these models without sacrificing performance.

3) Ethical and Privacy Considerations:

- **Bias Across Modalities:** Just as with text-based LLMs, multi-modal models are susceptible to biases in their training data. However, when combining multiple modalities, these biases can be more complex and harder to detect. For example, a model trained on biased visual data might reinforce stereotypes not only in image recognition but also in the text it generates based on those images. Addressing these biases requires careful data curation, model auditing, and the development of fairness-aware training techniques.
- **Privacy Concerns:** The integration of different data types raises additional privacy concerns, particularly when models are trained on sensitive or personal data. For instance, a multi-modal model that combines text, images, and location data could inadvertently reveal more about a person than intended. Ensuring that these models comply with privacy regulations and ethical standards is crucial for their responsible deployment.

4. The Future of Multi-modal LLMs

1) Advancements in Multi-modal Research:

- **Unified Multi-modal Models:** The future of multi-modal LLMs may see the development of unified models that seamlessly integrate multiple data types into a single, coherent system. These models would be capable of handling any combination of text, images, audio, and video, making them incredibly versatile and powerful. Such advancements could lead to breakthroughs in fields ranging from healthcare and education to entertainment and communication.
- **Cross-Domain Applications:** As multi-modal LLMs continue to evolve, we can expect to see their application in more diverse domains. For example, in healthcare, multi-modal models could analyze medical images, patient records, and genetic data to provide more

accurate diagnoses and treatment recommendations. In journalism, these models could generate comprehensive multimedia reports by combining text analysis with video and audio content.

2) Expanding the Boundaries of Human-AI Interaction:

- **More Natural Interactions:** Multi-modal LLMs have the potential to make human-AI interactions more natural and intuitive. By understanding and responding to multiple forms of input, these models can engage with users in ways that more closely resemble human communication. For example, a virtual assistant could respond to spoken questions with a combination of text, images, and video, creating a richer and more informative interaction.
- **Enhanced Accessibility:** Multi-modal LLMs can also play a key role in enhancing accessibility for individuals with disabilities. By generating content in multiple formats, such as text-to-speech for the visually impaired or sign language avatars for the hearing impaired, these models can make information more accessible to a wider audience.

The future of LLMs is multi-modal, with the integration of text, images, audio, and video offering exciting new possibilities for applications across various domains. While the development of multi-modal LLMs presents challenges in terms of data alignment, model complexity, and ethical considerations, the potential benefits are immense. By continuing to innovate in this area, researchers and developers can create more powerful, efficient, and versatile AI systems that better reflect the richness of human communication and understanding. As these models become more advanced, they will play a central role in shaping the next generation of AI-powered applications, driving progress in fields as diverse as education, healthcare, entertainment, and beyond.

17.3 LLMs and Human-AI Collaboration

As Large Language Models (LLMs) continue to advance, their role is expanding from being merely tools for automation to becoming collaborative partners with humans. The potential for Human-AI collaboration powered by LLMs opens up new possibilities across various industries, from creative work to complex decision-making processes. This section explores how LLMs are shaping the future of collaboration between humans and machines, highlighting both the opportunities and challenges that come with this evolving relationship.

1. The Evolution of Human-AI Collaboration

1) From Tools to Partners:

- **Enhanced Productivity:** Traditionally, AI has been used to automate routine tasks, improving efficiency and freeing up human workers for more complex activities. However, LLMs are moving beyond simple automation to become active collaborators. These models can assist in brainstorming sessions, generate creative content, and even offer strategic advice, making them valuable partners in tasks that require both human intuition and AI-driven analysis.
- **Complementary Strengths:** Human-AI collaboration leverages the strengths of both parties—humans bring creativity, empathy, and contextual understanding, while LLMs contribute speed, data processing capabilities, and vast knowledge. This combination allows for more informed and innovative outcomes than either could achieve alone.

2) Collaborative Workflows:

- **Creative Industries:** In fields like writing, design, and music, LLMs are being used to enhance creativity rather than replace it. For example, a writer might use an LLM to generate plot ideas, suggest dialogue, or

refine text, while retaining control over the final narrative. Similarly, designers might collaborate with AI to create unique visual elements or explore new design possibilities.
- **Decision-Making Support:** In corporate environments, LLMs can assist in decision-making by analyzing large datasets, identifying patterns, and generating insights that might be overlooked by human analysts. This collaboration allows for more data-driven decisions while still benefiting from human judgment and experience.

2. Applications of Human-AI Collaboration

1) Content Creation and Curation:

- **Co-Creating Content:** LLMs are increasingly being used in content creation, where they can generate drafts of articles, blog posts, or marketing copy. These AI-generated drafts can serve as starting points that human writers refine and personalize, speeding up the content creation process while maintaining a human touch. This collaborative approach can be particularly effective in fields that require a high volume of content production, such as journalism, digital marketing, and social media management.
- **Content Moderation:** In addition to content creation, LLMs can play a role in content curation and moderation. They can help filter out inappropriate or low-quality content from user-generated submissions, ensuring that only the best content is presented to the audience. While the final decisions often rest with human moderators, AI can handle the initial screening, making the process more efficient.

2) Healthcare and Medical Research:

- **Augmenting Clinical Decision-Making:** In healthcare, LLMs can assist doctors and medical researchers by analyzing patient data, suggesting diagnoses, and recommending treatment plans. These models can sift through vast amounts of medical literature and patient records to identify relevant information, helping clinicians make more informed decisions. However, human oversight remains crucial to ensure that AI recommendations are accurate and tailored to the patient's unique circumstances.

- **Accelerating Research:** LLMs are also being used in medical research to accelerate the discovery of new treatments and therapies. By analyzing existing research papers, clinical trial data, and genomic information, LLMs can generate hypotheses, identify potential drug candidates, and even design experiments. This collaboration between AI and researchers can significantly speed up the research process, leading to faster breakthroughs in medicine.

3) Customer Service and Support:

- **AI-Assisted Support:** In customer service, LLMs are being integrated into chatbots and virtual assistants to provide instant responses to customer inquiries. These AI-driven systems can handle a wide range of queries, from simple FAQs to more complex issues. When the AI reaches its limits, it can seamlessly hand over the interaction to a human agent, who can take over with full context. This collaboration allows businesses to offer faster and more efficient customer support while still providing a human touch when needed.
- **Personalized Experiences:** LLMs can analyze customer data to provide personalized recommendations and support, enhancing the overall customer experience. For instance, an AI assistant might suggest products based on a customer's purchase history or provide tailored advice based on their preferences. This level of personalization can help build stronger customer relationships and increase satisfaction.

3. Challenges in Human-AI Collaboration

1) Balancing Automation and Human Input:

- **Over-Reliance on AI:** One of the challenges in Human-AI collaboration is ensuring that AI does not overshadow human input. While LLMs can provide valuable assistance, there's a risk of over-reliance on AI, where human workers defer too much to the model's recommendations without applying their own critical thinking. It's essential to maintain a balance where AI serves as a tool to enhance human capabilities rather than replace them.
- **Maintaining Human Creativity:** In creative industries, there's concern that relying on AI-generated content might stifle human creativity. To mitigate this, it's important to use LLMs as sources of inspiration or as tools for exploring new ideas, while keeping the creative process firmly in human hands.

2) Trust and Transparency:

- **Building Trust in AI:** For Human-AI collaboration to be effective, users need to trust the AI's outputs. This requires transparency in how the LLMs work, including understanding the data they're trained on, the algorithms they use, and the potential biases they might have. Building this trust involves not only educating users but also developing AI systems that are explainable and transparent in their decision-making processes.
- **Bias and Fairness:** LLMs can inadvertently introduce biases into their recommendations, particularly if they're trained on biased data. In collaborative environments, this can lead to biased outcomes, especially in areas like hiring, loan approval, or legal decisions. Addressing these biases is crucial to ensuring that AI augments human decision-making in a fair and equitable manner.

4. The Future of Human-AI Collaboration

1) Evolving Roles:

- **AI as a Creative Partner:** As LLMs become more advanced, they are likely to take on more prominent roles as creative partners, particularly in industries like media, entertainment, and marketing. These models will not only assist with content generation but also with idea refinement, trend analysis, and audience engagement strategies. Human workers will need to adapt to these evolving roles, focusing on high-level strategy, oversight, and the creative aspects that AI cannot replicate.
- **Collaborative Intelligence:** The future may see the rise of "collaborative intelligence," where humans and AI work together in real-time, each complementing the other's strengths. In this model, AI might handle data processing and pattern recognition, while humans provide the context, intuition, and ethical considerations. This symbiotic relationship could lead to new forms of problem-solving and innovation, where the combination of human and AI intelligence produces results that neither could achieve alone.

2) Ethical and Regulatory Considerations:

- **Guidelines for Collaboration:** As Human-AI collaboration becomes more widespread, there will be a growing need for ethical guidelines and regulatory frameworks to govern these interactions. This includes establishing clear boundaries for AI's role in decision-making, ensuring that human workers retain agency, and addressing the potential for AI to perpetuate or exacerbate existing biases.
- **Ongoing Education and Training:** To ensure effective collaboration, ongoing education and training will be essential for both human workers and AI systems. Humans will need to develop new skills to work alongside AI, while AI models will require continuous updates

and retraining to stay relevant and aligned with human values. This dynamic approach to learning will be critical to maintaining a productive and ethical partnership between humans and AI.

The collaboration between humans and AI, particularly through LLMs, represents a significant shift in how work is conducted across various fields. By leveraging the strengths of both humans and machines, this partnership can lead to more innovative, efficient, and personalized outcomes. However, realizing the full potential of Human-AI collaboration requires careful consideration of the challenges, including the need for transparency, trust, and the preservation of human creativity and judgment. As we move forward, the relationship between humans and AI will continue to evolve, shaping the future of work and society in profound ways.

17.4 The Role of LLMs in AGI (Artificial General Intelligence)

Artificial General Intelligence (AGI) represents the ultimate goal of AI research: the creation of machines that can perform any intellectual task that a human can, with a level of understanding and adaptability that goes beyond narrow, task-specific AI systems. While AGI remains a theoretical concept, the rapid advancements in Large Language Models (LLMs) have sparked discussions about their potential role in achieving AGI. In this section, we will explore the relationship between LLMs and AGI, examining how current developments in LLMs might contribute to or fall short of the broader ambitions of AGI.

1. Understanding AGI and Its Challenges

1) Defining AGI:

- **General vs. Narrow AI:** Unlike narrow AI, which is designed to excel at specific tasks (such as image recognition or language translation), AGI aims to replicate the general cognitive abilities of humans. An AGI system would not only perform well on a wide range of tasks but would also possess the ability to learn, adapt, and understand the world in a manner akin to human intelligence.
- **Core Capabilities of AGI:** For a system to be considered AGI, it must demonstrate several key capabilities, including reasoning, problem-solving, abstract thinking, and the ability to transfer knowledge across different domains. Additionally, AGI would need to exhibit a deep understanding of context, a sense of self-awareness, and the ability to interact with humans in a meaningful and empathetic way.

2) The Challenges of Achieving AGI:

- **Complexity of Human Cognition:** One of the primary challenges in developing AGI is replicating the complexity of human cognition. Human intelligence is not just about processing information—it involves emotional intelligence, ethical reasoning, creativity, and an understanding of social dynamics. These aspects of intelligence are difficult to model computationally and require advances in areas such as cognitive science, neuroscience, and AI.
- **Ethical and Safety Concerns:** The development of AGI raises significant ethical and safety concerns. An AGI system with the ability to operate autonomously could potentially make decisions that are harmful or unethical if not properly aligned with human values. Ensuring that AGI is developed in a way that is safe, transparent, and beneficial to humanity is a critical challenge that researchers must address.

2. The Contribution of LLMs to AGI Development

1) Current Strengths of LLMs:

- **Language Understanding and Generation:** LLMs have demonstrated remarkable abilities in understanding and generating human language. They can engage in conversations, translate languages, summarize text, and even generate creative content such as poetry or stories. These capabilities are essential components of AGI, as language is a core aspect of human cognition and communication.
- **Knowledge Integration:** LLMs are trained on vast amounts of data, enabling them to integrate knowledge from diverse sources and apply it to various tasks. This ability to synthesize information and provide relevant responses across different contexts is a step towards the generality required for AGI.

2) Limitations of LLMs in Achieving AGI:

- **Lack of True Understanding:** Despite their impressive performance, LLMs do not possess true understanding or consciousness. They generate responses based on patterns in the data they have been trained on, without comprehending the underlying meaning or implications of their outputs. This lack of true understanding limits their ability to perform tasks that require deep reasoning or contextual awareness, which are essential for AGI.
- **Absence of Common Sense and World Knowledge:** LLMs often struggle with tasks that require common sense reasoning or an understanding of the physical world. For example, they might generate plausible-sounding but factually incorrect or logically inconsistent responses. Achieving AGI will require models that can reason about the world in a way that aligns with human understanding and experience.

3) Potential Pathways for LLMs to Contribute to AGI:

- **Hybrid Models:** One potential pathway towards AGI involves combining LLMs with other AI systems that specialize in areas where LLMs are currently lacking. For instance, integrating LLMs with models that excel in visual perception, motor control, or ethical reasoning could create a more comprehensive system that approaches the generality of AGI.
- **Continuous Learning and Adaptation:** To move closer to AGI, LLMs will need to incorporate mechanisms for continuous learning and adaptation. This would involve the ability to learn from new experiences, update their knowledge base, and refine their understanding of the world in real-time, much like humans do. Advances in reinforcement learning, self-supervised learning, and transfer learning could play a crucial role in enabling this capability.

3. The Future Role of LLMs in AGI Research

1) Ongoing Research and Development:

- **Expanding the Scope of LLMs:** Researchers are continuously working to expand the capabilities of LLMs, exploring ways to improve their reasoning abilities, enhance their understanding of context, and integrate more sophisticated forms of knowledge representation. These efforts are laying the groundwork for the development of more general AI systems that could contribute to the eventual realization of AGI.
- **Interdisciplinary Approaches:** Achieving AGI will likely require interdisciplinary collaboration, drawing on insights from fields such as cognitive science, psychology, neuroscience, and ethics. LLMs, as part of this broader research effort, can serve as a valuable tool for exploring how language and knowledge representation contribute to general intelligence.

2) Ethical Considerations and Responsible Development:

- **Aligning AI with Human Values:** As LLMs become more advanced and take on roles that resemble AGI, it is crucial to ensure that they are aligned with human values and ethical principles. This includes addressing biases in training data, developing mechanisms for accountability, and ensuring transparency in AI decision-making processes.
- **Preventing Misuse and Ensuring Safety:** The potential misuse of AGI poses significant risks, including the possibility of unintended consequences or malicious applications. Researchers and policymakers must work together to establish guidelines, regulations, and safeguards that prevent the misuse of AGI and ensure that its development is guided by principles of safety and human welfare.

While LLMs have made significant strides in natural language processing and knowledge integration, they are still far from achieving the level of understanding and generality required for AGI. However, their ongoing development provides valuable insights and tools that can contribute to the broader pursuit of AGI. By addressing the current limitations of LLMs and integrating them with other AI systems and interdisciplinary research efforts, we can move closer to realizing the vision of AGI. As we continue down this path, it is essential to prioritize ethical considerations and ensure that the development of AGI is aligned with the values and needs of humanity.

17.5 The Impact of Quantum Computing on LLMs

Quantum computing, with its promise of exponentially faster processing power, has the potential to revolutionize many fields, including artificial intelligence and, more specifically, Large Language Models (LLMs). While quantum computing is still in its early stages, its development could have profound implications for how LLMs are trained, optimized, and deployed.

In this section, we will explore the potential impact of quantum computing on LLMs, discussing how this emerging technology could enhance the capabilities of LLMs and what challenges and opportunities it presents.

1. Understanding Quantum Computing

1) What is Quantum Computing?

- **Quantum Bits (Qubits):** Unlike classical computing, which relies on bits that represent either 0 or 1, quantum computing uses quantum bits or qubits. Qubits can exist in a superposition of states, meaning they can represent both 0 and 1 simultaneously. This property allows quantum computers to process vast amounts of data in parallel, potentially solving complex problems much faster than classical computers.
- **Quantum Entanglement and Interference:** Another key feature of quantum computing is entanglement, where qubits become interconnected in such a way that the state of one qubit can instantly influence the state of another, regardless of distance. Quantum interference allows for the constructive or destructive combination of quantum states, enabling more precise calculations. These properties make quantum computers particularly powerful for certain types of computations, such as factoring large numbers or simulating molecular interactions.

2) Current State of Quantum Computing:

- **Early Development:** While quantum computing holds immense potential, it is still in the experimental phase. Current quantum computers, known as Noisy Intermediate-Scale Quantum (NISQ) devices, are prone to errors and limited in the number of qubits they can effectively manage. However, ongoing research and development are rapidly advancing the field, with significant progress expected in the coming years.

- **Potential Applications:** Quantum computing is expected to impact various domains, including cryptography, material science, drug discovery, and AI. For LLMs, the implications of quantum computing are particularly intriguing, as it could dramatically alter how these models are developed and utilized.

2. The Potential Impact of Quantum Computing on LLMs

1) Enhancing Model Training:

- **Faster Computations:** One of the most significant impacts of quantum computing on LLMs could be in the training process. Training large models like GPT-3 or BERT requires enormous computational resources and time. Quantum computing could potentially accelerate this process by performing the necessary calculations much faster than classical computers. This would enable the training of even larger models with more parameters, leading to more powerful and sophisticated LLMs.
- **Optimizing Algorithms:** Quantum computing could also introduce new optimization techniques for training LLMs. For example, quantum algorithms like Grover's algorithm could be used to search for optimal hyperparameters more efficiently, improving the performance and accuracy of the models. Additionally, quantum-enhanced gradient descent methods could potentially accelerate convergence during training, reducing the overall time and computational cost.

2) Improving Model Inference:

- **Real-Time Processing:** Quantum computing could enable real-time inference for LLMs, even for the most complex tasks. This would be particularly valuable in applications where low latency is critical, such as real-time language translation, conversational AI, and autonomous

systems. By leveraging quantum computing, LLMs could process and generate responses almost instantaneously, enhancing the user experience and expanding the scope of AI applications.
- **Handling Complex Queries:** Quantum computers excel at handling complex, multidimensional problems. This capability could be leveraged to improve the inference capabilities of LLMs, allowing them to better understand and respond to complex queries that involve multiple layers of reasoning and context. For example, quantum-enhanced LLMs could provide more accurate and nuanced answers to questions that require deep understanding and synthesis of information from diverse sources.

3) Addressing Computational Challenges:

- **Scaling LLMs:** As LLMs continue to grow in size and complexity, scaling them becomes a significant challenge. Quantum computing could help address these challenges by providing the computational power needed to train and deploy extremely large models efficiently. This would enable the development of LLMs with unprecedented capabilities, capable of understanding and generating human language with even greater accuracy and sophistication.
- **Energy Efficiency:** Training large LLMs is not only computationally intensive but also energy-consuming. Quantum computing could potentially offer a more energy-efficient solution, reducing the environmental impact of training and deploying LLMs. This would make the development of AI more sustainable, aligning with broader efforts to reduce the carbon footprint of technology.

3. Challenges and Considerations

1) Integration with Classical Computing:

- **Hybrid Systems:** In the near term, it is likely that quantum computing will be integrated with classical computing in hybrid systems. These systems would combine the strengths of both technologies, with quantum computers handling specific tasks that benefit from quantum speedups while classical computers manage the rest. Developing effective hybrid systems that leverage quantum computing for LLMs will require significant research and innovation.

- **Interoperability Issues:** Integrating quantum computing with existing AI infrastructures presents interoperability challenges. Ensuring that quantum and classical systems can work together seamlessly will be critical to realizing the full potential of quantum-enhanced LLMs. This may involve developing new software frameworks, protocols, and standards to facilitate the integration.

2) Accessibility and Cost:

- **Limited Access to Quantum Hardware:** Currently, access to quantum computers is limited to a few research institutions and technology companies with the resources to invest in this cutting-edge technology. As quantum computing becomes more widespread, democratizing access to quantum resources will be essential to ensure that the benefits of quantum-enhanced LLMs are available to a broader range of developers, researchers, and organizations.
- **Cost Considerations:** The high cost of quantum computing infrastructure is another barrier to widespread adoption. Over time, as the technology matures and becomes more commercially viable, costs are expected to decrease. However, in the short term, the expense of quantum computing may limit its application to only the most critical and resource-intensive tasks.

3) Ethical and Security Implications:

- **Ethical Concerns:** The integration of quantum computing with AI raises ethical considerations, particularly regarding the potential for quantum-enhanced LLMs to be used in ways that exacerbate existing societal challenges. For example, the increased power of LLMs could lead to more sophisticated misinformation campaigns or more invasive surveillance systems. It is crucial to develop ethical guidelines and safeguards to ensure that quantum-enhanced AI is used responsibly.

- **Security Risks:** Quantum computing poses a threat to current cryptographic systems, as it could potentially break widely used encryption methods. This has significant implications for the security of AI systems, including LLMs, which rely on secure communication and data storage. Addressing these security risks will require the development of new quantum-resistant cryptographic techniques and the implementation of robust security measures.

Quantum computing holds the promise of dramatically enhancing the capabilities of LLMs, offering faster training, more efficient inference, and the ability to handle more complex tasks. While the technology is still in its infancy, the potential benefits of integrating quantum computing with LLMs are immense, paving the way for more powerful and versatile AI systems. However, realizing this potential will require overcoming significant technical, ethical, and economic challenges. As quantum computing continues to advance, its impact on LLMs and the broader field of AI will be a key area of focus, shaping the future of how we develop and interact with intelligent machines.

17.6 Preparing for the Next Generation of LLMs

As Large Language Models (LLMs) continue to evolve, the next generation of these models promises to be more powerful, versatile, and integrated into various aspects of our lives. Preparing for this future involves not only advancing the technology itself but also addressing the broader implications of their deployment. In this section, we will discuss how researchers, developers, and organizations can prepare for the next generation of LLMs, ensuring that these advancements are leveraged responsibly and effectively.

1. Advancing Research and Development

1) Pushing the Boundaries of Model Architecture:

- **Innovative Architectures:** The next generation of LLMs will likely involve new architectures that build on or even go beyond the Transformer model. Research is already underway to explore more efficient models, such as sparse transformers, which reduce computational requirements without sacrificing performance. Additionally, hybrid models that combine the strengths of different architectures (e.g., combining convolutional networks with transformers) could lead to breakthroughs in efficiency and capability.
- **Incorporating New Modalities:** Future LLMs will increasingly integrate multiple data modalities, such as text, images, video, and audio, to create more holistic and context-aware models. Developing these multi-modal models will require new techniques for data alignment and processing, as well as innovative training strategies that can handle the complexity of multi-modal information.

2) Scaling and Optimization:

- **Efficient Scaling:** While current LLMs are already massive, the next generation will push the limits even further. However, simply scaling up models is not enough; efficiency in training and inference must also be prioritized. Techniques such as model pruning, quantization, and knowledge distillation will play a key role in making larger models more practical for deployment.
- **Automation in Model Development:** The future of LLMs may also

involve greater automation in the development process. AutoML (Automated Machine Learning) techniques, which allow models to automatically tune their hyperparameters and architectures, could become more sophisticated, leading to the creation of models that are better optimized for specific tasks or environments without requiring extensive manual intervention.

2. Ethical Considerations and Responsible AI

1) Addressing Bias and Fairness:

- **Mitigating Bias:** As LLMs become more embedded in decision-making processes, ensuring fairness and reducing bias in their outputs is critical. The next generation of LLMs must be developed with enhanced bias detection and mitigation techniques. This involves not only curating more balanced training datasets but also developing models that can self-assess and adjust their outputs to reduce biased responses.
- **Transparent Decision-Making:** Transparency will be a key requirement for future LLMs, particularly in high-stakes applications such as healthcare, finance, and legal decision-making. Users and regulators must be able to understand how LLMs arrive at their conclusions, which will necessitate advancements in explainable AI and the development of models that can provide clear, understandable reasoning for their decisions.

2) Ensuring Security and Privacy:

- **Data Security:** The more powerful LLMs become, the more data they require, raising concerns about data security and privacy. The next generation of LLMs will need to incorporate stronger encryption methods and adhere to stricter data protection standards to ensure that sensitive information is handled securely throughout the model's lifecycle.

- **Robustness Against Attacks:** As LLMs are increasingly deployed in critical applications, they must be robust against adversarial attacks and other forms of manipulation. Research into adversarial defense techniques, including robust training methods and anomaly detection systems, will be crucial in preparing LLMs for safe and secure deployment in the real world.

3. Preparing the Workforce and Society

1) Upskilling and Education:

- **Training for AI Professionals:** As LLMs become more complex, the demand for skilled professionals who can develop, deploy, and manage these models will grow. Educational programs and training initiatives must be updated to equip the next generation of AI professionals with the knowledge and skills needed to work with advanced LLMs. This includes not only technical skills but also an understanding of ethical considerations and the societal impact of AI.
- **Public Awareness and Literacy:** Beyond the AI community, there is a need to increase public understanding of LLMs and their implications. As these models become more integrated into everyday life, fostering AI literacy among the general population will help individuals navigate the changes brought about by AI and make informed decisions about their use.

2) Policy and Regulation:

- **Developing AI Governance:** Governments and regulatory bodies must prepare for the next generation of LLMs by developing policies that promote the responsible use of AI. This includes creating frameworks for transparency, accountability, and fairness in AI systems, as well as addressing issues related to data privacy, security, and the ethical use of AI.

- **International Collaboration:** The global nature of AI development requires international collaboration on governance and standards. Future LLMs will be used across borders, making it essential for countries to work together on establishing common guidelines and best practices for AI development and deployment.

4. Exploring New Applications and Opportunities

1) Innovative Use Cases:

- **Emerging Industries:** The next generation of LLMs will likely open up new opportunities in industries that are currently underexplored by AI, such as advanced manufacturing, environmental monitoring, and space exploration. By applying LLMs in these areas, we can unlock new potential for innovation and growth, leading to advancements that benefit society as a whole.
- **Cross-Disciplinary Applications:** Future LLMs will also enable cross-disciplinary applications, where AI can be used to solve complex problems that require expertise from multiple fields. For example, LLMs could assist in climate modeling by integrating data from environmental science, economics, and social sciences, leading to more comprehensive and effective solutions.

2) Collaborative Innovation:

- **Public-Private Partnerships:** The development of the next generation of LLMs will benefit from collaboration between public institutions, private companies, and academic researchers. Public-private partnerships can drive innovation by combining resources and expertise, leading to more rapid advancements in AI technology.
- **Open Research and Development:** Encouraging open research and sharing of findings across the AI community will be essential for

accelerating progress. Open-source initiatives, shared datasets, and collaborative research projects can help democratize access to cutting-edge AI technology and ensure that advancements benefit a wide range of stakeholders.

Preparing for the next generation of LLMs involves not only advancing the technology itself but also addressing the broader societal, ethical, and educational challenges that come with it. By pushing the boundaries of model development, ensuring responsible AI practices, and fostering collaboration across sectors, we can harness the full potential of LLMs to drive innovation and improve lives. As we move forward, it is essential to balance the pursuit of technological progress with a commitment to ethical principles, ensuring that the next generation of LLMs serves the best interests of humanity.

Chapter 18: Conclusion and Final Thoughts

18.1 Recap of Key Concepts and Techniques

As we reach the conclusion of this comprehensive guide to building, optimizing, and deploying Large Language Models (LLMs) for production, it's important to take a step back and recap the key concepts and techniques we've covered. This summary will reinforce the foundational knowledge and practical insights that will be essential as you continue working with LLMs in real-world applications.

Understanding Language Models

We began by establishing a strong foundation in the basics of language models. This included an overview of their evolution from statistical methods to the powerful neural network-based models that dominate today, particularly the Transformer architecture. We discussed the theoretical underpinnings of why LLMs work, diving into the core concepts of tokens, embeddings, and attention mechanisms that enable these models to process and generate human language.

Architectures and Frameworks

Next, we explored the architectures that form the backbone of LLMs, with a deep dive into the Transformer model and its variants like BERT, GPT, and T5. We also compared different architectures to understand their strengths and weaknesses in various applications. Alongside this, we examined the frameworks and tools essential for building LLMs, such as TensorFlow, PyTorch, and Hugging Face Transformers, and discussed considerations for scalability in model architecture.

Mathematics Behind LLMs

We then delved into the mathematical concepts that underpin LLMs. This included linear algebra, probability, and statistics, which are crucial for understanding how models learn and generalize from data. We also covered the importance of optimization techniques, attention mechanisms, and regularization methods to prevent overfitting and ensure robust model performance. Gradient descent and its variants were discussed as key methods for training models effectively.

Data Collection and Preprocessing

The quality of an LLM is heavily dependent on the data it is trained on, making data collection and preprocessing critical steps. We examined how to source high-quality data, preprocess text through tokenization and other techniques, and handle challenges like imbalanced datasets and noisy data. Ethical considerations were also highlighted, emphasizing the importance of responsible data practices.

Training and Fine-Tuning Models

With data in hand, we moved on to the process of training LLMs from scratch, covering everything from setting up the training environment to distributed training across multiple GPUs or TPUs. We explored hyperparameter tuning for optimal performance and discussed common pitfalls and monitoring techniques during training. Fine-tuning pre-trained models was also covered, including the use of transfer learning, selecting appropriate pre-trained models, and employing techniques like layer freezing and learning rate schedulers to adapt models to specific tasks.

Optimization for Production

Deploying LLMs in production environments requires careful optimization to ensure efficiency and scalability. We discussed model compression techniques like quantization, pruning, and distillation, which are essential for reducing model size and inference latency. Memory optimization and efficient serving of LLMs were also key topics, along with tools and frameworks designed to facilitate model optimization for real-world applications.

Debugging, Troubleshooting, and Deployment

No development process is complete without addressing the challenges of debugging and troubleshooting. We provided strategies for identifying and resolving common issues in LLM training and deployment, addressing performance bottlenecks, and managing edge cases. We also explored best practices for logging, monitoring, and maintaining LLMs post-deployment, ensuring that models remain reliable and effective over time.

Emerging Trends and Future Directions

Finally, we looked ahead to the future of LLMs, exploring emerging trends and technologies that will shape the next generation of models. This included the potential impact of quantum computing, the role of LLMs in Artificial General Intelligence (AGI), and the integration of multi-modal data to create more comprehensive AI systems. We also discussed the ethical and societal implications of these advancements, emphasizing the importance of responsible AI development.

Throughout this book, we have covered a vast array of topics that are essential for anyone looking to build, optimize, and deploy LLMs in production environments. From foundational concepts to cutting-edge techniques, you now have a robust toolkit at your disposal. Whether you are a data scientist, AI engineer, or researcher, these insights will help you navigate the complexities of working with LLMs and contribute to the ongoing evolution of this transformative technology. As you continue to apply and build upon what you've learned, remember that the field of AI is dynamic and ever-changing, and staying informed and adaptable will be key to your success.

18.2 The Process of Implementing LLMs: Lessons Learned

Building, deploying, and maintaining Large Language Models (LLMs) is a complex task that requires careful planning, technical expertise, and a deep understanding of both the technology and the practical challenges it presents. Throughout this book, we've walked through each step of this process, but it's also important to reflect on the broader lessons learned from implementing LLMs in real-world scenarios. These lessons not only reinforce key concepts but also highlight the nuances and practicalities that come with working in this fast-evolving field.

1. Importance of a Solid Foundation

One of the first lessons learned is the critical importance of starting with a strong foundation. This includes understanding the fundamental concepts behind LLMs, such as the architecture of transformers, the role of attention mechanisms, and the mathematical principles that underlie model training. Rushing into implementation without a solid grasp of these basics can lead to avoidable errors and inefficiencies down the line. Taking the time to thoroughly understand these core principles pays dividends throughout the entire lifecycle of the model.

2. Data Quality is Key

Another crucial lesson is the undeniable impact of data quality on the performance of LLMs. High-quality, well-curated data is the backbone of any successful LLM implementation. During the data collection and preprocessing stages, it's essential to focus on sourcing diverse, representative datasets and applying rigorous preprocessing techniques. Handling imbalanced datasets, dealing with noisy data, and addressing ethical considerations are not just technical challenges; they are foundational to ensuring that the LLM you build is both effective and responsible.

3. The Balance Between Experimentation and Optimization

When it comes to training and fine-tuning LLMs, finding the right balance between experimentation and optimization is a critical lesson. It's easy to become overly focused on tweaking hyperparameters and chasing marginal gains in model performance. However, this must be balanced with a practical approach that recognizes the law of diminishing returns. Knowing when to stop fine-tuning and focus on deployment is a skill that comes with experience and an understanding of the specific goals of your project.

4. Scalability and Efficiency Matter

As LLMs become larger and more complex, scalability and efficiency have emerged as key considerations. Whether it's optimizing for memory usage, reducing inference latency, or ensuring that your model can handle large-scale workloads in production, these factors can make or break the success of an LLM deployment. Techniques such as model compression, distributed training, and efficient serving are not just technical niceties—they are essential practices that enable the practical application of LLMs in real-world settings.

5. Expect the Unexpected

No matter how well you plan, there will always be unforeseen challenges when implementing LLMs. From unexpected bugs in the training process to performance bottlenecks during deployment, the ability to troubleshoot effectively is invaluable. Logging, monitoring, and having robust debugging processes in place are lessons learned through experience and are crucial for maintaining the reliability of your model. Being prepared to adapt and respond to these challenges is a key part of successfully working with LLMs.

6. The Role of Collaboration and Community

Another important takeaway is the value of collaboration and leveraging the broader AI community. The field of LLMs is advancing rapidly, and staying updated with the latest research, tools, and best practices is critical. Engaging with the community through open-source contributions, research papers, and forums can provide insights that help you overcome challenges and improve your models. Additionally, collaboration within your team, across disciplines, and with other organizations can lead to innovative solutions and shared successes.

7. Ethical and Responsible AI

Finally, the implementation of LLMs is not just a technical endeavor; it's also an ethical one. Ensuring that your models are fair, transparent, and secure is a responsibility that cannot be overlooked. This involves continuous reflection on the impact of your work, adherence to ethical guidelines, and proactive measures to mitigate bias and protect user privacy. These considerations are not just about compliance—they are about building AI systems that are trustworthy and aligned with societal values.

The process of implementing LLMs is a multifaceted challenge that involves a blend of technical skills, strategic thinking, and ethical considerations. By reflecting on these lessons learned, you can better navigate the complexities of working with LLMs and increase the likelihood of success in your projects. As you move forward, keep these lessons in mind, and continue to adapt and learn as the field evolves. The journey of working with LLMs is ongoing, and each project offers new opportunities for growth and innovation.

18.3 How to Stay Updated in the Fast-Paced World of LLMs

The world of Large Language Models (LLMs) is constantly evolving, with new research, tools, and applications emerging at a rapid pace. For professionals working in this field, staying updated is not just beneficial—it's essential. However, keeping up with the latest developments can be challenging given the sheer volume of information and the speed at which the field advances. In this section, we'll discuss practical strategies for staying current and making sure you remain at the forefront of LLM technology.

1. Regularly Engage with Research Papers

One of the most effective ways to stay informed is by regularly reading research papers. Many of the key advancements in LLMs are first introduced in academic papers, which often serve as the foundation for future tools and models. Websites like arXiv and Google Scholar are invaluable resources for accessing the latest papers. Setting aside time each week to read new papers or even summaries can keep you up to date on cutting-edge techniques and innovations.

For those who find it difficult to keep up with dense academic writing, there are also plenty of resources that provide summaries and explainers of recent research. Blogs, newsletters, and online forums often distill complex ideas into more digestible formats, making it easier to grasp the key concepts without getting bogged down in technical details.

2. Follow Thought Leaders and Influencers

Social media platforms, particularly Twitter and LinkedIn, are rich sources of information on the latest trends in AI and LLMs. Many researchers, engineers, and thought leaders in the field actively share their insights, discuss new papers, and offer their perspectives on ongoing developments. Following these individuals can give you real-time updates on what's happening in the world of LLMs.

In addition to individual thought leaders, subscribing to AI-focused newsletters and podcasts can also be incredibly useful. These resources often provide curated content that highlights the most important developments, saving you time while ensuring you don't miss out on significant advancements.

3. Participate in Conferences and Workshops

Conferences and workshops are excellent opportunities to immerse yourself in the latest developments and network with other professionals in the field. Events like NeurIPS, ICML, and ACL are some of the top conferences where the latest research is presented, and attending them can give you direct access to new ideas and trends.

If attending in person isn't feasible, many conferences now offer virtual attendance options or publish recordings of the sessions. Additionally, following the conference proceedings and reading the papers presented can provide a wealth of knowledge, even if you can't attend the event itself.

4. Engage with Open Source Communities

The open-source community is a driving force behind much of the innovation in LLMs. Platforms like GitHub host a wide array of projects where you can see firsthand how new models and techniques are being implemented. Contributing to these projects, or even just following their progress, can keep you connected with the latest developments.

Engaging with open-source communities also offers the benefit of hands-on learning. By contributing code, experimenting with new models, or even just participating in discussions, you can deepen your understanding of LLMs and stay ahead of the curve.

5. Continuous Learning and Skill Development

The fast pace of AI means that continuous learning is a necessity. Online courses, certifications, and tutorials can help you keep your skills sharp and ensure that you're proficient in the latest tools and techniques. Platforms like Coursera, edX, and Udacity offer courses that are regularly updated to reflect the latest advancements in AI and LLMs.

Beyond formal courses, experimenting with new technologies in your projects is a great way to stay current. Whether it's fine-tuning a new model, testing out the latest optimization techniques, or integrating LLMs into new applications, practical experience is one of the best teachers.

6. Join Professional Networks and Communities

Networking with other professionals in the field is another key way to stay updated. Joining AI-focused groups, attending meetups, and participating in online communities can connect you with peers who share insights, ask challenging questions, and offer support.

Platforms like Stack Overflow, Reddit, and specialized AI forums provide spaces where you can discuss challenges, share experiences, and learn from others. Engaging in these communities not only keeps you informed but also helps you build relationships with other experts in the field.

Staying updated in the fast-paced world of LLMs requires a proactive approach that combines continuous learning, active engagement with the research community, and practical experience. By regularly reading research papers, following thought leaders, participating in conferences, engaging with open-source projects, and continually developing your skills, you can ensure that you remain at the forefront of this exciting and rapidly evolving field.

18.4 The Future of LLMs in Society

Large Language Models (LLMs) are no longer just cutting-edge tools for AI researchers—they are becoming integral parts of everyday life, influencing how we communicate, work, and interact with technology. As we look to the future, the role of LLMs in society will only grow, presenting both exciting opportunities and significant challenges. In this section, we'll explore some of the key areas where LLMs are likely to make a lasting impact and the considerations that will shape their future use.

Transforming Industries and Workplaces

LLMs have already started to revolutionize industries like customer service, healthcare, and finance by automating tasks, enhancing decision-making, and providing insights from vast amounts of data. In the future, we can expect this trend to accelerate, with LLMs becoming even more deeply integrated into business processes. For instance, in sectors like legal and education, LLMs could take on more complex roles, assisting professionals by generating legal documents, offering personalized learning experiences, or even conducting preliminary research.

However, as LLMs become more embedded in various industries, there will be a growing need to address concerns around job displacement and the shifting nature of work. While LLMs can handle many tasks more efficiently than humans, they also raise questions about the future of certain professions and the skills that will be most valuable in the workforce. Preparing for this shift will require not just technological advancement, but also thoughtful strategies for workforce development and education.

Ethical Considerations and Responsible AI

As LLMs play a more prominent role in society, ethical considerations will become increasingly important. Issues such as bias, fairness, transparency, and accountability in AI systems will need to be addressed to ensure that LLMs are used responsibly. The potential for LLMs to generate misinformation, reinforce harmful stereotypes, or make decisions that affect people's lives highlights the need for robust ethical guidelines and oversight.

One of the key challenges will be developing methods to ensure that LLMs are not only technically sound but also aligned with societal values. This includes creating models that are explainable and transparent, so that users can understand how decisions are made. It also involves ongoing efforts to mitigate bias in training data and to design systems that are inclusive and fair. As LLMs become more influential, the responsibility to use them ethically will rest not just with developers and researchers, but with society as a whole.

The Role of LLMs in Global Communication

LLMs have the potential to bridge language barriers and facilitate global communication in ways that were previously unimaginable. By providing real-time translation and context-aware communication tools, LLMs can help connect people across different cultures and languages. This could lead to greater collaboration and understanding on a global scale, as well as new opportunities for international business and diplomacy.

However, this potential also comes with challenges. Ensuring that LLMs accurately capture the nuances of different languages and cultural contexts is a complex task. Moreover, the widespread use of LLMs in communication raises questions about privacy, data security, and the control of information. As LLMs become more integral to how we communicate, it will be crucial to address these issues to maintain trust and safeguard individual rights.

LLMs and the Evolution of Creativity

One of the most intriguing aspects of LLMs is their ability to generate creative content, from writing and art to music and design. As these models become more sophisticated, they could play a significant role in the creative industries, collaborating with humans to produce innovative works or even generating content autonomously.

This raises interesting questions about the nature of creativity and the role of AI in the arts. While LLMs can mimic human creativity to a certain extent, they do so based on patterns learned from existing data, which may limit their originality. The future will likely see a blend of human and machine creativity, where LLMs are used as tools to enhance human creative processes rather than replace them. As this collaboration evolves, it will be important to consider issues of authorship, intellectual property, and the ethical use of AI-generated content.

The Impact on Education and Lifelong Learning

LLMs also have the potential to transform education by providing personalized learning experiences and making knowledge more accessible. From tutoring systems that adapt to individual learning styles to platforms that generate educational content on demand, LLMs could make education more tailored and inclusive.

In addition to formal education, LLMs could support lifelong learning by helping individuals stay updated with new skills and knowledge throughout their careers. However, this also means that educators and institutions will need to adapt to new methods of teaching and learning, ensuring that students are not only consumers of AI-generated content but also critical thinkers who can engage with and understand the technology they are using.

Preparing for a Future with LLMs

As we look ahead, it's clear that LLMs will play a central role in shaping the future of society. Their influence will extend across industries, affect how we communicate and create, and even challenge our ethical frameworks. To navigate this future successfully, it's essential that we approach the development and deployment of LLMs with a focus on responsibility, inclusivity, and innovation.

By fostering a culture of continuous learning, collaboration, and ethical awareness, we can ensure that LLMs contribute positively to society and help us address the complex challenges of the modern world. The future of LLMs is full of potential, but realizing that potential will require careful consideration and thoughtful action from all of us.

Made in the USA
Columbia, SC
11 March 2025

55041684R00298